S0-AVD-567

A Lover's Guide

By the same author:

Star Quality

MARJORIE ORR

A Lover's Guide

Aquarian/Thorsons
An Imprint of HarperCollins*Publishers*

The Aquarian Press
An Imprint of HarperCollins*Publishers*
77–85 Fulham Palace Road,
Hammersmith, London W6 8JB

Published by Aquarian Press 1994

1 3 5 7 9 10 8 6 4 2

© Marjorie Orr 1994

Marjorie Orr asserts the moral right to
be identified as the author of this work

A catalogue record for this book
is available from the British Library

ISBN 1 85538 315 2

Phototypeset by Harper Phototypesetters Limited,
Northampton, England
Printed in Great Britain by
HarperCollinsManufacturing Glasgow

All rights reserved. No part of this publication may be
reproduced, stored in a retrieval system, or transmitted,
in any form or by any means, electronic, mechanical,
photocopying, recording or otherwise, without the prior
permission of the publishers.

To Blackie and Tom, with love

CONTENTS

1

A LOVER'S GUIDE
TO THE STARS

Is your love life predetermined by the stars? Will they lead you to your one and only perfect partner, custom-built for you?

Plato has said that we are split in two before birth and that we spend our lives searching for our missing half – our soul mate. Is astrology the key to finding this needle in a haystack? The bad news is – probably not. The good news is that in astrological terms there are many more possible partners out there for you – not just one ideal mate.

Sun and Moon Signs

When you were born the sun was sitting in one particular constellation of the zodiac. That constellation is your birthday sign, the one you consider when reading your daily horoscope – Cancer, Sagittarius, etc. Your sun (birthday) sign tells you about the more 'masculine' side of your personality: your interests, talents, your identity.

The moon plays its part too, as it was also against a constellation in the heavens at the time of your birth. Your moon sign tells you about your 'feminine' side, what nourishes you, what comforts you, how you relate to your body, your childhood and your feelings. Your moon sign can be found accurately in the lists beginning on page 344.

The combination of your sun and moon signs tells you a great deal about how you relate within yourself and what you long for in a lover. The connection between the two tells you how your head and your heart are connected – vital if you want a real love affair that breathes. You must consider the two signs together to find a romantic match that might actually last a lifetime.

You may be an Aries sun because your birthday is in early April – but your moon could be in Scorpio, which subtly alters how the sun energy lives itself out. An Aries sun, Scorpio moon personality is a curious hybrid: fiery, energetic and confident yet also deeply secretive, moody and emotional. Such Aries/Scorpio mixes need equally curious partners who can feed their deeply sensual Scorpio moon without overwhelming all that fiery Arien energy.

On the other hand, Aries sun, Sagittarius moon personalities will be non-stop ravers and high-powered go-getters, real entrepreneurs who say whatever flits across their brains and are not exactly sensitive about other people's needs. They need amiable, practical partners who will put up with their shenanigans and keep the domestic show running smoothly during their long absences!

The first step along the astrological road to relating is a preparatory one: to check up on how you get on with yourself and, equally, how well-designed your intended is for a settled match. Look at your own sun and moon connection (Chapter 2) and that of your partner (if you have one). This is your 'reliability rating'. If your sun and moon are at odds then your relationships will also be disjointed, no matter how perfect a specimen of humanity you are involved with.

Some (not all) of the problems in relationships come not because you are inadequate or a delta-double-minus at love but because you simply picked the wrong mate. Not everyone in the world can love everyone else. The chemistry is often just plain wrong, as astrology can clearly show. The patterns you learn from your parents will continue to rule your choice of partner, not always with happy results – unless you unlearn these patterns. The appallingly difficult fact for a child (or an adult) to face is that you and your parents are simply different people with needs that are not always in tune.

Children always feel it is their fault somehow that they are not loved. As adults they feel that if only they had tried harder, achieved more and fulfilled Mum's expectations and Dad's dreams then everything would have been wonderful. But Mum was an Aquarius who tried to push you out of the nest as soon as you could toddle, while you, a Cancerian, preferred to stay close. You had to learn, against your nature, to be more independent than felt comfortable. Dad, meanwhile, was a Capricorn – a stickler for discipline, achievement and thrift – all of which meant nothing to your wildly wayward Gemini spirit. Somewhere deep inside you felt a failure for not matching up to what he wanted. Trouble was, neither of them saw you as you actually were. What they wanted was to fulfil their own needs, so you never learned how to look after your own.

All this means that now, in adult life, you keep trying to prove deep down inside yourself that you can actually make disjointed relationships work. You pick for yourself exactly what you had in childhood. It may not have worked when you were a child but it sure as hell is going to now, even if it kills you.

Your sun/moon combination can reveal why your fantasies of love are so different from the reality. You dream of grand passion yet spend your life knee-deep in dirty socks or grass cuttings. Lust and love both go sour rapidly. What you adored at the beginning you have now started to loathe. The young Penelope/Adonis who started the voyage with you is beginning to look all too like your dreaded mother-/father-in-law. You absolutely know you chose someone who was the exact opposite of your parents, yet the old scenario is playing itself out before your horrified gaze.

Freud thought that the compulsion to repeat bad experiences/

relationships was rooted in a desire to re-enact and therefore gain control of a situation that frightened us as children when we were powerless. That is why you may continue to try resolutely, bravely but hopelessly, even masochistically to pull together precisely the same relationship that could not be pulled together in childhood.

Why are you still making yourself unhappy? Why are you blaming yourself for failing in a relationship that never had a remote chance of working? At some point you need to get off the roundabout, face up to the pain of not having what you needed in childhood (easy to say, hell to do) and then try to find what really *is* going to make you happy.

Sun to Sun

In astrology, simple rules of thumb work remarkably well. For instance, the signs of the zodiac are divided into four elements – fire, earth, air and water. Water drowns fire, so the watery signs of Cancer, Scorpio and Pisces are bad news for the fiery Aries, Leo and Sagittarius. Earth and air make for a cool mix, so Taurus, Virgo and Capricorn make a practical but none too rapturous match with Gemini, Libra or Aquarius.

Astrology works at all sorts of levels, from the simple to the deeply complex. At a party all you are likely to learn about this new person you fancy is his or her sun sign. But even this tells you a great deal about a person and how you are likely to rub along together. You are Taurus, he is Aquarius. Is there hope? Probably not. You are earthy, sensual and possessive. He is out of touch with his body, freakishly independent and quite detached. Then you meet a Capricorn – things are getting much warmer. Or perhaps you are Aries, she Gemini – count down to take off! Scorpio/Scorpio? Almost definitely a hit. But Leo/Leo? The pits – forget it!

Some opposites attract. Take, for example, Virgo and Pisces: sweet, kind and refined together. Others don't, such as Leo and Aquarius: too stubborn, strictly chalk and cheese. Some adore their own kind, like Aquarians and Scorpios. Others loathe their own kind, like Leos (both too attention-seeking). Sun-to-sun comparisons reveal how the core of your two identities match up (see Chapter 3).

Moon to Moon

Your two moon signs, when compared and contrasted, give you quite a different perspective. Your moon sign tells you what comforts and nourishes you, how you relate to your body, to sexual pleasure, to cleanliness and to your home, family and childhood. Take the Prince and Princess of Wales. He is sun Scorpio, she sun Cancer – not a bad match as far as this goes, though prone to misunderstandings, sulks and storms (both signs being deeply emotional). But the real problem lay in the presence of his highly tactile Taurus moon, which is physically indulgent, deeply jealous, rather stubborn and in need of cuddles, as against her Aquarius moon, which prefers to stay away from bodily things where possible, is scared of intimate one-to-one commitment and flies off at the slightest provocation.

Thus Chapter 4 tells you how your moons click – or don't. Aries moon to Cancer moon: disaster. Pisces moon to Cancer moon: domestic bliss. Leo moon to Scorpio moon: horror time. Libra moon to Pisces moon: elegance, refinement and calm.

Moon to Sun

The final combination of your moon to your partner's sun reveals more still (see Chapter 5). Ideally the moon sign of one lover should be the same as the sun sign of the other. For example, the long-running match between Paul Newman (Aquarius sun, Pisces moon) and Joanne Woodward (Pisces sun, Aquarius moon). His sensitive Pisces moon needs her gentle, caring Pisces sun personality. Her Aquarius moon is quite happy to have the space his Aquarius sun personality gives her.

Astrology and Psychology

Astrology does not predetermine your life. There is no great fate involved. But it is a supremely useful source of information. It tells you what you cannot easily find out without two years' solid conversation, by which time it may be too late. It will certainly tell you if you are trying to mate a grasshopper with a bull. It will never work.

Relating is not just about knowing astrology – it is about understanding the psychology that lies behind it. Liz Greene is fond of remarking that astrology gives us the road map – it does not make the journey for us. Most of us are brought up woefully ignorant of the dynamics of relationships, which is why so many end in failure. Our expectations, based on too many films, romantic novels and perhaps inappropriate role models, do not give us the solid base we need either to pick the right partner or to sort out tangles when they come.

Relationships need to breathe, to be alive, to be able to cope with anger, sadness, failure, inadequacy, success (surprisingly difficult), jealousy, resentment, selfishness, love and hate. Real relationships involve risk. They involve pain and insecurity as well as tenderness, passion and protection.

Many people settle not just for second-best but for a shell of a relationship. Insecurity keeps them clinging to this wreckage of a match that is doing them no good at all. They grew up expecting little and that is what they settle for now. Many people think of themselves as unable to survive as independent human beings. Anything is better than loneliness; even a sour mismatch. But the plain truth is that nothing is as lonely, futile or destructive as staying in a relationship that has gone wrong.

You are two separate people who have a responsibility first and foremost to yourselves. If you know your needs and are willing to fight for them against your partner's wishes, which may seem at times more worthwhile or needy, then you can begin to sense how a robust, adult relationship is going to work. This may sound selfish and self-centred to you, or even crazy to people involved with highly infantile partners who want, want, want in a ruthless way. But every human being has essential needs; giving them up or hiding them means they are not being true to themselves. If these needs are continually overridden then a relationship will ultimately fail. Certainly if neither side gives way it will never work, but more relationships fail because one side is not dynamic or assertive enough. The resentment builds up, secretly, and when it finally breaks out – usually destructively – the damage is done.

This is where astrology can be so useful, because it pinpoints and can validate what you know deep inside you is right for you.

This can be used as a 'before' book for those about to embark on the slippery slope of a new relationship, to help you understand in what ways your lover is exactly what you need even though different from you. Or to help warn you that he or she is so out of step with you that the relationship will just wither away or explode out of sight. This can also be used as an 'ongoing' book, for those trying to understand why their relationship has hit a snag, or to confirm that it is as good as it feels. And this can be an 'after' book, for those who want to feel some small gratification in knowing that it was never likely to have worked anyway.

Rules of Relating

If the first rule of relating is to sort yourself out before you start, the second is that it takes two to make a romance float. One partner trying to sort out all the emotional storms and tensions in a relationship will fail. Generally women carry more of the emotional burden in a (heterosexual) partnership, partly because of biological/psychological reasons and partly because that is the way cultural conditioning has pushed them. Men genuinely do find it more difficult to get close to or contain their feelings. They feel overwhelmed by them. So many women are handed a package marked 'time bomb'. Not only do they have to cope with their own mood swings but those of their partners as well.

Both sexes have to realize that some of their expectations are unrealistic. Freud does remark that far from marrying their fathers, women quite often marry someone who represents their mother, or perhaps the mother they wish they'd had. Which is why some women complain copiously about not having a deeply sensitive, intuitively understanding mate. What they are looking for is the telepathic connection a baby has with its mother, who understands its every need without having to be told. If you do find a man who can act as your mother you will not like what often comes along as part of the package – an indecisive, dependent, martyr with no backbone.

Men *are* different from women. They have different needs, motives, aims and ways of functioning than women have. Jung was fond of pointing out that the 'contrasexual' part of us, which is what our heterosexual mates really are, is the part we never truly understand. Male and female bodies are designed differently and these physical differences mirror the inner, psychological ones. Sexually, men are outer-directed, while women take in. That in itself says a great deal about the differences in essential psychology.

In astrology certain sun signs are highly different depending on which sex is involved. Libran men are sweet, soft and rather 'feminine' where Libran women are cool, rational and quite 'masculine' in their approach (à la Maggie Thatcher). Some Cancerian men can stay Mummy's little boy for ever, while Cancerian women grow into matriarchal queen bees. Both sexes in Aries are quite macho, competitive and hard-driving. Capricorn men are on the whole more gentle creatures than their female counterparts. Gemini men are wilder and more promiscuous than Gemini women, who tend to be detached. So gender does make a difference.

These roles are of course not clear-cut, admittedly, because women are now developing their career strengths and more 'masculine' side, while men are struggling to come to terms with their true emotional role. But in the midst of this what is crystal clear is that we are different – and a relationship is about trying to find 'the other', not a carbon copy of yourself.

This is not to say that opposites in personality type should settle together. Too much difference means no connection. So rule three says relationships should not be narcissistic – looking for another version of yourself because there will be total understanding and no hassle. Though equally you cannot mate an octopus with an eagle. Somewhere in between there is a relationship that is a mixture of common interests, shared hopes, emotional resonances, similar sexual needs and an acceptance that this other is a whole human being who is not you, nor is he or she designed just to fulfil your needs.

Do opposites attract? In astrology some do and some do not. Often people early in adult life pick lovers who are very different from themselves because they fill in for what they feel they lack. An example of this would be Tatum O'Neal (Scorpio sun, Pisces moon) – all water, deeply emotional and adrift like a rudderless raft on the ocean – who picked John McEnroe, with an air sun and moon (Aquarius/Gemini), someone who certainly steers clear of deep feelings in relationships. To her he felt like safe, dry ground. But really there was not enough similarity for there to be any understanding. So the relationship did not stay the course.

You need a bit of 'sameness' to feel familiar and comfortable. Too much of the same is bad news, though – partly because you get bored with someone just like yourself. You need a bit of a mystery to keep the sparks flying and, with someone too much like you, all of your faults get doubled if not quadrupled. Too much fire and no one does the tax returns. Too much earth and no one dreams the dreams. Too much water and the relationship overturns in a storm. Too much air and no one feels anything at all.

Nothing about relationships or human psychology is simple or clear-cut. There is ambivalence and contradiction wherever you look. Astrology is a highly complex information system that copes remarkably well with the intricate mechanisms of two human beings trying to link hands, minds, bodies, hearts and souls. Not everyone manages to plumb the depths of the soul in a perfect love match. But then, not everyone wants to. First learn what your likes, limitations and ambitions in the love stakes are. Then travel hopefully. If you know what you want and it is right for you, go for it in your mind, give yourself permission to have it and – hey, presto! – it will happen. Read on, and good luck!

2

YOU AND YOUR MATE:
HOW DO YOU RATE AT
RELATING?

Sun and Moon in the Individual

Relationships may be about two people, but the horrible truth is that if you do not relate well within yourself then you are not going to make it together with even the most perfect specimen of humanity. Also life and sod's law being what they are you will, with the magnetic instincts of a homing pigeon, aim straight for an alternative version of your own muddle.

We all mate with our own mess. The only reason we do not see it is that we do not see ourselves clearly. So step one is self-knowledge and therefore a deeper understanding of the person you are clinging to so firmly as your perfect partner. Strip away the illusions before you make that irrevocable commitment. As someone once remarked – no matter whom you marry you always wake up next day to discover you are in bed with someone totally different. This here is preventive medicine. So read on. Your sun tells you about your identity, how you relate to the world and about career – basically it is your inheritance from your father. The moon tells you about what nourishes you emotionally, what kind of home life you like, how you relate to your body – it is your inheritance from your mother.

The relationship between your sun and moon signs tells you

how you relate within yourself, how your parents related to each other and thus what old patterns you carry in your head. Most importantly the sun/moon contact tells you what you will be looking for and what you will attract in a lover. You may loathe the mates you normally attract, but believe me they are part of your pattern. If you can understand the connection and get yourself more together the chances are you can hope to find a better match.

Understanding the *element* associated with your sun and moon signs also helps.

- Fire = Aries, Leo, Sagittarius – It acts first.
  A noisy, confident, flamboyant, imaginative, rather self-centred energy which lives in its hopes and aspirations.
- Earth = Taurus, Virgo, Capricorn – It makes things tangible.
  Earth signs are hard-working, practical, sensual behind a prudish exterior, rather tunnel-visioned and tuned in to the body and the material world.
- Air = Gemini, Libra, Aquarius – It thinks first.
  Air signs live in their heads, are full of thoughts, ideas, opinions and endless talk; they can be too cool and detached, though have perspective.
- Water = Cancer, Scorpio, Pisces – It feels first and reacts on gut intuition.
  Highly impressionable, sympathetic, caring, sometimes self-absorbed, moody and creative types.

The sun changes sign every month, usually on the 21st, 22nd or 23rd of the month though this varies every year by a day or so. This is why the dates given for sun signs in magazines or daily papers vary slightly. These sources can only give you the average date. If you are born 'on the cusp' it can be critical to know on which date the sun changed signs in your particular birth year.

The moon changes sign every third day. It has 12 signs to move round in the 28-day lunar month, so it spends only two and a quarter days in any one sign. Knowing the exact time of your birth can be vital in identifying precisely which moon sign you are. Look up the moon sign dates in the lists beginning on page 344.

If you are in any doubt about your exact sun or moon sign, a simple check with a consulting astrologer or a computerized personal horoscope will put your mind at rest (for details write to Marjorie Orr, PO Box 3125, London NW3 5QB).

Aries Sun Aries Moon

A bouncing, vital, energetic, hideously noisy new moon baby you have possibly less need to relate to or at least to lean on others than most. You do not feel a limb is missing if you do not have a permanent partner in life, though being a true romantic Aries you always want a dashing romance on the go, the more adventurous the better. It takes you a fair way through life to learn the sensitivity needed in close relationships. Thinking of the other is not part of your essential nature. Self-centred? Well . . . not to put too fine a point on it, and since you always admire honesty even if it causes a fight – yes. Competitive to the point of exhaustion – everyone else's, that is – you are a little too combative for the tender souls in life. Though oddly enough you will attract rather submissive geisha-like creatures who seem delighted to make themselves doormats for your convenience and let you win every time. Marlon Brando is the classic example.

Fidelity is not a strong point since you are a great starter, not such a hot long-distance stayer. Your enthusiasm wanes very fast. Aries men may remain delightful though maddening Peter Pans far into middle age – growing up is so boring! You need a very special kind of compliant lover who does not object to being abandoned for long periods, will not fuss about odd peccadilloes on the side, yet remain intriguing enough to be a continuing attraction. It is a tall order!

Female Aries will not be attracted to frills, flounces and the joys of domestic routines. You have very strong opinions which you let fly at the slightest provocation. You will need a tolerant mate with whom you can compete on an equal basis but who diplomatically lets you win, and most importantly still retains your respect. Another real one-off. The softening down of middle age helps. Sometimes.

Aries Sun Taurus Moon

Your head cries out for ever more adventure, risk, excitement and danger but your heart really wants total security. You are better grounded, more tactile and more earthbound than most Aries but you fight a constant battle within yourself about your need to be free and your need to be possessed and possessive. Jealousy crops up more here than you might expect. You are likely to attract lovers who are equally ill-at-ease with their own needs and desires. So at times even with a perfect coupling you are likely to feel that slight jarring of two souls not quite in harmony. What nourishes you is a happy home life, lots of people to cuddle and a great deal of money to buy the ultimate luxuries in life. You adore beautiful clothes in sensuous fabrics, extra comfortable furniture, wonderful food in largish quantities, and drink.

Part of you loathes change and too much upset of the quiet routines of pleasuring your senses. You can be fairly selfish about doing what suits you. If your pleasures also happen to suit your mate – great. But you can be very immovable. You need a reasonably flexible lover. One who can fulfil your very physical needs for great sex but who is also able to be out of the way when you want to be free to pursue your other interests. Famous examples include Diana Ross, who combines a jazzy, high-speed career with a large family to whom she is obviously devoted. Elton John is another, though he has not yet settled into finding what he needs. Also Vincent Van Gogh, who never did find it.

Aries Sun Gemini Moon

Talk? – You had better believe it! You absolutely must have a lover who can stand the sound of your voice since you never stop. You are bright (beyond belief), noisy, energetic, always on the go (a grasshopper to the nth degree) and exceedingly charming. On a superficial level you have a winning way with others especially at parties but when it comes down to the nitty-gritty of committing yourself to anything beyond a 10-minute joke, it is quite a different matter. The difference to you between a rut and a grave, as someone once said, is only a matter of degree. You simply must have constant variety, change and excitement otherwise you will die of boredom. But the problem is if you attract a mate who has the same needs you will very soon burn yourselves out. You do need some ballast in your life though you are not essentially attracted to earthy people – too tediously practical – and certainly not to watery emotional types – they make you feel as if you were being swamped or drowned. Romances will tend to be short, sharp and fast in younger adult life. What instantly attracts will soon become rather blasé and not substantial enough to hold your interest.

There is a two-dimensional quality about your emotional responses which is not enough. The knocks of life will bring you deeper into your feelings and make you realize that sacrificing some freedom and excitement is worth the stronger relationships which develop.

Aries Sun Cancer Moon

At odds with yourself you are constantly on edge, never being able to satisfy your head and your heart at the same time. You did not see your parents as being exactly in tune with each other and because of that you cannot quite get your own relationships together.

Certainly you are full of initiative and get-up-and-go and have highly romantic fantasies about what you want, but your rather abrasive Aries Sun does not let you settle enough to nourish your highly sensitive Cancer moon. You need a constant, secure happy home life and a great deal of freedom. So what you want is a family-orientated lover who can wander independently as much as you. Someone who is not possessive though will not mind your odd flashes of jealousy. An oddly designed animal to be sure, but in a way that matches your rather lop-sided needs. You can be both highly sympathetic, caring and sweet natured as well as being rather unemotionally self-centred about doing your thing no matter what. You will have difficulty committing absolutely to any one person and may, once settled, start to stray, which will bother your conscience.

Men, you will manage better being able to go out into the world to do your macho act yet still be able to slither home at high speed to find comfort when the mood strikes you. Women, you will find it more difficult to find your lover, being ill-designed for domesticity in one half of your nature yet craving it with the other. Your Aries machismo is less likely to be fuelled into fantasies about knights on white chargers, more into boardroom battles and beating the competition. You need to be less driven, more receptive, less winning-orientated and more tolerant. You also need a fairly soft mate.

Aries Sun Leo Moon

A larger-than-life, fiery, fast-moving, never-say-no, rather dashing personality who will leave weaker souls wilting in the ditch as you fly along at a million miles an hour. Burnout is a real possibility in life since all your energy is in your imagination, your fantasies. Confidence is all. Your instant reaction to any situation is not to feel or to think but to fly instantly into action. You desperately need a lover who grounds you and can cope with the practicalities of life, yet you terribly fear between trapped. You need freedom, grandeur, a first-class style of living (preferably in five-star hotels), oodles of excitement, thrills, and no spills.

You are, for all your confidence, very easily embarrassed and must, must, *must* have a mate who will not show you up badly. You think everything reflects back on you. You need a lover who does not mind being a satellite to your sun, or a courtier grovelling at the foot of your throne, though he or she also has to be a credit to you so not any snivelling slave is going to do. Getting your own way is not just a self-centred thing, it also springs from your genuine inability to change very quickly. You tend to get stuck in ruts emotionally and it takes a real hurricane to push you off course. However this has its merits. More faithful than most Aries you have a long-distance quality about you and you are refreshingly honest. Once in a good relationship you tend to stay. Sevvy Ballesteros, the international golfer, is one of you.

Aries Sun Virgo Moon

An odd mix for sure this, since you are brave to the point of idiocy in certain areas of life and timid to the point of paranoia in others. Your Aries sun could not care less about other people's opinions, needs and lifestyles, while your Virgo moon worries endlessly about absolutely everything and makes you a hypochondriac to boot. However you are more practical and certainly more sensible and sensitive than most of the over-competitive, over-fiery Aries breed. But it will take some time in life to get your head and your heart together in love. What you want to mate with is not what you feel you ought to be mating with. Your Virgo moon does not like infidelity yet you may find that the relationship you want at any one time is not the one you are in.

You have to understand that you have two completely different images of yourself and each needs a different lover! You want fire, fairy-tale romance and a constantly changing scenario on the one hand, and a refined, rather withdrawn existence where you can be protected on the other. What you require is a down-to-earth, rather sensual lover who can fulfil your needs for physical affection yet who will not offend your Aries sun, which dislikes anything too grossly physical. Someone who will let you wander but be there to calm down your endless stream of questions, anxieties and invented ghosts who haunt your life. The jet-set life obviously holds its attraction since the two famous examples are Philippe Junot (first husband of Princess Caroline of Monaco) and Princess Ira Von Furstenberg, renowned socialite.

Aries Sun Libra Moon

A full moon baby, you veer between opposites at a great rate of knots. Your life feels constantly tense as if half of you is never satisfied at any given time no matter whom you are with. Your conscience and duty are always at odds with your desires. You constantly wish for a composite of the various lovers you have had. 'If only I could have Jane's brain and Joanna's body I could be happy.' Or 'I adore Joe for his chat over dinner but he's so hopeless in bed. Mike is great between the sheets but I wouldn't be seen dead with him in public.' One is never enough.

The problems spring from early on, where you experienced your parents as very different kinds of people, not really compatible. What they did not get together in their marriage you cannot get together in your head. So you are constantly out of step with yourself – until, that is, you decide to leave childhood and the old patterns behind. But that means rising above your dilemmas to see that life is not a choice between either this person or that person, neither of whom seems perfect. There is a third way where you can find your composite lover. But the change has to come firstly from you.

Your Aries sun demands total freedom, great excitement and a fiery relationship that does not last for ever. Your Libra moon craves peace, niceness, social respectability and a fairly cerebral mate. You need someone just as contrary as yourself and hope the pieces fit when you come together. But relationships will always be a bit of a struggle. Actor Richard Chamberlain is one fellow-Aries/Libra mix.

Aries Sun Scorpio Moon

You are a real puzzle – flying along the cloud tops with a head full of fantasies yet also drawn to the depths where you can indulge your romantic dreams in the most physical and emotional way possible. You never ever admit to being hurt and will hide your feelings away with a determined ferociousness. You will probably have handled this conflict early on in adult life by repressing your need for deeply passionate relationships, being seemingly a light-hearted sprite who does not care about such things. Then one day – you fall – straight into the bottomless pit and are gripped by such agonies of jealousy and possessiveness that for a while you hardly notice the ecstasies that come along with them.

You hate yourself for being so hooked into these love affairs. Yet they give you what your normal dash-in/dash-out flash-in-the-pan flare-ups cannot. Your Aries sun demands that you find someone who will let you win, not mind your rather self-centred, 'me first' approach, and not worry when you wander independently off to do your own thing. But your Scorpio moon wants someone you can wrap your octopus tentacles round and never let go. You need an oddity like yourself who is transcendently romantic in such contradictory ways and just hope the same facets are on show when you want to be together.

You are likely to attract yourself to mates who seem to be as unlike you as anything your friends could ever imagine. But somehow it works. Friends will never see what goes on in the highly secret recesses of your life. Famous examples have a fair track record in the multiple relationship stakes: Warren Beatty, Dudley Moore and Sir David Frost.

Aries Sun Sagittarius Moon

A fiery flibberty gibbet, you are completely incapable of sitting still for long. Anything that smells remotely like possessiveness or being fenced in will have you running for the open plains. You absolutely must have your freedom – but herein lies your dilemma. No restraints at all usually means no relationship either, so life is one long lesson of learning that sacrifices are sometimes worth the hassle. Commitment will never be easy for you since your enthusiasms are notoriously short lived and once you sense that initial ardour waning you start getting itchy feet again. You need to learn to hack it through the boring patches and understand that obligations need not necessarily be the same as a prison sentence.

Not inherently talented at understanding the needs of others you may have problems with more sensitive emotional souls who need you to tune in to their every nuance. Although excitable and exciting, a thoroughgoing adventurer in fact and a real charmer on the social scene, you can also be abrasive and rather rough in your approach to one-to-one relationships. You must learn a little diplomacy. Honesty is one of your plus points but too much of it at the wrong moment can be a real downer. You need someone more practical than yourself but who has enough flair not to make you feel stuck in stodge, who is emotional enough to soften you down without becoming over-hurt by your rather abrupt manners. The acid-pen biographer Kitty Kelley is one example. A less obvious one is Dirk Bogarde.

Aries Sun Capricorn Moon

Hard-working, highly ambitious and rather cool to the touch, you rarely do anything without looking first to see what you can gain. You are probably one of life's winners – but happy? Not early on, that's for sure. You rarely give in to emotional whims and indulgences. Indeed you rarely sit still long enough to find out what those are!

Your Aries sun wants to be first past the post and your Capricorn moon thinks you will never be loved for just being yourself. You feel you have to achieve to earn love. Which is, of course, a non-starter, because the more you drive yourself to accomplish the further away from your feelings you get and the less likely is it that you will settle down to ongoing romantic bliss. You could settle for rather loveless matches which are good for your social standing. Capricorn moons do that sadly, until one day they fall madly, passionately and very physically in love and all their conventional morality goes straight out of the window.

You are a fire/earth mix, which is more practical and sensible than most Aries. But you lack air's reflective abilities and water's sensitivity to feelings. You can be rather cold and hard-edged. You need a lover who thinks and communicates, who is warm enough to heat you up a bit. You need to learn not to kill passion stone dead. But that probably comes with age. Capricorn moons have the happy knack of improving with age, though you may have to swap partners late in life to find your true depths. It should come as no surprise to find two politicians who have sacrificed a great deal of personal life to ambition among your Aries/Capricorn fellows: British Prime Minister John Major and American Vice-President Al Gore.

Aries Sun Aquarius Moon

Charming, zany, witty, adventurous and rather racy, you sound like everyone's dream of an exciting lover but the truth of the matter is that you are not at all clear you want a relationship that connects at all most of the time. You like thinking about love, talking about romance and sex endlessly, fantasizing about great passions, even writing novels about the whole affair. But as for actually doing it? Falling in love, making a commitment, trying to find your feelings – not such a hot notion at all.

Your Aquarius moon loves to be bizarre and even slightly shocking just to see the effect it has on others, so you definitely need lovers who will not be rattled. In fact your approach is so cool you probably need someone just as impersonal as yourself. It is not that your Aries sun cannot be fierce, fiery and passionate but sometimes you have difficulty turning what is in your imagination into real substance. Flesh and blood bodies tend to turn you off for one thing, and too many swampy feelings frankly scare you. Once you have got over the adrenalin-pumping, love-addict phase and into discussing mortgages, in-growing toenails and the best brand of laxatives, you really do not want to know anymore. A relationship with plenty of freedom and independence with an intellectual equal is what you need. Any sniff of possessiveness or jealousy will have you taking off like a space rocket. Joan Crawford was this type.

Aries Sun Pisces Moon

A brash, brazen, go-get-em type with a heart so desperately sensitive you can hardly bear to let it out to play at all. You fight a constant war in your head between your Aries sun – which despises any kind of cowardice or weakness and thinks you should head straight for what you want and grab it – and your Pisces moon – which operates a bit like an oyster without its shell. It cringes and tries to hide all the time.

Most often when your moon is operating you are too timid to even voice your feelings for a new person in case of the awful possibility of rejection. More than almost any other Aries type you need a long-term relationship to provide you with your shell. Then you can sally out into the world to look macho. Only those close know the real truth. But you need a lover who is exciting enough not to bore you, submissive enough to let you win, yet strong enough to give your feelings the protection they need.

You are that ultimate contradiction – a mix of fire and water. What you lack is air for reflection and earth for stability. But an over-airy lover will freeze you with too much analysis and not enough action. An over-earthy lover will seem too gross and rather blinkered. A practical but emotional type would be your best bet. Hugh Hefner, founder of *Playboy*, is your clue. An Aries sun Pisces moon, he played the field, then settled down very sedately.

Taurus Sun Aries Moon

An uneasy combination which seeks both total stability/security and constant change/excitement. Your Taurus sun wants a solid, unchanging, settled family life where you can root yourself, preferably for ever. But your Aries moon wants nothing of the sort. When it is in charge you never know quite what you want – except that the routine and constancy which your other half yearns for is certainly not it.

In early adult life you probably attract yourself to zany, wacky, wild adventurers who love you and leave your heart bleeding. You are much more possessive and jealous than you ever want to admit. The lover you need is home orientated yet freedom loving, physically warm yet able to leave you free to fantasize as you want.

Taurus is a highly physical energy, very sensual at a body level, which does not suit your Aries moon. What nurtures you has to be free of the grosser aspects of life and love. So you need a very special combination in your mate who will probably be as muddled and contradictory as you are yourself. A solid home base is a must but from there you must be able to flee when you please, to roam the wide open spaces and do what suits you. You are not essentially tuned in to other people's needs so you probably would do better with a reasonably undemanding lover or at least one who will take your whims and desires as being his or hers.

Taurus Sun Taurus Moon

A very earthy new moon baby, you have less need to relate outside yourself than most. Which does not mean you will not have good relationships. Just that you are less desperate than most to find your other half. A strong sense of mission usually goes with you through life and sometimes gets in the way of love. You undoubtedly adore the good things of life, especially the ones which pleasure the body – food, drink, clothes, a luxurious home. You are extremely tactile even in non-sexual situations so you must have people around you who are not too reserved about body contact. Love to you must be expressed in highly physical ways. It is not an imaginative experience as it is for fire signs, or one to be thought and talked about as it is to the air signs or even felt deeply in a watery, emotional way. You must see tangible expressions of love and affection before you will be satisfied that it exists.

The problem is being both sun and moon in Taurus you would naturally be attracted to other Taureans but it is a rather dull pairing. You need flair, sparkle and variety from the lighter signs. You can be immovably stubborn so you need a flexible, sometimes submissive mate. You can be ever so slightly self-centred when it comes to getting your own way, so there is no sense in settling with a prima donna. Jealousy and possessiveness can be problems. You can sulk for ever at slights and hurts. You are a real one-off. Pope John Paul II, Karl Marx, Katharine Hepburn and singer Glen Campbell are the unlikely quartet of examples.

Taurus Sun Gemini Moon

You are solid, stolid, very earthy yet a real grasshopper at the same time. Part of you is so securely anchored it hardly moves at all and would be happy rooting itself to one spot for ever. Your Gemini moon, however, regards all this unchangingness with horror. To a Gemini moon the difference between a rut and a grave is only a matter of degree. So your life is one long dilemma of how to keep your head and your heart happy at once.

Your prime requirements for a lover are an intelligent mind and a witty flow of conversation with enough physical passion to keep you satisfied but not so much you feel pulled down by it. You absolutely must have someone who shares your rather decadent approach to life – adoring good food, drink, clothes and luxurious furnishings. One tricky area is sex, about which you are highly ambivalent. Your Taurus sun is very physical and needs tangible displays of affection. Your Gemini moon is very cerebral and would rather think, talk and analyse than do. So you need someone who understands only too well your fleeting mood changes. What you wanted last night or last week or even 10 minutes ago is not what you want now.

Being an earth and air mix you may veer over into being a tiny touch cool at times so you probably need a partner who is slightly fiery to give you a bit of sparkle, or just passionate enough to stir your deeper feelings without scaring your Gemini moon into flight. Sigmund Freud, who thought a great deal about sex, more than he ever indulged in it, was one.

Taurus Sun Cancer Moon

Aren't you just a jealous one? You hide it pretty well, all things considered, but when the chips are down and you see what you want disappearing into the distance you certainly make a major fuss. This sun/moon combination looks to others very well balanced. You feel as if you were at ease with yourself. Socially you operate very smoothly, flirting and having fun especially with potential sexual partners. But you do not always have the smooth life on the inside that you crave.

You are fairly stubborn and a past master at the art of passive resistance. Nothing can shift you when your mind is made up. Your earth/water mix means that you recharge your own batteries very successfully indeed, though you can at times be a little heavy. You need some fire to sparkle you up and a little more reflectiveness to keep you detached. That would stop you hanging on quite so tightly. Physical passion is always hugely important to Taureans, but to Cancer cuddles are more gestures of family affection than anything deeply sexual. So you will never be quite sure what it is exactly that you want. What you will undoubtedly end up with is a solid home life. You adore the idea of staying rooted in the one place surrounded by a large brood. When you do settle you are faithful, definitely designed for the long-haul relationship rather than anything that is likely to chop and change. Disloyalty is neither in your best interests nor really in your nature. You need a lover who is tactile and indulgent but willing to put your indulgences at the top of the priority list. A home-loving raver, in short.

Taurus Sun Leo Moon

Wow! A really strong combination but not an easy one. Always at odds with yourself, you never feel totally satisfied with anything or anyone. Your head wants a practical, earthy, sensible, sensual mate while your heart really wants a flashy, flamboyant, rather regal personage. You always feel you get one or the other, but never both at the same time. What you want to have is never what you ought to have. As they say, you will meet your perfect mate in life – six months after you get married to someone else!

This rather gritty, restless, at-cross-purposes streak in you should ease as you mature and separate yourself from childhood. You certainly saw your parents as being highly different people not totally in tune. You need in time to rise above their differences to find your own way of relating. You are obstinate to the nth degree, determined to fulfil your own indulgences and to be always the centre of attention.

An earth/fire mix, you are known in the astrology business as a 'steamroller' type – always charging ahead when everyone else is sagging by the wayside. So you obviously need a lover with stamina. Your ego or at least your insistence on living life at a first-class (not to say five-star) level could cause problems – you also need a rich mate. But you are at heart a sign who needs love, passion, romance and real connections before you feel alive. Queen Elizabeth II, Barbra Streisand, dancer Martha Graham and round-the-world yachtsman Chay Blyth are all Taurus sun Leo moon people.

Taurus Sun Virgo Moon

Socially very much at ease, given to the good life and never happy if your body is not being indulged, you are lucky that your earthy mix makes you work hard. You could otherwise end up as a real louche character. In early adult life you were probably rather restricted by a lack of imagination and too practical an outlook. If anything you were probably a little heavy as a personality, needing mates who would sparkle you up a bit.

Your Virgo moon worries endlessly about everything under the sun and invents quite a few things to agonize over that do not even exist. You need a mate who is calm enough to handle your jitters, tolerant enough to stand your hypochondria, yet flexible enough to let your Taurean side have its way most of the time. What is also highly necessary is a good lifestyle that will give you the good food, drink, clothes and luxurious house that allows you to feel comfortable. You are not flashy but you are acquisitive and need to indulge your sensations. Jealousy can be a problem though you hide it well since your refined Virgo moon does not like to admit to such primitive feelings.

You need to learn to be more objective about yourself. Standing back far enough to see yourself clearly is not easy and self-analysis always seems a waste of time to you. But relationships will not work until you learn to see yourself as others see you. Shirley MacLaine, Jack Nicholson and Candice Bergen are fellow travellers.

Taurus Sun Libra Moon

Although you are never quite at ease with yourself this can be a rather lovely combination since both Taurus and Libra are ruled by Venus so you can be charm itself, rather creative, always superbly in good taste and very calm. You are at the refined end of Taurus – no grossly sensual desires upset the even tenor of your love life. You loathe the great unwashed, the lazy, the idle and the unemployed. What you need around you are the luxuries, indulgences and extravagances of life and the beautiful people.

Being earth and air you are practical, sensible, communicative and fairly detached. What you lack at times is warmth, dash and craziness. You need a lover who will push you towards the edge. That Taurus grit of yours and need for total stability sometimes makes you just a touch dull, safe and rather boring. That Libra moon too can make you just a touch superficial. If you always want life to be nice, sociable and clean, you miss out on a great deal that can be alive, human and invigorating. A rather restless spirit within you never quite lets you settle. You are never totally satisfied with life or your mates. Your Taurus sun really does want a cuddly armful but the Libra moon makes you standoffish. Finding an accommodation between your two conflicting sides is your life's challenge.

Taurus Sun Scorpio Moon

Strong, often silent – especially on the subject of your feelings – you are definitely a force to be reckoned with. A potent combination of sultry desire, simmering jealousy and unresolved tension ensures that your love life will never be boring. It may not always make you happy but you do live life in depth. You are stubborn – which is the understatement of the year. Having a fixed sun and moon, your normal reaction to change is to dig your heels in and steadfastly refuse to budge an inch. Since acquisitiveness and possessiveness lie at the core of your being, you never let go of old love affairs easily. What you want is yours and that is all there is to it. If anyone hurts you, though, there will not be a flicker of emotion shown. You hide away from public gaze what wounds you.

There is nothing milk sop or middle of the road about your feelings. You take them extremely seriously. You either love people to distraction or you loathe them. Once you have finished an affair you can never be friends. You ought to have a lover who is flexible to fit round what you want but you need someone who can stand your depths, so a weakling won't do. What you probably find is someone as stalwart as yourself and end up in a continual power struggle. Life will not be easy emotionally but you never give up trying.

Taurus Sun Sagittarius Moon

You want almost everything your other side does not want and vice versa, so life is not easy on the relationship front. Your Taurus sun wants to hang on to an unchanging, long-term relationship that provides earthy stability and lots of cuddles. Your Sagittarius moon on the other hand wants freedom first and foremost. You do not expect to have to ask permission to roam the world. Possessiveness makes your hackles rise and you reach for your running shoes. What you require is the impossible lover who is sensual but not too physical, loves being cuddled but will stand being abandoned frequently, can offer you security but does not make you feel fenced in. In return he or she will be given a wonderfully fiery, flamboyant relationship with indulgences, extravagances and luxuries thrown in since you adore the good life.

Restlessness will always be part of your nature so you need to have a lifestyle that keeps you on the move. Entertaining is one of your skills since you are both practical and given to colourful displays of largesse. Your parties are the talk of the town because you feed people so well in a highly original way. So lovers and future mates must be reasonably sociable creatures and communicative. That Sagittarius moon loves to philosophize about life. Being an earth/fire mix you have tons more energy than everyone else. Krishnamurti, the religious leader and writer, is this combination.

Taurus Sun Capricorn Moon

Earthy, practical, very attached to the body and over hard-working, you will be more at ease socially than you will be in close relationships. Somehow you have the idea that to be loved you have to achieve. You think no one loves you for just being you, which is a great mistake it will take most of your life to unlearn. Your Taurus sun wants to be hugely indulgent but your Capricorn moon is a hard taskmaster keeping your nose to the grindstone or sending you after lovers who are socially useful though hardly a bundle of laughs. You need to unhook your upwardly mobile tendencies from your love life and go for sensual pleasures.

Being an earth/earth mix you have tremendous potential for real physical passion though you need also to learn of the realms that lie beyond the body in the spirit, the heart and the mind. You will be inclined to pick rather serious, sometimes older lovers, but what you need in your life is more sparkle, fire, craziness and general *chutzpah* (guts). Your sense of humour will probably develop late in life. You will, also, find the last third of your love life makes up for all the austere chilliness of the first third. You will with a little encouragement turn into a merry, mischievous geriatric who oozes sex appeal. You probably do not want to know that Adolf Hitler was this astrological mix.

Taurus Sun Aquarius Moon

A rather square-edged combination this, which makes you resolutely earthy, solid, stubborn and quite sensual on the one hand, fighting a conflict with your other half which is airy, talkative, detached and rather anti anything too physical. How did you come by and how to resolve this dilemma? Well, take a good hard look at your parents – they were hardly in tune. What they could not get together between themselves you cannot get together in your head. So you constantly want what you do not have, or have what you do not want. Lift yourself out of your childhood battles and see life from a new perspective. It is possible to have your cake and eat it; to get what you want and still be doing what you ought to do at the same time!

You will always be slightly restless in relationships and you certainly need an oddly constructed mate – someone who can let you have your way since your Taurus sun is both super-indulgent and slightly self-centred. (Both your sun and moon are fixed signs so you expect the world to adapt to you.) But your lover will also have to be detached enough to let you fly free when you want and not mind being shocked along the way. You love being eccentric and slightly wild just to see the effect on people around, so partners need to be of an unshakeable temperament. Your earth/air mix could probably do with a partner with some sparkle and a little emotional warmth. The great and the good who share your combination include Nikolai Lenin, Machiavelli and the rather pugnacious actor Ryan O'Neal.

Taurus Sun Pisces Moon

Steadfast, stalwart and unflappable on the outside, you are a real shrinking violet where your feelings are concerned. You hardly dare voice your inclinations for fear of the dreadful hurt of rejection. So sometimes in life you miss out on relationships because you are scared to reach out. Emotional courage needs to be fostered though you will never be upfront about your feelings.

Your earth/water mix makes you sympathetic in a highly practical way, which is wonderful for those whom you trust. You have a great deal to give if you can get over your feelings of self-pity. You belong to the refined end of Taurus and though you share this sign's general characteristics of indulgence and love of the good life you conduct yourself in a highly tasteful manner always. The grosser, hugely stubborn side to Taurus is largely lacking or at least mellowed because you know the heart is just as important as the body and its pleasures. What you need is a lover who will be flexible enough to let you have your way yet strong enough to protect your sensitivities, which are legion. You need an intimate confidante to whom you can unburden your heart and soul without being scared that the instant you open up you will be savaged or abandoned.

It takes time for you to find and ultimately trust another. Once you settle you will do so for a lifetime or what is left of it. You want security, roots, unchangingness and a feather-bedded home.

Gemini Sun Aries Moon

Fun-loving, chatty, butterfly-brained and grasshopper-footed you are not exactly the stay-at-home type. On the social scene you appear at ease with yourself and happy to flirt. Nothing about you stays the same for long since you crave variety in yourself and in your companions. What you want now is not what you wanted 10 minutes ago, never mind 10 days ago. You can appear like a will-o'-the-wisp, one moment here, the next moment there, so you absolutely do not want a deeply possessive mate.

Being an air/fire mix you easily burn yourself out since you do not have a natural way of recharging your batteries. You are neither earthy and grounded nor are watery and emotional. You probably want a lover who can provide you with some ballast, a bit of practical know-how and an anchor. Other fire/air types are marvellous fun for you to be around since both of you brim over with liveliness but it is a fire that flares up and dies down quickly because it consumes itself. Long-term fidelity is not always your strongest suit since Geminis always like to hedge their bets and keep three of anything running at once whether it is jobs or love affairs. Your Aries moon also wants freedom and constant excitement. What nourishes you is getting all the attention and coming first, which is easier in a constant series of new relationships than in one that has had to learn about compromise. So you need a mate who will give you a very long rein indeed.

Gemini Sun Taurus Moon

Air-headed and clay-footed might be the uncomplimentary description of you, but it is true that you are made up of very different elements. Your Gemini sun is quick-witted, rather cool, freedom-loving, restless and given to sudden whims. Your Taurus moon is of a heavier cast. Solid, stalwart and affectionate, it loathes change, especially the kind of sudden change that your Gemini sun often precipitates. What nourishes your heart is a secure, rather physically passionate, certainly sensual match, but the other half of you is frankly not too tuned in to the body. So you will need to find relationships that give you just enough cuddles, kisses and tangible gestures of love without smothering you or making you feel tied down by more earthy matters.

You have a jealous streak and a wandering eye, which is a quirky combination. You crave faithfulness and loyalty in others but are not always good at finding it in yourself. What you really need is an anchor at home to provide you with all the indulgences of life – good food, drink, beautiful clothes and luxury furnishings – but leave you free to roam at will. Your darker side sometimes draws you into frankly undesirable relationships because you need to experience the profound depths. But luckily you quickly flit on somewhere else. Michael J. Fox and Bob Dylan are two Gemini sun Taurus moon types.

Gemini Sun Gemini Moon

Airy in the extreme you think everything through before you even dare to feel it. You prefer to talk, analyse, debate and argue over life rather than actually get in and live it. Cool to the point of chilliness at times you learn eventually that detachment has its drawbacks. If you do not give emotionally to others, you will not get support and affection back. But being born at the time of the new moon you are more self-sufficient and have less need for close relationships than most. You do not feel half a person without a partner. You do have a strong sense of mission that drives you on and can push relationships to one side, so you need a long-suffering mate whose ego will survive being rejected or abandoned every so often in favour of the grand plan.

If this makes you sound like the Iceman or the Snow Queen you are far from it. As far as short-lived affairs are concerned you can heat up along with the best of them. You adore the excitement, the risk and the thrills of a new romance blossoming. But long-distance staying is never going to be your strong point. Neither is fidelity. You need room for experimentation. Variety really is the spice of your life. Part of this need for variety stems from your wish to avoid facing the desert in the middle of your emotional life, which you do want to fill with a meaningful relationship at some point. You just do not have enough faith to believe that will ever be possible. Lovers absolutely must have a sharp mind and be good conversationalists. A meeting of the minds is the *sine qua non* of any match for you. Brooke Shields and Tom Jones are the restless pair who share your double dose of Gemini.

Gemini Sun Cancer Moon

A stay-at-home Gemini is a contradiction in terms, yet this is precisely what you try to be. Family relationships and a secure, unchanging base in life are your anchor, yet your Gemini sun yearns to fly free, to stray at will and for ever to be unfettered. A compromise is what you feel your love life always is, never quite everything you want. Whatever the emotional atmosphere of your childhood it stays around you for most of your adult life and colours what you think relationships can and should provide. You find it difficult to stray far from what is known or you stop feeling nourished. So you fight this continual battle in your head about wanting two entirely different ways of life. It is tiring but in a curious way it also keeps you alert.

Being an air/water mix you are more emotional than many Geminis, not so cool and detached. But you lack earth and fire so partners who can provide you with a little *chutzpah* (sparkle) and some practical grounding would help. Though not too much. Your Cancer moon can make you jealous since at heart you are so desperately insecure and terrified of losing what is nearest and dearest to you. Attachments to mother continue too long and can cause problems in relationships. But letting go causes such pain. You need security and a long lead.

Gemini Sun Leo Moon

Communicative, attention-seeking, restless, fiery and determined to live life the five-star way you are certainly no shrinking violet. Highly persuasive, blissfully charming when it suits you and rather entertaining on the social scene, you can unfortunately take offence very easily. Your vanity is a real weak spot. Standing on your self-importance can unsettle partners who do not have your sense of ego.

Not always too sensitive to the needs of others in early adult life you may take a while to settle. Faithfulness is not easy for your Gemini sun but your Leo moon is essentially loyal and honest. Which does not mean to say you will not stray, but at least half of you will disapprove or at least feel that the lying and petty deceptions are beneath your dignity. Your air/fire mix is a heady one, keeping you constantly on the go, always looking for excitement, variety and thrills. What you need from a mate is stimulation and adoration, but also some common sense to keep you anchored down occasionally otherwise you are likely to take off like a hot air balloon, or just plain burn out. Recharging your batteries is always necessary for you.

Another fire/air type would drive you wild but exhaust you rapidly. You need a touch of earth in your lover to get you tuned in to your body, and maybe a touch of water to let you find your heart. But too much of either and you will feel you are being weighed down or swamped by soggy feelings. Prince Philip, Paul McCartney and Clint Eastwood are the megastar variety.

Gemini Sun Virgo Moon

Fidgety, restless, highly adaptable and quite incapable of sitting still, you need a rock of Gibraltar on which to anchor yourself. You are communicative with an extremely bright mind. Your witty rather precise way with words makes you entertaining on the social scene but you never seem satisfied with yourself or anyone else. You want what you do not have and have what you do not want. In childhood you were aware of tensions in the atmosphere at home and have internalized these in your adult life with the result that you feel relationships will always pull you in two. They will not, but you do need to try some lateral thinking. Life is not about either or. There is a third solution, if you leave childhood behind and rise above those conflicts.

You worry incessantly about everything on earth and quite a few things that exist nowhere. Trying continually to impose order on the chaos of your life tends to make you over rigid. Sometimes you can even appear prudish – almost impossible for a Gemini but you manage it. Hypochondria can send you rushing off anxiously for advice, remedies and reassurance so you need a calm, stable partner who will listen sympathetically but not get irritated by your constant harping on. Your nervous system is over-wound up, causing your digestive system to act up at times. So you need a physically supportive lover as well.

Being an air/earth mix you can be a little dry at times but you are warmer than some Geminis because of your earthy Virgo moon. Fidelity is always an issue because your sun and moon take opposing views on the subject. So you stray and worry about it or do not stray and regret it. John F. Kennedy (who appears on the evidence *not* to have worried too much about) and Paul Gauguin belonged to this breed.

Gemini Sun Libra Moon

Cool, communicative and rather cut off from feelings is how you come across to others. You can be extremely sociable, very friendly and charming, yet you reach out to people with your head and your tongue, not your heart or your body. Flirting comes easily, almost as second nature to you as long as it is conducted with decorum since you have a horror of social embarrassment. You are extremely sensitive about how other people see you. Your status in society is a crucial factor in all your deliberations, whether about work or relationships. Being a slight snob does not bother you at all since you know your tastes are impeccable.

Gemini does have a dark, sometimes sensual side, but your Libra moon is not happy about plunging into the depths of passion, nor about anything too physical or claustrophobic. You abhor people who do not wash or who are somehow socially unacceptable. You need a mate who is happy to meet at a more surface level and allow you the freedom you need to be exploring continually new vistas, new interests and new acquaintances. You adore meeting successful, fairly wealthy and rather well-bred people so your friendship circle will be wide, varied and rather elegant. Traditionally having the sun and moon in the same element – here in air – is supposed to make you comfortable with yourself and others. But it often indicates a social ease rather than a real yearning to connect. So you have to watch that you do not become too 'up in your head', too parchment dry and detached. A fiery lover would make you sparkle though you might cringe at his or her brashness. A watery one would make you feel swamped. But you do need anchoring and grounding. A rather earthy type might help to give you warmth and a connection to life. George Bush and Henry Kissinger are two notable 'air heads'.

Gemini Sun Scorpio Moon

Drawn to the dark side you are undoubtedly among the most heavyweight of the Geminis, certainly the most secretive. You never ever let on when you are hurt, keeping your wounded pride to yourself, but allowing yourself the minor pleasure of getting your revenge at some point. Air and water are an odd mix since your Gemini sun basically prefers talking and thinking to touching and feeling whereas your Scorpio moon adores passionate clinches, intensely lived emotions and even deeply messy love affairs. Finding a balance that will suit both sides of your conflicting nature will not be that easy. Early adult life will contain wild and way out relationships and passing flings which you would not like to see in print or have brought up in front of your mother-in-law. But your need, quite compulsive at times, to find another half, a perfect mate for your desires will push you into a determined search to find that special someone.

Although Gemini is a notoriously wayward sign when it comes to fidelity, your Scorpio moon will provide you with stability. It gives you a streak of jealousy and possessiveness which will eventually teach you that your insecurity demands a reliable lover. Loyalty is a real Scorpio quality, which is a blessing though you will always feel slightly uneasy about being trapped. It hardly seems hopeful to mention that Xaviera Hollander, New York's most renowned madam, has this duo of Gemini and Scorpio, but it tells you what the dangers are.

Gemini Sun Sagittarius Moon

Restless, flighty, fiery and liable to burn out from non-stop go, there is no danger of you ever being bored or boring because you never sit still long enough. You talk endlessly and entertainingly with a real gift for piquing other people's interest yet you are terrified of being trapped in a committed relationship. Being fenced in is close to your idea of suffocation and at the first whiff of jealousy you are off at the run. Freedom is what you thrive on but you tend to be naïve. You learn about the harder side of life through knocks and bad experiences. Disillusionment comes hard, though, as your sense of humour will always bounce you back. There is an inner conflict between what your head wants and what your heart yearns for, which comes from a childhood sense of tension between your parents. When you get the lover you thought you wanted you start wanting someone totally different. You need a mate who can bring you down to the ground a little without restricting you too much. You need to learn to recharge your batteries rather than trying to stay high all the time.

You are warmer than many Geminis because of your fiery moon and more flamboyant so you will have little trouble in attracting a stream of lovers. Finding the right one will take more time. Donald Trump and Judy Garland are two examples.

Gemini Sun Capricorn Moon

Talkative, ambitious, hugely determined yet inclined to be just a tiny bit dull unless you can find a lover who will drag you away from work and your need to be socially acceptable. Gemini can be zany enough but you grew up thinking that achieving was the be-all and end-all. Success would make you loved and deep down you never think you do enough to earn your happiness. Which is, of course, all the wrong way round. You need a lover who is warm and centred enough to make you realize how magnificent a human being you are in yourself.

You will always want a solid lifestyle with the better things liberally sprinkled around. You are not one for slumming or mixing with life's failures. Being an air/earth mix you thrive on situations and people who are not too fiery, impulsive or erratic. Your sharp mind demands partners who are intellectually stimulating rather than bundles of passion. But you do need someone who makes you take yourself less seriously. You mellow with the years, gaining a livelier sense of humour and becoming quite a snazzy geriatric, but it does take time. Relationships are important to you but you need to gain more confidence. You may look cool, controlled and together but inside you often feel lonely, vulnerable and insecure, taking slights to heart more than others realize. Barbara Bush is a stalwart example.

Gemini Sun Aquarius Moon

Zippy, zany, wildly communicative and quite impossible to tie down, you are a real 'head case' in the strict sense that emotions are thought about, talked about but not always felt too deeply. An air sun and air moon together make you dabble endlessly in a wide variety of interests but you often need prodding to help you turn your ideas into reality. Lovers with fire in their belly or an earthy attachment to reality will help you get into life more. A watery emotional mate would make you run a mile because anything that smells like possessiveness has you very much on edge, ready to flee.

You are more nervous than you appear, at times even hyper-sensitive, which belies your cool, chatty exterior. But you positively must get away from routine at times, especially out of domestic ruts, to clear your mind from its eternal worrying, planning and fidgeting. Friends are hugely important to you and often you irritate more romantic lovers by always inviting the gang along just when a moment for cosy intimacy offers itself. Your fear of close one-to-one commitment veers toward the paranoid. Overcoming this fear is your real challenge because your Gemini sun deep inside really wants another half in life, the mythical twin you feel you have lost way back before the beginning of time, and craves very much to water the desert that seems to exist where your heart should be. Richard Wagner and Marilyn Monroe are examples to ponder.

Gemini Sun Pisces Moon

Highly adaptable, rather gentle, always fidgeting and a more emotional Gemini than the norm you really do want to find a tender love in life. But it is not easy to settle your wayward tendencies and ease your fear of being trapped, never mind your fear of being rejected. Often you cannot find the courage to voice your feelings so prospective lovers pass by never knowing they were the object of your desire. In childhood you were aware of a difference in outlook between your parents and it may take you well into adult life to settle the inner conflict that rages inside you as a result. Your heart points you in one direction and your head in another. You marry one person and promptly fall in love with someone else. What is over the fence always looks more attractive – until you hop across and get what you thought you wanted. Then the whole process starts over. You need to find a way in your emotional life of doing what you want and what you ought at the same time.

An air/water mix between your sun and moon helps you be creative, makes you good at counselling others and is a highly sensitive combination. You just need to watch that you do not dream too much. Your escapist tendencies can get out of hand. A fiery lover would help you act out your fantasies and an earthy one would pull you into reality more. Though they need to be tactful on the one hand and not too physical on the other. You dislike brash ill-mannered partners, as well as dull clods. You need variety alongside stability. But someone who can centre you and anchor you without making you feel fenced in really is the ideal.

Cancer Sun Aries Moon

Emotionally super-sensitive and home-loving, you also have a real determination to get out into the world and make it happen. A watery sun and a fiery moon make it difficult for you to settle to what you need. One part of you yearns for family togetherness and suburban bliss, the other part of you is a hard-driving, over-excitable, go-getting raver. It may take you half a lifetime to find the balance but you will – once you learn to rise above the either/or conflicts in your life. Your head and your heart can be made to agree. What usually happens early on is that you commit to one person and immediately find you want someone else. Nothing satisfies you totally. Your Aries moon wants nourishing by a lover who is fierce, courageous, romantic and a great adventurer. But your Cancer sun is looking for a more stable, suburban mate altogether. Someone to cling to who will be dependent on you.

You can be completely contradictory in your moods, even more so than the usually fickle Cancerian, so you need a steady partner who will protect your more sensitive feelings yet can also give you the excitement you absolutely must have. Getting out to make your career happen is almost more important to you than anything. You over-react to criticism, even where none is intended, so a tactless lover is a dead end. Great physical passion is not really your scene. You like cuddles and you dream of wonderfully ecstatic clinches but you get bothered by partners who want total exclusivity.

Cancer Sun Taurus Moon

Home-loving, security conscious, possessive, indulgent, caring and considerate you are one of the world's family people. The better things of life are a must for your happiness and fulfilment – a comfortable home, classy and sensuous clothes, good food and drink, plush friends and an abundance of cuddles. Being a water/earth mix you are creative in a highly practical way. Starting new projects is never a problem and once on track you have more staying power than most Cancerians. You like to wrap yourself round lovers, anchor them to the spot and never let them go. Jealousy runs deep in your nature and you react with great speed to any threat to your emotional well-being.

Part of you is amazingly physical and passionate but part of you wants the emotional contact as much as anything. Cancer is not given to deeply erotic relationships though Taurus is, so you need to find a balance in your mate. You can be stubbornly determined to get your own way in relationships and at home, which can cause problems. You need a pliable, flexible partner who does not mind giving in. Throwing tantrums is not really your style except at the full moon, but you are a past master at the art of passive resistance. Cancer the crab digs itself into the sand at the first whiff of danger or disagreement and Taurus, the bull, stands firm at all times. You are slow to anger but quite a sight when you do erupt. You absolutely must have a faithful mate. Imelda Marcos of the several thousand pairs of shoes, highly talented but family-orientated actress Meryl Streep and family man/sitcom actor Bill Cosby belong to your tribe.

Cancer Sun Gemini Moon

A fairly untypical Cancerian you can blanch sometimes at too much emotion, hate being swamped in sentiment and really long for the wide open spaces. You are supposed to be a home-lover yet at the first opportunity you fly the coop. Restlessness is inbred. Gemini moon people regard ruts and routines with something akin to horror. You feel as if you might die if you have to keep at the same repetitive drudgery for ever. So you have a conflict on your hands going on inside you between your Cancerian half which wants home, family and the suburban life and your Gemini half which wants excitement, travel and mental stimulation. You can be jealous though you loathe to admit it. You need an oddly assorted lover who will not cling on too firmly and who can give you enough security without making you feel trapped.

You are not terribly good at intensely intimate physical relationships where it is all heavy breathing and hot passion. You need space and a lighter touch. In your partners the ability to communicate is a must. If they cannot talk, think and sparkle they will not last long. You are a water/air mix so maybe you need a touch of *chutzpah* (sparkle) and common sense in your mate. Being highly sensitive can make you a dreamer and rather fantasy-prone but you are still able to get your act together very effectively. You can laugh at yourself better than most Cancerians.

Cancer Sun Cancer Moon

Deeply emotional, hyper-sensitive and curiously rather self-sufficient, you feel as if you were almost too swept around by your feelings at times to be able to open up easily. Like a raft cast adrift on the sea you are blown hither and thither by the winds and the currents. Consideration and care of others in a general way is central to your nature but sometimes you find it easier to relate to the sufferings of the world and give to everyone rather than give to someone very close. You need to pick partners who will not hurt you in any way. It is said that Cancer is the sign most deeply afraid of being hurt. Fear of separation is the worst and you have it in double quantities. Jealousy runs strongly in your nature and you can sulk endlessly if things do not go your way.

Leaving the past behind is difficult and at times feels almost impossible; you can be wildly, wonderfully sentimental.

Curiously enough, being a new moon baby you do not have a driving need to have a partner around all the time. You can prop yourself up quite happily and your self-absorption may upset partners because you do not rely enough on them. You have all of the Cancerian's love of family though you may make partners feel more like children or siblings after a time than intimate lovers. You are full of initiative and get-up-and-go and will doubtless have an active career. When life gets tricky you pull your socks up and start a new project to keep you occupied. Little Prince William, actor Harrison Ford and pioneer in working with the dying Elizabeth Kubler-Ross are all double Cancerians.

Cancer Sun Leo Moon

Water and fire do not mix, they say, but you have to find a way since you are emotional and intuitive at the same time. Living life to the full in the most flamboyant way is your aim. Extremely creative, very colourful and full of initiative you keep your life moving along at a fair pace. The grand style is important to you. Life as you see it should be travelled first-class and lived only in five-star places. You adore surrounding yourself with wealthy, elegant friends. Charm is second nature to you and entertaining is one of your great joys. Your reputation is very important (perhaps a touch too important) to you so a partner who can up your status is a must. Home and family are deeply important to your well-being and you cling firmly to those you love. Jealousy can be a problem but in addition to loathing separations of any sort you also loathe criticism, even the merest whisper of it. So you need a mate who is the soul of tact and diplomacy, endlessly patient and willing to put up with your foibles, dislikes and mood swings.

At best you can be simple, direct and very straightforward. At worst you can be given to loud outbursts. You can be amazingly stubborn at home, so lovers have to be flexible.

Cancer Sun Virgo Moon

Kind, considerate, highly practical, socially charming, a mover and a shaker in a very quiet, refined way, you are one of the world's special people. Worrying is your great downfall. You are a past master at nit-picking over every tiny anxiety and when they are used up you invent a few more! You crave order a little too much and need to watch a tendency to be prudish. Luckily your Cancer sun keeps you on the move, starting new projects, creating a little beauty or comfort for yourself and others. Being of service is extremely important to you though you are remarkably good at standing up for yourself when the moment comes. You are no pushover and indeed have more inner determination than most.

A family is important to your well-being, both when unmarried and married. You need a lover you can introduce round to your relatives as well as one who wants to settle with children eventually. You also need one who understands your deeper fears and phobias. On your off days you can be amazingly tetchy, even sometimes slightly paranoid, and need to be made feel secure. You can be both possessive and quite adaptable. What could be a problem as you age is a tendency to turn lovers into just another member of the brood at home or to become slightly shrivelled up with worry. You do nag at times. You have to stay open to life and live that Virgo moon out to its fullest physical expression. The Dalai Lama is your most notable model.

Cancer Sun Libra Moon

Successful, creative, sensitive, considerate, charming and rather elegant, you are definitely one of the world's beautiful people. You love surrounding yourself with tasteful objects and even more tasteful people. The great unwashed hold no fascination whatsoever for you. Dare it be said – you can be just a touch snobbish and at times too much on the surface. Home-loving but definitely not the stay-at-home type, you are constantly on the move, working for success. But you also are consistently trying to find the answers to your inner dilemmas because you always have a sense that you never get quite what you want. Your life is always half wonderful. You feel a despair about ever getting total satisfaction. What you want is never what you ought to do.

Your Cancer sun pushes you towards emotionally sensitive, home-loving people who can be part of your larger family but that Libra moon wants a one-to-one partner who is also fairly expansive and detached. Finding the right balance is tricky and much of the dissonance comes from the incompatibility which you sensed as a child between your parents. They did not feel that together so you cannot feel that together within yourself until you leave childhood behind and begin to find your own identity. You are an escapist so you need someone rather practical and grounded, within limits.

Cancer Sun Scorpio Moon

Creative, caring, strong, intense and very determined, you always know inside yourself exactly where you are aiming though often you do not let on. You are awash with emotion and sometimes feel cast adrift like a small boat on the ocean, blown hither and thither by the winds and currents. Your feelings run deeper than almost everyone else's but you never ever admit when you are hurt. Taking great pride in concealing your vulnerabilities you sometimes come across as uncaring or rather tough but quite the reverse is the case. Standing far enough back from yourself is not easy so you can rarely be objective. Over-reacting to slights or hearing criticism where none was intended makes life not only difficult for you but also for your partner. Some people need to balance up by finding lovers the opposite of themselves but you could not stand an airy, unemotional sort. Or one who was too fiery and up in the clouds. Earth types can ground you a little and make you feel more stable and secure. But at the end of the day you really want a mate who can join you in those oceanic feelings which at times threaten to swamp you.

You never take your love life lightly. It's all love or war! Once you are off people that is it. At times you may not want any mate at all because you do get so pulled into your depths. Often you find yourself giving and getting emotional nourishment from larger groups of people. But you cannot live without love for long. Families are hugely important to you. Nelson Mandela is your type, which indicates that for him his almost lifelong imprisonment must have been particularly unbearable.

Cancer Sun Sagittarius Moon

No one could ever accuse you of being boring or stodgy. A wonderfully colourful mix of fire and water you thrive on fun, constant activity and impulse decisions. A contradictory mix is what you are – fiercely emotional, home-loving and caring on the one hand but also freedom-loving, independent, devil-may-care and tactlessly honest on the other. You fight a constant battle within yourself. One part of you wants family, security, stability and roots – the other wants the wide open spaces, stimulating friendships and the odd thrill to keep life exciting. You need an equally odd mix in a lover: someone who will give you space and support at the same time.

Hot, strong, physical passion is not your scene. What you really prefer is emotional warmth and perhaps the romantic illusion of an adventurous relationship. You certainly will never settle for anyone dull. But you do not like to be too crowded. As you grow older lovers may feel as if they have been added in as just another member of the family, which could cause problems. On your best days you are wonderfully, refreshingly direct and on your worst given to firework displays of bad temper. You love to entertain both socially and professionally. You will never feel totally satisfied about your emotional life because you need such totally different things in a mate.

Cancer Sun Capricorn Moon

Emotional and earthy, caring and practical, creative, successful, you are always on the go. You have oodles of initiative and never sit still. New ideas, new projects and new people float constantly through your life. Whatever is not working well is abandoned as you sail off to start afresh. Beginnings are relatively easy. It's keeping going which is difficult for you. Routine and long-distance jobs are a bore. But somehow you never feel quite satisfied with life or love. A full moon baby, you are constantly living on a see-saw. You veer from extreme to extreme, wanting what you have not got. Once you have it you want something else. In childhood you felt your parents were quite opposite types. You have ingested the split between them into yourself so that what you ought to do is never what you want to do and vice versa. You commit to one person and promptly want another.

At times in life you will not have stopped working long enough to find a satisfactory love life. You never feel acceptable for just being you. You feel you have to earn love by achieving all the time. Your Cancer sun yearns for roots, protection and the reassurance of a family while your Capricorn moon pushes you out into the cold, hard world to keep working. You need a mate who will drown you in love and boost your self-esteem to the extent of making success less necessary. Ernest Hemingway is one of yours. Suburbia was hardly his cup of tea.

Cancer Sun Aquarius Moon

Bright, sharp-witted, caring, creative, very restless and rather sensitive, you are never quite sure what it is you want in life. Emotionally quixotic you want quite contradictory, incompatible qualities in your lovers. They need to be into their feelings enough to give you security and protection yet open enough to let you roam free. You are desperate to continue your childhood family life into adulthood yet you shy clear of one-to-one involvement and commitment because you fear being trapped. You are a compulsive joiner of groups, teams, crowds of friends. Safety in numbers is one of your mottos.

You are constantly pulled between your head and your heart. At times the only solution seems to be to disappear into your daydreams. Escapism is a failing and brings discontent and dissatisfaction. You do have a fertile imagination which can be put to better use than creating fantasies. What you lack is real trust in life and practical common sense. But if you try to find these qualities in lovers you get unsettled by their fiery over-confidence or their boringly mundane approach to life.

Great physical passion is not at all to your taste. Indeed your Aquarius moon really wants to be separate from the body altogether at times. Role models are the Princess of Wales, whose split hopes for family and public career are obvious, as is her need to distance herself from her body. Also Soraya of Iran, actress Leslie Caron, novelist Iris Murdoch and singer Linda Ronstadt.

Cancer Sun Pisces Moon

Deeply sensitive and caring to a degree which hurts, you feel pain for almost everyone to the extent that you sometimes need to shut yourself away from the world and people just to settle down your surging emotions. At times you are so impressionable you feel cast adrift on a wide sea, helpless to anchor yourself or be at rest. Your extraordinarily creative and considerate temperament can be put to good use either in artistic careers or in helping others. But you sometimes shy away from revealing your feelings in intimate relationships because you fear rejection, abandonment or worse. At the same time you are very seducible and often find yourself dragged into relationships out of pity.

Finding the courage to voice your feelings is a challenge for you. You absolutely need a lover who is not a rough clod around matters of the heart. Someone who can soothe away your worries, protect you against the troubles of the world and give you a secure harbour. Mates also need to be strong enough not be blown around by your extremes (which can be very severe). At times you can appear and probably are very self-absorbed just because your feelings do swallow you up. Maturity usually brings you some ideal in life to dedicate yourself to which helps to pull you out of yourself. Resentment can be a tiny failing since you so often feel a martyr to other people's needs. Escaping off on a day-dream trip is your way out but not always helpful. You need love and a family. Ginger Rogers is one of your watery kind.

Leo Sun Aries Moon

Bright, brash, colourful and highly active, you live life at a pace that would exhaust most people. At times you even threaten to burn out yourself. An energetic go-getter, you are great at creating, at starting up new projects and thinking of new ideas and you have all the courage and daring in the world. Common sense is not always your long suit and neither, it has to be said, is emotional sensitivity. You just never sit still long enough to consider other people's needs, which obviously can bring relationship problems in its wake. As a red hot Leo you need an audience of adoring, admiring fans and courtiers. With an Aries moon you need even more to stand out as an individual. Co-operating, sharing, caring and being half of a duo is a difficult concept for you especially in early adult life. So you tend to aim for rather submissive lovers who will grovel, agree and anticipate your every whim. They also have to be classy enough to fit in with your idea of your station in life.

You always think of yourself as being highly romantic and often wish you had been born in a more glamorous era. You will have some sizzling escapades but they may not survive for ever. Since love is essentially about being and not doing you are somewhat at a loss. Your reactions change constantly, you loathe restraint in any form and the idea of compromise makes your hackles rise.

Your pride often gets in the way of love. The knocks and disappointments of life will hopefully eventually soften you down a touch, giving you a connection to your own suffering and thus to the suffering of others. Then partnerships really begin to work. You are basically faithful, want a solid home and family life and once settled can be loyal. But you also will need space to do your own thing.

Leo Sun Taurus Moon

Fun-loving, power- and attention-seeking, determined to follow your own pleasures in life, there is no doubt that you carve your own path. A determined steamroller of a personality you will do whatever is necessary to fulfil your ambitions. Your fiery sun can make you just a touch vain or pompous but luckily your earthy moon adds a touch of grounding, common sense and humility. Self-indulgence is, however, a large part of your make-up and you rarely listen to advice which tells you to cut back, give up or be hard on yourself. Pleasuring your senses is high on your list of priorities. So you eat and drink well, insist on living in style and comfort and really cannot survive without an abundance of cuddles. Your great strength can be a blessing or a curse. Hugely stubborn, you obviously need a mate who will adapt to your needs rather than the other way round. If you hit difficulties you stand rooted like an oak tree until other people and circumstances adapt to you. But once on track you have a great deal of staying power. Indeed there is little that will shift you.

Your head and heart rarely agree so you often settle in one relationship and then your wandering eye starts to look over the fence. You can be loyal and faithful once settled, though you will always be jealous and fairly possessive. You do need to acquire an appreciation of the finer subtleties of life and love, perhaps at some point dedicating yourself to serving others rather than the other way round. You need tough partners who will not be pushed around by you. An unholy yet intriguing mix of personalities are this type. Sex, drugs and rock 'n' roller Mick Jagger for one. US President Bill Clinton is another. Swiss psychotherapist Carl Jung, whose infidelities are well documented, is a third. All three personalities have been lucky in their choice of extraordinarily solid and forgiving partners.

Leo Sun Gemini Moon

A never-sit-still individual, you are everyone's idea of heaven at a party. You talk entertainingly and non-stop, feeding titbits of fascinating information (quite often about yourself) to anyone who will listen. You revel in attention and admiration, the more the merrier. Routine and drudgery are but one step away from the grave to you. Your life must be filled with variety, spice, excitement and glamour otherwise you get very bad tempered. Committed relationships are a mixed blessing in your view. Your Leo side really wants a burning passion which will fill your life from now to infinity, and in that mode you can be extremely faithful. But your Gemini moon is a real social butterfly. What you want one moment is not what you want three seconds later. You need a partner who is just as erratic, unpredictable and quirky as you. You also need a mate who will put up with your need to be centre stage and in the limelight. Lovers have to be grand enough to share your regal lifestyle (Leo being king/queen of the beasts) but not so uppity that they threaten to upstage you.

It often takes you a while through life to learn compassion or sensitivity to the needs of others, which can prove a stumbling block to early relationships. What you lack, being a fire/air type, is water and earth. So you must get more in touch with your feelings in tiny ways in all aspects of life. Lack of earth makes you impractical and rather unrealistic so it would help to find a mate with some common sense to balance you. You give them fiery enthusiasm and trust in life. They keep your feet on the floor. Mussolini was your type.

A Lover's Guide

Leo Sun Cancer Moon

Two words spring to mind – one is family, the other is grand. You certainly love the better things of life, you need socially elevated friends, the more the merrier, and you want a solid, settled family base. No one is going to upstage you at home, that is for sure. Leo always wants to be top dog in the family and your Cancer moon makes very certain that the older you get the more you will pull the strings of power in the family. Being a fire/water mix you are a person of extremes, excitable, impulsive, intense and highly sensitive to criticism.

You over-react even where no slights were intended, which can make you a prickly minefield for lovers. They have to tread very delicately around you. Jealousy can be quite a problem. Certainly you hate being separated from those you love both in the emotional sense and because you absolutely loathe being humiliated. Your mood swings can be quite severe though you are usually able to express yourself with a refreshing directness. You can be highly unpredictable or thoroughly warm-hearted. Show business personalities often are of your type and you certainly would adore the glamour, razzmatazz and romance of the public life. What you possibly need more than anything else is an earthy type who would offer you warmth tempered with common sense. You do lack air and the objectivity it brings, but airy types – Gemini, Libra and Aquarius – would seem too cool, heartless and detached. Princess Margaret is an exact Leo/Cancer type.

Leo Sun Leo Moon

A difficult combination this, both for yourself and for partners. You are so centred in yourself and your needs, so determined to be grand, be admired and be loved that you genuinely find it difficult to step beyond the boundaries of your own world to see the needs of others. It will get better as you grow older and learn a few tough lessons about love, suffering and life. Few people recognize quite how insecure, unconfident and empty you really feel you are. They only see the regal gestures, the flash, the show, the public performance. Inside you are often very frightened, not knowing whether you really exist at all, so you absolutely must have a mate who can boost your fragile ego and who does not mind being a slave to its demands.

Your moods can be extreme opposites – one moment demanding, proud and arrogant, the next humiliated, feeling worthless and powerless. You can be stubborn to the nth degree but are not always sensible, to put it mildly. You lack earth to give you a sense of your body and to put your feet on the floor. You lack water so you are not always well in touch with the feelings that could nourish you. Burnout is a real problem since you have no sense of when to slow down. Being a new moon baby you are more self-sufficient than most, with less need to have a constant other half. But you do need a passion. Not for nothing is Leo known as the sign of the burning heart. Megastar actors (which is what you might expect) Patrick Swayze and Peter O'Toole are your type.

Leo Sun Virgo Moon

You work very hard to stay in a prominent position in life. Two quite contradictory traits vie with each other inside you. One wants the glamorous life full of attention, admiration and money. The other is rather self-effacing, workaholic, almost timid and a great worrier about the tiny trivia of life. But you are a great deal more realistic than most Leos, which is a help since you pay attention to your body and do not delegate the boring tasks of life loftily to others as is the norm with most other of your sun sign compatriots.

Being fire/earth you are what is known in astrology as a steamroller type who keeps going long after everyone else has dropped by the wayside out of sheer exhaustion. You have the energy and determination of 10. Obviously you need a partner with stamina to keep up with you though not, of course, to knock you off centre stage, which is the cardinal sin in your book. You do lack contact with your feelings and are often not good at standing back far enough to see yourself clearly. But a highly emotional mate would make you feel too swamped and an airy mate would feel too cool and detached. You need a flexible partner who will give way when you dig your heels in. The starry cast of Princess Anne (more attention-seeking than she sometimes appears), Madonna (harder working and more self-effacing than she appears), Robert Redford and Dustin Hoffman (exceptionally hard-working perfectionists) are members of your type.

Leo Sun Libra Moon

You could never be poor, unwashed or a down and out. You need to be grand, to move in the best circles, to live a luxurious lifestyle with a group of highly elevated friends. Upwardly socially mobile is the name of your game. Your Leo sun wants attention, excitement and colour. Your Libra moon wants peace, harmony and elegance. You certainly have great taste – in clothes and interior design.

Being fire and air you move at speed, rarely slowing down to ask your body or your feelings what they want. You need a partner who can anchor you a little without making you feel suffocated or swamped. You find it difficult to connect with the darker side of life. If anything you can come across as being slightly superficial because you like to stay sociable, stay on the surface and not face depressions, pain or misery. Hard experience in life will teach you to connect to the depths which can give you more stability and solidity. Your sense of humour is usually a strong point and you can always look on the bright side of life. But over-optimism sometimes trips you up. You often accuse others of being critical or gloomy when in fact they are just being realistic. Fidel Castro is your type.

Leo Sun Scorpio Moon

Sunny on the outside and deep, dark and determined on the inside, you rarely show that you are hurt, indeed you rarely show your feelings at all. Your Leo sun is all show and you certainly adore being centre stage when admiration and attention are going. But emotionally you play your cards very close to your chest and are a much more complex being than the normally straightforward Leo. Your Scorpio moon makes you hang on to grudges and you can even be vindictive when people have hurt you. Forgiveness does not come easily. You are stubborn to an extraordinary degree so need a mate who can bend and flex to your will without feeling aggrieved.

Change is not easy for you and in general you will withstand most pressures, digging your heels in to maintain the status quo. You assume circumstances and other people will give way before you do. You are the most controlled of the fire/water types but even your moods swing from extreme to extreme. Unpredictable, excitable and rather impulsive you often have little discipline about life. What you want is what you want and that is all there is to the matter. You can express yourself very directly at times and can be warm and supportive, though you will always hold part of yourself back. You will jealously guard what is yours. The Queen Mother, not quite the sweet bundle of sugar candy she looks, is one of your type.

Leo Sun Sagittarius Moon

Wild, restless, charming, self-centered and absolutely determined to do what you want at all costs, you are in danger of burnout because you will not settle down ever. You ignore the signals from your body that it has had enough, ignore advice from everyone around and generally ignore life's warnings until you are forced to face up to reality with a bump. Sometimes you come across as warm, charming, outgoing and generous but you do have a genuine difficulty seeing others' points of view or understanding a partner's needs so you can also seem crude and insensitive. You are an entrepreneur at heart, a real go-getter and promoter so you need a mate around who can support you in your aims and who does not mind being abandoned for long stretches while you go chasing after your visions.

What can let you down in relationships is your inability to stay with your heart. Very watery, emotional partners make you feel swamped but you do need to learn to take in nourishment from your feelings and not fly along the cloud tops all the time. Lovers and partners will often be accused by you of being critical or gloomy whereas they are probably only being sensible in refusing to be totally caught up in your wild enthusiasms.

Leo Sun Capricorn Moon

You want to look grand but are willing to put your back into making it happen, rather than indulging in vague dreams. The attention and admiration of others are your life's blood but you are much more insecure, under-confident and deprived than you let on. You have always felt that you need to achieve to be loved rather than being accepted for just being yourself. You certainly make more of a success of your life than most but along the way you do not always feel as happy as you should. You can come across as vain, even arrogant, but in reality you are terrified no one will notice you. Criticism hurts you deeply.

Being a fire/earth type you are what is known in astrological parlance as a steamroller, able to keep going long after weaker souls have dropped by the wayside. You have formidable energy and the vision to sustain your interest. Love may be pushed to one side for the sake of work and ambition for longish periods in your life but you are basically a warm-hearted person underneath all that rigid self-discipline. Your Capricorn moon can be sensual, cuddly and pleasure-seeking when you let yourself relax, which does happen more easily as you get older. You need a partner who will adapt to your needs since you are fairly stubborn, and perhaps also someone who can survive those times when your interest is either on yourself or your ambitions. Tough guy actor Arnold Schwarzenegger, (Stormin') Norman Schwarzkopf and Rasputin, the Russian priest, madman and arch-manipulator who pulled the strings in the Tsar's family are your type.

Leo Sun Aquarius Moon

A full moon baby, you never know what you want. Your head says one thing, your heart quite another. When you have a lover, you promptly want someone else. But that never quite works either. Your Leo sun wants attention and admiration and is rather traditional and quite self-centred. But your Aquarius moon is friendly, happy to be one of the crowd and could not care less about the limelight. It is also zany, wacky, eccentric and unconcerned about the social niceties of life. So you are constantly at war with yourself. This conflict stems from a childhood in which you saw your parents as being incompatible. What they could not get together in their marriage, you cannot get together in your head. So you need to rise above their differences of long ago and find new solutions to your problems. It does not have to be a question of either this or that. There is a third way.

Very close relationships make you claustrophobic and you fight shy of anything that smells remotely like jealousy or possessiveness. You want to be free to follow your own unconventional lifestyle. Often you set out to startle or shock companions just to make an effect, so you need a mate who is expansive, tolerant and fairly unflappable. Being a fire/air type you could probably do with a lover who is slightly earthy to give you warmth and grounding. Watery, emotional people make you run a mile.

Leo Sun Pisces Moon

Fun-loving and attention-seeking on the outside, in reality you are a deeply sensitive, rather timid soul inside. Those who know you well (and few probably do) realize that you often pass up chances for relationships because you are so scared of rejection. Often you indulge more in day-dreams than in actual romances. You need to make more of an effort to get into reality. Being a fire/water type you are excitable, impulsive, restless and prone to fairly extreme mood swings. Over-reacting to others' comments can make you seem prickly and unreasonable, but you do genuinely hear slights in anything that is not unabashed admiration. Feeling a martyr often makes you seem self-pitying and you need to make an effort to pull yourself away from the past. Restraining yourself is not always easy and you are possibly more addiction-prone than some.

At best you can be refreshingly straightforward and direct, though you can also be way off beam at times. You are highly creative, probably musical, and would fare well in a show business or entertainment career. You need a partner who is adaptable and willing to put his or her needs aside to allow you centre stage. But you are more giving than many Leos, able to understand the distress and needs of close partners. Emotional types would suit you well, though some earth in your lover would also help to bring you down to the ground occasionally. You are not remotely practical.

Virgo Sun Aries Moon

A restless personality, you are in truth a slightly odd mix. Your Virgo sun makes you hard-working, modest, rather refined and a great worrier. Your Aries moon makes you excitable, slightly brash, go-getting and fairly pushy. Being an earth/fire mix you are a real steamroller of energy, crashing on when other weaker souls have dropped by the wayside. You have determination, persistence, an eye for detail and an appetite for grand schemes. In love you want excitement and a slight element of danger. Sitting still at home tending to the domestic chores is not your idea of heaven.

You somehow manage to be highly critical, a bit of a perfectionist and wildly impractical all at once. You never feel you have everything you want in life. Something is always missing. You certainly need a similarly unsettled personality as a mate. Ideally an Aries with a Virgo moon would be your choice. You adore work and you channel your energies with great dedication. But your reactions change constantly and you tend to leap into activity often without thinking matters through carefully enough. You need a partner who is more fixed than you, able to stand still while you dash around like someone possessed. Stalwart veteran actress Lauren Bacall, long-time companion of Humphrey Bogart, and Stefan Casiraghi, the second husband of Princess Caroline of Monaco killed in a speed boat accident, are examples.

Virgo Sun Taurus Moon

Earthy, warm, charming, hard-working and very rooted you are certainly concerned with giving yourself what feels good in life. Luckily your Virgo sun gives you a strong sense of service otherwise you would be totally given over to your own comfort. Although reasonably adaptable you essentially loathe change of any sort, especially in your home life.

You are affectionate and more demonstrative than some Virgos. The Taurus moon makes you extremely tactile and always in need of a good cuddle. Life to you is about the pleasures of the senses and as long as you find a mate whose pleasures coincide with yours then you should have relatively little trouble.

You do lack slightly in imagination, being all earth. You can have a rather narrow vision of life and do need to channel your formidable energies into some challenging task. A perfectionist where others are concerned you can be a touch critical or analytical and that sometimes freezes emotions before they have had a chance to develop. Luckily your Taurus moon warms up that rather detached side of Virgo. You need an emotional mate who can breathe some real life into your heart. Fire types will drive you wild with their impracticality. Quiet but competitive Prince Harry and the enigmatic Greta Garbo (who was less ascetic than she appeared) are examples of your type.

Virgo Sun Gemini Moon

Restless, adaptable, a great worker and worrier, you find concentrating over a long span difficult. More likely to be a jack-of-all-trades than a specialist you always have several strings to your bow. The difference to you between a rut and being half-dead is only a matter of degree. You need to learn to settle in life just a little and would be the better for a fixed partner – Taurus, Leo, Scorpio or Aquarius in either sun or moon sign – to give you some anchorage. Though sometimes this very security makes you feel suffocated and trapped. Nervousness can be a problem because you are highly strung, possibly more so than others realize. So you also need an unflappable mate who can cope with your panics and phobias without getting exasperated.

You can be both intellectual and practical but what you are not is impulsive or emotional. You come across as cool, reasonable, even a little chilly. You need to attract more fiery excitement into your life and a little more feeling. There is no sense in you mating with an over-watery type, however, since too many emotions would threaten to swamp your finely balanced system. You need to get fully into life at some point. You are in danger of drying up if you do not. Virgo has a tendency to be too much the observer, not enough the participant.

Virgo Sun Cancer Moon

A charming, helpful, hard-working, home-loving person you are not one of the world's ravers but all the better for it. Being practical and adaptable you can fit into most situations rather happily and go well out of your way to make sure companions are well looked after. You do tend to be over-serious at times and self-protective but you have the capacity to hang on in there through almost any crisis. Your inner strength is considerable but you can be too attached to the past or may feel the need to maintain your security to an obsessive degree. This can cause problems in relationships – as can your tendency to manipulate. But you have an adaptability and a sense of initiative that are highly useful. What you lack sometimes is staying power and the insight to understand your unconscious fears.

Your Cancer moon makes you sentimental rather than realistic about your past and present family life, which is not always helpful. Breaking away from your childhood family is difficult for you. You absolutely need to settle down with a family as an adult, so keep your Virgo perfectionist streak well under control. It sometimes destroys feelings before they have had a chance to blossom.

Virgo Sun Leo Moon

You want to live life the five-star way and are willing to work extremely hard to make it happen. You are a curious mix being both modest, self-effacing and rather shy and also charming, entertaining and at times vain. Your ego never quite knows where it is – being pushed into the background or being allowed centre stage. More outgoing than the normal Virgo, you love putting on a show and being flamboyant. Your vanity is easily dented and you loathe criticism in any form, though being a Virgo you can be quite a perfectionist about others. You appear more flexible than you really are. That Leo moon does not give way easily to anyone else's needs or wants.

Your personal magnetism gets you your own way most of the time. Being an earth/fire mix you charge through life, leaving weaker souls exhausted by the wayside. Your workaholic tendencies combined with flair and vision make you a formidable achiever. But you need sometimes to look at the subtler side of life and not be so determined to keep on the move all the time. A partner with a touch (not too much) water would help to nourish you, slow you down a little. Staying in touch with your feelings is important. Louis XIV (known as the Sun King), who certainly liked show (as his palace at Versailles proves), was your type.

Virgo Sun Virgo Moon

A workaholic and a worrier, practical, self-contained and rather critical, you do not always need a partner in life. Being a new moon baby you can survive better on your own than most. Being in addition a Virgo you are fairly good at staying within your own boundaries. This does not mean you do not want to relate, just that you are not desperate for a soul mate in the way some are. A double earthy aspect can give you too narrow a vision in life and an obsessive concern with what works. If your career lets you down you panic, so it always has absolute priority.

You do not always let your imagination free to push you in the direction of your dreams and visions. You need to find more trust in life, more sparkle and daring, and to stop worrying. They always say that the Virgo moon raises worrying to an art form. You have it in double doses! Emotions can sometimes be analysed to freezing point before they have had a chance to blossom. You need to allow your feelings more space. A spontaneous, outgoing lover would probably do you the world of good – though you will object to having your neatly ordered life upset. Getting into life is important since you can turn out to be rather 'spinsterish' (no matter which sex you are) if you stay on the sidelines and only ever observe. An intriguing mix of this type are Sean Connery (much less James Bondish in his private life than his looks would suggest), talented singer Mama Cass, now sadly gone, and gifted but unstable 1930s actress Frances Farmer, whose life was portrayed by Jessica Lange in the film *Frances*.

Virgo Sun Libra Moon

Refined, elegant, rather retiring and very hard-working, you would never knowingly put a foot out of line socially. You are one of the world's goodies though you need to watch that you do not become too precious or indeed too much of a superficial observer of life's scene rather than an active participant. You are fastidious, slightly snobbish and loathe the great unwashed and the idle. Your Virgo sun makes you a perfectionist about other people and your Libra moon makes you want everything to be 'nice' – blissfully harmonious and peaceful. This can make relationships tricky since it leaves no room for flaws, faults and the odd off day. You are adaptable, however, and full of initiative so you usually pick yourself up and keep things ticking over.

What you are exceptionally good at is creating a beautiful home full of beautiful things, and you entertain like a dream though you are not an indulgent party person yourself. You like working at everything including your social life. Being an earth/air mix you can sometimes come across as too practical and cool. You lack impulsiveness and emotional sensitivity. Perhaps you need a lover who is just a touch more daring and has more connection to the feelings. Getting down into the depths of yourself is not easy for you.

Virgo Sun Scorpio Moon

An intriguing combination, you can appear rather prudish on the surface but passions burn deeply within. Your workaholic tendencies obscure your deeply emotional nature, at least to the outside view. What is sure is that you will not be one of life's dried-up, 'spinsterish' Virgos who view it all from the sidelines. You throw yourself intensely into whatever you are doing, be it emotional or professional. Your Scorpio moon is deeply secretive and few ever know the turmoil of feelings that churn inside you. You will never let on when you have been hurt. 'Forgive and forget' does not come easily to you. At times you have been known to be vindictive though you dislike yourself afterwards.

As an earth/water type you have tremendous stamina and endurance. You can survive any calamity but have a tendency to cling too firmly to what is past rather than moving ahead through changes. What you need is a lover who wants to live life at the same emotional depth as you, preferably a water sign, ideally a sun Scorpio who can put up with your slightly manipulative tendencies. Fire does not sit happily with your nature but maybe a mate with a touch more daring than yourself could give you the courage to be less fearful.

Virgo Sun Sagittarius Moon

Restless, fidgety, talkative to a startling degree and rather wise, you are certainly not a stick-in-the-mud personality. But you never feel quite settled with yourself. Your head and your heart always want different people and different things. As soon as you settle with a lover, you promptly lose interest and look elsewhere. You need to find a way of combining your duty with your desires.

Jealousy and possessiveness make you run a mile so an insecure mate who tries to fence you in absolutely will not do. You need to have intellectual and emotional freedom to wander as you please. Friends are hugely important to you but they need to be relatively thick-skinned since you are honest to a staggering degree.

Being an earth/fire person you keep going constantly. In astrology you are known as a steamroller, able to forge ahead when everyone else is dropping by the wayside. You have a way of combining flair with practicality so you can turn your visions into reality, though at times you do get bogged down in details. Work is your main interest and a life of settled domesticity is one of your ideas of hell. You need a lover who can introduce you to the subtler aspects of life and maybe even get you more in touch with your feelings. Alan Dershowitz, the New York lawyer immortalized as counsel for the defence in the Claus Von Bulow case, and who specializes in winning 'no hopers', is your type.

Virgo Sun Capricorn Moon

Earthy, over-worked, a worrier, a touch too practical, you can be surprisingly sensual if you let yourself go. But you tend to assume you will only be loved if you achieve, so you can go through ambitious workaholic phases and even remain celibate for longish periods. You are undoubtedly charming though you never relax much on social occasions. You have a sneaking feeling that indulgences are sins that other people can manage but you cannot. You come across as someone who is relatively at ease with himself though this is partly an illusion.

Being a double earth type you are a touch narrow in your vision of life and obsessed with what works and what is practical rather than what could be a dream or an ideal. Money could become too much of a god for you, as could social status. You need to let your imagination roam free and to have more faith in life. Take the odd risk. A partner with a water sun or moon (Cancer, Scorpio or Pisces) would get you in touch with your feelings more. But you really love a partner who makes you feel needed and secure – someone who is worth while. Your self-esteem is not great. If your career fails at any point you panic like mad.

Virgo Sun Aquarius Moon

You constantly surprise yourself by being what you are not. An odd mix of the highly traditional and the frankly way out you manage to be at the same time rather prudish, fairly retiring and wild, wacky and eccentric. You almost deliberately set out to shock mates at times just to see the effect. Friends are the mainstay of your life and you are never happy with the idea of claustrophobic, possessive relationships. At the first whiff of jealousy you are off.

Being an earth/air mix you can come across as too cool and practical. Although impulsive in some respects you are not given to emotional flights of fancy. In fact you often stand so far back from feelings that others wonder whether you have them at all. You run the risk of never getting into life, instead becoming the expert observer and analyser who stands on the sidelines all the time to watch. Dissecting every lurch of your heart before it has taken time to root will freeze a relationship. You need to learn to trust feelings more and to go with the flow. Highly watery, emotional mates would be too difficult and might threaten to swamp you. But a touch of sensitivity to that side of life would help.

Virgo Sun Pisces Moon

A full moon baby, you are constantly out of step with yourself about what you want. Your head wants one person and your heart quite another. You settle and suddenly the grass looks greener elsewhere. You need to rise above the conflicts of your childhood to see that you can get your duty and your desires together – though this will not be easy. Adult life can be a long search for emotional happiness and stability. You are restless, adaptable and rather kind in nature so you should be able to find what you want ultimately.

You have a self-sacrificing streak and genuinely want to be of service. Because you are so sensitive to rejection, however, you sometimes shrink from exposing your feelings. Romantic opportunities are often missed because of your timidity. Day-dreams can often fill in for what your relationships fail to provide. Often you feel self-pitying, almost slightly martyred because of your predicament. You need to find the courage to get out into life. You have warmth and sensitivity. A lover who is fixed would give you an anchor. Maybe one with a touch (not too much) of fire would give you a sense of daring and trust in life. But you need a lover who is as refined as yourself. No one brash, crude or too direct would suit you. Sad, reclusive Michael Jackson, who does not find exclusive one-to-one relationships easy, is your type.

Libra Sun Aries Moon

A full moon baby, you never know quite what you want. It usually is not what you have got. Settle with one lover and the grass immediately looks greener on the other side of the fence. You rarely get your head and your heart together, which is a great shame since you desperately need a mate in life. Librans are never good at being solo flyers. You just do not feel whole without another half. But you are insecure, rather excitable, move around far too much and tend to be rather outspoken at points, which ruffles feathers. (This goes for Libran women more men since they are rather 'masculine' in their approach to life anyway, and an Aries moon adds to their dynamic, rather aggressive energy. Libran men tend to be sweeter and softer.)

Being an air/fire mix you are rather combustible and can flare up very rapidly. You also tend to burn out because you never slow down enough to recharge your batteries or listen to your body. Partners with a touch of earth about them to ground you and give you common sense, or with a hint of water to teach you to nourish yourself emotionally, would help. You tend to come across as rather superficial because you are highly sociable and shy away from the deeper, darker sides of life and love. It is only through painful experiences and being disappointed that you learn to plunge into those very feelings that can give you strength and stability.

Your sense of humour and wonderful way with words are real blessings for you. Your types include the rumbustious, none-too-sensible Duchess of York, tennis star Martina Navratilova (whose love life is also a constant upheaval), Luciano Pavarotti (the world's most beautiful voice and temperamentally combustible) and Friedrich Nietzsche, the philosopher who ended his days in mental decline.

Libra Sun Taurus Moon

Both your sun and moon are ruled by Venus, otherwise known as Aphrodite, the goddess of love, parties, indulgences and the high life. You certainly know how to enjoy yourself and no mistake. You have superb taste in clothes, décor and entertaining and you eat and drink rather to excess. You were never designed to be poor and absolutely must have a mate who either provides you with the luxuries of life or will allow you to spend as you please to pleasure yourself.

You need another half in life, so a partner is a must. You are more earthy, sensual and body-orientated than some Librans so must have a good sex life. You can be stubborn (hugely) about getting your own way at home and you loathe change in any form. Being an air/earth mix you can come across as rather cool. Certainly you are not given to wild impulses or flights of fancy except where your comfort is concerned. A hard worker you are never happy with lazy lovers, certainly not those who are idle about personal hygiene. You dislike the great unwashed. Your Taurus moon can make you possessive though Libra on the whole is not a jealous sign. A refined sun Taurus would suit you down to the ground. But you cannot stand crudity in any form so he or she would need to be civilized.

Libra Sun Gemini Moon

An airy, detached, talkative, nervy, restless personality you certainly know how to put yourself across to people in a highly persuasive manner. You rarely sit still and loathe settled routines of any sort so you need a mate who can fly along at your pace or at least let you have your freedom. Being a double air person you tend to live up in your head, in your ideas, opinions and thoughts. You will tend to attract yourself to similar kinds of people because you absolutely must have stimulating conversations, but two air types together become very cool and so detached that eventually you will hardly touch at all. Emotions do, however, make you nervous and you basically distrust watery people (Cancer, Scorpio, Pisces). Earthy types also make you feel weighed down and suffocated. Fiery types are much more exciting but together you are too reckless and burnout could be a problem. You need to compromise and find a way of connecting to what can nourish you in life without being overwhelmed by it.

Happily your Gemini moon, though exceedingly restless, does have an inclination to the darker side of life and this could be your saving grace because you will be pulled at some point towards the depths which will give you some stability. But staying too high will always be a problem. Brigitte Bardot is your type – though she may have looked deeply sexual never settled emotionally.

Libra Sun Cancer Moon

You are basically at odds with yourself so will never find it easy to get your head and heart together. What you lust after is not always what duty tells you is right. But both Libra and Cancer have relatively similar interests in life so you will not fare badly as long as you can set up a comfortable, beautiful home, a coterie of elegant, sophisticated friends and a career that allows you elbow room to keep constantly on the move.

Being an air/water mix you swing between detachment and deep sympathy, between thinking and feeling. You are highly sensitive and can be a real dreamer and escape merchant. What is vital is an outlet for your helping skills. Your Cancer moon does make you security-conscious and at times jealous. You loathe the idea of separation, indeed any kind of emotional pain makes you wince so you need a highly sensitive mate. But you also need one who will put up with your cool, airy, rather detached side – which frankly does not want to swim around in too many swampy feelings. This is your inner conflict and the challenge that you must face up to in your relationships . . . how to combine air and water? You must just find a way of living out both.

Libra Sun Leo Moon

Vibrant, sociable, colourful, charmingly persuasive, not a shrinking violet you are certainly one of life's more noticeable people. You want to live the five-star way with the best of everything. Certainly you were never designed to be poor and you loathe the idle, the unemployed and the great unwashed. You have great taste in clothes, décor, friends and entertaining. A gourmet – not to say gourmand – you may have trouble with your waistline at times because you party so much and so wholeheartedly. Vanity can be a tiny problem and you certainly react very badly to any kind of personal criticism. People who put obstacles in your way also get to be highly unpopular. You need another half in life who will pander to your whims as well as being a great support.

Being an air/fire mix you are not likely to listen to your body's needs and will exhaust yourself at times. So a mate with an earthy touch who can ground you would help. Emotional people make you nervous so avoid them like the plague. Libran women are always more 'masculine' where Libran men are more 'feminine', so the female of this species with a regal moon thrown in will be a considerable challenge. You need a lover who can cope.

Interestingly Margaret Thatcher, the Iron Lady (married to an earthy Taurus) is one of this mix. The writer Oscar Wilde, hounded for his homosexuality with a member of the aristocracy, was another.

Libra Sun Virgo Moon

A sweetly diplomatic, rather refined, possibly fairly quiet individual who will put him- or herself out for other people's needs – that is how you come across. Libra always thinks of the other and Virgo is deeply into service and self-sacrifice. You can be at times rather cool, sometimes highly critical and always a great worrier. But you are warmer than most Librans, though possibly less sociable. You never find you can relax totally at parties though you adore them. You always feel the need to be doing rather than just being. Being an air/earth mix you can think in a highly practical way though you do worry too much about the details of problems and are an obsessive tidier. A tendency to become too 'parchmenty' and dry through life is a danger. Getting down into the murky depths of life, into the blood and guts of it all, is not really your scene yet you need to find your roots otherwise you will shrivel up eventually.

Lovers need to be slightly more fixed than you to give you an anchor, perhaps with a tiny hint of fire to give you daring and zest. If anything you will be too conservative, traditional and slightly snobbish. Mates certainly should not be brash nor social embarrassments, but you do need a little jolt once in a while to liven you up.

Libra Sun Libra Moon

A new moon baby, you should have less need to relate to others than most and yet the idea of a Libra without a mate is like a cart without a horse. So you need a relationship in which you can maintain your boundaries, where you can feel half of a whole and yet be self-sufficient at times within yourself. Being a double air person you live up in your head, in your ideas and your thoughts. You are not well tuned in to your body or your feelings and perhaps do not trust life quite enough. Libran women are usually quite 'masculine' in their approach to life – crisp and cool, not frilly and 'feminine' – and this is a double emphasis of that rather cool, argumentative temperament. Libran men, on the other hand, tend to be sweet, rather more tactful and less assertive than their counterparts. So double the difference here.

You are more highly strung than your appearance would suggest. At times you need to step away from your worries to wind down. You will tend to attract yourself to similarly cool, airy types but this is a mistake because you eventually hardly relate at all. Your suspicions are aroused by emotional lovers and earthy ones make you feel trapped. Fiery types will excite you more, though together you can take off like hot air balloons and as a combination lack common sense. A hint of water or a hint of earth would help. You will spend your life trying to find the right balance. Lord Alfred Douglas, Oscar Wilde's lover, was your type.

Libra Sun Scorpio Moon

Interesting combination this, since you seem cool, detached and rather laid back but only those in your intimate circle know quite how deep, dark and passionate you really are. Nothing in the world will make you admit when you are hurt. Indeed, your feelings are rarely on public display at all. But you are a little at war with yourself. What your Scorpio moon wants is intensity, depth and an emotional tussle . . . the agonies are worth it for the ecstasies that come along for the ride. But your Libra sun hates all that angst and really wants permanent peace, bliss and harmony with nothing to ruffle your calm. There is no way you will satisfy both sides of yourself totally. A compromise is needed somewhere along the way. Perhaps a mate with a touch of elegant, sensitive Pisces, which is at the lighter end of the water spectrum, would keep your moon nourished while not swamping your Libra sun.

Being an air/water mix you swing between thinking and feeling, but you have a way of putting your ideas into practice with sympathy. You have a very jealous streak which you dislike intensely but can never quite stamp out, so why try? You can be vindictive, which comes out of this rather unforgiving side of your nature as well. Sex interests you more than it does most Librans. At times you can be positively preoccupied with it. Julie Andrews, not quite the pure virginal English rose she often portrays, is your type.

Libra Sun Sagittarius Moon

High-flying, highly sociable and rather scatterbrained, you rarely sit still. Life to you is about staying on the move, having fun, chatting up a million different people. As you mature your ideals become more important to you and you aspire to greater ambitions. Usually fair and honest, you can be trusted with making sensible decisions though the process may take some time. But you do stay too much on the surface of life. Burnout can be a problem for air/fire people like yourself since you are not tuned in to your body enough to listen to its demands. You need to stop once in a while to recharge your batteries. Only through the years with disappointments and suffering do you begin to plumb your depths to connect with those feelings that will give you stability and solidity.

Finding a mate like yourself would be a mistake as you would take off like a hot air balloon together. You need a lover who can ground you, a little, and teach you to become more sensitive to your emotions. Partners who are too emotional will terrify you and if too earthy would bore and suffocate you. But just a hint would help. You loathe being fenced in or made to face up to petty details but a mate with more staying power than yourself could help to anchor you enough to make you commit.

Libra Sun Capricorn Moon

Definitely upwardly mobile you are a restless personality, full of ambition and initiative and determined to get to the top professionally and socially. You grew up believing that only by succeeding would you be loved, so you really do not accept that you are worth while in yourself. You need to patch your self-esteem together before you will get the relationships you need and deserve. The Capricorn moon though earthy and quite sensual can also be so work-orientated it switches off altogether from emotional and sexual relationships for longish periods. But being a Libra you basically need another half in life. You need to watch a tendency to pick partners who will help you up the social or professional ladder. You cannot compromise your feelings for ever.

Essentially you are in a minor war with yourself about what you want. Your head and your heart never seem to agree. Find a mate and the one over the fence promptly looks more attractive. But you are highly motivated to find the answers to your problems and eventually will rise above your desire/duty dilemma to find what you need. You probably want a mate with a touch of emotional sensitivity who can put you in touch with your feelings and one with a little fire in the belly to give you the courage to risk more. Michael Douglas, famous son of famous father Kirk Douglas (who has admitted to not being the ideal parent), is your type.

Libra Sun Aquarius Moon

Traditional and slightly snobbish in your outlook at one level you can also be outrageously rebellious. You want a mate and yet you fear close committed relationships. You want life to be balanced, blissful and peaceful yet you also adore startling and shocking people around you just for the effect. So you find it difficult to understand yourself – how can others cope? Being a double air person you live up in your head, in your ideas and thoughts. You are not tuned in to your body or your feelings. You run on extraordinarily high levels of nervous energy. But finding your opposite will not do. Earthy, practical mates who might ground you will also stifle you and make you feel weighed down. Watery, emotional lovers will make you nervous since you fear being swamped by emotions, which you basically distrust. Finding another of your own sort will not do since you would disappear eventually into a pair of bookends either side of the shelf – full of ideas, words and visions but lacking in feeling or physical contact. Fire is probably your best bet, so a lover with Aries or Sagittarius as a sun or moon sign is what to seek out – though watch for exhaustion since neither of you will know how to slow down.

You will always need to keep a wide circle of your own friends since you hate being fenced in. Lovers need to be pals as well. John Lennon, who picked a sun Aquarian in Yoko Ono for his mate, was your type.

Libra Sun Pisces Moon

A sweet, sensitive, creative and highly diplomatic soul you can be really timid when it comes to love since you are terrified of rejection and often pass up romantic opportunities because you are scared of failing. But you need a mate in life. Librans cannot function alone. Being an air/water mix you are slightly at odds with yourself. Half of you thinks and the other half feels. Your Pisces moon is deeply romantic and wants a real day-dream of a love affair. But Libra is cool, detached and rather laid back about anything too smoochy. So your moon may become evasive and disappear into your fantasies rather than try to go out into the world to make it in reality.

At times you feel self-pitying, almost martyred because of your fears and phobias, and you need to find courage. This is easier for a Libran woman, who will be reasonably 'masculine' in approach, than for a Libran man, who tends to be sweet, soft and more timid. Certainly you need a mate who has superb taste in clothes, décor, art and entertaining. You are supremely elegant yourself and loathe being embarrassed socially. A sensitively emotional lover who is not too clinging would suit you. Black magician, rock climber, genius and nutcase Aleister Crowley was one of your type, obviously at the more unstable end of the spectrum.

Scorpio Sun Aries Moon

To say you are a person of extremes is putting it mildly! You are deep, dark, passionately intense and high-flying, fiery and very upfront. Your mood swings are a sight to behold as you flip from one end of the spectrum to the other. Hugely stubborn at times and rather immovable you can also be constantly on the move seeking new challenges at every turn. Emotional, excitable and impulsive you rarely put restraints on yourself. On good days you are refreshingly direct and can express yourself freely. On bad days you explode with frustration and anxiety. You almost always act out of a sense of insecurity or a sense of vindictiveness. You dislike your need to get back at those who have hurt you but it always seems to pop up. You are never wishy-washy in your approach to love – it is all or nothing. Once an affair is over you let it drop. Being friends with old lovers is not really your style.

You can be warm, supportive and highly entertaining. What you need is a lover who will cope with your agonies and ecstasies, the highs and the lows, the erratic whims and the need to win. A Scorpio moon is probably a must in your mate though you have to realize you will never find your ideal fantasy lover. You need too many contradictory things. A compromise has to be reached. The agonizingly funny but rather tortured comedian John Cleese is one of your type.

Scorpio Sun Taurus Moon

A full moon baby, you can never quite get your head and heart together. What you desire is not what your duty tells you is right. When you settle with a mate you promptly want another more attractive lover on the other side of the fence. You are deeply passionate, very jealous and stubborn to a staggering degree. You absolutely need a mate who is flexible and adaptable, but finding one who is intense enough to satisfy your highly sexual and sensual needs yet not so jealous that he or she objects to only having half of you is going to be tricky.

The problems lie in your childhood where you felt your parents were inherently incompatible. What they could not get together in their marriage you cannot get together in your head. You will need to separate from the past and rise above those conflicts before you find that there is a third way of relating. Your head and your heart can be satisfied at once. Your Taurus moon needs a tactile, cuddly lover who can really look after you (your physical comforts are hugely important to you). But you also want a lover who can transport you to positively transcendental realms. At times you wallow around in the depths of your darker feelings. You must have a lover who is able to meet you there. The emotionally unsettled Prince Charles, who satisfied his Taurus moon with the cuddly Camilla rather than the ice queen Aquarius moon Diana, is one. Highly talented film director Luchino Visconti is another.

Scorpio Sun Gemini Moon

Intensely emotional, hugely determined and very restless you are an enigma even to yourself. The darker side of life definitely appeals to you though you are more of a 'butterfly brains' than most Scorpios. Your restless streak fights a war with the part of you that wants to stand rooted to the spot. You can be immensely secretive and very swayed by your deeper impulses but your airy Gemini moon pulls you back from the edge more often than not. Being a water/air mix you swing between feeling and thinking. This can give depth to your ideas and at times will detach you from your overly strong feelings to lend perspective to your actions. But you do feel pulled and pushed by your conflicting needs to stay high and to dive deep. Your Gemini moon does not want to be fenced in, nor to be closeted in a claustrophobic relationship, while your Scorpio sun wants love that is hot, passionate, jealous, possessive and angst-ridden. A compromise is inevitable and you may never feel wholly satisfied with your love life, so some needs have to be met elsewhere.

Luckily Gemini, though airy, does have a leaning towards the murkier side of life albeit in a rather laid back way. It likes to know rather than to experience directly. But it is an easier combination than an Aquarian or Libra moon would be. You need a lover who can offer you the impossible. The ecstasy without strings. Wacky, petite actress Goldie Hawn and wacky, oversized comedian Roseanne Barr are your types.

Scorpio Sun Cancer Moon

Wonderfully emotional, deeply sensitive, certainly intensely jealous you are a water person through and through. Though you give the appearance of being strong, dark and silent you feel half the time as if you are on a raft on the high seas being driven hither and thither by the winds. For you the hidden undercurrents are deeper than almost anyone else on earth. You act on compulsion, at times quite blindly and you certainly never forget a hurt. Your vindictive streak gets you into trouble and does not always make you any friends, but you cannot help yourself. Often you hear slights when none were intended so you create more emotional tension than is necessary. Being deeply impressionable you soak in the atmosphere from those around you so always have to be choosy about whom you keep in your close circle.

You need both an intimate soul mate and a family, which sometimes creates dilemmas. Scorpios adore one-to-one exclusive relationships that are so intertwined there is no room for anyone else. But you absolutely must have a tribe of your own around as well, both in childhood and in your adult life.

Jealousy is a great stumbling block for you and there is no middle way in romance. You love them or you loathe them. Lovers never become friends later. They are erased. An earth/water person might suit you since he or she would provide you with an anchor – or even a water/air type to give you a sense of perspective on your actions. You are often so swamped by your feelings that you cannot see yourself clearly. Tatum O'Neal, known when a child actress as 'Miss Tantrum' and ex-wife of tennis star John McEnroe, is one of your type.

Scorpio Sun Leo Moon

A powerhouse of determination, energy and (dare it be whispered) vanity, you are an enigma even to yourself. Your Scorpio sun is intensely emotional and secretive, yet your fiery Leo moon wants to let it all show. You are a real contradiction and find it difficult to marry the desires of your heart to the dictates of your conscience. What you want is never what you ought to do. If you settle with one partner you promptly fancy someone else like mad. And so it goes on. Your head and your heart are split because you grew up in an atmosphere of mutual incompatibility or at least great difference between your parents. What they could not get together in their marriage you cannot get together in your head. You can – with effort – separate from the past and rise above those conflicts to find a third solution. But it will take time and you find change enormously difficult.

You are stubborn (extremely) so need a flexible, gentle partner yet one who can cope with your ego and your slightly manipulative tendencies. Your mate also needs to be reasonably unflappable to cope with your mood swings and lack of restraint.

Living life the five-star way is always your wish so a wealthy mate – or at least one who will not cost you – would help. You can get explosively frustrated about life's setbacks so you need a warm, comforting lover who will reassure you. But you need first to find peace with yourself before you will find it with another.

Scorpio Sun Virgo Moon

Intense, highly determined but more practical than most Scorpios, you have a way of making life work for you that others envy. Certainly you worry incessantly but that often pushes you into building up more security for yourself. You are extremely self-protective with the ability to survive difficult times and catastrophes. Endurance is your middle name.

Where romance is concerned you can be passionate and rather prudish by turns, so lovers never quite know whether you will be blowing hot or cold. An obsessive tidy streak can also exasperate more chaotic companions, but you do like everything in its place. If you can unhitch the prim side of your Virgo moon you can be warmly physical as well as emotionally sensual. Being a water/earth personality you lack a clear vision of yourself. You also could do with more *chutzpah* (zest), daring and recklessness. A touch of sparkle from a fiery mate would help – though not too much since you are essentially opposites. Jealousy can be a problem since you loathe losing control over close partners and you basically hate the idea of being humiliated by rejection. You are less vindictive than some Scorpios but the kickback is still always there. A warm Capricorn could do you the power of good. Jodie Foster, the actress whose crazed fan attempted to kill Ronald Reagan and whose choice of film work has veered towards the stark – including *The Silence of the Lambs* – is your type.

Scorpio Sun Libra Moon

An odd mix this, since you live in the depths of your feelings yet can be superficially sociable. You never quite know what to do with your feelings. Part of you wants to be passionately, emotionally intertwined with another. Another part of you wants a somewhat distant, chatty, harmonious relationship that includes friends and not too much hassle. Unfortunately while your Scorpio sun is prepared to put up with the agonies for the sake of the ecstasies, your Libra moon is not. It wants everlasting peace and niceness. Scorpio knows you have to go down into the gutter sometimes to find the gold nuggets. Libra is so snobbish and fastidious it cannot conceive of anything being bearable that is not elegant, expensive and socially acceptable. You will find trouble marrying the two parts of yourself together, never mind finding a mate who fits. But it will happen because your Libra moon needs another half and your Scorpio sun certainly wants a strong connection.

Being a water/air person you veer between feeling and thinking. Because you are a highly sensitive being you sometimes disappear into your day-dreams and fantasies as a way of escaping the difficulties of real life. You are peculiarly sensitive to the opinions of others. The Kray twins Ronald and Reginald are your type – but there have to be nicer examples as well.

Scorpio Sun Scorpio Moon

A new moon baby, you are intensely self-protective, self-sufficient and self-contained. Not only do you have less need to relate outside yourself than most people, being a double water personality you have a fear of being swamped or overwhelmed by others. So you retreat into your own private emotional world and some fair persuasion is needed before you will venture forth into relationships.

You are secretive, stubborn and hugely jealous but never ever admit when you have been hurt. You take your emotional life incredibly seriously and anyone who ever hurts you will never be forgiven. With you there is no halfway house – it is all or nothing, love or hate. Once lovers have blotted their copybook or been abandoned, it is final. There is no turning back. Your problem is in finding a mate who will cope with your terrible intensity and deep undercurrents. Ideally another Scorpio would suit but the pair of you would wrap yourselves in your own dark, secret world and never emerge. It would not be too healthy. A touch of earth to ground you would help, so a Scorpio with an earthy moon might be the best compromise. You need to watch your manipulative tendencies.

Scorpio Sun Sagittarius Moon

A wondrous combination this, full of fiery intensity and conflicting urges. You want passionate closeness yet you loathe being fenced in. You want to plunge to the murky depths to find your soul and yet you are equally convinced that only by sailing high on the cloud tops will you satisfy your spirit. A water/fire mix you are emotional, excitable, impulsive and remarkably sensitive about how others see you. Your mood swings are frightening to behold. On good days you are refreshingly, even scorchingly, direct and encouraging. On bad days you are ready to explode with frustration. You can be warmly supportive but you need to learn moderation in all things.

Lovers will need to be sensual enough to fulfil your deepest longings for transcendental sex yet have the sense to give you a long rein. You are jealous yet you hate being possessed. You are a born entertainer at heart but not easy to live with. You need a strong sense of purpose in your life. Flamboyant, much travelled opera singer Dame Joan Sutherland is your type, as was the highly talented but emotionally over-excitable artist Pablo Picasso.

Scorpio Sun Capricorn Moon

A real heavyweight personality, you rarely let the grass grow under your feet. A supreme strategist you always have your eye on the main chance or your secret ambition and you will shift heaven and earth to get to where you want to be. Scorpios are known as the miracle makers of the zodiac because they never take no for an answer, and Capricorn is the sign of the dictator – so whichever way you look you are hardly a timid rabbit. But you are always torn about your love life. Your Scorpio sun wants a love so intense and so passionate you will never be parted. Your Capricorn moon believes sadly that you will never be loved unless you achieve, so you disappear off into your career ambitions for longish periods leaving you and your mate dissatisfied.

Being a water/earth personality you have fairly traditional values and need security. You have the ability to survive calamities and catastrophes and have great inner strength. But you can be manipulative and too attached to the past. You need a mate with more of a sense of detachment and perhaps a bit of sparkle. Your strong sense of destiny sometimes pulls you away from love but you always bounce back. Mega-strong mother of India Indira Gandhi was your type.

Scorpio Sun Aquarius Moon

The oddest combination of them all, you hardly know what to make of yourself. Your Scorpio sun wants emotional intensity and deep, dark, passionate affairs yet your Aquarius moon shies away from any kind of commitment in close one-to-one relationships. It wants to be friends, not lovers and prefers a platonic group to a sexy clinch any day. You have to sort out the conflict within yourself before you will settle into a happy duo. Part of the problem stems from childhood where you felt your parents were not in tune. They were opposites. What they could not get together in their marriage you cannot get together in your head. What you want is never what you feel you ought to be doing. You find a lover then immediately fancy someone over the fence (preferably someone committed elsewhere). You must find a way of resolving this desire/duty dilemma within yourself.

Being a water/air personality you veer between feeling and thinking. One moment you act blindly from your guts, the next you are so detached you freeze every feeling before it has a chance to blossom. You are sensitive to the degree that you will escape into your day-dreams and fantasies to get away from hard reality. You need a mate who will love you to the end but give you space and a long rope to wander. In short you need someone as oddly assorted as yourself. Ultra-modern artist Andy Warhol was your type, as is Sharon Tate's murderer, Charles Manson.

Scorpio Sun Pisces Moon

Deeply emotional, passionately intense yet very sensitive you swim around in a universe full of feelings. You are so impressionable that at times you feel like a raft adrift on the ocean, blown this way and that by the winds and the currents. Because of your instability you sometimes withdraw into your own little universe, or find it easier to be a healer and counsellor to those around than to make very close relationships which might conceivably overtax your highly charged emotional system. Because your Pisces moon makes it difficult for you to approach others out of a fear of rejection you sometimes miss out on romantic opportunities. But at the end of the day your Scorpio sun really needs a close, committed relationship and it certainly does not lack courage.

Being a double water personality you have to watch your tendency to become too self-absorbed. Finding an ideal mate is tricky because although other water types would share your sensitivities you would sink each other in the swamp of your feelings. You need a water/air type who can give you a little distance and perspective on your life. Or a water/earth type who will anchor you to the ground. You are certainly charming on the social circuit so should have few problems ultimately in finding a soul mate. Intriguingly two seeming ice queens with much more going on behind the scenes than appearances would suggest – Hillary Clinton and the late Grace Kelly – are your type.

Sagittarius Sun Aries Moon

Lively, loud, energetic, boisterous and exuberant you are one of the world's movers and shakers. Never one to hold back when you could be leaping into action, you can get yourself into extremely hot water. You frequently do not engage your brain before letting your tongue loose and find it difficult to empathize with other people's feelings. You have a reputation for being just a touch brash or crude in the way you relate. Life's harsher lessons of pain and disappointment may well mellow your sharper edges and teach you compassion along the route. You often act out of insecurity and your reactions change so fast and frequently that partners become confused. Certainly they feel they cannot trust you to be in the place they want you to be. You adore challenge and excitement – too much.

As a lover you obviously need someone of an unflappable and reasonably un-jealous temperament. You are allergic to anything that even hints at possessiveness. Being fenced in is close to your idea of suffocation. A very grounded earthy lover would make you feel weighed down and possibly offend you. Too much of a concentration on earthly physical pleasures is not your thing. You like fantasy in romance, not sweat and dandruff. Emotional types you distrust. They make you feel swamped. Airy, up-in-the-head chatterboxes do suit you but as a combination you are likely to take off like hot air balloons. You need ballast.

Sagittarius Sun Taurus Moon

Fiery, restless, outspoken, demonstrative and affectionate you are a bit of a dilemma. You may feel odd because of your contradictory and conflicting attitudes to life, love and sex but there is merit in having the grounded energy of Taurus added to your flyaway Sagittarius sun. The only trouble is that you need to be both free and rooted at the same time. You live half the time in your ideas, dreams and fantasies. The other half of the time you are greedy for your physical comforts. Sometimes you are desperate for variety, excitement and challenge. Then you flip into moods where you yearn for sameness, security and the status quo.

Being a fire/earth mix you are what is known in astrological parlance as a 'steamroller' personality, able to keep going long after weaker souls have dropped into the ditch with exhaustion. You are a powerhouse of determination and can translate all those wonderfully fiery visions into tangible realities. What you are not enormously good at is starting new projects. You are stubborn yet flexible; initiative is a touch lacking. Getting in touch with the subtler aspects of life – possibly through a lover with just a hint of water – would help you enormously. A whiff of the airy signs also might just do some good. In neither case do you want too much, however.

Sagittarius Sun Gemini Moon

A restless, over-talkative full moon baby you never know quite where you are at or what you want. You are butterfly-brained and grasshopper-footed, loathing settled routines, obligations and heavy commitments. Whenever you find one lover who sparks your interest and you start thinking about mating long term you promptly find your fancy wandering off across the fence to another. And so life goes on. You grew up seeing your parents as basically opposites and what they could not get together in their marriage you cannot get together in your head. The only solution long term is to separate from the past and rise above those old childhood conflicts. Then you will find that life is not about either suiting your head *or* your heart. Duty and desire can be made to coalesce in the same mate. But it takes time, effort and energy. It will not happen if you look the other way and just hope.

Being a fire/air mix you are volatile in the extreme. Think of the mixture of helium gas and flame in a hot air balloon. You can take off effortlessly enough – but you find it difficult to stay attached to the ground, reality or your body. Love is fantasized about or thought about but it does not really blossom in your feelings or your physical senses. You could do with a lover who has a hint of water or earth just to help you recharge your batteries once in a while, otherwise you will burn out from being constantly on the move.

Sagittarius Sun Cancer Moon

Fire and water are a mix that, handled properly, can produce a boiling kettle – but allow it to go wrong and you find the flame goes out. You are impulsive, excitable and emotional with wild mood swings and a marked inability to restrain your whims. Your lack of self-control lands you quite literally at times in hot water. You veer between fantasizing and feeling. You want freedom, then you want security. You are an enigma even to yourself, you cannot ever make up your mind what you really want. Your Sagittarius sun needs to be able to roam to the ends of the earth without being fenced in. It is basically not a domesticated animal at all. But your Cancer moon desperately wants a happy home base, a tribe of children and close relationships to wrap yourself round. Somehow you need to satisfy both parts of yourself. It makes sense to find a good family set-up and then give yourself the elbow room to fly free when you want. The other way round really will not work. So give your Cancer moon what it wants and needs but reserve the right at all times to be without strings.

You probably need a lover who is willing to provide that anchor at home and will not fuss too much when you disappear off across the perimeter fence for days at a time. Too much physical sex is not your style but you do need closeness at times.

Sagittarius Sun Leo Moon

Over-active, restless and probably over-concerned with making things happen in the world you are a real go-getting entrepreneur . . . one of life's movers and shakers. Relationships are not that easy, partly because you hate being fenced in and partly because being all fire you genuinely have difficulty empathizing with the emotional needs of others. Fire is basically a self-centred energy; you can approach lovers in a way that seems crude or insensitive. In the process of maturing through life's darker passages and disillusionments you do learn more compassion, which helps. Humility is not a strong feature of your nature and you do think you deserve to live the five-star way. Your reputation is hugely important to you and vanity can be a weak spot. Criticism wounds you deeply and you certainly do not tolerate people who get in your way. But you can when you try be charmingly persuasive, highly entertaining and very generous.

Lovers have to be flexible enough to move around your needs, which are quite demanding. They also, of course, need to give you constant admiration. The problem is assessing what kind of personality you need. A little earth to ground you but not so much that you feel suffocated. You are not a deeply physical lover. Perhaps a little water to give you more subtle sympathy, though a highly emotional lover would cringe at your scorching directness and you would feel swamped by his or her hidden undercurrents. A lover with an air moon would offer you intellectual stimulus without too many problems added. Actress Jane Fonda, who seems to have landed on every bandwagon going, is your type. So was Winston Churchill, who was certainly a great propagandist but bad at handling his Black Dog depressions.

Sagittarius Sun Virgo Moon

You are certainly restless, very talkative, slightly at odds with yourself but on the whole a pleasant combination. Your Virgo sun helps to anchor that flyaway Sagittarian nature which never happily settles to anything for long. You can be over-verbose and at times sharply critical but there is a warmth about your fire/earth mix that mellows your rougher edges. You have the strength of 10 and are usually still going strong when weaker souls are dropping by the wayside. But you do worry – endlessly and inventively. Once all your anxieties are settled you think up a few more.

Sometimes chaotically fragmented, you can also have moods of obsessive tidiness. Partners have to put up with your contradictions since you are fickle and wayward at times. Because you had from childhood a sense of parents who were not exactly in tune you cannot get your head and your heart together in adult life. Where duty lies is not what you desire and vice versa. So settling with one exclusive partner always feels like an unsatisfying compromise. A sun Virgo could suit you. An emotional watery type would be a disaster. A hint of Gemini about your mate could appeal.

Sagittarius Sun Libra Moon

Wonderfully communicative, lively, energetic and sociable you never let the grass grow under your feet when it comes to making new friends or seeing new places. You like to keep on the move. Partly scorchingly honest and partly highly diplomatic you can be mellower than some Sagittarians because you genuinely care about other people's approval. You have high ideals and in general dislike dishonesty and sleazy behaviour. You like a life that is clean, above board and straightforward. Partners need to be hard-working, well-scrubbed and solid members of society.

The idle, the unemployed and the unwashed are not your cup of tea. Being a fire/air mix you are not good at coming down to ground level. Learning about the darker side of life is important for your development but it will not be easy. Through disappointments and emotional suffering you will learn compassion and sensitivity. If you do not then you will continue to fly high and run the danger of exhausting yourself. Recharging your batteries is a must.

You generally have a wonderful sense of humour and a wicked way with words but you do need more depth. Lovers need to give you a long lead since you hate being fenced in. The first whiff of jealousy and possessiveness and you are off like a shot. But with a Libra moon another half in life is a must for you. You need a sweet, harmonious, easy-going mate who will not hassle you or rock the boat too much. He or she must also have a keen intelligence.

Sagittarius Sun Scorpio Moon

Sunny, outgoing and communicative on the surface you are also secretive, stubborn and fairly controlling at an emotional level inside. A curious combination of contradictions makes up your personality. Your Sagittarius sun makes you freedom-loving, tolerant, scorchingly direct and highly sociable. Your Scorpio moon can be jealous and possessive and will never let on what is going on inside your turbulent feelings. If you are hurt you will stand coolly and never let on. But you never forget or forgive.

Being a fire/water mix you are impulsive, excitable and given to extreme mood swings. You can be surprisingly sensitive to what others think of you. On good days you are straightforward and highly encouraging. On bad days you are explosively frustrated and unpredictable. It is a good combination for a show business career and business affairs in general.

Your lover will need to give you the intensity required by your Scorpio moon, which adores deep, dark passions. He or she will also have to give you space to roam free. Only a complex personality will please all of your different needs. A hint of earth in your mate would help to anchor your extremes of mood, perhaps even a hint of air since you often lack the detachment which might give you some perspective on your actions. Comic actress with a sweet/sour approach to life Bette Midler, megatalented Steven Spielberg (who keeps making movies to compensate for his deprived childhood), tennis player Chris Evert and philosopher Laurens Van Der Post, mentor of Prince Charles (Scorpio sun) are your type.

Sagittarius Sun Sagittarius Moon

Impulsive, overly active and hugely restless you are one of the world's non-stop movers. Being double fire you tend to hare into situations without stopping to think before you leap. At times your way of relating to others can seem crude or insensitive just because you get so fuelled up with your own enthusiasms that you do not see their needs. It is genuinely difficult for you to empathize with others or indeed to stay in contact with your own feelings. You probably do not see this as a problem but it becomes one through life if you do not slow down enough to nourish yourself. Burnout from exhaustion or addictions is sometimes a problem. Being a new moon baby you have less need to find the support of another half in life, so finding relationships does not have the edge of desperation it does for certain people. You certainly dislike being fenced in and since your enthusiasms are notoriously short lived you like the kind of affairs where you can move on very rapidly. Long-term commitments are not easy for you. Most of your energy is kept for work projects, which you attack with formidable courage and determination.

You are a self-motivated go-getter, a real entrepreneur at heart. But for all that you are immensely popular. You have a way of keeping other people stimulated intellectually. Your ideas are wide ranging and you do have strong beliefs. You hate being involved with petty details, so partners with a tiny amount of earth about them would be of use, since they could handle the practical side of life for you.

Sagittarius Sun Capricorn Moon

More serious than some Sagittarians, you work very hard in life to achieve because that is the only way you think you will be loved. You constantly strive to justify yourself and gain approval. It all comes from a rather restricted childhood where you did not feel valued. You need to learn self-acceptance before you will be happy in your relationships, otherwise work will always come first.

For all this you have a helpful mix of fire and earth which allows you to be practical as well as enthusiastic. You are what is known as a steamroller personality, able to keep going long after weaker souls have dropped in the ditch from exhaustion. You have a way of turning your ideas and ideals into reality. But you do need to develop a sense of the subtler side of life. Sometimes a Capricorn moon can settle for security or social advancement rather than love, but your passions will catch up with you one day because underneath all that driving ambition is a streak of purely self-indulgent sensuality.

You are a slightly odd mix since one half of you is wacky, upfront, very honest and uncaring about approval, while the other side of you is genuinely traditional and easily embarrassed at a social level. Your lover needs to be able to give you a long rein and a stable base in life. You need physical contact and cuddles, but not too much. You do tend to blow hot and cold, which can be confusing. The hugely travelled Christina Onassis, sadly gone, whose emotionally deprived childhood would have made most child psychologists blanch, was your type, as is movie producer Carlo Ponti, husband of Sophia Loren.

Sagittarius Sun Aquarius Moon

Zippy, zany, friendly and highly talkative you have a million ideas, endless enthusiasms and a restless lifestyle. You are rather scared of highly committed one-to-one relationships, which feel claustrophobic to you. You would much rather be one of the crowd with friends than stuck in a passionate clinch. At times you can be startling or shocking just to see the effect it has on others. A born anarchist at heart you love to rebel and upset the status quo. Being a fire/air mix you are inclined to fly too high above life and need to come down to see the dark side at some point. Burning yourself out through exhaustion is a real danger since you rarely give yourself a chance to be grounded or to stay in touch with your feelings, when either course would give you stability and inner strength.

You are optimistic in outlook and hugely idealistic though not very realistic. You need a mate who can give you an extra long lead because you absolutely must be free to do what suits you. You loathe jealousy or possessiveness in any form and will run at the first sniff of a restriction or a tie that might bind you. Settling long term is difficult since you worry about commitment. But because of your social charm you should have little problem keeping a constant supply of partners running. Woody Allen, whose difficulty in settling is legendary, is your type.

Sagittarius Sun Pisces Moon

Restless, excitable and impulsive you tend to go to extremes and do have severe mood swings. But you are highly adaptable and good at fitting round most situations. Most often you are at odds with yourself over what you want. Your head and heart rarely coincide. What duty tells you to stick to is not what you desire. You find one lover and promptly one much more fanciable pops up elsewhere. And so it goes on. This stems from a childhood where you saw your parents as being basically incompatible personalities. Because they were not in tune in their relationship you cannot quite get in tune in your head. These inner conflicts can be left behind if you rise above them and leave childhood behind. It will take a fair way through life, however, before you are able to commit yourself wholeheartedly to a settled relationship.

Your Pisces moon is not brave, indeed you will miss romantic opportunities because you are too scared of rejection to even voice your feelings. Being a fire/water mix you are surprisingly sensitive to others' opinion of you and will hear slights where none were intended. You can sometimes wallow in self-pity because you resent your current situation. Day-dreaming or escaping into fantasies is one of your ways out. You need a compassionate, intuitive mate who will understand your anxieties. He or she needs to be stable enough to ground you a little but not so possessive as to make you feel fenced in.

Capricorn Sun Aries Moon

Ambitious, restless, always starting new projects and very, very determined to reach your goals in life, you can sometimes come across as rather hard-edged. You have a very sensual, earthy side which you keep well hidden behind your workaholic tendencies. You can go without companionship for longish periods while you concentrate on your more materialistic aims, but then you fall deeply, violently and passionately in love.

Standing still for long-term commitments is not easy for you. You need constant challenge and change. Often you act out of a feeling of insecurity and because your reactions change all the time you often confuse companions, who feel they cannot rely on you. Being an earth/fire mix you have the energy of 10 and keep going long after everyone else has dropped by the wayside from sheer exhaustion. You need to learn about the subtler aspects of life which you tend to miss by flying along at such high speed.

Lovers obviously have to be reasonably self-sufficient to stand the times you are away working and ignoring them totally. They also have to be unflappable to put up with your flare-ups. Because your sun and moon are rather at odds with one another you often feel you are never totally satisfied. What you have is never quite what you want. You have to overcome these inner conflicts before you can settle happily. Aggressive go-getter Al Capone, who never let anything stand in his, way was your type.

Capricorn Sun Taurus Moon

Charming socially though too much of a workaholic to settle easily into emotional relationships, you are very definitely in touch with the material world. You love to have a challenge to sink your teeth into and to channel your formidable energy towards. But you can be too narrow in your outloook since you see the world in highly practical terms. You dislike abstractions and day-dreams but really you need to have an uplifting vision in life to give you a sense of purpose. If your career sags at any point you panic because it is this that gives you your sense of self-worth.

A tendency to be too cynical or sceptical can upset close relationships, but underneath it all you are very earthy and have a strongly sensual streak. A Taurus moon certainly gives you a liking for the physical comforts in life, including cuddles. You can be warm and affectionate when in the mood, and highly possessive. You loathe change in your home or emotional life and will dig your heels in hard if forced to shift for any reason. You need a lover who can broaden your view of the world – perhaps one with a hint of water. Your emotional sensitivity is somewhat lacking and he or she could introduce you to a softer approach to relationships. You are highly conventional and must never have a mate who will embarrass you socially.

Capricorn Sun Gemini Moon

Although enormously restless and a real social butterfly you also have a dedicated, determined streak when it comes to work, ambition and achievement. You will do almost anything to fulfil your aims and have been known to cut corners. But your overly active mind sometimes makes it difficult for you to concentrate over the long term. You really prefer to be knowledgeable across a wide range of interests than specialize too heavily. You are a wonderful propagandist but your interests rarely stay still for long.

Being an earth/air mix you can be rather cool – unemotional almost – and need a lover who can give you more sparkle, more daring and a feel for taking risks. Underneath your driving ambition you have a sensual streak which needs to find an outlet. For periods in your life you can be almost celibate then all of a sudden you fall into times of physical indulgence and sensuality. But you do find emotional commitment tricky because your wants are so changeable. Your moods flit around and what you wanted two days ago is not what you want now. Sometimes you have been known to settle for partners who are helpful at work or in boosting your social reputation, but this never works in the long term.

Capricorn Sun Cancer Moon

Being a full moon baby you are constantly pulled in two opposite directions in life. What your head wants is not what your heart needs. Wherever you are is not where you want to be. Find one lover and another across the fence promptly looks more fanciable. Your Capricorn sun makes you work-orientated, highly ambitious and determined, at times rather cold. Your Cancer moon on the other hand wants nothing more than a happy home and family life, is highly emotional, rather jealous and desperate to hang on to anything that belongs to the past.

You are at odds with yourself because you had a sense in childhood that your parents were not compatible. Since you inherited traits from both of them you cannot get together in your head what they could not get together in their marriage. You need to leave the past and childhood behind, rise above those conflicts and find a new way of relating that is entirely yours. But it is not easy. Being an earth/water mix you tend to be self-protective and rather over-serious. Indeed you often do not feel happy unless you are carrying a heavy burden through life. You have a great deal of inner strength, so surviving through difficulties is never a problem. You are highly traditional in your outlook and want to maintain the high standards of the past. Lovers who are wacky, eccentric or likely to embarrass you socially will *not* do. The hugely talented but unhappy singer Janis Joplin was one of your type. So is Andrew Parker Bowles, husband of Prince Charles' friend Camilla. His track record on fidelity does not seem ever to have been too great.

Capricorn Sun Leo Moon

Very grand, rather snobbish, highly ambitious, you are determined to work as hard as it takes to give yourself a five-star lifestyle. You loathe doing anything cheaply and will move mountains to boost your reputation. You can be charmingly persuasive as well as generous to others but you do like to receive admiration in return. Your vanity is a weak spot and you absolutely cannot stand being criticized. Being an earth/fire mix you are a real steamroller of a personality, able to keep going long after weaker souls have dropped by the wayside. But you do need a lover who can teach you about the subtler side of life which you often miss because of your driven lifestyle. At times you have a tendency to settle for partners who can offer you advancement through work or a leg up the social ladder, but compromising your feelings in this way is always a mistake in the long term.

You are extremely traditional in your outlook and fairly

stubbornly attached to the status quo emotionally. Sudden changes unsettle you. Lovers must be able to adapt to your determined, sometimes slightly self-centred wishes and willing to devote themselves endlessly to your needs, yet still not worry too much when you fly off on work ventures leaving them abandoned for long periods. You have got fairly strong physical needs, which you deny at times but always come back to fulfilling. Your Capricorn sun is earthy, sensual, at times almost wickedly indulgent. Actress/singer Dolly Parton, whose long-standing detached marriage to a husband who rarely appears on the show business scene is one. Singer David Bowie is also your type, as was actress Marlene Dietrich.

Capricorn Sun Virgo Moon

Seemingly at ease with yourself you can cope well socially though your primary drive in life is towards work. You are highly ambitious, very determined to fulfil your aims and willing to put in any amount of energy in that direction. A great worrier, you do sometimes invent anxieties where none exist. They always say that Virgo moon types raise worrying to an art form, and when you have cleared the decks of everything that has been plaguing you, you seek out new problems to burden yourself with.

Being a double earth personality you can be too narrow in your outlook in life. You want everything to be practical and your aims tend to be materialistic. You can lack imagination and a sense of vision in life. You need a lover who can broaden your approach and give you a little sparkle, *chutzpah* (zest) and maybe even an inclination towards risk. A water type might threaten to swamp you emotionally but a lover who is a hint more in touch with his or her feelings than you would help to connect you to the subtler side of life. You also need a lover who will not be manipulated by your excessive need to keep order in life. You have a prudish streak which in early adult life can make you seem rather 'spinsterish' (no matter which sex you are). Launching yourself wholeheartedly into the middle of life with all its muck, muddle and problems will, curiously enough, make you a happier person and better able to enjoy your emotional life.

Capricorn Sun Libra Moon

Full of initiative, restless, energetic, work-driven and rather snobbish you certainly never let the grass grow under your feet. You will seek to better yourself professionally and socially at every turn. You were not designed to be poor. The idle, the unemployed and the great unwashed are not your cup of tea at all. You abhor drifters, derelicts and under-achieving members of society. Being an earth/air mix you can appear rather cool, logical and not given to impulsive gestures, but in fact you have a fairly earthy, sensual streak underneath. You just repress it far too much.

You are surprisingly sensitive to others' opinion of you. Social approval is exceedingly important, perhaps too much so. You need to relate more to the essential values of other people and indeed your own feelings. Allowing yourself to be pushed around by everyone else's value judgements eventually makes you seem superficial and lacking in integrity. Your sun and moon are at rather gritty angles to each other so you do not find it easy to get your head and heart together. What you want and what you ought to do are usually two entirely different things. Overcoming this desire/duty conflict is not easy since it is rooted in a childhood where you felt your parents were incompatible, but as you leave your past behind you should find there is a solution.

Capricorn Sun Scorpio Moon

An intense personality who is both deeply emotional and very work-orientated, you are highly self-protective. Your tremendous inner strength and stamina mean you can survive any calamity. Your ambitions usually come first and you are able to look as if your feelings do not matter to you. In fact you are just highly controlled and rarely let the seething turmoil of emotions inside you be seen, even by those closest to you. Your privacy is almost more important to you than anything else. You are jealous, possessive and sensual but you never ever let anyone see when you are hurt. It is a matter of pride for you to look calm, but you rarely forget or forgive a slight. Plotting revenge can be a weak spot in your temperament.

Your Capricorn sun is highly ambitious and will usually go to any lengths to achieve its aims, but underneath it is very earthy and indulgent. Your physical comforts are given a high priority. Your Scorpio moon can make you preoccupied with sex, though usually in secret. You act often from secret compulsions that others do not understand. Your undercurrents are deeper than most people's. You need lovers who can cope with your intensity, your need for passion and your need to be free at times to follow your ambitions. Hollywood sex symbol Kevin Costner and French sex symbol Gerard Depardieu are your type, as were the prophesier Nostradamus and controversial author Henry Miller.

Capricorn Sun Sagittarius Moon

More happy-go-lucky than some Capricorns, you never quite know how to settle your restless spirit. You are very work-driven but you also need to be able to roam free. Your Capricorn sun makes you practical, earthy and determined to fulfil your ambitions in life, whether professional or social. You love being regarded as someone of status and high reputation. But your Sagittarius moon makes you a bit of a gambler, a great talker and someone who is disinclined to pay attention to too much detail. The two opposing sides of your nature do not always sit happily together, though being an earth/fire mix you do have tremendous stamina and once you find beliefs in life that matter to you, nothing can stand in your way. You have the energy of 10 and can keep going long after everyone else has sagged with exhaustion.

What you are not good at is empathizing with the needs and sensitivities of others. You need a lover who can connect you to the subtler aspects of life and love – someone who will not be dismayed when you disappear after your own projects. You adore friends in large numbers and can chat endlessly. Once you have learned to devote yourself to some cause you will find yourself much steadier in love.

Capricorn Sun Capricorn Moon

Deeply serious, very practical and too much of a workaholic you will be half way through life before you begin to mellow, find a sense of humour and give yourself time to relax. You were a very old child but the good news is that you will be a young geriatric. Life may have seemed a struggle early on, either through emotional or financial deprivation, but your old age will be paradise by comparison. What may stop you finding an ideal lover early on in adult life, apart from being too tied up with your material ambitions, is that you are quite self-sufficient. Being a new moon baby you have less of a desperate need to find another half in life than some people. You can be celibate for long stretches or settle for a mate who can bring you social or professional advancement.

Your view of the world is too narrowly practical. You need to find a broader sense of vision, to make your imagination work more. There is more to life than work, money and social position. Unfortunately early in life you got the message that love only came if you earned it. So you struggle to achieve to get attention but along the way you may lose partners because you give them so little time. A lover with a hint of water would get you in touch with your feelings, though you do not want a highly emotional mate since you basically distrust feelings, and in any case a water person would never settle for coming second to your work.

Capricorn Sun Aquarius Moon

An odd mix, you are both highly conventional and rather eccentric. Your social reputation is important to you and yet you can leap off into rather startling activities because you adore shocking companions. Close one-to-one committed relationships are not easy for you and as a way of avoiding them you tend to surround yourself with crowds of friends. Your early life was probably fairly tough so you distrust relationships that put value just on you as a person. You feel you have to achieve to earn acceptance.

Being an earth/air mix you tend to be cool, rational and unemotional. You examine feelings rather than letting them blossom, which can sometimes turn you into an observer rather than a participant in life. Stubbornness is a fault in your emotional life and you can be immensely hard to shift. You need a lover who is adaptable and can put up with your highly variable whims. Partners also need to be of unflappable temperament for those times when you set out to be rebellious. Often you put on a show of being outrageous or slightly eccentric just to make others sit up and take notice. You do mellow through life and become warmer as middle age approaches. A lover with a hint of water to give you more connection to your feelings would help – or perhaps one with a hint of fire to give you more sparkle. Pugnacious Mohammed Ali – who was always good at putting on a startling display – is your type.

Capricorn Sun Pisces Moon

Serious, self-protective and a very hard worker you can give the impression of being unemotional. Yet behind your rather ambitious front you are deeply sensitive. Often you miss romantic opportunities because you are so scared of rejection. You can easily become a martyr to work and complain of your lot in life.

But you just need the courage to ask for what you need from your love life.

You are good on the social scene, able to charm and flirt with an ease that often surprises you – but when it comes to closer relationships you can become a little manipulative. You are basically highly insecure and attach yourself firmly to the traditional values of your past. You have a great deal of stamina and can cope well with crises. What you find more difficult is coping with the more pleasant, more settled aspects of an ongoing emotional relationship. Luckily you mellow through life, gaining a stronger sense of humour through middle age and approaching your older years with a warmth that was missing early on. Escapism can curiously be a problem for you, whether it be through day-dreaming or the addictions. Capricorn is usually known as a practical sign but it does have a highly indulgent physical side and the Pisces moon very definitely wants to lose itself in some orgiastic or boundary-loosening activities. You need a lover who can keep you gently in touch with reality and give you more courage. Elvis Presley, who, sadly, succumbed to his addictions, was your type.

Aquarius Sun Aries Moon

Zany, funny, wildly energetic, highly talkative and desperately keen always to keep on the move, you are one of the world's live wires. Rebellious and quite an anarchist in your own way you do not sit still and accept whatever comes your way. You often act out of insecurity and your reactions change constantly. Others sometimes think you cannot be counted on because you are never in the same place twice. Constant challenge and excitement keep you alert, but settling down to committed relationships or a stable existence is not easy for you.

On the social scene you always appear at ease with yourself and others but digging deeper into your feelings through intimate relationships is something you shy away from. You are idealistic and rather high-flying but you need to face up to the darker side of life. Usually through the years, with the disappointments and suffering that goes with love, you do begin to connect to the deeper feelings and needs that can give you inner strength and stability. You need more grounding and more emotional contact in your life otherwise you burn out because you have no way of recharging your batteries. Being an air/fire personality you take off like a hot air balloon and really need a lover who can give you ballast and anchor you to the ground. Dame Edna Everage's impersonator who just has to be wild, Barry Humphries, is one of your type. So are operatic delight Placido Domingo and *MASH* actor Alan Alda.

Aquarius Sun Taurus Moon

Stubborn, solid but curiously in constant disagreement with yourself you can never decide whether to stay aloof and friendly or to aim straight for cuddles and physical comforts. Being born at the time of the waxing quarter moon you never quite get your head and your heart together. What you want is never what you have got. If you find a lover you promptly want someone else. Part of this duty/desire dilemma is rooted in a childhood where you saw your parents as quite incompatible. Because you've inherited their traits you cannot get together in your head what they could not get together in their marriage. You will need to leave the conflicts of the past behind before you will be able to find the wholehearted emotional satisfaction you seek.

Being an air/earth mix you come across as cool, logical and unemotional. Underneath that front, however, your Taurus moon is very warm, affectionate and demonstrative. This can create a difficulty for your Aquarius sun, which is basically friendly rather than passionate. You need a lover who feeds your needs for physical closeness but is happy to give you a long rein. Although you can be jealous and possessive, you hate being fenced in yourself. Argumentative writer and feminist Germaine Greer, who never seems to settle emotionally is one of your type. Ronald Reagan, whose long-running marriage to Nancy is obviously not a bed of roses, is another.

Aquarius Sun Gemini Moon

Communicative to an extraordinary degree, you are a real jack-in-the-box personality who never sits still if there is a chance of excitement, variety or fun. You feed off challenges and constant upheavals. Being both stubborn and very changeable you are an enigma to most people. A born rebel at heart you do not often take other people's approval into account when deciding on a course of action. Indeed frequently you will aim to disrupt the status quo as a way of making yourself feel better and trying to establish a better future. You are tolerant about other people's foibles, which makes you popular, though you are not easy to tie down in close, committed relationships. You basically hate sitting still so you need affairs that give you elbow room to race around at high speed. You are more nervy than you appear because you are a double air personality. Running down your nervous energy is very easy since you are so highly strung. You do not always have a way of replenishing your batteries because you are so out of touch with your body and with your feelings.

You need a lover who is more sensitive than yourself emotionally – though not too much so. You basically distrust feelings and a highly emotional type would not take kindly to your up-in-the-head approach, which rather freezes emotions before they have had a chance to develop. Highly strung, tantrum-prone tennis player John McEnroe is your type. He married the highly emotional Tatum O'Neal (a Scorpio sun Cancer moon) but to no avail.

Aquarius Sun Cancer Moon

A contradiction in your own lifetime you both want space and a happy home life. You fight for your freedom yet you are jealously possessive of those close. You need a long lead but it always has to come back to a protective niche that is filled with your own tribe of people. Your Aquarius sun basically is happier being friends with an enormous number of people and not getting into claustrophobic clinches. But your Cancer moon definitely wants the 'wrap round factor'. Neither your sun nor your moon is physically very passionate but your moon needs cuddles, affection and a feeling of belonging. Letting go of the past or childhood is exceptionally difficult for you, which can make you sentimental in the extreme. Being an air/water personality you have a highly sensitive, rather escapist streak. You often want to get away from harsh reality by disappearing into day-dreams and fantasies or even addictions. You need a mate as contrary as yourself who will give you the warmth and security you seek but not tie you down or object to your having your own circle of friends. A mate who is highly emotional will appeal to half of you but frighten the other half witless. You must compromise and find a family-orientated but laid back individual. Actress Farrah Fawcett, married to Ryan O'Neal, is one. Boris Yeltsin, deeply attached to his mother is another, and the highly talented, sadly departed cellist Jacqueline Du Pre was also your type.

Aquarius Sun Leo Moon

Fiery, restless, talkative and rather flamboyant you definitely like living the five-star way. Nothing but the best for you. You are much grander than the usual run-of-the-mill Aquarian and more sensitive to the approval of others. You are curiously pulled in two directions since half of you is eccentric, wayward and a real rebel at heart while the other half desperately wants to be accepted as the crème de la crème.

A powerfully stubborn full moon baby you are never clear what you want in life. Whenever you find a mate you promptly think the grass on the other side of the fence looks greener, so you wander restlessly from one partner to another. This conflict between what your head tells you and what your heart wants stems from a childhood where you saw your parents as being quite incompatible. Because you inherited traits from both of them you find that you cannot get together in your head what they could not get together in their marriage. You need to leave childhood behind and rise above their conflicts to find your own solution for a totally satisfying emotional life. This is not easy, however, especially since you are resistant to change. You need a lover who is flexible and can adapt to you rather than the other way round. Also one who can make you see the darker side of life.

Being an air/fire personality you tend to fly too high and be wrapped up in your ideals and visions. Being brought down into the depths of your feelings and having more connection to your body will give you more inner stamina. You will also not exhaust yourself so much by constantly giving out all the time. Hollywood star Tom Selleck is your type.

Aquarius Sun Virgo Moon

Wildly rebellious, rather eccentric and quite modest, you worry yourself sometimes by your outrageous gestures. You do have a strong need to be of service to people and to make a better society for others to live in, so you can channel your revolutionary tendencies in acceptable ways when you try. Being an air/earth mix you can appear rather cool, logical and unemotional. But behind your rather distant image you have a warm heart.

You worry too much and are a perfectionist, and can come across as critical. But you only want the best for those you love. It is said that the Virgo moon raises worrying to an art form. Whenever you have cleared your desk of problems you promptly invent a few more anxieties to gnaw over. You can be a touch prudish or over-obsessed with neatness and order but there is a streak of pure anarchy in you which can at times reduce life to chaos. You fight a private war with yourself. You need a lover who will give you a long rein because you hate being crowded or possessed. You may also need a partner who can give you a touch more sparkle and fire. You are fairly out of touch with your feelings and need a connection to the more sensitive realms of love.

Aquarius Sun Libra Moon

Airy, communicative, restless and rather more socially adapted than some Aquarians you very much want the better things of life for yourself. Aquarius is a rebel at heart, an anarchist and a revolutionary – but your Libra moon shudders in horror at anything that would upset the status quo. You desperately want to be accepted by all the proper people in your circle and you have fairly traditional values. Home to you should not be a hang-out for hippies or the wild eccentrics of life but for nice people with elegant tastes, cultural values and upwardly mobile tendencies. You loathe the idle, the unemployed and the great unwashed.

Although you are socially at ease and appear happy within yourself, you are in fact a contradiction in many ways. Certainly you are more highly strung than you appear and have to watch out for nervous exhaustion. You very much need periods of calm, meditation or retreat in your life to take you away from your constant worries, anxieties and endless thinking. You live too much up in your head and need a lover who can bring you a little more in contact with your body, your feelings and perhaps give you more trust in life. It is all very well being brilliant but you are more than just a brain. Too much emotion makes you suspicious and uneasy. Too much physical contact makes you feel weighed down and suffocated, but you must allow a little more feeling and cuddles into your life – in small doses.

Aquarius Sun Scorpio Moon

An intense personality you think widely, feel deeply and find change rather difficult. You are stubborn to a staggering degree and must find partners in life who can adapt to your way rather than the other way round. You are at odds with yourself since your Aquarius sun makes you expansive, friendly and fearful of close one-to-one commitment, whereas all your Scorpio moon really wants is passionate clinches, intertwined relationships and a fairly transcendental sex life. What your head wants is never what your heart yearns for. What duty tells you is not what you desire. This inner conflict is rooted in a childhood where you felt your parents to be very different people. Because you inherited traits from both of them you cannot get together in your head what they could not get together in life. You need to leave your childhood behind and rise above those conflicts to find your own way of relating. This it will not be easy since you hate change.

You loathe being possessed and yet are fairly jealous yourself. You never show when you are hurt and take pride in concealing the turbulence of your emotions. But you never forget hurts and rarely forgive. You plot revenge years later though you hate yourself for it. You are sensitive and can be an escapist day-dreamer. You need a lover who can ground you and give you more courage. Princess Caroline of Monaco, who rebelliously went her own way in her first marriage to spite her Scorpio mother and who has never quite settled since, is your type.

Aquarius Sun Sagittarius Moon

Wacky, wild, energetic, highly talkative and always scorchingly honest, you rarely sit still or fit into accepted moulds. You want to be a one-off who is not fenced in, especially by the domestic scene. You have wonderfully expansive ideas and are a stimulating conversationalist. Your enthusiasm allows you to be a good teacher and you must always have a strong sense of purpose about your life, though at times you do come across as being quite irresponsible.

Being friendly and open with a large crowd comes more easily to you than close one-to-one commitment or passionate, sexy clinches. You are not well connected to your body or your feelings and avoid at all costs facing up to the harsher realities of life. You prefer to fly high with your head in the clouds. You need a lover who can bring you gently down into the depths of your feelings and in contact more with the ground. That way you will gain in inner strength and be able to recharge your batteries. Otherwise if you stay high you will burn yourself out from exhaustion. You can be fairly stubborn out in the world, though at home you are more adaptable. Your sense of humour and wicked way with words makes you popular at a social level and probably eases you over domestic hiccups. But you need a partner who will give you a long lead and allow you to keep up your own circle of friends.

Aquarius Sun Capricorn Moon

A wonderful mix of wildly way out and rather conventional, you often have a fight with your opposing traits. Part of you could not care less about social acceptability and is really a rebel at heart. Part of you desperately wants to be respectable, indeed to be upwardly mobile on the social ladder. Sadly in childhood you got the message that you had to earn being loved by achieving, so you work too hard. Your self-esteem is not high and you do not understand about just being valued for being yourself. This early feeling of being under-loved has resulted in you seeking emotional security at every turn, but you sometimes pull yourself away from the very nest you seek by struggling out in the world to do everything you feel you must.

Being an air/earth mix you appear cool, logical and practical rather than emotional. You need a mate who can gently pull you more into contact with your feelings and give you sparkle. You lack trust in life and need to develop faith that everything will be all right. You can be very ambitious and use any means to achieve your ends, which does not always bring you happiness. You will mellow through middle age, gaining a stronger sense of humour and a sense that you do not have to try quite so hard. Mia Farrow, who is obviously the ultimate tryer and who settled for a while with the Aquarius moon of Woody Allen, is your type.

Aquarius Sun Aquarius Moon

A zany, highly individualistic personality who cannot bear restraints of any sort, you buck convention and the status quo at every opportunity. Being a new moon baby you have less need to find a partner in life than some. You feel whole within yourself. Being a double Aquarian you prefer space and friendly crowds of people than being stuck in passionate, sexy relationships over a long period. You are rather cut off from your body and your feelings and live more in your head and ideas. You may give the impression of being highly sexed but much of that is an illusion. You know it all in your head but are not always so keen in practice. Examining emotions intellectually comes easier to you than feeling them intensely.

You certainly need a mate who is flexible since you are immensely stubborn and cannot adapt easily to other people. Your nervous system is more highly strung than others ever see and you are prone to butterflies in the stomach or emotional digestive disorders. You need times of retreat, rest or meditation to pull you away from your constantly active mind, which runs over and over plans, anxieties and worries all the time. You need a lover who will give you a long rein but who will also bring you, slowly, more in touch with your feelings and the more sensitive side of life. You also need to connect to your body in a more grounded way. Princess Stephanie of Monaco, whose love life has been a catalogue of short-lived enthusiasms and endings and who obviously cares little about her startling effect on others, is your type.

Aquarius Sun Pisces Moon

A more emotional Aquarian than some, you often hide your feelings away because you fear rejection. You give the impression of being open, friendly and rather rebellious but behind the scenes you are deeply sensitive and want a really romantic match. You are perhaps too prone to disappearing into your day-dreams or acting out your life as a performance as a way of protecting your soft underbelly. You want very much to help people and are prepared to sacrifice yourself to that end, but it can make you resentful and self-pitying at times.

Handling reality is not always easy for you, which is why you often want to escape somewhere else. But your Aquarius sun does give you at times the courage to make a determined stand. Being an air/water personality you are pulled between thinking about life and feeling. This can be helpful because it gives depth to your ideas, but it can also create problems since part of you fights shy of close one-to-one commitment. You need a lover who will give you a long lead yet be there for you when you are feeling timid and in need of sustenance. You like keeping up your own circle of friends. You also need a lover who can be firm with you when you are being too evasive and are trying to duck out. Mega-star of the sexy blue eyes Paul Newman, who settled brilliantly with a Pisces sun Aquarius moon lady in Joanne Woodward (and in so doing found a mate with his own curious traits in reverse), is your type. Smart man.

Pisces Sun Aries Moon

Emotional, excitable and wildly impulsive, you never sit still for long. You somehow manage to be deeply sensitive, refined and sympathetic at the same time as being brash, very upfront and self-centred. You are a contradiction to yourself because your sun and moon signs are so different in type. Your mood swings are extreme as you veer between your feelings and your aspirations, your need for security and your need to be free. You rarely think matters through coolly and logically but leap to conclusions and then leap straight into action without engaging your brain first. Your courage (or foolhardiness) surprises even you at times. On your good days you are refreshing straightforward. On bad ones you become frustrated and resentful. But you have an enormously kind, helpful streak. It is just that your moods change so rapidly that others never quite know what to expect and sometimes find you unreliable.

You need a lover who can anchor you a little more, perhaps someone with a hint of earth – not too much, though, since practical people make you feel weighed down and suffocated. You certainly do not want highly emotional or reckless mates, since that just pushes you into even more challenging situations. You need calming down.

Pisces Sun Taurus Moon

Charming, emotionally sensitive and warm, you love to demonstrate your affection. You want a great deal of physical comfort and cuddles in life. You are not one to hide your needs away. Change is not something you find easy, especially at home, and you cling to the status quo fairly grimly. You are better grounded and more practical than most Pisces, able to balance all your wonderful day-dreams and fantasies with a bit of action. You can turn your visions into reality so are less likely to be an escapist or addictive Pisces.

Self-protection comes high on your list of priorities and you are likely to work very hard to survive. Calamities and crises are not such a big deal for you since you have endurance and inner strength. But you can hang on too firmly to the past and your need for security. You can also be quite manipulative when it comes to getting your own way, usually with great subtlety, but it can cause relationship problems. You need a mate who will share a beautiful, comfortable home with you and give you the support to do whatever you want in the outside world. You need a lover with a touch of air who can give you detachment and a sense of perspective about your life.

Pisces Sun Gemini Moon

Restless, changeable, never one to settle to routine when you could be following more interesting roads, you can sometimes be too blown around by events or your own short-lived enthusiasms. Your boredom threshold is very low indeed. Starting new projects is not easy for you, nor is staying the course over the long distance. But you are highly adaptable and will generally fit in amiably enough with what is going on around you. Being a water/air personality you are pulled between your feelings and what you think. You are highly sensitive and prone to escaping into day-dreams or even addictions as a way of avoiding harsh reality. You lack trust in life, yet at times sparkle.

You need to become more grounded in your body to stay healthy and to develop your rather inadequate practical side. Getting better organized is tricky but crucial. Maybe partners with a hint of earth about them might get you in touch more with the real world – though you could not stand too earthy a mate since you would feel weighed down and suffocated. You do need a lover who will put up with your unpredictable whims. Your head and your heart are often split about what you want. Desire and duty often pull you in two opposite directions. This is a lifelong battle for you, but it can be won.

Pisces Sun Cancer Moon

Deeply emotional, very intuitive and very easily hurt, you sometimes clam up and hide away from emotional difficulties because they feel too much to handle. You are so impressionable to the outside atmosphere you feel like a raft cast adrift on the high seas, blown hither and thither by the winds and the currents. You can escape into day-dreams, even addictions, as a way of blocking out what is painful. At times you have real difficulty in facing up to situations that are beyond what you've experienced before. The Cancer moon is very rooted in the past in a sentimental way. You never like to look back and see the pain, with the result that you cling firmly to your childhood and old values but in a rather mindless way. You need to gain great detachment and distance from your life. Once you see it more clearly then you will be able to move ahead more freely.

A happy home life is essential to your well-being and you love the idea, not just of an exclusive relationship but of a whole tribe of family members to whom you can belong. You need to overcome your self-absorption, which in a double water personality is almost inevitable. Then you can give unreservedly to others. But you will probably always go to great extremes because your feelings are so deep. You need a mate who is emotional enough to understand your fears and protect you from the rougher edges of life. But you also need one who can anchor you and not be distracted by your roller-coaster emotional life. Intense and talented actress/singer/dancer Liza Minnelli, daughter of the tragic Judy Garland, is one of your type.

Pisces Sun Leo Moon

A dreamer and an escapist, you want a life that is romantic, glamorous and very definitely five-star. You are charmingly persuasive on the social scene and like to be admired. Your vanity is very easily wounded by criticism and you can at times appear arrogant, though the truth is you are more timid than others imagine. You usually have a grand vision about your life, a vision that is not always very practical. You lack grounding either in reality or in your body and could probably do with a lover who would anchor you a little more.

Being a water/fire personality you are emotional, excitable and wildly impulsive at times. Your mood swings can be fairly extreme as you veer between feeling and hoping, between your need to be attached and your need to be free. Having a solid, settled family base is exceptionally important to you. With a Leo moon you need to be top dog at home with a den of your own and pride of place among your own tribe. You can express your feelings more directly than most Pisces, who on the whole are a timid breed, but at times you can be deeply frustrated at what is blocking your life. You give vent to unpredictable outbursts of opinions or feelings and this rather upsets your sensitive side when you look back. You desperately want not to hurt others. Sir Ranulph Fiennes, the round-the-world explorer, is your type.

Pisces Sun Virgo Moon

An overly restless full moon baby you rarely sit still and often do not quite know what you want. Both emotional and practical, you can veer from being too sensitive to being too cool. You rarely feel totally satisfied with your life. When you settle with one partner, you promptly find someone across the fence who looks more fanciable, and so it goes on. What you ought to stick with is never what you want. This desire/duty dilemma stems from a childhood in which you saw your parents as being fairly incompatible. Since you've inherited traits from both of them you cannot get together in your head what they could not get together in their lives. You need to leave the past behind in order to rise above this conflict.

You are one of the world's great worriers and if you ever clear your plate of problems you dream up a few more anxieties to burden yourself with. You can be escapist either into day-dreams or addictions as a way of winding down your rather nervy state. But what gives you strength is your ability to survive calamities and crises. You want a settled home and family life but you need a mate who can give you more sparkle and a little faith in life. Edward Kennedy, never a settled mate until recently, is your type.

Pisces Sun Libra Moon

Rather refined, always good-mannered, sympathetic and eager to please you are both emotional and rather thoughtful. You certainly want a 'nice' lifestyle which is upwardly socially mobile, and find facing the harsher side of life rather difficult. You loathe the idle, the unemployed and the great unwashed in almost equal measure. At times you 'space out' into day-dreams or even addictions to avoid reality, which to you feels rough-edged and painful. You need to protect your sensitivities always against difficult people and difficult situations. Beauty is hugely important to you, either through well-designed clothes, tasteful home décor or music.

You are not always strong physically and need to keep stress at bay as best you can. A lover with a touch of earth can help to ground you and protect you from what you perceive to be outside dangers – though you cannot cope with people who are too physical. They feel gross, crude or too suffocating. You are less emotional than some Pisces but do certainly need another half in life. You like hard-working partners who also have a feel for harmony. You hate arguments and bad temper. You could perhaps do with more courage and a touch more faith that life will always be there for you. Patty Hearst, the heiress who was captured by the Symbionese Liberation Front and held for five years, is your type. Her Libra sun must have loathed the rough lifestyle, and little wonder with her impressionable Pisces sun that her former identity almost completely disappeared in the process.

Pisces Sun Scorpio Moon

Deeply, intensely emotional you are driven to extremes of behaviour because your feelings can be so unpredictable. At times lovingly sympathetic and caring, you can sometimes shut other people out because you feel so swamped by feelings. You are too impressionable to the atmosphere around you and soak in everyone else's feelings. At times you can feel like a raft cast adrift on the high seas, blown around by the winds and currents.

You can come across as cool, very self-absorbed and rather distant but that is only your way of trying to keep control of your deep yearnings and insecurities and your tendency to over-react to the slightest pinprick in the outside world. You take pride in never letting it be seen that you are hurt, but you never forget those who have slighted you and you never forgive. Often you plot revenge years later and you certainly have a vindictive streak. You can give a great deal to others since you have fathomless depths of compassion but you need to have found your own balance before you are happy with a life of giving.

Your Scorpio moon can make you preoccupied with sex, seeking a transcendental union with another which allows you to feel whole. You need a mate who is less emotional than you though sensitive enough to understand your anxieties and needs, someone who can provide an anchor in your storm-tossed world. The tempestuous Liz Taylor and the obviously less stodgy than he looks Prince Andrew are your type.

Pisces Sun Sagittarius Moon

Restless, emotional, excitable and given to wild impulses you never feel totally satisfied with anything you have in life. Your sun and moon are at gritty angles to one another so you constantly feel your head go one way and your heart another. What you ought to do is never what you want to do. This desire/duty dilemma is rooted in a childhood where you saw your parents as being very different people. Since you've inherited traits from both of them you have become almost two separate people inside yourself. You have to rise above the problems of childhood to find your own individual way of relating. Otherwise you will never settle, since every lover you find will promptly become less interesting than the one across the fence. Being a water/fire type you are pulled between your feelings and your hopes, between your need to be secure and your need to be free. Your Sagittarius moon wants to roam the wide open spaces and not be tied into heavy commitments. If it feels fenced in it will be off like a shot. Yet your watery Pisces sun really wants a sensitive emotional connection and a protected family base into which you can escape.

On good days you are direct and very honest. On bad days you can be explosively frustrated with life. You need a mate who can anchor your mood swings and give you some grounding, though not too much. You do lack staying power but you can be highly adaptable. Czech celebrity Ivana Trump is your type, as was the brilliant Albert Einstein.

Pisces Sun Capricorn Moon

Deeply sensitive, you worry constantly that you are not good enough. Sadly you grew up believing you would not be loved if you did not achieve, so you push yourself too hard. Often you miss out on the full satisfaction of relationships because you are working so hard to prove yourself acceptable. On the other hand you are more practical and better grounded than some Pisceans and less likely to escape into day-dreams and addictions. You can turn your dreams and visions into reality.

You tend to be too self-protective and rather serious in your approach to life. But you have strength, endurance and the stamina to walk through any catastrophe or crisis. You hang firmly onto the old traditional values in life and very much want to be accepted by the respectable members of your society. Social upwardly mobility is one of your aims. What you lack is sparkle, *chutzpah* (guts) and the courage to trust in life. You need to loosen up and be more reckless. A mate with a tiny hint of fire would help to lift you up and improve your sense of humour. Not too much, though, since fiery people seem unrealistic and foolhardy to you. You will mellow through your middle years, anyway, because any Capricorn influences improve with age. You need to learn to stand back from your life and see your actions with more perspective. Mikhail Gorbachev is your type, as was Adolf Eichmann.

Pisces Sun Aquarius Moon

Emotional and 'up in your head' at the same time you are an enigma to yourself, never mind to companions. You are insecure, deeply sensitive and need a loving relationship, yet you are also scared of close one-to-one commitment. You frankly prefer being one of the crowd to being in a passionate, sexy clinch all the time. You would rather think about life at times than feel it. Your emotions are often not allowed to develop since you immediately distance yourself from them and start analysing. You can be an observer rather than a wholehearted player in life. At times you can be rebellious just to see the effect. You love startling or shocking others in a mild way to make them sit up and take notice. At heart you are an escapist (either into day-dreams and fantasies or even into addictions). The harsher realities of life seem too tough, painful and hard-edged for you. You lack practicality and grounding. Physically you are not always strong, being prone to allergies and other rather un-diagnosable ailments. You also lack sparkle, courage and *chutzpah* (zest). A lover who can bring you out of yourself and make you trust in life more would be a great asset.

You are deeply creative and love to help others, and these pursuits can be outlets for your impressionable feelings. The artistic but rather aimless Prince Edward and the talented Joanne Woodward, who cleverly married an Aquarius sun Pisces moon in Paul Newman for one of Hollywood's longest-lasting marriages, are your type.

Pisces Sun Pisces Moon

Highly emotional and impressionable, at times you feel too timid for the world though you have an enormous amount to give in the way of sympathy and creative talent. Like an oyster without its shell you feel exposed and try to shut out anything that is too rough-edged or painful or that means facing harsh reality. Being a double water personality you over-react to the slightest stimulus and can feel like a raft adrift on the high seas, being pushed hither and thither by the winds and currents.

Since you were born at the time of the new moon you feel less need to relate outside of yourself than some. You can be quite self-absorbed – perhaps because it feels safer that way than establishing emotional commitments with others. But at the end of the day you are a water person and need emotional security, warmth and protection. Your behaviour can sometimes go to great extremes just because you find it difficult to control the storm-filled tempest that rages inside you. You need to find an ideal or a vision to dedicate yourself to; then it becomes easier to venture forth into the world of people. If you don't you are in danger of becoming an escapist, either through day-dreams or even addictions. You need a lover who can provide an anchor for you, perhaps one with a hint of earth. But you also need some fire to give you faith in life and some air to give you a sense of distance and perspective on your actions. Your timidity often stops you expressing your feelings because you fear rejection so. Thus you miss out on romantic opportunities. You need more courage.

3

AND SUN SIGN
SHALL SPEAK
UNTO SUN SIGN

Your Sun to Their Sun

Taking it step by step, this is the simple checklist first. Having pulled yourself together and identified your contradictory needs, lusts, loathings and desires you can get to work on finding your perfect mate, who has to be out there somewhere. At that first contact across a crowded pub/party/tennis match all you are likely to find out is his or her birthday sign. But this will tell you a great deal about the person and what your 'interface' is likely to be – smooth, gritty, explosive or defensive. Only later will you plunge into the depths of the complexities of sun and moon compatibilities (Chapters 4 and 5).

You Are Aries

As the first sign of the zodiac you are often referred to as the baby of the star signs – and you can be almost as noisy! You want attention no matter how many tantrums you have to throw. What you want, you want *now*. Patience is in short supply and is a virtue you gain only later in life – if at all. You have an infant's refreshing sense of being the most important person in the world. No false modesty or delicate anguish about the feelings of others gets in the way of your main aim. Number One is organized first, the rest can follow.

You are straightforward to a fault, you can be brash and have been known to be insensitive, but you are a joy to have around when a strong opinion is needed. Normally you take no side and have no devious strategy; you certainly will not try to please others by telling them what you think they want to hear. Relationships are not inherently your strong point, especially early in life since you genuinely find it difficult to consider the needs and feelings of another. This is not to say that you do not have a strong sex drive or can't be highly romantic. You adore the adventure, the intrigue, the excitement and the thrill of the chase and the seduction in love. Your passions flare up quickly and must be indulged. Staying power, however, is not your strong point. You bore easily and want to wander off to find a new love interest to keep your adrenalin flowing.

You thrive on arguments and confrontations. You hate wimps who will not stand up to you, but on the other hand you do not like being dominated either. You need a good clean fight, although you'd prefer to be the victor at the end. Diplomacy and tact are added to your repertoire through life as you discover ultimately that you can win more easily and often with a modicum of charm.

Your Aries Sun to Their Aries Sun

Imagine the flash, crackle and pop of a rock concert on a boiling summer's day, or of Scud missiles whistling on target for a direct hit – that is Aries on Aries. Very noisy, very explosive, very hot but not designed to last for a lifetime. Indeed, burnout could happen extremely quickly since both of you are speed freaks, adrenalin junkies and fairly ungrounded. Together you will egg each other on to greater risks, upping the stakes and ultimately falling out since neither of you is willing to step aside for the sake of peace and quiet. As geriatrics, mellowed by the passing years and softened by life's catastrophes you might just manage it – but not before 80 at the very youngest.

Your Aries Sun to Their Taurus Sun

You fire, them earth. You soar, they stand rooted. You enthuse, they point out practical flaws. You fantasize, they scoff. You get into trouble, they sort it out. You're careless, they have common sense. There is merit in this combination though it is not exactly designer compatibility. You are almost complete opposites – the hare and the tortoise. You have initiative and starting power but are a lousy finisher. They are achingly slow to get moving but have the stamina of a marathon runner. You dislike being trapped, they are jealously possessive. You are not wildly physical, they are terribly tactile. Can opposites survive together? Initially they attract you but really in the long term you do not truly understand what makes the other tick. You have much to offer that the other lacks but unless your moon signs have a connection then this is probably a non-runner.

Your Aries Sun to Their Gemini Sun

A sparkling combination where your wit, intelligence, fire and imagination strike a chord immediately with their fun-loving, communicative, devil-may-care outlook on life. You will certainly never be bored, nor be silent for very long together. You both thrive on gossip, new ideas and an intense curiosity about life. What may lack a little from your relationship is common sense, practicality or great depth of feeling. Neither of you is good at staying down in your passions for long. Aries soars up into romantic fantasies, while Gemini stands back to be fairly clinical. Neither of you is hugely physical except in the first flush of love. Neither of you (dare it be whispered) is exactly renowned in the fidelity stakes. Both of you have notoriously short enthusiasms and attention spans. You could fly away together into the stratosphere or fizzle out like a spent firework. Give it time before you commit. If you have anchoring from your moon connections it might just be what you are looking for. But banish jealousy from your mind. It is not helpful.

Your Aries Sun to Their Cancer Sun

Put fire and water together and the water may boil or the fire may go out. Your rather abrasive style gets under Cancer's thin skin and threatens its security. All that soggy emotion of Cancer slightly frightens you, making you feel you will be trapped for ever, pulled under water by hidden currents. Both of you are brimful of initiative and are rather restless, so as a working combination this can sometimes satisfy. But Cancer is the most emotionally sensitive (even hyper-sensitive) sign in the zodiac and especially afraid of letting go. You hate being fenced in. You do not share the same fantasies. You want glorious Technicolor adventure, knights on white chargers rescuing princesses, etc. They want rose-covered cottages (large ones) full of children, grandchildren, aunts, uncles and cousins – with themselves in full matriarchal control (no matter which sex they are). You will clash over who is boss.

Your Aries Sun to Their Leo Sun

Wow! What a connection. All that fire, fantasy, heat and passion coming together in one glorious conflagration. Leo's solidity and stubbornness is a useful anchor to your zippy, never-sit-still flyaway streak, but there is still a fair danger of burnout since neither of you is practical, grounded or that interested in reality. Who would empty the rubbish? Or clean the bath? Leo would at least read the bank statements, which is more than you do. This is a combination that often attracts. You share a refreshingly direct approach to life, love and danger. Both of you thrive on risk (Leo slightly less so than you), revel in romantic fantasy and adore the good life. The downside (apart from exhaustion) is that each of you in different ways not only likes to win, you absolutely need to win. Egos will grind loudly and long. You cannot bear Leo's tendency to sulk and their surprisingly fragile vanity does not always take kindly to your trenchant honesty or brutal sense of humour.

Your Aries Sun to Their Virgo Sun

Bit of a chalk and cheese mix this. You thrive on fight, flight and constant excitement. You have a gloriously insane faith in life and your own good luck. Virgos are timid, slightly over-sensitive to too much stimulus and have an inbuilt suspicion about life's ability to be there for them. They nag out of insecurity and worry endlessly over a million nit-picking details. You do not basically understand their anxieties and they resent deeply your lack of sympathy, empathy and mother-hen qualities. What this combination does have going for it is Virgo's common sense and ability to keep everyday life ticking over with great precision, which Aries almost totally lacks. You can also add sparkle and courage to Virgo's tendency to dullness and cowardice. But at the end of the day this match is not designed in heaven for eternity, unless your moons give a hint of other, deeper connections.

Your Aries Sun to Their Libra Sun

You lead and they follow – you think of yourself and they think of their partner. Suits everyone! It works best with Aries woman, Libra man, since the male Libra tends to be a softer, sweeter person who does not mind being bossed around. The other way is slightly more problematic, since Libra women can be real viragos – à la Maggie Thatcher and the Duchess of York. They have a fairly 'masculine' approach to life which can clash horribly with an Aries warrior, though they might make it better with an Aries Peter Pan. Not all signs get on with their opposites but this is a match often seen. Communication is good between you since you both have bright, sparkling minds. Your fire sits happily with their airy approach to life, though their slightly fastidious, sometimes snobbish outlook can cringe with embarrassment at your more direct approach. You could not care less what others think and always do precisely what suits your purposes. You will cut corners to win. Neither of you is jealous though Libra is more faithful than Aries, which could cause problems.

Your Aries Sun to Their Scorpio Sun

Not to be recommended unless there are major advantages coming from other quarters. Aries is like Icarus, who wanted to fly to the sun. Scorpio is more connected to Pluto, god of the underworld. Scorpio is deeply determined, power hungry and possessive – all of which sounds like a day in hell for you. You like winning, racing around at high speed, being free to do whatever suits you and with whom (no matter what your long-term commitments are). Scorpio takes over control early on and has the tenacity of a King Kong-sized scorpion when roused. Which is not to say that the early passions could not be wild, way out and quite transcendental, just that the long-term outlook is for a rough, stormy road. You are basically wary of too much emotion where Scorpio thrives on turbulent, teeming, throbbing feelings. You are honest to the point of naïvety. They are secretive to the point of paranoia. There would come a time when you got tired of living down in the depths and blocked them out. They could not live with that.

Your Aries Sun to Their Sagittarius Sun

A wonderful, happy-go-lucky, devil-may-care, feckless combination that works surprisingly well. You are both fire so prone to wild fantasies, taking huge risks and treating life as a bit of a practical joke. But since both of you are overloaded with luck even when you do not deserve it, you do better than most at pulling gambles off. You do both lack practicality and common sense so need an anchor from somewhere, hopefully your more earthy moon signs. Otherwise the boring domestic tasks never get done.

Luckily Sagittarius, though just as fiery and manic as you, does have more adaptability so they will let you win more happily. Burnout and exhaustion could be hazards since neither of you knows how to slow down. Pacing yourselves is a real problem. Sagittarius women are not remotely domestic and hate being fenced in and you are not always great at keeping your enthusiasm up for long-term commitments, so 45-year marriages could run into the odd problem. Oscar-winning actress Emma Thompson, flamboyant and outspoken, is happily married to wonderfully expansive Kenneth Branagh.

Your Aries Sun to Their Capricorn Sun

This can work wonders as a good business combination. Both of you have initiative and drive. Aries has flair and imagination where Capricorn has earthy practicality. You both like the better things of life. Aries likes winning and Capricorn adores status, social acceptability and luxuries. The match does, however, lack something in the way of the deeper feeling required for an emotional pairing. Capricorn can be a touch lofty about Aries' rather more idiotic ideas about life and can be deeply embarrassed by Aries' lack of social sensitivity. The last thing in the world Aries cares about is respectability, whereas with Capricorn it is the first. On first meeting Capricorns often come across as cold and could be written off as repressed, prudish or downright frigid. Their hidden fires sometimes take a while to break free. Whereas with Aries what you see is what you get – it is all out front. Timing and a lack of mutual rhythm could be a problem. What Aries wants it wants *now*. Capricorn has a much more ordered set of priorities.

Your Aries Sun to Their Aquarius Sun

This is a wild, wacky, way out and fairly common pairing. Everyone knows you are not like other couples and they secretly envy your madcap approach. Neither of you cares a hoot what other people think. You know what you do has to be right for you. But both of you are such individualists that you sometimes find it difficult to find the flexibility needed for a relationship. Give and take is a problem. Aries in a tight corner picks up its jacket and moves on. Aquarius just sits tight and waits for life/partners to come round to their way of thinking. If they don't? Well, Aquarius knows it is hugely self-sufficient. Total dependency is not part of this relationship and indeed it could wither away at some point just because both sides drift off after their own interests. But on the upside you do communicate well and laugh a great deal together. Neither of you is overly physical nor too possessive, though sometimes Aquarius can be so distant you wonder if they want to relate at all.

Your Aries Sun to Their Pisces Sun

This should not work well as a pairing but I suspect it sometimes does because you both want the same things though you come from very different places. Both of you are hugely imaginative – so much so you can spend a great deal of time wrapped up in your day-dreams – which is hardly a bother if both of you are at it. Both of you are fairly distant from the physical realm so you would not worry about being shut in a claustrophobic, too earthy relationship. Aries loves to win. Pisces will fit in fairly sweetly to whatever the prevailing order is. But it is an offbeat coupling. Aries' brash, dynamic outlook does not always fit well with vague, super-sensitive, emotional Pisces. The odd Pisces can also be a voracious, devouring sea monster. All that watery feeling could completely submerge your fiery spirit. Basically you fear all that chaos inside Pisces which threatens to dismember you if you get sucked into it. You are in this respect very opposite. You are about getting your ego together and standing rock solid for yourself. Pisces is about self-sacrifice, giving up the ego altogether and dissolving into the cosmos. The mix is not a natural one.

You Are Taurus

Second sign in the zodiac, you are earthy, stubborn, practical and pleasure-seeking. You are one of life's slow starters but once you get going you are impossible to shift. Think of an oak tree or a enormous bull: that is Taurean strength at its best. You can be slightly infantile in your approach, especially to relationships. 'Me first', or at least 'my pleasure first' is what you think. Other's wants and needs come distinctly second. Which is not to say that it is not a highly pleasurable experience being around you, since good food, hugely comfortable and luxurious surroundings and good company are the stuff of your life.

Sensation is what you love, especially touching. It need not necessarily be with sexual intent. You just love that warm, animal feel of being in contact with another human being. But all the senses are important to you. Thus you love music for the ear, nature or art for the eye – colour is crucial, perfume to savour, the feel of fabrics like velvet, satin and silk, and of course the taste of almost anything indulgent to eat and drink.

Possessiveness and greed can sometimes be a problem. You hate letting go. You like to control and to dominate and you can get rather blocked and bloated. The positive side of this is your ability to hold on through thick and thin, your loyalty. You make an excellent friend and can be extremely faithful as a partner, if a little jealous at times. Relationships can be tricky since you are so stubborn. Giving and taking does not come easily to you. But you can make the most marvellous foundation for a happy home life since you can be warm-hearted, affectionate, physically demonstrative and very down to earth.

Your Taurus Sun to Their Aries Sun

Can you tie a firefly down or chain a hummingbird? What you want is security, warmth, human contact. What Aries wants is freedom, adventure and the high road to places unknown. They bring out quite the worst of your controlling, possessive instincts and you make them feel a little like Cio-Cio San in Puccini's opera – a butterfly pinned to a board. Not the most ideal pairing, this one. It does have its merits, however, because you can give ballast, common sense and practicality to Aries' flyaway tendencies. If you do not mind being the anchor at home while they flit around off the lead then it could work, though it would stretch your capacity for jealousy to breaking point at times. They also give you a little zip, sparkle and daring, which is healthy since you are a very solid earth sign and inclined to get too stodgy if left to your own devices. Direct opposites do not often make ideal long-term living relationships, however. Sex could be a problem since you are very physical and they are not.

Your Taurus Sun to Their Taurus Sun

Solid, so solid this combination that you might get glued to the spot and never move again. You certainly both need security, hate change and enjoy the good life and a good cuddle. But both of you tend to lack imagination and your vision might narrow and narrow down until you turn into vegetables. Too much practicality in a relationship is certainly better than too little, but an overdose can kill feeling, spirit, fire, passion and communication. Neither of you would question the whys and wherefores of life, love and your togetherness, so you would never sort the problems out as they came along. You would expect to live your lives in the same unchanging pattern as your families have lived for generations. Constipation would probably clog romance up eventually. You would only survive together with maybe a fiery moon connection to bring an element of danger, or an airy moon link that gave you more objectivity and dilute all that earth.

Your Taurus Sun to Their Gemini Sun

In astrological lore you are supposed to fear the sign before you and regard the one ahead as somehow having developed qualities that you lack. You come before Gemini in the zodiac so its flighty, flyaway qualities fear your solidity, need for security and deep rootedness, while you secretly envy their agile, quick-witted mind and ability to reflect on life. But while opposites sometimes are initially attracted it is always a questionable basis for a long-term commitment. You need more common ground. You are highly tactile, very physical in your expression of love. Gemini is distant, often preferring to think about sex rather than get too deeply involved. Not that some Geminis are not highly promiscuous, but it tends to be of the here-today gone-tomorrow variety. You prefer the unchangingness of the same partner. They find you a little stodgy and lacking in courage, where you think them foolhardy and lacking in depth. You would get very jealous of their wandering feet, always wondering where their thoughts were even when their body was within your grasp. Solid, stolid Queen Elizabeth is married to flighty Gemini Prince Philip – not an easy match given her jealousy and his wandering feet.

Your Taurus Sun to Their Cancer Sun

This can be a happy combination since you both adore security, happy family homes, the better things of life and living in luxurious style. You are practical and determined while they are full of initiative and great at starting new schemes. It works differently depending on gender. Taurus men are strong on the whole and Cancer women can be positively matriarchal as they age so there could be a fight for control, especially on home territory. Cancer men are softer, sweeter souls who could quite happily be pampered by a Taurean earth mother who did not want her power base eroded, though he could also be eaten alive. You are both jealous to quite a destructive degree if you do not keep a firm grip on your insecurities. Together you could also be a tiny touch over-materialistic putting too much stress on the indulgences and outer appearances of life. Sex could be one area where negotiation is required, since you are very demonstrative at a physical level. Cancer likes cuddles but of a fairly generalized nature and is not always too drawn by prolonged physical intimacy.

Your Taurus Sun to Their Leo Sun

A stubborn, very heavyweight pairing, where the high points – at least early on – could be very elevated indeed. But as the highs are high so are the sulks likely to be very dark clouds indeed over the long term. Neither of you gives way easily. Both of you approach life and relationships as events that will eventually have to adapt to your way if you just stand still long enough. It is a game that you could go on playing for ever and ever. You like to control and to hold the power, and have immense stamina. Leos thrive on attention and only needs to *appear* to have the power. They will happily delegate the boring tasks of life to someone else, so you can win if you just play to their vanity. You do offer them a practical anchor to reality while they offer you sparkle, fire and a sense of fun. But it will work better (not perfectly but better) with Taurus man and Leo woman. Leo women are marginally more able to flex, bend and give in than their male counterparts. A Leo man would be too much the autocrat for a Taurus woman, who is not well prepared to suffer ego trips or foolish vanities.

Your Taurus Sun to Their Virgo Sun

A wonderfully sympatico combination this, with all the earthy warmth coming together and Virgo adapting where you stand solid. Indeed Virgos will positively bless your rock steadiness as an anchor for their jittery, nervy sensitivity. You can be amazingly stubborn but they are good at wending their way round oak trees. Both of you appreciate a practical, well-ordered life and love small animals, nature, gardening and the better things of life. Virgo being the sign of service will race around to see to your every need, and you can turn a deaf ear to their nagging, nit-picking and endless worrying. You would need a touch of sparkle from your moon connections, though, otherwise life could become terribly earthy and sensible and lack fun.

Your Taurus Sun to Their Libra Sun

This pairing is not supposed to match but you both share the same ruler in Venus so it can work surprisingly well. Venus was the goddess of parties, loved the good life, dressed well, ate, drank, flirted and was wonderfully elegant. You can share your love of the luxurious life and both of you have a real sense of style and taste. But there are also wide differences. You can find Librans a little too chilly and detached, not very physical, fastidious to the point of snobbishness and sometimes lacking in depth. In fact Librans are not superficial but they do tend to try to please too much, which can comes across as a lack of integrity. Their thoughtfulness can be a positive advantage where your stubbornness is concerned, however. They will give in! You would need to watch that the relationship did not become a little dry, since neither of you has sparkle from fire nor emotional depth from water unless this is supplied by your moon signs. You can be jealous, which they will neither understand nor appreciate. You may also be made to feel rather gross at times since they are fairly detached from the body and all matters physical. Taurean Denis Thatcher, a model of rooted English stock, married the flightier but always precise Libran Maggie, the Iron Woman.

Your Taurus Sun to Their Scorpio Sun

The powerhouse of all combinations, this could start in earth-shaking ecstasy – but where it might end up is quite another matter. You are both hugely stubborn, very passionate, possessive, power-hungry, determined personalities. Not much exists in the way of adaptability. It could be a fight to the death with a great deal of bitterness swept under the carpet as you struggle for supremacy. When the resentments break cover they could be very destructive indeed. On the other hand both of you like being in the depths of a very tangible relationship. Neither of you is designed for a wispy, here-today gone-tomorrow affair. What could be a real problem is that you need a degree of unchangingness to give you security while Scorpio is never happy unless life is going through a massive sea change every so often. Both of you are highly sexual though in different ways. You are highly physical. Scorpio knows the body is the vehicle to move into more transcendental realms. It could be overwhelmingly wonderful or quite gruesomely horrible – probably both.

Your Taurus Sun to Their Sagittarius Sun

You will adore their light, fiery spirit, their fun-loving approach to life. They make you feel less stodgy, more alive. They adapt to your needs and make you laugh. That is in week one. What happens in week 450 is quite another matter! You now begin to dislike everything you envied before. They are impractical gamblers who are never going to settle to a steady routine or carry responsibility. They joke when they should be working or worrying. Even worse they fly away when you want to pin them to the spot. They loathe being fenced in and you are possessive by nature so you have picked yourself a hair shirt to start with. You are highly physical and they are unhappy about being too intimate. They fantasize wonderfully romantic dreams. You want to live them out in the flesh. You can provide the gaps in the other's armour since you are opposites but in the end it is not a happy combination unless there are good moon connections.

Your Taurus Sun to Their Capricorn Sun

Happy as bunnies in the field, your earthy qualities draw you together. You adore the Capricorn way of making things happen and getting new projects started though you may worry about their defensiveness initially. You thrive together eating, drinking, home-making and cuddling as long as you have not picked yourself a cold-souled, workaholic Capricorn, in which case you will probably not get together in the first place. But there are pitfalls here. All the world's major dictators (and heavyweight boxers) are either Taurus or Capricorn, so some power struggles are almost inevitable though they need not be physical (but they could be). You will not be allowed to sulk much around a Capricorn, which will help, and Capricorns have a way of pushing you on to new paths that are beneficial. Both of you are very physical in the expression of your love, though it can take Capricorn longer to find this out. You are more possessive and jealous so they can put a restraining hand on you. But both of you are loyal once you settle.

Your Taurus Sun to Their Aquarius Sun

This is Earthlings trying to mate with Martians. You do not inhabit the same planet, speak the same language or approach life with similar thoughts. You live for your body, pamper your senses, are jealous, feel attached to nature and can never see any point in thinking about things that are not practical. Aquarius tries to distance itself from the biological at every opportunity, loathes anything that smells like possessiveness and loves nothing better than a wonderfully abstract discussion about life, philosophy and the cosmos. You inhabit the physical realm. Aquarians inhabit the mind. You would not find what they consider a relationship suitable at all. They think that touching fingertips or blowing a kiss across a crowded room full of friends is passion. You expect that from your postman. If you do not get full body contact – forget it. The rather full-blooded marriage of Taurean Ryan O'Neal and Aquarian Farrah Fawcett is a stubborn match. Luckily he has an Aquarius moon to lessen his jealousy and need for total possession.

Your Taurus Sun to Their Pisces Sun

This can be a felicitous combination since Pisces' sensitive adaptability can smooth away your cares and wend its way skilfully round your more obstinate points. You adore being pleased and looked after and Pisceans can be deeply intuitive. They can also be so distant they hardly know you exist, which would *not* please you abundantly. It depends slightly on which gender is which sign and what kind of Pisces you have. There are little fish Pisces who are sweet and accommodating, and then there are large fish Pisces who are voracious, man-eating monsters. Pisceans of the latter type will have picked quite the wrong person in you, since you have a core of solid oak and no intention of being swallowed alive. Taurus men and Pisces women are the better combination, or at least a more old-fashioned – he walks in front, she walks behind – kind of mating. Taurus women and Pisces men could be trickier. She strong and master of the art of passive resistance. He timid to the point of evaporation or grasping helplessly for control. Either way not quite as easy as Pisces men with Taurus women, but on the whole it is a combination that offers both of you a great deal. You give practical, common sense to a creative but ungrounded Pisces. They offer you vision and hope. Sex might be a problem since you like it and they sometimes would rather day-dream about it than experience it in reality. Pisceans can either be platonic or very orgiastic. It depends again whether it is the little minnow or large whale variety you land.

You Are Gemini

As third sign in the zodiac and first of the airy ones you are flighty, restless, communicative and curious. Your mind and your tongue are always active. Your adaptable nature finds it difficult to settle down or commit itself for long to any one situation or relationship. Behind a great deal of your restlessness, however, is the fear that you may never find your other half in life. You feel split and yearn for that perfect match which will make you feel whole. You hate that sense of a dry desert inside where your emotions ought to be.

But it is your strength to be detached, to be able to stand back and observe, to gain perspective. You do need to be fairly free in spirit to fulfil your needs. Your favourite occupations are reading to pick up information, thinking and most importantly talking. Nothing is more attractive than a stimulating chat during which your knowledge is paraded and titbits collected for future use. You are not desperately intellectual because you never stand still long enough to become a specialist but you have an amazing breadth of knowledge.

Unless sunk in the glooms of your dark side you make a great party guest – witty, bright, full of jokes. By the end of the evening you will have chatted to the entire guest list. You are happiest when doing three jobs and when flitting around leading an active social life. You perhaps need to learn the virtues of being a little more straightforward.

Your Gemini Sun to Their Aries Sun

You talk, they act. You never sit still, neither do they. You are not remotely practical, neither are they. Neither of you is especially jealous, possessive, over-emotional, hyper-sensitive or given to long sulks. This combination is good news. You love constant excitement and stimulation and they provide you with a running adventure story. You are reasonably adaptable so will not fall over if they insist on having their own way and winning (which they will). You adore their capacity for making life work and their courage at bouncing back, which you share. Where you lack as a pair is in being able to connect with deeper emotions. Your lives move so fast that you have little time to settle down to find out what you really feel. At some point in life you may discover that running thrills, spills and adventures are not enough for your heart to flourish on. But then again you may not. Fidelity does not come naturally to either of you. That has to be worked on. Your enthusiasm span is fairly short.

Your Gemini Sun to Their Taurus Sun

You know you need to be anchored, to have someone who can control your flyaway tendencies. But will you like it when you get it? Taureans certainly supply much of what you lack but they are such opposites to you that you never really feel spontaneous, light-hearted and alive around them. All that earthy solidity makes you feel suffocated, trapped and over-burdened. Both of you share an interest in the fun side of life, but from very different perspectives. You like variety, stimulation and excitement. They adore pleasuring the body, which (after a while) you find rather off-putting. You live in your head, your ideas and your wit. They live in their body, in nature and the very practical realms of life. Sex might be a problem after a while since you are not keen on prolonged physical intimacy. They are fiendishly jealous and possessive, which you are not at all. But you can adapt well to their stubbornness, which in the right setting can give you a solid core to your life. Not a first choice, however. Prince Philip is a flighty Gemini and the Queen a very solid Taurus.

Your Gemini Sun to Their Gemini Sun

Very heady, up in the air and communicative, but does it have much feeling going for it? Both of you are rather restless wanderers who lack deep connection to your bodies, your emotions or indeed a sense of sparkle in life. There will be an initial attraction because you have no difficulty conversing endlessly about every subject under the sun. Both of you are butterflies, jacks-of-all-trades who know a mite about a million different things, so boredom is unlikely to settle in. The male of the species is a little inclined to wander and the female is not hugely domestic so you could drift apart unless there is a dedicated effort to hold together. There is a dark side to Gemini so it is possible for there to be a wildly, way out, seamy affair, but not for long. If you stay on the light side then you could have a superficial social marriage that looked fine on the surface but that, once you hit the stormy spots and had to come down to face darker feelings and harsher realities, could disintegrate. Your coolness and tendency to analyse feelings before you have had time to experience them can result in a relationship that is paper dry and as passionate as a computer. George and Barbara Bush are just such a Gemini/Gemini couple. She has a Capricorn moon which is workaholic and self-doubting about her emotional worthiness but is at least earthy. His Libra moon craves social position and will settle for social status rather than great passion. Intriguingly, though both John F. Kennedy and Marilyn Monroe were also Geminis – they liked walking on the wild side – they were too volatile to last long together.

Your Gemini Sun to Their Cancer Sun

This is a rather chalk and cheese mix – or, rather, air and water. On the upside you are both restless, get-up-and-go types out in the world, so there is much of general interest to hold you together. Cancerians are by no means just stay-at-home-and-read-the-knitting-patterns-and-recipes types. But they are home and family loving, deeply possessive and inclined to make you feel uncomfortable with all their fluctuating feelings. You like to think difficulties through. They react with their emotions and can be quite contrary because of that. Their mood swings will exasperate you, their sympathy will sometimes feel smothering. You love to escape and they will not want to let go. You adore having a wide circle of friends and are never that happy about what you regard as claustrophobic commitment. They adore friends as well but want to turn life into one big, happy family – not always your scene. You need to have a watery moon or they an airy or fiery one before this will even have a hope of working.

Your Gemini Sun to Their Leo Sun

You adore the fire signs for their verve, vigour, courage and sparkle. You spark off each other in a stimulating way and boredom is never a problem. But Leos are possibly the least your type of the three fire signs (with Aries and Sagittarius). They can be a touch pompous, have a dreadfully fragile vanity that your incisive wit sometimes ruffles, and can sulk hideously, which you cannot abide. They absolutely need to be centre of attention, which your flexibility can cope with though it probably works better with a Leo woman and Gemini man. Neither of you is practical, which can be a problem round the house, taking care of domestic business, looking after long-term planning, and anywhere that matters physical are concerned. But both of you can be passionate in a fairly detached kind of way. You may not take kindly to being put down by Leos' innate sense of superiority, nor of being ticked off for social gaffes since they want to be accepted as the crème de la crème of polite society while you basically do not give a hoot. But it is a fair match and could work well. John F. Kennedy was Gemini to Jackie's Leo. She loved the grand life. He kept moving around.

Your Gemini Sun to Their Virgo Sun

A restless but amiable combination since Virgo is the lightest and most adaptable of the earth signs. Virgos give you practical help without smothering you, warmth without too much possessiveness, and great communication. You can both talk the hind legs off a donkey, are interested in people, curious about life and enjoy swapping titbits of information. Boredom is not usually a problem. Both of you are adaptable, which means there are no week-long sulks and obstinate silences, though you do not always find it easy as a couple to make major decisions. One constantly defers to the other. On the downside you may not always take kindly to their nagging and constant worrying. You are much less fussed about the everyday details of life. And neither of you is especially good at calming the other down. Both of you tend to be highly strung. With Gemini women and Virgo men the combination could become a little dry and unemotional and wither away eventually for lack of sparkle. The other way round has more chance of staying alive, lively and breathing. Your Virgo other half will need not to become too fastidious, since you live life exactly the way you want, which does not always pay attention to convention.

Your Gemini Sun to Their Libra Sun

If you do not communicate you do not exist so Libra, another air sign, is made in heaven for you at least across the dining table. Both of you share the same detached, slightly unemotional, chatty approach to life. You are more of a flibberty gibbet, slightly less respectable sign than Libra, who has been known to exhibit snobbish traits and be a touch superior. But really you do resonate along the same wavelength. Librans bring taste, elegance and charm into your life and put themselves out for your convenience. They are restless like you but probably better at starting new projects and keeping life moving. Their indecisiveness will at times drive you potty. Neither of you is jealous though they may not take kindly, if you are a wandering Gemini, to your flights from the straight and narrow since they worry endlessly about what the neighbours/boss/friends will think. Neither of you is practical nor terribly physical so your relationship may lack grounding and, over a prolonged period, physical intimacy – unless you have warmer moons. Marilyn Monroe was a flighty Gemini married to intellectual, socially respectable Libran Arthur Miller. Both had airy Aquarius moons. It was all too heady and unconnected to last.

Your Gemini Sun to Their Scorpio Sun

This should not work but oddly it sometimes can. You are airy, detached, chatty and rather unemotional while Scorpios are deep, secretive and highly turbulent. Because Gemini is a split sign, however, with one half bright, the other half dark you can be attracted to all that depth and blackness in Scorpios (who fight their own endless inner battle between the forces of light and dark, good and evil). But in the long term you are very different types and you would begin to find the abyss between your outlooks on life rather wide. The undertow from Scorpios' emotional life is very strong. They may look strong and rather impassive on the surface but the undercurrents could pull the unwary under. You are essentially distrustful of feelings. They are also hugely jealous while you are footloose, fancy free and dislike being tied in to one claustrophobic relationship for too long. You love crowds of friends. They want a hothouse affair that runs for a lifetime. Eventually you might find you need more space to breathe than they allow you. Prince Rainier of Monaco is Gemini. His late wife Princess Grace was Scorpio, not quite the ice queen she appeared. Nor was their match the idyllic fairytale of compatibility it looked.

Your Gemini Sun to Their Sagittarius Sun

An adorable match with all the zany lack of common sense you might expect from the liveliest of the air signs and the luckiest of the fire signs together. You are attracted to their sparkle, sense of fun, risk-taking and general lack of concern for convention. Like you they are not stuffy. They hate being fenced in so will never question your whereabouts for fear that you might retaliate. You just love their bright minds, spread of knowledge and way of thinking about everything in global terms. You are restless and they love to travel. No one will ever know where to find you since you are both constantly on the move. You are curious and they will fill you in with interesting facts. What you have to watch with all this movement, stimulating conversation and general busyness is that burnout is a possibility. You fly along at such speed that one day you wake up plain exhausted. Feelings need more of a look in, so does common sense. Earthy moon signs would help.

Your Gemini Sun to Their Capricorn Sun

This is not supposed to fit together well but often does, mainly due to your own flexibility. It can be a rather dry, chilly or unemotional combination with work taking over too large a space. But if Capricorn can be persuaded to drop its workaholic tendencies and become more indulgent and you do not mind getting really physical then it can work well. You are airy and not very attuned to your body though you like living well; Capricorn can positively wallow in the flesh (à la Elvis Presley). So it rather depends where on the spectrum you both exist within your own signs. In the long term it is not an instinctively good match since you have differing outlooks. You are a restless spirit who cares little for convention. Capricorn is easily embarrassed socially, is quite a snob and thrives on tradition. You can find Capricorns stick-in-the-muds at times. But they do have deep in their core a warmth that you probably could benefit from if you can dig for it. It probably works better with Capricorn men and Gemini women than vice versa.

Your Gemini Sun to Their Aquarius Sun

You are instantly attracted to their wayward eccentricity, their uniquely one-off personalities and their way of caring even less than you do for respectability. They sparkle with wit, intelligence and rebelliousness and never give you a whiff of a feeling that they are going to trap you. Along the way you may even begin to wonder if you do mean much more to them than their other 93 friends, but maybe that detached quality suits you just as well as it suits them. This is no claustrophobic, hothouse affair. They do seem to know everything there is to know about sex, but practising it means getting into their bodies which is not their favourite habitation. Even you may feel the lack of physical intimacy, which is odd since you are airy and shy rather clear of anything too continuously earthy. It probably works better with Gemini woman and Aquarian man – a cooler, more intellectual match. The other way round can be a problem since Gemini men are sometimes real Don Juans and do not appreciate a dissertation on their favourite occupation rather than the real thing.

Your Gemini Sun to Their Pisces Sun

Air and water are not supposed to mix but you are both mutable signs and therefore highly adaptable. Also Pisceans' emotional nature is often channelled into their day-dreams and fantasies so you will not be swept away by tidal waves of smothering feelings, which can be the case with Cancer and Scorpio. You need to fill your life with multiple jobs, dozens of interests, friends and lines of inquiry, whereas Pisceans have a more gentle, intuitive way of floating through life which intrigues you though you do not basically understand what makes them tick. You could co-exist rather happily for years without ever getting into any great depth since Pisceans tend to hold their inner worlds fairly private. But whether it is a good relationship is quite another matter. You may find them cringing and withdrawing from your rather abrasive approach to life, love and romance. You may find their sensitivities rather silly or neurotic. It works best with Gemini men and Pisces women, though you need earthy moons to keep contact with reality. Donald Trump is a typical wandering Gemini and Ivana, his Czech ex-wife, a Pisces. Alas both had fiery flyaway Sagittarius moons not destined for a lifetime together.

You Are Cancer

As number four in the zodiac and first of the water babies you are the most emotionally sensitive sign of all, terrified of letting the past go. You cringe at the prospect of separation or of being hurt by the actions of those brasher souls who surround you. The security of a happy domestic and family life is vital to your well-being. But you have a driving spirit that also takes you out into the big, wide world. You have buckets of initiative, are great at starting new projects and thrive on enthusiasm. Because of your emotional sensitivity you can suss out what is in the public fashion at any given moment. Your love life is always a matter of great seriousness for you and rarely do you joke about love. Once threatened either with ridicule or rejection you retreat at high speed and snap your shell shut.

Although wonderfully charming when it suits, you can also be sulky, withdrawn and very stubborn. Like the crab, your symbol, you can dig yourself firmly into the sand and refuse to budge. Passion for intimate one-to-one relationships does not run deep in your nature and over the years you add partners onto the brood as just another member of the family. Close physical intimacy is fine as long as it is cuddles but anything too sexual is not exactly your scene. Sometimes you have a way of trying to create perfect children, little works of art, which is not accepting of their spontaneity. On the whole, however, you are an attentive parent – though never good at letting go.

You are wonderfully adept at setting up a beautiful home life since you have a highly creative sense in interior décor as well as clothes. You cook well and certainly like entertaining at home.

Your Cancer Sun to Their Aries Sun

As a working combination this could be rather productive. Both of you have flair, get-up-and-go, ability and drive. As an emotional combination it does not have a lot going for it. You need warmth, security, tenderness, sensitivity and a certain attention to your needs. Aries, bless them, are rather brash, can be self-centred, excoriatingly honest, loathe being fenced in, are not always faithful and are certainly not well designed to think about the needs of others without a fair amount of force. Have you a masochistic streak? It could just work as a mother-hen Cancerian woman taking on board a Peter Pan Aries man who refuses to grow up. But it is a certain disaster the other way round, with a rather sensitive Cancerian male faced with a dismissive, tough-minded Aries woman who wants a mate who is her equal especially when it comes to fighting. You hear criticism where none exists and magnify slights out of all proportion. Aries puts its foot in its mouth with great regularity since people born under this sign rarely stop to engage their brain before uttering what may well be true but could very well have been left unsaid. Your nerves will end up in tatters.

Your Cancer Sun to Their Taurus Sun

This is a sweetly designed pairing which should do well. You love security, a happy home life and minor luxuries around. Taurus hates change, needs to be rooted, wallows in pleasurable sensations and usually has good taste. You are both jealous and possessive but once settled both of you are reasonably faithful so it should not matter – though you can both sulk monumentally. You have the drive and determination to keep your lives together moving in exciting directions where Taurus has the hang-on-in-there ability that keeps you on track when you might become distracted. You are a great starter, not so hot a finisher. Taureans are achingly slow to get on track but un-shiftable once there. It can be a very complementary mating. You lend emotional sensitivity and creativity to the mix. They add practical common sense and an anchor for your tearful, tantrum-prone days when the emotional storms overtake you. They are more physical than you in their affections, which could prove a problem in the long term unless you have an earthy moon. It is better with a Cancer woman and Taurus man, though there could be power struggles since both of you like to be in charge. Cancer men might get pushed around a little by tougher Taurean women.

Your Cancer Sun to Their Gemini Sun

The astrological rule of thumb which says you fear the sign before yours would indicate rightly that this is not a totally in tune mix. Unless you are a very untypical Cancerian you fear all that icy detachment, that cool, dispassionate, unemotional, slightly dry Gemini approach to life. You thrive on feelings, empathies, sympathies and togetherness. Geminis thrive on thoughts, ideas, space and distance. You adore the notion of a family tied together by bonds of affection. They want a circle of friends held loosely together by common interests. What you find nurturing, they find smothering. What you think is natural interest in the affairs of those close, they find claustrophobic, invasive or controlling. Water and air are in many ways a worse mix than water and fire. Fiery signs (Aries, Leo, Sagittarius) may be brash, insensitive and self-centred at times but they can also be amazingly warm. Gemini can cut you to the quick by being so cold, so unfeeling. If there is warmth in your Gemini's moon it could work better. Indeed a good earthy connection here could save your bacon.

Your Cancer Sun to Their Cancer Sun

More signs than you might imagine get on well with their own kind. Here you could imagine a cosy scenario of all happy families together, since you both adore the domestic scene and a large, extended tribe of relatives. All your attention would be focussed on establishing roots and a beautiful home. Certainly you understand each other's emotional sensitivities and weak spots and could provide a cushion for each other. Your interests are wide; both of you are restless, successful personalities. Over the course of time, however, Cancerian women get stronger and more matriarchal and there is a real danger of the slightly sweeter Cancerian man getting sucked into the vortex to end up just another mini in the brood. Also one problem of both being the same sign is that you undergo upheavals at the same time, which can be wearing. There is never one partner relatively stable to act as an anchor. Full moons once a month would be a double hazard since both of you will be hyper-manic at the same time. You could end up feeling like rafts on the ocean blown hither and thither by the winds and currents, unable to hold yourselves steady. You need more detachment from an airy moon connection to stop you swilling so much in feelings. Or an earthy moon to give you stability on dry land and an anchor in reality.

Your Cancer Sun to Their Leo Sun

Signs that lie side by side in the zodiac are never supposed to get on, but you could do worse. Both of you have flair, colour, creativity and drive. Certainly you both revel in the better things of life and adore entertaining a wide range of interesting and elevated friends. You want security, warmth, comfort and a happy home life. Leos are known as the sign of passion or the burning heart. They adore children and, being a fixed sign, really want to have roots. Of all the fire signs they suit you best. They can certainly be insensitive to anyone's needs but their own at times but they can be generous in their own way as well. The downside is that both of you want to be top dog at home. Leos certainly need to be the one on the throne domestically. Cancerian women get more matriarchal with the passing years, so there could be headaches in store. Cancerian men are more likely to fit themselves meekly in with the rest of the brood and lean happily on a stronger mother/mate. Both of you are jealous but both are faithful and loyal once settled so that is no problem. Jerry Hall, the model, is quite a domesticated Cancerian, one whose attempts to bring Mick Jagger into the fold seem to have failed.

Your Cancer Sun to Their Virgo Sun

This mix offers a great deal in the way of contentment, security and affection. You want a sensitive mate who understands your knots and wrinkles and can adapt on your stormy or hyper-sensitive full moon days. Virgos are the sign of service and very adaptable to the needs of others. You dislike sudden changes or separations at home and they are forever trying to keep chaos at bay by being ordered and routine, so you should coincide over keeping excitement and upsets at bay. You are affectionate and sympathetic and respond well to their warmth and refinement. Both of you have good taste in décor, clothes, friends and the minor luxuries of life. Virgos are not likely to embarrass you socially or indeed outshine you. They work exceptionally hard and will be helpful at home in a highly practical way, so in a long-term commitment you will be able to put together a rather solid, elegant home. Their nagging and worrying may bother you at times, however. They can also be critical, which ruffles your feathers unduly since you loathe anything that sounds like a slight. Sometimes they analyse emotions too much rather than feel them, which makes you feel edgy. But the pluses undoubtedly outweigh the minuses.

Your Cancer Sun to Their Libra Sun

You share a similar approach to life, are sympathetic to each other's taste in clothes, design, friends and lifestyle. Both of you have initiative, are great at keeping new projects rolling along and want to be out there in the world succeeding. This can be a sympatico match though you do find their rather airy, detached approach to life somewhat unemotional. You thrive on feelings, on the intangible atmosphere, and can feel nourished in the silences. They thrive on thoughts, ideas and conversation. But they are the most relationship-orientated of the air signs and very definitely like another half through life. They need security as much as you albeit for different reasons. Neither of you is into overwhelming physical passion. You like kisses and cuddles from everyone in the extended family and they will not feel rejected if you concentrate on others beside them. They will never understand your over-reactions to emotional situations, especially around the full moon, but on the other hand you hardly want the two of you swept around in the turmoil of your feelings. They can anchor you and cool the tantrums. It is not an ideal match but with compatible moons it could just work.

Your Cancer Sun to Their Scorpio Sun

This has depth, passion, an ocean of feeling, tremendous sensitivity and a potential for quite extraordinary telepathic communication. You just know what they are feeling without having to ask. But it also does have one or two drawbacks. Both of you are so emotionally hyper-sensitive that tiny slights can blow up into three-week long sulks with neither of you willing to give way. Neither of you has much detachment or the ability to analyse a situation logically to bring a sense of perspective into arguments. 'I feel this . . . You feel that . . .' can run into endless stalemates because there is no common sense prevailing nor any rationale for finding a settlement. You are also both too open to the atmosphere and over-impressionable. Your relationship will swing high and swing low but rarely sit still. Like a raft blown around on the high seas you often feel rudderless and out of control. Still you do have an innate understanding of each other's difficulties with a cruel, hard world. You may want a more generalized family relationship, however, where Scorpio wants an exclusive, one-to-one, no-holds-barred passionate clinch lasting to eternity. This can be a problem since Cancerian women get matriarchal with the passing years and do not like being controlled. Cancerian men can sometimes soften and not feel up to the constant Scorpio turmoil. But with an earthy moon among you and a hint of air to give you an overview this match could be marvellous. Princess Diana is Cancer but the sulks and resentments grew too much in her marriage to Scorpio Prince Charles. He refused to be controlled. She refused to be placated.

Your Cancer Sun to Their Sagittarius Sun

You want security, warmth, affection, a mate to cuddle and one who will help you set up home. They want adventure, freedom and as little responsibility on the domestic scene as they can get away with. On the face of it there are not too many similarities here. Initial attractions can exist because you are both zippy, colourful and fun-loving personalities, but Sagittarius has a reputation for excoriating honesty which will leave your tender sensitivities wincing. They say Sagittarians need friends with the skins of rhinoceros hide – you are notoriously fragile when it comes to unintentional slights or brutal criticism. They never mean harm but they do blunder around. They also thrive on fantasy, foreign travel and abstract conversations about philosophy, world politics and the future of the cosmos. You want more immediate connections, warmer feelings and more family ties. They are flexible as a general rule but they will never adapt to jealousy, possessiveness or a sense of being trapped, which is how they see your idea of commitment. Not really to be recommended.

Your Cancer Sun to Their Capricorn Sun

Opposites attract initially though they sometimes wither away eventually because you truly do not understand each other's approach to life. But this pairing can and does work not badly at times. Both of you have initiative, flair, creativity and the ability to work hard. Both of you admire traditional values, enjoy the luxuries of life, like rising up to the social ladder and will never embarrass one another on the dinner party circuit. But you can find Capricorns cold, workaholic, judgemental and decidedly unsympathetic. They have an opportunistic streak that cuts across feelings at times, which you cannot stand. They can put practicality before love and affection. On the other hand they do provide an anchor for your tumultuous feelings, especially around full moons when you feel a tidal wave threatening to engulf you. If they are out of their repressive phase and into feeling full-blooded and passionate (which does happen) you can find them very exciting. Capricorns can remain celibate for years if they are in their ambitious phase – then all of a sudden passion strikes. Both of you can be fairly diffuse for different reasons when it comes to relating, which suits you both. You put the family as first priority, they put work, so neither of you feels deeply rejected not being the exclusive object of the other's interest. Prince Michael of Kent is a rather sweet, gentle Cancer married to imperious, socially ambitious Capricorn Princess Michael.

Your Cancer Sun to Their Aquarius Sun

Could not be worse. It would take a mountain of support from moon signs to get and keep this together. You walk in opposite directions down the road of life. You head for home, family and security and clutch firmly to the past while Aquarians head for the great unknown adventure of exciting new possibilities, freedom, few ties and as few commitments as possible. You would feel at times as if you were trying to form a relationship with a computer, which is what an Aquarian really wants to be – all high-charged electrical energy, a super brain and no body or messy feelings. They would regard you as a strangely unstable creature with quite irrational reactions. They like a logical life. Both of you are highly changeable but in different ways. You are always emotional, sometimes outgoing, sometimes withdrawn. They switch on and off like a light bulb but also like an absentminded boffin – all thinking process. Feelings are rigorously suppressed. They are not too happy in their bodies either, so prolonged cuddles make them nervous. They shy away from jealousy and possessiveness. You might as well be mating with an alien.

Your Cancer Sun to Their Pisces Sun

What a dream you make together – all love and light, affectionate sympathy and telepathic awareness of each other's needs. Pisceans are blissfully emotionally sensitive and highly adaptable. They will float round you like a cloud of ectoplasm ready to fit in with your wishes, needs, desires and lusts. You want security, a home, family and a luxurious lifestyle. They have taste, elegance, usually a creative flair to match your own, and need an anchor in life. Together you can be too impressionable to the emotional atmosphere, so full moon days can be a horror as both of you float around adrift on an ocean of feeling. But both of you innately understand the other's fear of rejection, humiliation and abandonment so you will not wilfully hurt one another. Both of you can be quite vague in the application of your love. You spread it right round the family. They disappear into their inner world of dreams and fantasies or relate to the entire universe. But neither of you wants totally exclusive calls on each other's time and feelings once you are settled together anyway. Pisces can be an orgiastic sign so you may fight for control if at times you feel swallowed up. But that is a small price to pay.

You Are Leo

As fifth sign in the zodiac, a fixed fire sign, you are outgoing, obstinate, warm-hearted and like to think of yourself as generous. You love being the centre of attention in any situation. You are a born entertainer or boss. Authority sits well on your shoulders, though you will settle for the throne and leave the actual power to others if it means less work. Practical you are not.

What only those closest to you see is that underneath your confident exterior lies a highly insecure personality. You can crumple remarkably quickly, deflating like a punctured balloon. Criticism hurts, wounds your vanity and makes you bridle. You need an audience around to tell you who you are and you are over-dependent on other people's praise. Humility is not your strong point and you need to watch a tendency towards pomposity, or towards sulking when everything does not go your way. Failure sits more unhappily on your shoulders than with any other sign in the zodiac. Apart from anything else failure is not nearly dramatic enough. You adore a life full of colour, pageantry and fantasy. They call you the sign of the burning heart though it can be halfway through life before you acquire the compassion needed to make relationships work really well. Being self-centred can get in the way. You have a very steady sexuality and need to keep it working.

You thrive around children, love, laughter, parties, sport and entertainment.

Your Leo Sun to Their Aries Sun

What a volatile, fun-loving, risk-taking, flamboyant pair you make! Life is all romance, glamour, excitement and pizazz – extremely noisy. There is little time or inclination for peace, quiet, calm and soothing balms. The noise comes from clashing egos since you want all the attention and Aries likes to win. This can cause conflict and probably works better with an Aries man and Leo woman since culturally women are more moulded to step aside. Not that the other way round is a disaster since Aries women are all too competent at standing up for themselves. Both of you thrive on fantasies of life being a thrilling adventure movie which you want to be starring in. The problems can begin when reality creeps in since neither of you is practical or good at stepping back to analyse what the real meaning of a situation is. Common sense can be lacking in large measure. Both of you rely heavily on luck to pull you through because you know you are the special people who get good fortune. This sometimes holds good but when it does not you can be left disgruntled and resentful. Burnout can happen since neither of you slows the other down. Quite the reverse. It could be a great passion that flares, then flickers and dies – but with no hard feelings left.

Your Leo Sun to Their Taurus Sun

This is a solid, heavyweight pairing but horribly stubborn. Neither of you budges an inch in an argument. Both of you stand rooted, firm in the assumption that eventually the other will give way. But Taurus is more than a match for your obstinacy. You are not inherently in tune with each other's energy. You are fire: enthusiastic, imaginative, sociable and high-flying. Taureans are earth: cautious, slow-moving, rooted and sometimes quite narrow in vision. They can give you an anchor and a grounding in reality. They cope with the practicalities of life while you dream the dreams and throw the parties. You give them sparkle and a sense that life has more to offer than chopping logs and drawing water. But they can be scornful of your brighter ideas, pointing out all the flaws, which makes your teeth grind and your ego wince in agony. You find them at times a touch cruel even with their very earthy approach. Both of you can be warmly affectionate but they are more physical and this can be a hazard eventually. You have a steady sexuality but theirs can seem gross at times because they need everything to be so tangible. You need lighter, adaptable earth or water moons to leaven the mix.

Your Leo Sun to Their Gemini Sun

A delightful combination since your fire resonates with their air providing a communicative, lively, fun-loving and rather reckless relationship. Gemini is adaptable by nature so will not argue everything endlessly like Taurus, Scorpio or Aquarius. Geminis might be a touch too honest for you and are certainly no diplomats, so your ego or your vanity will no doubt scream in agony at points. But you do egg each other on to great excitements so difficulties pass by quickly. Both of you approach life head-on with the idea that it should be lived to the hilt for enjoyment. You are probably more straightforward, certainly more naïve than they. Geminis can be like a barrowload of monkeys at times and not easy to pin down. But they amuse you so they soothe away your irritation in laughter, and their constantly changing antics certainly keep boredom at bay. You need to be boss at home, which suits them since they rarely stand still long enough to claim territory. You may find them a little chilly at times since they dislike getting too close to feelings and can be extremely detached. Fidelity is not their strongest point, especially among the males, while you are loyal and steadfast once settled. But across the board is makes a good match for you. Leo Jackie Onassis got the grand life and no boredom marrying Gemini John F. Kennedy.

Your Leo Sun to Their Cancer Sun

Cancer women can be very strong indeed as they mature and Leo men are equally so, which could create a real power struggle since both of you like to dominate at home. Cancer men can be softer, sweeter creatures more inclined to bend, so that way round might not be such a problem. But you are not really in tune. You always fear the sign before and you are rather wary of getting sucked into Cancer's emotional web. Cancerians really want to make you just another of the extended family whereas you know your place is on the throne – the only really special person around. They are water and you are fire. But you do have attitudes in common. Both of you want security and a happy home life. For different reasons both of you adore children: you because you remain a child at heart, they because they are basically mothers at heart (no matter which gender they are). Both of you are loyal and steadfast once settled. You are the most emotional of all the fire signs and you adore being looked after, which Cancerians do to perfection. You are more passionate and could find them evasive when it came to intimate cuddles. They much prefer having a family group to throw their arms round. This could make you feel very rejected and flee for more exclusive companionship.

Your Leo Sun to Their Leo Sun

Tearing flesh! – as both of you fight for all the attention and spotlight. This pairing can sometimes happen but it creates constant tension, acrimony and bickering. Inevitably one half ends up pushed out of the limelight and becomes resentful. Two Leos cannot easily be spontaneous in the same space. The passions may have flared instantly initially and you seem to share so many interests that for a while it looks like a great idea. But you cannot both be top dog at home. One will ultimately end up the courtier and have to be servile, which will not sit happily. Wounded vanities will ultimately erode the initial attraction. Competitiveness about who is doing better at work will also create areas of friction. There will be no soothing hand for moments of failure or inadequacy because the other will be so pleased to have exclusive claim to the success spotlight. Eventually you would find that envy was the real passion-killer. That and obstinacy. Sorry.

Your Leo Sun to Their Virgo Sun

An astrological rule of thumb says that you do not get on with the sign before you. Virgo, which is a fairly meek, retiring sign, should not therefore take kindly to your healthy egocentricity. Yet this is a combination that often works. Virgo adapts well and is good at serving so you feel your pride of place is not being eroded. Virgos are also refined enough to suit your grand ways, though not so flamboyant they will detract attention. They cope with all the practical details you find so boring and you give their lives sparkle and excitement. They do nag and criticize, which is your biggest complaint since your vanity does not like being ruffled. You much prefer mates who treat you as being perfect while racing around to sort out all the loose ends. Virgos will look after your health (being great experts on all matters medical because of their own hypochondriacal streak). You can usually persuade them to be more outgoing. They are good at organizing parties, which suits you, but never very good at relaxing at them. Courtship can be tricky since they hate relaxing and always want to be working. Even later their workaholic tendencies can get in the way. But this is a 7 out of 10 pairing. Princess Anne's first marriage to self-effacing, hard-working Virgo Mark Phillips died a death – perhaps because he was never truly happy away from his horsy interests.

Your Leo Sun to Their Libra Sun

This can be a dream mating, though best with a Libra male and Leo woman. Librans are relationship-orientated, usually good at thinking of their partner's needs and not too stubborn, which suits you down to the ground. Not too many ego conflicts here. They are light, sociable, colourful, charming, highly refined, will not embarrass you at parties and will provide you with a suitably well-bred escort worthy of your status. Their tact will gloss over your shortcomings. What more could you ask? At times they may seem a little distant, chilly or detached but that is what air signs are all about. At times they seem to lack courage just when you want to take a flying risk but that may be a positive help if they slow you down. They are generally a wise sign though hideously indecisive, which will irritate you. Neither of you is practical which could prove a problem where the business aspects of life are concerned, though less so than with any other fire/air combination. And there is less danger of burnout since Libra will strive to bring an element of balance into your life. Libra women can be a little fierce, which is why they sometimes rub abrasively against Leo men. Arguments about who is right can be heated.

Your Leo Sun to Their Scorpio Sun

A tough, stubborn, chalk-and-cheese combination. Both of you will fight for control and Scorpio will probably win, being more underhand than you. You also like to live life on the outside, shining in the spotlight at parties or playing games. Scorpios thrive on secrecy, manipulation and power games and like to live life in depth, which makes you nervous. All those hidden undercurrents and black passions are not your cup of tea at all. Their watery turmoil will threaten to extinguish your fire, while your happy-go-lucky, rather arrogant approach to life will drive them to boiling point. Both of you certainly share a passionate approach to life, but where you come out of your heart and your spirit and aim for the heavens they are much more sexual and inclined to view relationships as an intense struggle in which the agonies are as important as the ecstasies. You would wilt after a while and feel suffocated by all this angst. They are also jealous and possessive, more so than you might like. Both of you are fixed signs and therefore assume that if you stand firmly rooted long enough the other will adapt round to your way. It could be a long wait. Flamboyant Leo Bill Clinton certainly picked a solid mate in Scorpio Hillary. It has stood rooted, but how successful a match is it really?

Your Leo Sun to Their Sagittarius Sun

What a glorious couple – wild, feckless, carefree, irresponsible, imaginative, madcap and extremely funny. Sagittarians are highly adaptable so will not dig their heels in when you are being obstinate. They are fiery like you so you share similar fantasies and a sense of the ridiculous. They do not stand on their dignity as you are inclined to do, which is a help. There would be no shortage of jokes, except when Sagittarius decided to let rip with their famed honesty. They tell it like it is – without pulling their punches. You do not have a rhinoceros hide and much prefer tactful souls who edge their way round the minefield of your ego's vanities. That could be one problem. Also they hate being fenced in and shy away from domestic responsibilities and commitments when they can. You are more fixed, loyal and steadfast. Jealousy on your part could be a problem. Neither of you is practical so burnout could be a difficulty as you listen to neither common sense nor your bodies as you rush around all the time at top speed. Watery or earthy moon signs could help to give you a better balance. Your natural energies are certainly in tune.

Your Leo Sun to Their Capricorn Sun

Both of you are top people, share traditional values in life and love social climbing, luxuries and dining in the right places. You are not supposed to be a good match and yet you share such similar approaches to life it is not surprising you click. On the face of it you are more passionate, more heart-centred, but scratch a Capricorn and in time you find a depth of sensuality and passion that might surprise you. Capricorns work too hard and can appear chilly, standoffish and rather judgemental. They can go for years celibate, then all of a sudden they fall madly, deeply and truly in love in a hugely physical way. Their rather saturnine approach to life (which is basically pessimistic, cautious, defensive and self-doubting) does not always sit well with your sunny, trusting outlook. But you could complement each other.

They give you practical support and you lift their glooms. Capricorns are usually geriatric youngsters and become mellower with the passing years. By 50 they have positively developed a sense of humour. They are like good wine, better with age. Both of you like and are good with money.

Your Leo Sun to Their Aquarius Sun

Opposites in this case do not usually attract, nor complement one another. You are both hugely stubborn, unwilling to bend, give in or be flexible, which is not good news for close relationships. Also you face different ways down the road of life. You want attention, warmth, parties, the grand life and social status. Aquarians would embarrass you with their zany eccentricities. They do not give a hoot what anyone else or social convention thinks. Indeed they are born rebels at heart, where you are a traditionalist. You want to be a monarch. They want to be Che Guevara, a trade union strike leader or an unreconstructed hippie. You are prickly when it comes to criticism. They are notoriously straight shooters when it comes to the truth. You come out of your heart. They are creatures of their head and shy clear of anything that smells remotely like a feeling. They think brilliantly and you could certainly have stimulating conversations. But would it be enough? They are not good in their bodies and regard too much cuddling with distaste. If you do strike up an affinity you have to watch that you do not live life in overdrive. Neither of you has any sense of pace. Neither of you listens to common sense advice or your bodies, which often want to go slower.

Your Leo Sun to Their Pisces Sun

This can work better than it is supposed to since adaptable Pisces will wend its way gently round your need for attention and top billing. Pisceans fulfil many of their emotional needs in their day-dreams so will not swamp you with too much feeling. At times however you may get a disquieting feeling that they are not relating to you at all, which would be a worry since you like an attentive audience. Your fiery courage and faith in life will be good for their timidity. Their subtlety and artistic taste will appeal to your own creative flair. Both of you are great romantics at heart in different ways, so the courtship stage will be gloriously seductive. Pisceans can submerge their identities and melt into the other, which suits you down to the ground. No messy ego conflicts or power struggles about who is most important. There could be worries with large fish Pisceans (who can be rather voracious) as opposed to small fish Pisceans (who are vague, amenable creatures on the whole). But all are refined, thoughtful, tasteful and on the whole sweet natured. You are not inherently the same kind of people but you can sink your differences better than most. Leo Princess Anne's second husband Tim Laurence is a watery Piscean. Hopefully it will fair better than the marriage of Leo Princess Margaret and creative Pisces Lord Snowdon.

You Are Virgo

As sixth sign in the zodiac, adaptable and earthy, you are practical, restless, bright, observant and communicative but one of the world's great worriers. You like to be of service to others but often end up feeling martyred and resentful. You can be a workaholic and end up dull because of it. What you need to develop is a sense of humour and a connection to the messier side of life. Fastidiousness taken to extremes can turn you into an old maid, whatever your gender or marital status. Underneath your prudish, modest exterior lie hidden, sensual depths – if you can get at them.

Your observant and analytical mind along with your conscientiousness make you a solid and usually successful citizen, but these same traits in a negative sense make you a nark, a nag and a critic. You can drown in details and be so obsessed with the flaws or minor drawbacks of a person or situation you lose sight of the whole. You are a great perfectionist and often lose relationships because you cannot bear to settle for second best. You need to learn to accept people warts and all without turning yourself into a doormat. Emotions should not be constantly analysed. They can be killed stone dead by your tendency to think not feel. You are deeply interested in all matters medical, to the point of hypochondria.

Your Virgo Sun to Their Aries Sun

Fiery signs do lift your spirits up and give you courage, but Aries? . . . Too brash, too abrasive, too self-centred and too careless of your tender sensitivities. You are not concerned with your vanities but you do not understand Aries' driving, competitive need to be first all the time. You certainly object to the way they tramp straight across anyone or anything that gets in their way. Your more refined approach to life requires a gentler mate. Having a bright, agile mind you never quite understand their headlong rush to act, often before engaging their brains. They never seem to consider the consequences of their actions whereas you endlessly do. Opposites can often help to give the other what he or she lacks. You can give Aries a practical grounding and can sort out a great many domestic and administrative tangles for them. They push you out of your cowardice, insisting you get into life in a more wholehearted way. You should be a perfect foil for their 'me first' approach to life considering your need to be of service, but really you are so different you hardly exist on the same planet. You also object to their brutal honesty. A critic you may be but you are never keen on being under the microscope.

Your Virgo Sun to Their Taurus Sun

Cosy, cuddly, warm and rather sensual, this is undoubtedly one of the better combinations for you. Taureans are wonderfully tactile and refuse to let you disappear up into your head. They are a rock and an anchor for your excessive worrying and nit-picking. They stand solid while you race round in ever decreasing circles. Your flexibility is a help because their obstinacy makes them almost un-budgeable at times. But their very dislike of change offers you security. You could together be perhaps a shade lacking in fun, fire and spirit. You could work too hard, be too practical or too unimaginative. The warmer side of earth is life-giving but its colder end is tunnel-visioned, slightly gross and rather leaden. Taurus can be a dictator and fairly power hungry, which eventually could unsettle you since you never like fighting for supremacy. Taureans also need very tangible gestures of affection. Their approach to love is more physical than that of some Virgos. But you share a common outlook on life because you are both earthy; you also share a myriad of similar interests in nature, plants, small animals and medicine.

Your Virgo Sun to Their Gemini Sun

No one else will get a word in edgeways here since you are both the great communicators of the zodiac. A highly restless pair of real jitterbugs, you will never be at peace together but you will never be bored either. Your practicality will be a help to airy Gemini; Gemini's sense of fun and adventure will haul you out of your timidity and natural defensiveness. But you may not always appreciate Gemini's rather cavalier way of cutting corners emotionally and professionally. Honesty is not always a strong point with Gemini, nor is fidelity (among the males). You are not supernaturally jealous but you are straightforward usually and dislike subterfuge and betrayal. You could end up feeling 'doormatted' since Geminis will tend to leave you with the heavy end of the responsibilities. Since you have never been known to say no to work and are a bad delegator this could be a problem. This is a mix which slightly lacks feeling and could cool itself away to withering point, with you nagging and them evaporating into thin air. Both of you talk about feelings rather than feel them. After the initial flurry Geminis are not always interested in too much physical intimacy, which is a problem since you are earthy and in need of a constant cuddle. They are social butterflies when it suits them, which may not suit your more reclusive tendencies.

Your Virgo Sun to Their Cancer Sun

A steady combination this with much resonance, similar interests and a sensitivity to each other's needs. You are practical, earthy, refined, highly strung and hard-working while they are emotional, protective, highly domesticated but with a strong drive to succeed as well. It probably works better with a Virgo woman and Cancer man since you would then be more evenly matched, though you would probably nag him too much. Cancerian women tend to mature into stalwart matriarchs as the years progress and Virgo men, never the most courageous, can feel a little chewed up along the way. Both of you will be interested in setting up a happy home life. You are excellent at domestic details and Cancers have a genuine flair for home making that is second to none. Neither of you is brash, upfront personalities so you can protect each other's tender spots well. Both of you are rather jittery though in different ways. You get wound up in a nervy sense over trivia. They get over-emotional about tiny hurts and slights. You can probably balance each other's anxieties out, though they may find you a little chilly with your analytic approach to emotions. What is perhaps lacking is a strong sense of humour between you or an adventurous streak. You need a fiery moon to lift you up to greater heights.

Your Virgo Sun to Their Leo Sun

Astrological lore has it that you dislike the sign before you, or fear it. Leo is just prior to you and Leos' rather desperate egocentricity is not your way for yourself in life, but curiously your self-effacing need to be of service does mean you can survive them better than most. Secretly you may even envy their barefaced grabbing for attention, which you would never allow yourself. They are fire so come intact with a basic trust in life, a lively imagination and not much common sense. Your earthiness offers them practical guidance, a way of handling daily life with all its boring details, which they loathe. They will certainly drag you out into life and especially onto the party scene, which they adore and you normally try to avoid. There is a basic incompatibility in your outlook in life which will tell at some point, though along the way you are both warm-hearted and very straightforward. They can offer you security and an anchor for your endless, constant worries. Leos rarely bother to worry about the major things in life, never mind the trivia which so obsesses you. They have a steady sexuality and your earthiness responds well to that if you are not too offput by their selfishness. They hate your tendency to criticize.

Your Virgo Sun to Their Virgo Sun

Some signs do and some don't – get on with their clones. You would find yourselves worked and worried to a frazzle if you tried to co-exist. You need someone to pull you away from your anxieties not find a few more you had not already thought of. Your already workaholic tendencies would be emphasized and both of you would be constantly nit-picking each other's flaws. Feelings would freeze before they had a chance to breathe, with both of you pouncing to analyse them. You work exceptionally well together, respect each other's conscientious approach and would make good friends, but you are not designed for the grander passions of life together. You need more fire, more faith, more adventure. Life would grind to a halt since both of you are nose-deep in trivia and the tiny minutiae of everyday living and cannot see the broad scale. You would need a Sagittarius moon at least between you and that would just add to the generally restless feel. Initially you might feel that your refined earthiness gave you a chance of a good physical relationship but you need to be continually pulled out of yourself into a more wholehearted approach to life. With another Virgo you would end up constantly on the sidelines, spectating on life and commentating on it – but never really living it.

Your Virgo Sun to Their Libra Sun

A sweet, refined, good-natured pairing this, with both of you determined to suit the needs of the other. Virgo likes to serve and Libra always thinks of the other. You share similarly good tastes in friends, furnishings, clothes and cultural pursuits. Librans are more sociable, so are good for your reclusive streak. You are warmer and more practical, so good for their rather detached way of handling love, life and relationships. It works less well with a Libra woman with Virgo man since she can be brusquely sharp, wounding his pride and making him retreat from full-blooded involvement – always the death knell for Virgo men since they end up parchment dry and rather resentful. There can be slight problems (but only minor ones) because of Libra's indecisive streak and Virgo's highly strung tendency to worry about everything in sight and a few imaginary things as well. At the end of the day it can be a slightly dry combination unless both halves work hard to keep the passion alive. Libra prefers to stay on the surface and Virgo withdraws to the sidelines. It could all too easily become non-physical.

Your Virgo Sun to Their Scorpio Sun

This depends fairly and squarely on what kind of a Virgo you are. If you are fastidious, hygiene obsessed and rather prudish – forget it! Instantly! You will loathe Scorpio's muck-raking tendencies, its compulsion to drag everything down into the depths, its need to live life as a constant passionate power struggle. But if you are a Virgo who like your mythological counterpart Persephone has descended into the underworld and found your inner depths then it can work well. But you need to find a fairly worked out Scorpio. The only one who can cope with a raw, intensely determined Scorpio is another one. Best leave them to it. They understand each other. So with all the ifs and buts it can work with a passionate Virgo and a refined Scorpio who is willing not to indulge in too many underhand tactics to win control. You bring a light earthy warmth while Scorpio brings you a glimpse of the ecstasies beyond everyday life.

Your Virgo Sun to Their Sagittarius Sun

A restless, talkative combination but one that often works very well indeed. You adore Sagittarians' cheerful optimism and envy their courage at taking risks in life and having faith that good luck is always on their side. They will teach you eventually to worry less – unless you land a real gambling Sagittarius, which would be a disaster. You anchor them to the ground, offering the stability and practical common sense (as well as the basic tact) they lack. You may not always appreciate their blunt speaking, which can prick your sensitivities, but they are not malicious and never really mean harm. They just call a spade a spade and are accident-prone about putting their feet firmly in their mouths, mainly because they rush so much. Together you rarely sit still and are not wonderfully good at changing life together. Both of you are rather over-adaptive, finding it difficult to hold your ground. But long-running sulks are at least not a problem as long as you manage not to nag too much, especially about their impractical side. If you do keep on nagging you may find one day that they just fly away. They hate being fenced in.

Your Virgo Sun to Their Capricorn Sun

With only one real drawback this can be the most marvellous combination. There is a natural affinity. Both of you are earthy, practical, hard-working, well-mannered, fairly traditional in outlook and rather reserved. Neither of you will embarrass the other or make waves when duty calls. What can be a headache is the workaholic tendencies of both of you, which can often pull you away from romance. Both of you feel slightly guilty about indulgences, relaxation and light-hearted fun. Both of you can be slightly tunnel-visioned about the practical affairs of life. You need to keep the flames of passion alight by giving yourself (or forcing yourself to make) time for love. It works marginally better with a Virgo woman and Capricorn man since the energies are more evenly matched, though he is even more likely than his female counterpart to spend too many hours in the office. Since Virgo is fairly self-sufficient this in itself is not an instant disaster. The other way round (Capricorn woman and Virgo man) can make for a slightly less warm mating, with her in executive control and him rather hen-pecked.

Your Virgo Sun to Their Aquarius Sun

On a compatibility range of 1 to 10 this is about 0.5. You are warm, practical, good at helping people, sensitive to criticism, rather prudish socially and not keen on making a spectacle of yourself. Aquarians are cool, airy, rather eccentric (sometimes very eccentric), hideously honest (since they always tell the truth no matter the consequences) and not very interested in close relationships. You can communicate well together since both of you have active, intelligent minds. But you just approach life from such different standpoints. In can appear to work at times because Virgo is fairly self-sufficient and does not come across as over-emotional, jealous or possessive, but ultimately you would find it a little trying. Aquarians want friends, preferably en masse, not lovers in quiet moments. You like your own company and moments of peaceful romance as well. They know all about sex – in their heads – but prefer not too much physical contact. You like a good cuddle. But worst, you will never settle to their way of totally disregarding convention and doing absolutely what suits them. You will cringe with embarrassment at what you see as social gaffes.

Your Virgo Sun to Their Pisces Sun

You fit easily into each other's lives with few ripples. Not all opposite signs attract but both of you are naturally sympathetic, sensitive, adaptable and restless and you share cultural interests.

You are the more practical so can help Pisceans a great deal in their everyday life. They have vision so can drag your nose out of the minutiae of life to see the broad scale and maybe the inspiration as well. Neither of you is good at holding your ground, so sulks are not long lasting – though you can as a pair do with more anchoring. You will find it difficult to institute changes together because both of you are natural followers, not leaders. Pisceans bring you romance since they have wonderful dream-like imaginations. You bring them physical warmth of a light enough character not to make them feel weighed down. You are self-sufficient so will not mind them drifting off constantly into their inner worlds. Together your earth and their water make for a highly creative couple. Actor Richard Gere, an earthy, sex symbol Virgo, is happily married to supermodel Piscean Cindy Crawford.

You Are Libra

As seventh in the zodiac, a cardinal air sign, you are rather wise, full of initiative and bright chat. Always known as the relationship sign you are, curiously, emotionally quite detached. This cool quality fools others into thinking you do not care, but really you need another half in life whether at work or at home. You do not feel whole without it. Highly sociable you thrive on parties, friends and social gatherings. You adore living life at a rather superficial level where all relationships are friendly and there are no nasty rough edges. Your tactful, diplomatic approach (sometimes) makes you popular and an asset to most groups. Your drawback is a tendency always to find balance by putting the opposite point of view, which makes you seem argumentative.

Women Librans, it would have to be said, are much sharper than their male counterparts. Not all signs vary so much between the genders, but you do. The female of the species has a clear, 'masculine' mind and no-nonsense approach to life, while the male has a more 'feminine', sweet-natured outlook and can be a real softy. Both sexes can seem dithery and indecisive because you

like to think your way right round subjects. Sometimes by the
time you have made up your mind the opportunity has long
passed. At the end of the day, however, you can be extremely
wise. You are afflicted with extravagant spending habits, an
expensive and expansive taste in good food, clothes, furnishings
and lifestyle. You can be lazy but your career usually gets together
after the age of 29. You cannot stand a lazy mate. Balance is your
ideal and something for which you strive but rarely attain. Your
mental balance is sometimes more precarious than your
sophisticated image would suggest.

Your Libra Sun to Their Aries Sun

You admire their drive, *chutzpah*, courage, barefaced cheek and
loathe their brash straightforwardness, which tramps
undiplomatically through everyone else's sensitivities. It *can*
work, though you need to be extremely clear about what you can
cope with and what you cannot. Aries often do not change until
well into their fifties. That's when some of them grow up! Some
never do. So do not expect your harmonious approach to smooth
over their rougher edges instantly. They have romance, fire and
excitement in megadoses so may attract you initially just because
they can be highly appealing. They can also be highly irritating
and you do not take kindly to social gaffes, embarrassments or
their tendency not to engage their brains before they leap into
speech or action. Be warned. It works better with Libra man and
Aries woman, though the machismo is all on the wrong foot. The
other way round could be war!

Your Libra Sun to Their Taurus Sun

Sharing a ruler in Venus, you know you share similar tastes in
good living, food, drink, beautiful clothes and wonderful homes.
You are adaptable where Taureans stand solid and firm, so they
can provide you with an anchor. They can be hugely stubborn but
this is sometimes an advantage in a sticky corner since they do

not blow over easily. Always being the one who thinks about the other half in relationships, you do not mind a more self-centred partner (which they can be). As long as you fit in with their pleasures you will do fine. But woe betide you if you try to go against their wishes! Even better than Cancer they are masters at the art of passive resistance. They do not budge. They are earthier than you, which can provide problems since they undoubtedly want more cuddles, kisses and tangible signs of affection than most whereas you can be cool, detached and fairly up in your head. Communication is not always instinctive since they are not inward-looking and write off many intriguing aspects of life as being not practical and thus not worth considering. Maggie Thatcher, a model 'masculine' Libra woman, found her stability married to earthy Taurean Denis. Different types, with different interests, they go different ways but stick together.

Your Libra Sun to Their Gemini Sun

Light, bright and chatty you make the most sociable pair in the neighbourhood. Both of you thrive on friends, parties, reading books and swapping interesting facts. You are both air signs so live in your heads, your ideas and your opinions. Not inherently at home in your bodies, the more physical side of love may slacken off fairly fast. You could find Gemini a little gauche at times or socially embarrassing, because they do not have your innate diplomacy and need to keep the peace. They can also take short-cuts, which upsets your sense of natural justice. You are, on balance, more moral than they. It probably works best with a Libra male and Gemini female because he will be sweet-natured and she infinitely adaptable. The stronger Libra woman pitted against a wily Gemini Don Juan could be a stormy match. One problem with all the air signs is a tendency to coolness, which ultimately freezes feelings. The fires have to be kept alive.

Your Libra Sun to Their Cancer Sun

Air and water do not always mix well but you have more hope than some combinations. You can work in business well together since both of you have initiative, zip and vitality. You both adore large groups of interesting, well-bred and cultural friends. Both want a beautiful, settled home. You need a partner in life and Cancerians need a family. But you are more detached, airy and rather cool at times. You think rather than feel, whereas they approach life totally from an emotional standpoint and can threaten to upset the balance you so strive to maintain. They live life like a raft on the ocean's surface, rising and falling with their moods – one moment outgoing and the next moment withdrawn. You also can veer from extreme to extreme, which makes you a pair on see-saws trying to find an anchor in each other. They are jealous. You are not. A 6 out of 10 match.

Your Libra Sun to Their Leo Sun

Air and fire make a heady combination. Think of a helium balloon taking off. That's you as a couple – full of enthusiasms, bright ideas and romantic fantasies. Hugely sociable, both of you, and revelling in the better side of life. Parties (the bigger the better), friends by the yard and an approach to life that always looks on the light side. Relationships are what make your world go round and Leos are known as the sign of the burning heart. They are hugely egocentric – which could create problems though you can cope better than most. They want to do what they want and you to do what they want as well! But they will bring you a flamboyant lifestyle and a colourful spontaneity, which sometimes your airy coolness lacks. You could be just a tiny touch superficial together since neither of you is grounded. Neither of you wants to look into the watery, emotional depths or into the dark side of life. Nor are you very practical together. But a 7 out of 10 match all the same.

Your Libra Sun to Their Virgo Sun

Astrological lore has it that the sign before yours frightens or repels you. This may be the exception which proves the rule, since you rather like Virgo's refined warmth and sensitivity. Virgos go out of their way to be helpful, are generous, usually honest and hard-working and share your fairly light approach to life. As an adaptable sign they will leave major decisions to you and generally fit in rather than get too stubborn about their dislikes. They can nark on rather continuously, which is a bore, but their way of analysing feelings does not bother your airy detachment. They are the least heavy of the earth signs and good at bringing you down to face reality in a tactful way. Where you part company is over parties. You adore them and they do not. But if you can persuade them to organize the social events, run round with the canapés and do the dishes, all of which they adore, then you can get on with enjoying yourself chatting, charming and flirting with your guests.

Your Libra Sun to Their Libra Sun

How will you ever decide anything together? Each keeps deferring to the other and asking for advice. Both of you want to put the other first, which is wonderfully altruistic but could stop life in its tracks altogether. Despite your reputation for balance you know in your heart you are the most extreme of creatures, forever wobbling from one end of the see-saw to the other, which is precisely what your Libran other half does as well. So it could be a fairly unsettled existence. Both being air you could also be so detached and cool that the feelings would freeze altogether eventually. You would be great party-goers together since both of you are highly sociable, but your lives might tend to run along the surface rather than penetrate to any great depth. You need warmth from earthy moons or empathy from water moons to give you a feeling source.

Your Libra Sun to Their Scorpio Sun

You like living life on the surface, keeping everyone peaceful and harmonious and, generally speaking, steering clear of anything too messy or uncomfortable. Scorpio plunges compulsively into the depths, loathes superficialities and thrives on relationships where the agonies and ecstasies are inextricably mixed. How are you ever to agree? You are cool, airy, detached and think feelings through carefully before expressing them. You exude cheerful, colourful, light vibrations. Scorpio broods, is strong, dark, silent and fairly power-hungry. Scorpios express themselves through their turbulent and intensely felt emotions. You would constantly be pulling each other in opposite directions. You are indecisive but well balanced and interested in natural justice at the end of the day. Scorpios are hugely determined and keener on gaining control than worrying about the finer points of what is fair. With a Scorpio moon yourself you might just find a link, but even then you would be oddly matched.

Your Libra Sun to Their Sagittarius Sun

A light, bright, breezy, fun combination this which will keep you whistling cheerfully. You adore socializing, chatting, being part of a larger society. So does Sagittarius. Sagittarians have sharp, intelligent, wide-ranging minds – once you can get their comedy act shut down. Both of you are interested in matters social, political and philosophical. Being air and fire you are a heady couple, always on the go. They fire you with enthusiasm and a slightly more devil-may-care attitude to life. You add a little wisdom to their madcap schemes. What can positively put you off them is their disastrously honest approach. They need truly thick-skinned friends because they tell it like it is, in triplicate. You, being the soul of tact and diplomacy, are not always used to the brutal truth delivered unvarnished. That apart, all is well. You have bags of initiative. They adapt happily to whatever you suggest. Both of you are spendthrift and extravagant but since they are lucky the books should always balance. You are not jealous so will not worry about their need to roam freely. They hate being fenced in.

Your Libra Sun to Their Capricorn Sun

A vital, zippy combination for business with both of you full of drive, bright ideas and initiative. Neither of you is a slouch and you respect each other's strong sense of duty. It is a politically correct match socially but can be a little lacking in the deeper passions. Your mother will adore it but you may wish at times for slightly more excitement. Both of you are traditionalists at heart (snobs if one is to be truthful) and adore mixing in the best company. Your social life will be top-notch and always busy. But Capricorns can be workaholics and difficult to prise away from business meetings, which does not suit your need for an ever-present partner. Curiously, they can veer from a rather austere, almost celibate extreme to one of rather decadent sensuality. They are at heart an earth sign which you could find a little too physical at times, though they can also switch off for long periods as they become work obsessed. A 7 out of 10 pairing.

Your Libra Sun to Their Aquarius Sun

A wonderfully light, bright, airy and chatty pairing. Both of you are air signs and adore a good natter about almost everything under the sun. Both of you are interested in society as a whole and its future. But, but, but . . . there are drawbacks. You are sociable, refined, well bred, squirm with embarrassment over social gaffes and love a mate in life. Aquarians are certainly friendly and adore group functions but are born rebels and anarchists at heart. Give them a status quo and they will upset it. They can be wildly eccentric and do not give a hoot what anyone thinks as long as they are able to express their individuality. On the whole they do not like close relationships and will run a mile at the first sniff of jealousy, possessiveness or ties. They need space. If you do settle with them you need to watch that the entire relationship is not conducted at head level – all thinking, talking and no feeling. Neither of you is well grounded in your body. You need solid, earthy moons to give you a sensible link.

Your Libra Sun to Their Pisces Sun

Signs five removed from each other in the zodiac are not supposed to be complementary, but you are both sensitive, cultured, creative, sympathetic souls who care about people, the world and making a better life for yourselves. Pisceans are adaptable so they will follow your lead, which is wonderful when you are being decisive and not so great when you are dithering. Your airy, detached, rather cool approach may not seem custom-built for a water sign but they can be rather busy with their day-dreams so will probably not notice, and you will not be swamped with too many troublesome feelings. You have a fairly aesthetic feel for the better aspects of life and luxury which Pisces shares, though neither of you is wonderfully practical. You will be better at coping with the harsher realities of life than they; they will give you inspiration and vision. They will also romance you wonderfully in the early stages. Pisces is the most seductive (not to say orgiastic) of the signs, but not so physical that you would be turned off. Libran Duchess of York married the creative Piscean Prince Andrew, but her coolness and extreme behaviour (very Libran) finally unsettled the match. His intensely watery nature couple with his Scorpio moon finds it difficult to let go.

You Are Scorpio

Number eight in the zodiac you are fixed and watery, a powerhouse of emotional intensity. Deep, dark, determined and challenging, you know exactly where you are going in life though you rarely let anyone else know. Wilfully stubborn at times and deviously secretive, you never take no for an answer or listen to those who say something is impossible. It is not for nothing that you are known as a miracle maker. Power is what you really want in life. You are content to leave the glory and spotlight to others if you can just hold the whip and reins. More than anything in the world you loathe being controlled by others. You are excellent at handling confidential information and secrets though you rarely reveal yourself.

Relationships to you are about being plunged into the heart of your feelings, which can be fairly stormy. You need a similarly intense partner who does not mind a gut-wrenching partnership. The agonies are to you just as much a part of love as are the ecstasies, and it is not everyone who can stand life lived at this level. For all that you are surprisingly sentimental in affairs of the heart and are often quite hurt by people close to you in the family. Your great drawbacks are a tendency to sulk endlessly and, even worse, to plot revenge when you have been attacked.

Your Scorpio Sun to Their Aries Sun

Never in a million years will you understand what this restless, flyaway firebird is all about. It's like trying to mate an octopus with an eagle. You want passionate clinches that last a lifetime, or at least a decade, while they are happy to land lightly in one place for a milli-second and then flee for pastures new. Your thresholds of enthusiasm are very far apart. They are sprinters over a short distance. Boredom sets in fairly easily and they are never entirely happy in anything too physical. You are a steady marathon runner, secure in the knowledge that lust grows in time into deeper, more blissful states. The body for you is crucial to the love experience, the vehicle that carries you into transcendent places. You are jealous, possessive and driven by your emotional undercurrents. They hate being fenced in and if trapped will disappear into their day-dreams to evade you. This can only work if one or other of you is suppressing your essential nature. Or if you have moons that create such a strong link that you can override the sun. But it will still be an uneasy match.

Your Scorpio Sun to Their Taurus Sun

This is a heavyweight match. Two hugely stubborn signs together, but what is in your favour is that you both approach life with certain central objectives the same. You are both jealous, possessive and capable of living with great passion, though you slightly more than Taurus, who ever yearns for a peaceful existence. You can never be doing with wishy-washy, milksop signs who want to live life on the surface. But you have to accept that sulks can be weeks long, that Taureans are never going to budge easily and that their prime interest in life is generally pleasuring themselves. They can be immensely sweet, cuddly and sensual but they will not shift off base to fit in with your plans, at least not without a hurricane force wind behind them. They can make your life run more sensibly because they are earthy and practical. You force them to look beyond the surface to the greater dimensions of life. It is not an ideal match but at 6 out of 10 it can survive better than some.

Your Scorpio Sun to Their Gemini Sun

Curiously this can work not badly for a while. Your watery depths are not supposed to dovetail with Gemini's restless, airy nature and Geminis can be brightly superficial, which is hardly your scene, but they do have a very dark side as well which has an attraction. Both of you like to walk on the wild side of life, to explore the miseries as well as the joys, the agonies as well as the ecstasies. That can hold you together for a while. Though at the end of the day Geminis are grasshoppers and will move on rapidly when their interest fades, which does not suit your jealous nature. You have staying power and fidelity. They haven't. You are deeply emotional and exist in your feelings where they live in their heads, their ideas and their theories. They can be tantalizingly split or, to put it more bluntly, two-faced at times.

You never quite know whom you are relating to, which certainly does not suit your passionate nature which likes to possess body, soul and heart. Ultimately they will become scared of being swamped by your feelings and pulled under by the hidden currents. Princess Grace of Monaco, a heavyweight Scorpio, stood by a long and probably not easy marriage to the more butterfly personality of Gemini Prince Rainer.

Your Scorpio Sun to Their Cancer Sun

This can purr along very smoothly in the early stages. Both of you are watery, emotionally sensitive creatures so you understand each other's needs intuitively. There is no danger of either of you becoming scared of the hidden undercurrents or tidal waves of feelings that sweep over you. But you will at times feel like a raft cast adrift on a stormy sea with no anchor unless one or both of you have earthy or airy moons to calm you down and detach you from all those turbulent feelings. The passions will rage but ultimately this match could run into problems. Scorpios are always strong personalities but Cancer men tend not to be, which can prove an uneven pairing. The reverse, a Scorpio man and an increasingly matriarchal Cancerian woman, could turn into a battle royal for supremacy at home (like Prince Charles, Scorpio, and Princess Diana, Cancer?). Scorpio really wants one intense exclusive relationship. Cancer wants a family, and partners can end up feeling relegated to being just another of the tribe at some point. This would never suit you.

Your Scorpio Sun to Their Leo Sun

Not a match made in heaven or really suited to an existence on earth unless there are overwhelmingly compatible moon connections. You are deep, dark, secretive and power hungry. Leos are light, bright, attention-seeking and basically frightened of the emptiness in their depths. They would freak out at having to live life at the level where you feel satisfied. Both of you are hugely stubborn, so the sulks would be endless and no one would want to give way first – they for fear of losing face, you for fear of losing power. Certainly both of you are highly sexual, but in different ways. You because you want to move into the ecstasies beyond the body. They, being fiery, are more into the fantasies of a true love, knights on white chargers, etc. The two may sound as if they would merge, and possibly could do for a while, but the gritty side would have to be ironed out. Both of you are certainly faithful once settled, and home-loving, though Leos want to be top dog in the family and you never relinquish control lightly. Water and fire are a strange mix. You would be on a roller-coaster of emotions from one end of the spectrum to the other. Hillary (Scorpio) and Bill Clinton (Leo) are worth a look at to see how it works in practice.

Your Scorpio Sun to Their Virgo Sun

You have to pick your Virgo carefully for this to work. Select an old maidish (of either sex), dried up, parchmenty, nagging, nit-picking, over-fastidious Virgo and you would feel desperate within a day. Every feeling you had would be dissected, analysed and freeze-dried before you had a chance to sink into it. All your visions of the ecstasies beyond boring reality would be killed stone dead. But there are warm, earthy Virgos who have learned to live life to the full and have plunged into their depths. As long as you are willing to respect their refined sensitivities and fairly cautious approach, they can be a reasonably good match for you. You will not experience the intensity you would with another Scorpio but your Virgo will ground you, smooth out your practical problems and will adore a good cuddle. They will also be faithful, so will not upset your jealous streak. They will adapt to you so your obstinacy can reign unhindered. They will serve your needs since that is what they really like. They will also talk endlessly, which will not always suit you, and have a slightly unhappy habit of usually being right. But that is a small price to pay.

Your Scorpio Sun to Their Libra Sun

In the astrological rule book you are supposed to fear the sign before yours. In this case it is not so much paralysing terror as rather contemptuous indifference. You cannot understand why anyone would want to live life at that superficial level. All sociable smiles, sweet pleasantries and an instant balm to smooth away any ruffles in the atmosphere before they turn into arguments. Librans hate discord while you thrive on turbulent feelings. They like light. You head like a homing pigeon for the darkness. To survive together one or other of you would have to be operating well outside the milieu that suits your essential nature. Although known as the relationship sign Libra is airy, so is almost always detached, cool and sophisticated. You would feel very unattached and unconnected to your watery depths. You feel. Librans think. You want passions and are willing to put up with agony to get them. They wants peace, sweetness, harmony and what you consider to be a wishy-washy life where everyone agrees. You would feel you had nothing to grapple with, nothing to stretch you to your limits. With a heavy water moon on the other side you might just make half a go of it, but it does not feel like a match.

Your Scorpio Sun to Their Scorpio Sun

Heaven! Another soul mate who understands your terrible yearnings, is not scared of your deeper undercurrents and wants to live life to the full, plunged right down into the depths. You are both passionately jealous and possessive, so any hint of infidelity will blow up a major tornado. The sulks will be long lasting since neither of you gives in easily. There will inevitably be a ping-pong match of 'who won the last round and who is going to win this one?'. Both of you will fight for control and supremacy while understanding that the other has to win sometime. Vindictiveness in petty ways could eventually start to undermine the relationship since neither of you can resist the temptation to get back, nor indeed forgive very easily. More

Scorpios marry other Scorpios than happens among the other signs. Family life will be surprisingly sentimental since both of you are slushy at heart when it comes to kids. Once settled you can stay very loyal since you understand the pain of separation and betrayal. If it comes to a break, though, very destructive, vengeful feelings will spill out into the open. Yasmin and Simon Le Bon are a matched pair.

Your Scorpio Sun to Their Sagittarius Sun

You are ruled by Pluto, king of the underworld. Sagittarians are ruled by Jupiter, who was king on Mount Olympus, highest point in the heavens. Nuff said? You thrive on deep, secret passions and want endlessly binding clinches. They fly off at the first whiff of possessiveness, are not emotional except in their fantasies (which they are not happy to share) and never stand still for long. Being a fire sign they are naturally attuned to the body – and how are you to experience all those sexual ecstasies which are your life's blood if they cannot stay with you in the physical experience? Their restless feet and wandering eye would keep you in agonies as well. Water/fire mixes are very tempestuous, but not in the sense you appreciate. They just represent two opposites trying to mate – an octopus with an eagle, a scorpion with a firebird. Initially they may present you with reason for hope because they can be excitingly dramatic personalities and are keen to take risks. But where you are hidden they are bluntly honest and open to the point of naïvety. You will frighten them off fairly quickly unless you are acting in a manner very much out of character. Ted Turner, media mogul, is a Scorpio. His wife, actress Jane Fonda, an enthusiastic Sagittarius.

Your Scorpio Sun to Their Capricorn Sun

A strong workmanlike combination that has a real chance of working as long as you do not pick a workaholic, celibate Capricorn (and they do exist). Though, naturally, you may be the road to such Capricorns' salvation as you reintroduce them to the joys of loving and the pleasures of the flesh. If you can get their minds off money, status and achievements, they are an earth sign and hugely indulgent. You just have to rebalance them. Then your highly sexed, deeply passionate nature can be satisfied. Not in total, however, because they are earthy and therefore not intuitively emotional. They can be warm (though that is true more of the males than the females) but it is an earthy warmth, not a deeply felt experience. You might miss the descent to the agonies and the underworld which is so much a part of your fulfilment in life. But you do respect their initiative, their devotion to hard work and their ability to provide a good lifestyle. They are also not too stubborn, so would not clash with you that much. They are honest, at least emotionally, and faithful on the whole, so would not cause you too much insecurity.

Your Scorpio Sun to Their Aquarius Sun

You live life. Aquarians think about it. You feel. They theorize. You adore being close, in passionate clinches. They are distant beyond your comprehension and want friends, not lovers. You breathe jealousy and possessiveness. They exude tolerance, preach free love and frankly would prefer to keep relationships as platonic as possible. They know all about sex. Aquarians are the great sexperts. But they know it in their heads from the best books and sophisticated conversations, not from practice. You are both stubborn so would find compromises difficult, but you are on different planets when it comes to love. You are Mars Pluto – all fire, emotional depth, lust and longing. They are Saturn Uranus – cool, defensive, out of their bodies and so individualistic that anything that gets more intimate than a passing kiss feels like a violation of their selfhood. You would constantly be grasping at a partner who does not want to be there in spirit. It would need great moon connections for this even to make a stab at working. Seriously intense Tatum O'Neal is Scorpio, even worse with a watery Cancer moon as well, so double up on the jealousy factor.

Parting company with very airy Aquarian John McEnroe with his airy Gemini moon was sadly perhaps always inevitable. All water with all air – chalk and cheese.

Your Scorpio Sun to Their Pisces Sun

A blissful pair of intuitive watery types, you thrive together. Pisceans are highly sensitive so you need to be wary of grasping them too tightly or you could find them reversing off into their day-dreams and fantasies. But play them right and this can be a match made in heaven. You are fixed and stubborn where they are flexible and adaptable, so the sulks will not last long. Pisceans give in. They prefer to merge into their partners unless, of course, you find the odd large fish Piscean, who can be a trifle whale- or octopus-like in his or her approach to love, life and lust. But even this voracious, rather orgiastic appetite can suit your depth of passion. At times you may feel like a raft adrift on the ocean, rudderless and at the mercy of the winds and currents since neither of you has an anchor once the emotional temperature heats up. Pisces can sometimes be maddeningly evasive and even feel cool, which is strange for a water sign. But that is because Pisceans have such a yearning to merge with the cosmos and all of humanity that they sometimes lose their sense of relating on a one-to-one basis. But the pluses undoubtedly outweigh the minuses.

You Are Sagittarius

Ninth sign in the zodiac you are fiery, restless and flexible. Energetic, impractical, cheerful and wildly communicative, you are usually highly popular because of your eternal optimism. You always look for the silver lining in any black cloud and 'never say die' is your motto. But as a rainbow-chaser you dislike being made to stand still. Facing up to responsibilities and commitments in relationships makes you feel fenced in. Running off to roam the open plains is your best defence. Avoiding jealous, possessive partners is your first aim. Finding one who is a strong individual in his or her own right comes next, then at least you know he or she will be self-sufficient enough not to lean on you.

Doing things on the small scale is not your style. You always take the broad view. Some critics might call you 'over the top'. You loathe being forced to pay attention to practical details and minutiae. Flamboyance is the name of your game. You are always up front with your opinions, but not always too sensitive. Friends of Sagittarians, they always say, need rhinoceros hides because of your brutal frankness. Malice is not in your nature but you do lack tact. You are sociable, outgoing, usually goodhearted, almost always naïve. Interests in life include foreign travel, books and knowledge. You can be a real armchair philsopher when you are not exploring the four corners of the globe.

Your Sagittarius Sun to Their Aries Sun

Not quiet, not peaceful, not practical but what an amazing amount of fun – while it lasts. Burnout is all too likely since both of you go at life wholeheartedly and in overdrive all the time. Both of you run on fire energy, which acts first and thinks later (if at all) and finds feelings a little tricky. So you race around taking risks, looking for glamour, romance, excitement and adventure. Life according to your creeds should be out of a thriller. Neither of you is jealous or possessive – quite the reverse – though Aries does not like to be a loser so infidelity is likely to be regarded as an aggressive act. Your marvellously adaptable nature allows you to fit in with your Aries mate most of the time, though you will insist on the freedom to roam as you please when the mood suits. Neither of you is tuned in to the body so long-lasting physical passion may not be so easy to maintain. Indeed the boredom threshold on both sides is likely to be very low indeed. Honesty sessions could also wear the relationship thin at times, since both of you are bluntly frank to a startling degree. But whatever happens you are likely to remember the encounter with glee.

Wonderfully bouncy actor Kenneth Branagh, an ever-enthusiastic Sagittarian, is married to outspoken Arien Oscar-winner Emma Thompson.

Your Sagittarius Sun to Their Taurus Sun

You need a practical mate who can put your feet on the ground occasionally, but do you need being buried under a ton of earth? You like to fly free where Taurus needs to stand still. You loathe restrictions while Taurus hates change with a vengeance. You are the most restless fire sign while Taurus is the most solid of the earth signs. It is a gritty, rather ill-matched mix. In early adult life opposites often attract each other to fill in for what they lack in themselves. But as maturity rounds you out so do you discover you really have very little in common. Being out of sync at an essential level means you inevitably grow apart with different interests and different outlooks. Jealousy would be a problem in the relationship since you cannot stand it and Taurus hangs firmly on to what it regards as its own possession. On the upside your sunny, adaptable nature can cope with Taurus' stubborn stance, but for what? Unless your moons are highly compatible you really can do better for yourself.

Your Sagittarius Sun to Their Gemini Sun

You are opposite signs in the zodiac but not so different in temperament. Both of you talk endlessly, wittily, across a wide range of topics. You are gregarious, sociable, interested in what others think. You are restless and rarely sit still. Both of you are flexible, perhaps lacking a little in initiative and staying power but definitely of a temperament to bend round difficult people and circumstances. You do fit together better than many polar opposites. But you are a flyaway pair together, with not much common sense between you. You like flying high, taking risks and assuming your luck will always hold out. Gemini races around like a demented butterfly at times and thinks that quick wits will overcome most problems. Both of you need more of an anchor and more connection to your feelings. It could just work if you have an earth moon connection or maybe even a water moon. If you have fire or air moons you will burn out like a spent firework at some point. Too much heat never lasts.

Your Sagittarius Sun to Their Cancer Sun

You are not ideally designed for each other since you need to be given a long rein to roam free. Domesticity is not your bag of tricks at all and anything that smells of jealousy or possessiveness really gives you shudders of horror. Whereas Cancer is home-orientated, devoted to the sink, the stove and the hearth and can be immensely jealous if it feels its security is being threatened. Cancerians do not let go easily. You are fire and they are water. Together you will veer from high to low. Fire can boil water up to a heated passion but at some point the water will put out the fire. Basically you distrust feelings and are suspicious of the manipulation and control that tends to go with them. Cancerians will tear their hair out at your searing honesty. They hate criticism in any form and your lack of tact will feel like a lack of empathy to them. You tend to approach life with your theories and thoughts or enthusiasms, rarely your feelings. Not a happy combination over the long term. You would end up trapped and hen-pecked.

Your Sagittarius Sun to Their Leo Sun

Fire on fire is a very combustible combination. Both of you live life at high speed with little thought for reality, the practicalities of life or the state of your body. You like living high, full of passion, glamour and romance, with a burning vision of what you want. All of this can create a warm and wonderful relationship, but can it last? Without care it could burn out quickly. Of course, you are deeply attracted to each other. You are on the same wavelength. You can adapt to Leo's stubbornness relatively easily. Leos will adapt less well to your scorching honesty, since their pride and vanity are wounded by anything that is not outright flattery. But you do need an earth moon or even a water one between you to provide some ballast, otherwise the relationship will be undermined by lack of real feeling and probably lack of organization. One partner usually needs to be the practical one – neither of you is.

Your Sagittarius Sun to Their Virgo Sun

Both being mutable signs you are highly adaptable, restless and energetic. Not necessarily good at starting new projects together – you need a kick-start from outside – nor at staying over the long distance, you could do with more anchoring. Virgos will certainly be more practical than you and sort out the everyday details of life – obsessively so, to your irritation at times – but they will bring organization to the chaos of your existence. They are earthy and warm but fairly refined, so will not offend you with too much gross physicality in the relationship. You need to be allowed to roam free and they are among the less jealous signs in the zodiac. They will not appreciate your straight-from-the-hip comments because they are sensitive to attack. If you are together it is probably because you have an earthy moon, which will be a definite help.

Your Sagittarius Sun to Their Libra Sun

As long as you can keep a grip of your tongue, this is a heaven-sent combination. You are fiery, enthusiastic, interested in broad ideas, and sociable. Librans are diplomatic, wise, communicative and also happy among crowds of people (who have to be well bred). Both of you like to slide across the surface and are not too happy being plunged into the depths of feelings or the harsher realities of life. At times this will make the relationship seem shallow or insincere but it is how you like to operate. Neither of you is hugely physical where passion is concerned, so that is no worry. You need a tolerant mate who will let you roam free. Librans are not jealous, though they loathe social embarrassment and humiliation. You must watch your step at times. They can seem a little cool at times (especially Libra women), which may bother your fiery soul, but they will provide you with a beautiful, harmonious home base from which to take off.

Your Sagittarius Sun to Their Scorpio Sun

No. In a word. You are ill-designed for each other. You find Scorpios frighteningly dark, manipulative, secret and controlling. They find you a flibberty-gibbet who never settles down, who is unrealistically optimistic and will not come down to the level where real life exists. You basically distrust feelings and are suspicious of emotional types. None comes more with more hidden undercurrents and storm-filled tempests than Scorpio. They can be just as sharp as you with their opinions but there seems to be an edge of malice or vindictiveness in them that is entirely missing from your more gullible, naïve approach to life. They know that through sex and intense unions they can reach a really transcendental place. You feel frightened of being pulled that close to any one person and are in any event not that physical. You fire, they water. It can flare into passion early on but it will not last, since you need elbow room and they need the exact opposite.

Your Sagittarius Sun to Their Sagittarius Sun

A wild, way out and not very realistic combination. You could have an amazing time together for a short period and then it would all fizzle out since both of you go like space rockets. You rarely sit still and would lead a life together of dizzying activity, but you really need a mate who can ground you a little, put you in touch with your body and your feelings. Together you would endlessly swap ideas, philosophize and ponder on the future implications for society. But it would all be too up in your heads and in your hopes. Getting the practical loose ends of life tied together would be a major horror since both of you bore easily when it comes to details. Neither of you is particularly good at starting new projects or sticking to long-distance plans. You much prefer instant excitement, which is all very well but usually one partner needs to have common sense and grounding if the relationship is not to take off like a hot air balloon. A good short-term prospect but not sensible for a lifetime.

Your Sagittarius Sun to Their Capricorn Sun

There are pros and cons to this match though in essence the differences between you are so clear that it is difficult to see how you could ever be totally compatible. The plus points are that Capricorn would bring you down to earth and sort out the practical details of your life, not all of which will please you but which would help in the long term. Capricorns have initiative and get-up-and-go on the work front, where you tend to adapt yourself to whatever is already happening. The down side is that they tend to view you as unreliable, over-optimistic, unrealistic and a bit of a gambler – all of which in their book is bad news. And Capricorns do disapprove rather noticeably. They can be highly judgemental. Your brighter, livelier spirits would ultimately be weighed down by their very earthy approach. They do not share your wacky sense of humour at all. They would not tie you down, which would help, but they work so hard you might find their absence eventually irksome. If they have a fire moon it might just work.

Your Sagittarius Sun to Their Aquarius Sun

A gloriously exciting, not very stable or realistic combination but one that could work because both of you have the same zany sense of humour. Both of you are scorchingly honest and truthful, interested in society and the broad scope of ideas. Neither of you is keen on being crowded or possessed and you both adore freedom. So you fit each other's foibles remarkably well. The only problem is that neither of you is very realistic, so you can sometimes take off together like a hot air balloon, your fire fuelling their air into some rather reckless enterprises. But it is always fun and rarely does boredom set in. Physically there will not be great passion that lasts for ever since both of you are rather separated from your bodies. Aquarius lives up in its head and ideas while you live in your fantasies, ideals and hopes. Sagittarian Woody Allen made a match with Aquarian Mia Farrow which had a great deal going for it but burnt out along the way for these two highly self-sufficient people.

Your Sagittarius Sun to Their Pisces Sun

A pair of fidgets together, you will never sit still but you are a better fire/water mix than virtually any other. Partly because Pisceans, should they not get all the emotional nourishment they need, will quite happily space out into their day-dreams and not make you feel as trapped as the other two water signs, Cancer and Scorpio. Your direct truth-telling may, however, upset their delicate sensibilities. Pisceans cringe more than most at the harsher realities that you love pointing out. But you do understand their need for fantasy since you have so many of your own visions, ideals and hopes for the future and for the world. There may be a clash since you are essentially courageous and they can be extremely timid. You will give them more sparkle and *chutzpah* (daring) but they may find your boisterous exuberance tiring. You adore their rather passive, self-sacrificing approach to life since it allows you to do more or less what you want.

You Are Capricorn

Practical, ambitious and determined to rise socially and professionally through hard work, you can sometimes be a touch lacking in fun. You started life as an old child, feeling deprived emotionally or financially, but you will mellow through your middle years, gaining a sense of humour and ending up a thoroughly impish geriatric.

You are renowned as having a hard head for business and can at times be a real workaholic who has no time for romance or a sex life. But then you fall madly, passionately and not always wisely in love in a highly physical, sensual way.

Known as the stander on the threshold between the conscious and the unconscious you can be enormously creative with ideas, either teaching in a broad sense or turning dreams into money in business. Security is the most important thing in life for you. Retirement cottages are in your mind in your mid-twenties and you fully intend to have your nest egg stashed away with your fully paid up pension plan. A real traditionalist you can at times put too much stress on outer appearance and are quite class-conscious. You can be highly sensitive about your social reputation and the approval of the right people.

Your Capricorn Sun to Their Aries Sun

A robust combination but one made for work rather than romance. Both of you are bursting with energy, initiative, drive and the will to win. Aries because they need to be first. You because you want to climb up the social ladder and acquire wealth for security. You can thrive together but it will be gritty and competitive. Ego clashes are almost inevitable. You may not always find Aries' brash, rather self-centred approach to your liking. Ariens have no embarrassment when heading for their goals, no worry about what anyone else thinks and social niceties tend to be swept aside. You are keen to be seen as respectable, wince with humiliation if you are seen to be out of line and worry about not being quite the thing. Neither of you is especially emotional, though you are more physical. Ariens at the end of the day can be too out of touch with their bodies to suit you totally. You will frown on their unrealistic approach to life while they will feel weighed down by your ever-practical attitude. You will judge them harshly.

Your Capricorn Sun to Their Taurus Sun

An earthy combination this, which promises much in the way of physical closeness, a shared interest in work or in gardening and a fairly practical approach to life. You tune in to each other's energies, though at times you can be perhaps a little too narrow in your vision of what life is all about together. You will have to haul yourself away from work more to make the relationship thrive. At times you will find Taurus' stubbornness irksome. You are restless, energetic and more inclined to give life a shake and make it go. Taureans sit rock steady and assume problems will go away in time. Both of you are sensual, sensuous people and great gourmets. Taurus especially is keen on physical comfort and your home life together will be luxurious. You will want to refine your mate's taste in almost everything since Taureans can be a little basic at times, but they will warm you up and stop you turning into a workaholic.

Your Capricorn Sun to Their Gemini Sun

Not instantly recognizable as a good pairing this sometimes works very well indeed. Both of you are hard workers, keen on making money and very energetic. Neither of you is hugely emotional. You have a healthier interest in physical closeness but Geminis can have a wild way about them which could suit (though that is the male of the species rather than the female). You will not always appreciate their way of cutting corners. They can be a little devious, which upsets your strait-laced soul. At times you wince because you need social approval and a good reputation while they are born rebels at heart and could not care less what anyone else thinks. It could end up a rather cool relationship because you have workaholic tendencies and Gemini lives up in its head, in its ideas and thoughts. Geminis tend to detach themselves from feelings before they have time to develop. Not an absolutely ideal match but a 6 out of 10.

Your Capricorn Sun to Their Cancer Sun

Opposites sometimes attract, sometimes repel. Your base in life is undoubtedly work, while theirs is home. But both of you are energetic, hard-working signs and Cancerians can make their way in the world as well as setting up a happy family foundation for themselves. You are earthy, therefore more practical. They are watery, therefore highly emotional. You will seem chilly, critical and judgemental to them at times. Your practical, always purposive approach to life cuts through their more sentimental, empathetic approach. If it is a Capricorn man with a Cancer woman there can be power struggles as you age, as she will become more matriarchal and you may retreat more and more into staying late at work. The other way round will definitely have Capricorn as the dominant partner. Whichever way round, this is likely to be a busy partnership with both of you constantly dreaming up new ideas and starting new projects. Strong, determined Princess Michael of Kent, a Capricorn, is married to rather gentler Cancerian Prince Michael. Will it stand the test of time?

Your Capricorn Sun to Their Leo Sun

You are fairly opposite energies but strangely you like the same things. Both of you adore social respectability and the good life. Neither of you was designed to be poor, derelict or unwashed. Life needs to be five-star, perhaps more discreet for you and more flamboyant for them but definitely socially upwardly mobile. Leos will irritate you at times not just because of their monstrous egos and their vanity but because of their basically impractical outlook on life. You will find yourself picking up the bits which they litter behind them. They may find you chillier than they like because you tend to take a stalwartly practical view on everything and they loathe being judged. But for all that you will prosper because you will fill your lives with interesting, important friends. They will bring sparkle to your rather withdrawn personality and you will anchor them to the ground a little more, which they need. A 6 out of 10 match.

Your Capricorn Sun to Their Virgo Sun

If you can both drag yourselves away from work and obligations this can be a very good match indeed, but you both have workaholic tendencies which need watching. You are both earthy so share a similarly practical, realistic approach to life. You both like good food, gardening and a good cuddle. Virgo can be too nit-picking at times, too much of a perfectionist and an anxious worrier, so you will get exasperated. But Virgos will, more than most people, respect and tolerate your need to be working longer hours and you will offer them a protection against the world. They are also fairly adaptable and will fit round your needs. Both of you can go through chilly, almost celibate periods when deep passion and warmth are pushed to one side, but both of you are capable of very physical love if you let yourselves go. It will be a relationship that should mellow nicely with the years.

Your Capricorn Sun to Their Libra Sun

Different energies but similar interests can make this a good, if slightly cool combination. You are both keen on knowing the right people, being approved of and living a good social life. You both have oodles of initiative and rarely sit still. You very much appreciate Librans' good taste in décor, entertaining and clothes and their tactful way of keeping harmony wherever they go. They respect your hard-working abilities and talents, adore your growing respectability and share your traditional values. They can seem a little shallow at times because they basically try to avoid their feelings and stay on the surface of life, but you really do not mind that especially. They are airy, up in their heads most of the time. You are more earthy and in tune with your body than they are, which could cause difficulties in your sex life. But you are capable of switching off desire if need be for reasons of work or advancement, so this may be a hurdle that you can overcome. It will probably work better with a Capricorn woman and Libra man. The other way round could be a little too businesslike.

Your Capricorn Sun to Their Scorpio Sun

This is theoretically supposed to work well, but I wonder. Scorpio is deep, dark, intense, highly passionate, secretive and manipulative. Scorpios need relationships they can sink themselves into, intertwine themselves around. You certainly have an earthy, sensual side but you can also come across as rather cool because you put work first much of the time. They would feel dismissed and brushed off by you, hurt because you will not sink to their depths. Scorpios adore being down in the murk and although you can be extremely physical you do not appreciate being emotionally exposed to that extent. You are also very straight and rather traditional; their rather devious ways do upset you and make you suspicious. You always have a nasty feeling there is dirty linen that might one day be washed in public. That is a humiliation you would go to any lengths to avoid.

Your Capricorn Sun to Their Sagittarius Sun

One astrological rule of thumb says you fear or dislike the sign before yours in the zodiac. You exist in a world that is practical, straightforward, cautious, at times even pessimistic. Sagittarians are harum-scarum creatures who trust to luck, are quite unrealistic, have their heads in the clouds most of the time and tend to say the first thing that comes into their minds, polite or not. They are born optimists and luckier than you, which certainly makes you envious. Not a happy combination, though over the short term you could have something to offer each other. You would anchor them to the ground while they would give you a little sparkle, prod you into taking more risks and give you more trust in life. But at the end of the day you are such different animals it would hardly work well. You need physical affection.

They are not well tuned in to their bodies and need to roam free. You are hardly the jealous and possessive type but with your work schedule and their wandering feet you might meet only very infrequently.

Your Capricorn Sun to Their Capricorn Sun

This would be a rather dour, humourless, over-work-orientated combination which would gradually wither on the branch and die. Certainly both of you can be physical and sensual but both of you have to be prompted into it by livelier companions. Otherwise you fall back into staying at the office longer and longer hours. Both of you are so ambitious for security, achievement at work and social respectability you would forget to make time for relaxation and sheer indulgence. As an older couple it might work since you warm, mellow and gain a stronger sense of humour through middle age, but early on you are certainly both too serious, pessimistic and blinkered to be happy together. You need a mate who can awaken your sense of vision and fantasy, to let you see more is possible than the mere making of money. There are beautiful, worthwhile ideals to which you can aspire. Love is not just bodies meeting. It is also hearts and souls.

Your Capricorn Sun to Their Aquarius Sun

Essentially a chalk and cheese mix, this does not have a hopeful feel about it. You are traditional, cautious and rather anxious about social approval. Aquarians are wild individualists, true eccentrics, rebels and anarchists at heart. They hate fitting in and never see any point in worrying about other people's opinion. You would cringe with embarrassment at their startlingly direct way of speaking the truth. You are class-conscious. They are tolerant of all human foibles and willingly embrace the great brotherhood and sisterhood of humanity, whatever the class, creed or background. You are earthy, physical and can be quite sensual. They are airy, very distant and not tuned in to their bodies at all.

They know things about sex you've never even dreamed of but they rarely practice – it's all in the head. You would find them cool to the point of chilliness, friendly enough but just not keen on close relationship.

Your Capricorn Sun to Their Pisces Sun

A sweet match this, with you out in the world achieving and being protective while Pisces wanders round in its day-dreams but remaining always sympathetic to your needs. Pisceans are highly adaptable, which suits you, and will generally follow along behind. They are passive and can lack courage. You are on the other hand assertive, dynamic, full of initiative. Together you make a good business pair because Pisces has the dreams and you put them into action. You anchor them in reality and they pull you away from too narrow and practical an outlook. They give you imaginative flair and ideals to shoot for. You are more physical than they but they are a highly emotional, seductive and seducible sign that needs companionship. They may exasperate you because of their vagueness and their tendency to disappear into outer space in their fantasies from time to time, but this can be a positive advantage when you are away at the office for long hours. They will happily occupy themselves.

You Are Aquarius

You are a rugged individualist with a witty, inventive mind and, despite a really stubborn streak, are often seen as amazingly tolerant. Because you see no need to be one of the common herd you can be a great pioneer, treading unknown paths and being truly unique. You have a real sense of the great brotherhood/ sisterhood of humanity and want to make a better society in which independence and freedom are the keynotes.

The truth is highly important to you. Rarely do you cover over unpalatable facts for the sake of politeness. You tell it like it is, tactless or no. Your airy, communicative approach to life at times makes you appear emotionally cool or detached. Close relationships do try your patience since you hate being shut in a claustrophobic atmosphere and you also resent the give and take and compromises that are part of one-to-one unions. What you need is an independent mate who gives you space. Ultimately you just have to watch that space does not turn into distance and everything just withers away from neglect. Physical contact is not as necessary for you as for some signs. Although you know a great deal about sex (the great sexperts are almost all Aquarians) it is more of a head exercise than a frequent practice. You will keep your own friends after marriage.

Your Aquarius Sun to Their Aries Sun

A zippy, zany, very noisy combination but always a great deal of fun. Boredom is never likely. You will happily let them win, which suits them, and they in turn with their irrepressible bounce will keep you laughing, joking and sparkling. Ariens do not care if you are shockingly direct and honest because they are, too. Neither of you is jealous or possessive or indeed very physical. Ariens live in their fantasies while you live in your thoughts and theories. Sometimes your stubbornness will irritate them because of their passion for keeping on the move. Sometimes their very self-centred approach to life will irk you because you see the value in having an equal, happy society that is friendly and democratic. You tend to be more selfless. They may help to focus your ambitions more strongly. You will help detach them from their obsessions and give them perspective on their actions.

Your Aquarius Sun to Their Taurus Sun

Not a wonderful match since you are expansive, friendly and rather laid back emotionally and physically while they are close, cuddly, warm, jealous, tactile and quite sensual. Your sex life would cause problems after your early passion had worn off.

Taurus' constant need for physical attention and demonstrative affection would make you feel cornered and restricted. You hate claustrophobic relationships and much prefer to be one of a crowd. Both of you are hugely stubborn, neither would give way easily in arguments. Taurus is a past master at passive resistance. It just digs its heels in and does not budge, standing rooted like an oak tree. You are more explosive but are equally good at standing your ground. You would find Taurus too staid, too traditional, too concerned with the boring practicalities of life. Taurus would find you too concerned with abstractions, zany ideas and madcap schemes. A Taurean would pour cold water over you and try to control your more wayward tendencies. You need compatible moons for this to work. Talented actress Farrah Fawcett, an individualistic Aquarian happily endowed with a family-orientated Cancer moon, is married to obstinate, volatile Taurean Ryan O'Neal. What saves this match from instant self-destruct is his Aquarius moon – though it cannot be an easy relationship.

Your Aquarius Sun to Their Gemini Sun

A non-stop talk show, where both of you try to outdo each other with wild ideas, crackpot schemes and weird jokes. You both share a rebellious, devil-may-care approach to life which says to hell with convention, respectability and boredom. You are possibly a little too much together since neither of you is going to restrain the other with practical words of advice or caution. Both of you live up in your heads, not in your feelings or your bodies, so you might find it difficult to stay together in the long term once the initial hot flush of passion has worn off. You would gradually drift into such an airy relationship with so little connection to emotion that it would wither away and die. Your sex lives could become problematic since you prefer the theory to the practice, and a long rein to experiment as you please. Gemini is not known for its fidelity so you might end up with a relationship so open that it does not hold together.

Your Aquarius Sun to Their Cancer Sun

Not a good idea at all. Really you are such polar opposites in almost everything. You loathe jealousy, possessiveness or being trapped and are deeply suspicious of highly emotional people. You feel swamped by all those untrustworthy swamps and hidden undercurrents. You need to be allowed to roam free no matter what. Cancerians are home-based, emotionally deeply sensitive and moody, clutch on to mates like drowning men to straws and can be desperately jealous. In essence you both represent what the other most dislikes and fears. You possibly could be friends since both of you enjoy having crowds of people around. But Cancerians are traditional at heart and can be snobbish. You are direct, down to earth and tolerant of all human souls no matter their condition or class. You would probably embarrass them with your truth-telling since they are hypoallergic to anything that smells like criticism.

Your Aquarius Sun to Their Leo Sun

Opposite signs in the zodiac sometimes work together, sometimes not. In this case your central characteristic of stubbornness is not wonderful together. Neither of you gives way easily. You both assume if you stand still long enough the other will adapt to you. Also you are way out, laid back and a real ageing hippie at heart. Leo can be snobbish, pompous and a dreadful traditionalist. Leos are desperate for social approval, which you care not one fig about. You would clash as they would feel you were undermining their social status and reputation by behaving the only way you know how. You would not mind giving them centre stage, since your ego is not that important to you, but you would begin eventually to ask yourself why. What are you getting back in return? You are not custom-built as a slave or a courtier, which is what Leo really needs. Neither of you is practical and you would end up taking off like a hot air balloon, getting further and further removed from the necessary routines and organizations of everyday living.

Your Aquarius Sun to Their Virgo Sun

Not a good idea because you would feel nagged to death and hemmed in by Virgo's need to keep life in order. Virgo is precise, obsessively tidy, rather a perfectionist especially about other people and much more practical than you. But there are plus factors. Virgos are fairly self-sufficient most of the time and would not make you feel too guilty for being off after your own interests. They are not hugely jealous either, though they can be traditionalists at heart and would not appreciate an open marriage, partly because it seems messy and partly because it could be humiliating and they are highly sensitive to social approval. Neither of you is egocentric so there would not be endless clashes. They are adaptable while you are stubborn, so that would work well, and they do like to be of service. But it is a cool, rather pinched combination which would not bring out the best in either of you. They need more warmth and you need someone more reckless and less tidy-minded.

Your Aquarius Sun to Their Libra Sun

Airy, communicative, thoughtful people that you are this should make a good combination, but there are problems. For one, Librans are acutely sensitive about their social reputation and whether or not they are approved of. They are class-conscious, a touch snobbish and forever trying to keep the peace. You do not give a toss about anyone's opinion and insist on doing your own thing no matter how bizarre or eccentric. You know it is more important to be yourself than to be one of the common herd. You adore heated controversies, debates and general argy-bargy, which they loathe. Also, since both of you are air signs and rather up in your heads you are both detached from your feelings and your bodies, so the relationship could eventually wither away and die for lack of nourishment. Your social lives would be great since Libra entertains like a dream, but that is hardly enough and anyway you would disagree about each other's friends. Yours would be hip. Theirs would be oh so classy.

Your Aquarius Sun to Their Scorpio Sun

No. A truly dreadful combination unless one or other of you is not living out your essential energy, in which case it will suffer in the long run anyway. You need space, distance, detachment and much prefer friendships to close one-to-one commitments. Scorpios on the other hand adore being plunged into the murky depths of their feelings, are dark, secretive and passionate and need to be closely intertwined in an exclusive relationship. You would distrust their hidden undercurrents and their rather devious way of proceeding in life, and their jealousy would give you the claustrophobic horrors. They would find your friendly but decidedly laid back approach to relationships too cold, too airy. They need a body to clutch on to and a mate with their special kind of emotional courage, which you do not possess. Scorpio next to Cancer is the worst sign in the zodiac for you. The mismatch of Aquarian John McEnroe with Scorpio Tatum O'Neal is a sad example of why this cannot work.

Your Aquarius Sun to Their Sagittarius Sun

A great deal of laughs, not much common sense and non-stop activity. When you come together, which may not be that often, you will have a real firework display. Sagittarius needs a long rein and so do you, which is why the relationship may founder in the long term. Too much space can lead to increasing distance and then no contact at all. But while it lasts it is great fun. You are the more stubborn and rooted of the pair while Sagittarius is adaptable as long as it does not feel hemmed in or tied down. Sagittarians loathe domesticity, as do you, so practical, everyday details of running the house may become a bore. Neither of you likes chores nor thinking too deeply about money. But on the plus side neither of you is not overly physical or jealous. On the whole it is a combination that can work exceptionally well but you do have to watch each other's tendency to stray too far from the nest. Aquarian Mia Farrow, friendly rather than fiercely passionate, survived a while with zany Sagittarian Woody Allen before the rot really set in. Neither is good at coping with dark, tumultuous feelings, and both lack real insight.

Your Aquarius Sun to Their Capricorn Sun

One astrological rule of thumb says you dislike or fear the sign immediately before you in the zodiac. Certainly you and Capricorn are highly different temperaments. You do not like Capricorns' class-conscious, traditional approach since you are an unreconstructed hippie yourself. They also seem to lack a sense of humour and be far too materialistically inclined where you rather look down on money or indeed security as an aim in life. They seem narrow, blinkered, judgemental, pessimistic and far too earthbound. They see you as abstract, eccentric and a minor social embarrassment since you do not care about anyone's approval. If you have to get together or stay together the plus points are that they will anchor you and organize the practical side of your life, which certainly needs doing. They can also be highly self-sufficient and so work-orientated that they are not going to make you feel crowded. You will liven their lives up, though they may not want that. Not a sure-fire certainty this at all.

Your Aquarius Sun to Their Aquarius Sun

Some signs mate together, some destroy each other. You are, curiously, like Scorpio in that you actually adore your own kind (though for highly different reasons). Both of you need space, want to be friendly rather than deeply and continuously passionate and are prepared to give each other a long lead. You are both hugely stubborn, but that seems not to matter since you are tolerant at the same time and happy to let each other be their own person. You share an offbeat, oddball sense of humour so can be wacky together. You will never embarrass each other socially because both of you respect directness and have little time for social niceties or insincere compliments. What you do need to watch out for, since neither of you is well tuned in either to feelings or bodies, is that you do not become too disconnected. Eventually you could both drift off in opposite directions with your own interests and friends. You could separate almost without noticing it.

Your Aquarius Sun to Their Pisces Sun

Not an ideal match though there are several things going for it. On the down side – you are airy, detached and really quite suspicious of feelings. You fear hidden undercurrents and all those swampy emotions that could undermine you. So you stay up in your head and your ideas. Pisces is an emotional, sensitive creature, wanting sympathy, empathy and kindness. What makes Pisces easier for you than the other two water signs (Cancer and Scorpio) is that they are often content to disappear into their day-dreams and fantasies and not to worry too much if they are not clutching a real live relationship 24 hours a day. Both of you do have dreams for a better future and a better society, so that interest could tie you together. Pisces would exasperate you because it is timid, evasive and rather vague. You are none of these things. You would frighten Pisces at times with your directness. Your cool, airy approach would feel very cold at times. But Pisceans are hugely adaptable and keen to sacrifice themselves for others, so they would bend to your needs. One of Hollywood's most stable marriages (fingers crossed) is that of Aquarian Paul Newman and gentle Piscean Joanne Woodward. Happily both have moon signs that match the other's sun sign – he a Pisces moon, she an Aquarius.

You Are Pisces

Twelfth and last sign of the zodiac you are watery, adaptable, refined, sensitive, creative, a dreamer, maddeningly vague, rather timid and usually compassionate. You feel for other people's pain and are willing to make large sacrifices to improve matters. Sometimes you feel so much for the suffering of the world that it pulls you down. Although emotional, you do find it difficult to commit to long-term one-to-one relationships. Your feelings are so diffuse you want to merge with the cosmos, not just one individual. Your emotional longings are also quite spiritual in tone, so you really want a god or a goddess to relate to, not some ordinary human being with dandruff and ingrowing toenails.

There are two kinds of Pisces – little fishes and large fishes. The minnow variety can show a lack of courage that makes them evasive and preferring to take the round-about way to avoid confrontations. They can be long-suffering and feel martyred because of the weight other people put on their shoulders. Self-pity will hold them back in life if they do not rouse themselves. The larger variety can be positive whales – voracious, orgiastic monsters who like to take over other people, swallowing them up. Whichever is your type you like to escape from the realities of life into day-dreaming and fantasizing, sometimes into addictions. What you need is a practical partner to help you make these dreams live for you in reality. Music and the cinema also provide escapes for you that nourish your soul.

Your Pisces Sun to Their Aries Sun

Not a match made in heaven since you are sweet, timid and hugely sensitive. Ariens are brash, rather self-centred, inclined to put their foot in their mouth and to trample over other people's corns. You can certainly adapt to their energetic, competitive spirits, but do you need to? They can offer you much in the way of sparkle and courage, which you can lack. They also tell the truth, which you sometimes avoid. But at the end of the day they will be exasperated by your lack of direction, your over-cautious approach to life and your vagueness and will not understand your unfulfilled visions. You will wince at their rather startling directness and hear their version of the truth as criticism, which you hate. Their lifestyle will be constant activity and noise, which reduces you to a nervous wreck. You must have a haven of peace to which you can retire. For a brief fling they might do you good and shake you up a little, make you more outgoing. But over the long term you would withdraw into home and they would advance in the world, so you would drift apart.

Your Pisces Sun to Their Taurus Sun

Planets separated by only one other in the zodiac are supposed to get on well together, so you are amiably well disposed toward each other. You do share an interest in certain rather aesthetic aspects of life. Taurus adores the comforts of life, eats, drinks and dresses well and adores a good cuddle. Your interests are rather more ethereal but you do like to create a dreamworld of comfort around you. Sometimes you can be quite addictive and are attracted to Taureans' generous lifestyle though you do not share their need for constant physical reassurance. That is probably the greatest drawback because for you love can be something spiritual, rarified, almost platonic. For Taurus it must be passionate and very tactile, which you can sometimes find rather gross. It is not that some Pisces do not have an orgiastic streak but it is fairly switch on/switch off. Taureans who are fairly refined with artistic tastes will do very nicely. They will help ground you, attending to all the practical details of your everyday life. You will adapt round their stubbornness.

Your Pisces Sun to Their Gemini Sun

A restless pair together, you do get on reasonably well since both of you are adaptable, fairly flighty and hate boredom. They may seem a little cool to you at times, being an air sign and prone to analysing feelings rather than experiencing them. But you sometimes like to be left to conduct a rather internal emotional life in your day-dreams so they will not harass you too much. You will have to be self-sufficient since Geminis are constantly on the move and (especially the male of the species) not renowned for their fidelity. Over the long term you might find your interests drifting apart since you are water and air, which are very different elements. You represent for Geminis the emotional connection they feel they will never find in their lives. They yearn for another half but you must get them to open up first and not flit endlessly like butterflies or grasshoppers through life avoiding their emotional needs. Piscean Ivana Trump had fun with Gemini Donald, but eventually the restlessness had to tell.

Your Pisces Sun to Their Cancer Sun

Both highly emotional creatures you get on a treat together. You understand each other's sensitivities so are less likely to crash into criticisms or hurtful remarks. You are both highly self-protective, which can make it difficult for you to open up to each other initially, but once you have made the breakthrough then you can create a cocoon for yourselves that shuts the world out. Cancer will take more initiative than you and, though a water sign, is energetically competitive in the outside world. It will make the home you always dreamed of come true. Moodiness and sulks can be a problem since both of you retreat into your shells suddenly and with little obvious external reason. You are both highly impressionable to the atmosphere around you, so you will feel at times as if you were being tossed around by the high seas without any controls. You must always watch the company you keep. Difficult, anxious, nervy friends will pull you both down.

Your Pisces Sun to Their Leo Sun

Very different elements, water and fire, you can sometimes make a match because you share a similarly creative outlook on life. Both of you like living well, like entertainment, music, movies, art. In different ways both of you are highly romantic. You are adaptable so can fit round the needs of Leo's rather overblown ego. Leos need to be centre of attention all the time, wanting an audience and constant admiration, whereas one of your essential drives in life is to be self-sacrificing. You do end up feeling martyred and self-pitying but you do genuinely like putting yourself out for others. So you have complementary needs. They are fixed and rather stubborn so can provide an anchor for your rather aimless, at times over-timid progress through life. They are also fiery so have a trust that you lack that life will always be there for them. This trust sometimes comes across as arrogance but it is good for you to see someone who will push forward. You need more of that energy. Not a superb match but a 6 out of 10.

Your Pisces Sun to Their Virgo Sun

This is a reasonably common match and can work well. Some opposites attract, some repel. You just seem to fit together. Virgo is the most refined of the earth signs so can give you a practical help in life without making you feel suffocated or weighed down. Both of you are sensitive so will not unnecessarily crash through each other's protective barriers. Virgo can be fairly self-sufficient and, since you like disappearing into your day-dreams, that can suit both of you. Virgos do nark and nag on a bit, which is a bore, and your vagueness will exasperate them. But that really is because they fear sliding into the chaos in which you exist most of the time. Their response is to become obsessively neat and tidy. This combination has pluses and minuses. They will sort your life out but they can also run against your grain. If you can persuade them not to be so perfectionist they are warm and tactile. You can be exceptionally romantic and seductive, so there could be quite a wonderful connection. Piscean supermodel Cindy Crawford conducts a fairly separate working career with overbusy Virgo actor/Buddhist Richard Gere. The attractions are obvious but, they need to watch the restlessness.

Your Pisces Sun to Their Libra Sun

An elegant, tasteful mix this, one that has a great deal going for it. You both love art, beautiful people, pleasant social occasions and nothing too abrasive. You are sensitive to an extreme degree about the harsher side of reality and Libra absolutely must have harmony and balance. Libra can seem a little cool, being an air sign, which will not always suit your sympathetic, emotional nature. But you can withdraw happily into your day-dreams to compensate. You are highly adaptable where Librans have buckets of initiative so you will follow their lead happily. Both of you tend to be self-sacrificing in relationships, wanting the other to be happy, which can make for a caring long-term commitment. It possibly works best with a Libra man and Pisces woman. The male of the Libra species is softer, sweeter, almost 'feminine' in outlook where the Libran women are quite sharp, cool, almost 'masculine' in their thinking. It is not an absolutely ideal mix since you are very different energies, but it is definitely a 6 out of 10. Piscean Prince Andrew, a more sentimental animal than his stodgy appearance suggests, was obviously seduced by fun-loving Duchess of York, a rather rumbustious Libra. But she wore the trousers and did the wandering. He was not strong enough to keep her under control.

Your Pisces Sun to Their Scorpio Sun

Two water signs together make an excellent match but you have to be a tougher-minded Pisces than the norm to cope with Scorpio's intensity. Really Scorpios like to mate with their own kind who are happy to live in the depths of their feelings, with that kind of tortured anguish that also promises ecstasy. But it is not a pleasant trip for a vague, timid Pisces. You could feel yourself overwhelmed. Your sense of identity is not strong at the best of times. You are self-sacrificing by nature but Scorpios will needle you until you stand up to them. They do like power but they also like a robust, substantial relationship. However, you are both emotionally sensitive signs able to gauge each other's moods and you are certainly not given to treading on corns. You basically like peace and harmony. Scorpio's stinging responses can sometimes hurt you though your tendency to martyr yourself perhaps helps you hide it. This can be an invigorating match if you are up to it.

Your Pisces Sun to Their Sagittarius Sun

Totally different energies, you being water and they fire, this is not an instant first choice. Water and fire together can sizzle and boil but it usually ends up a damp mess with Sagittarius flying off to sunnier climes. On the plus side what it does have going for it is your shared ability to bend in the breeze. When the going gets tough you do not instantly dig your heels in but bend round the difficulties. You are both on the lighter end of the sun signs so will not instantly cause each other problems. But Sagittarius is notoriously outspoken and you can be extremely thin-skinned. Sagittarians mean no malicious harm but they are blunt. They are also allergic to long-term commitments and fly off at the first whiff of jealousy or possessiveness. This may not matter as much with you as with most water signs because you can disappear into your day-dreams and do not always like hugely committed relationships yourself. Both of you could do with a more practical partner. A 4 of out 10 match.

Your Pisces Sun to Their Capricorn Sun

Signs separated by only one other in the zodiac do match well. You provide the inspiration here, the emotional sensitivity, the flexibility and the need to be helpful. Capricorn will provide the energy and the drive, determination and practical common sense you sometimes lack. Capricorns can ground you and give you a lead to follow, which suits you down to the ground. At times they may feel too work-orientated, rather chilly and remote and weigh you down with judgemental comments about your vagueness. However you do need a mate who can help you turn your dreams into reality, and you can offer them a safe haven from the rigours of the world. They are softer than they appear inside if you can actually get them to open up. They are noisy at home, however, which may upset your need for peace, quiet and bliss. You do have shared interests in creativity and the arts, which can help to cement a bond.

Your Pisces Sun to Their Aquarius Sun

Not an instant hit, since you are a gentle water sign and they are the most abrasive air sign, stubborn, idiosyncratic, argumentative and not at all keen on one-to-one committed relationships. They need to be allowed to go their own road in life. It may work just well enough if you are a very absorbed Pisces lost in your own inner world and not one to worry about absent partners who have completely different interests. In your own way you also sometimes shy away from claustrophobic one-to-one relationships. You will not appreciate Aquarians' blunt truth-telling or way of analysing emotions before they have experienced them. You will not persuade them to get lost in your romantic glow. You are seducible and seductive. They just like to talk about the theory of sex. If you have, like Paul Newman and Joanne Woodward, a moon sign in the other's sun sign it obviously can work. He has a Pisces moon, she an Aquarius moon.

Your Pisces Sun to Their Pisces Sun

You should be divinely happy with another of your own kind, each of you sweet, sensitive, refined and always aware of the other's need for peace and protection. Yet you are both over-restless, over-adaptable, sometimes aimless creatures who would drift around as if blown by the winds and the currents. You really are too impressionable a sign to survive well in the world without an anchor, a practical mate who can give you help with the everyday details of life and give you more sparkle and courage. You would be like two orphan waifs in the storm. You are both moody and hyper-reactive to atmosphere and can be self-pitying. Two martyrs together is not good news. You need someone to jolt you out of your oyster shell into the world a bit. Certainly you would have the joy of someone who shared your obsession for music, cinema and art. But it probably is not enough in the long run.

4

DO YOUR
MOONS SPOON?

Your Moon to Their Moon

The sun is the core of your identity, the sign your moon was in at the exact moment you were born tells you about what emotionally nourishes you, what makes you feel comfortable and comforted, how you relate to your body and how you see your past, your childhood and your family. It is, if you like, the 'feminine' half of your personality.

Even if sun signs are compatible, if you and your partner's moon signs are out of sync you will have problems setting up a stable home together and will have wildly differing approaches to sex, children, eating, relaxing, cleanliness and home décor. You will also not have your moods in tune. You want sex when he wants to cut the grass. You want to work when she wants to be quiet together.

The moon changes sign every two-and-a quarter days, and its fickle nature is the reason why some Ariens, for example, lean this way rather than that. The core identity is still the same for all Ariens, but the moon sign shows up one facet of the personality more than others, and sometimes suppresses a vital element of that personality if the sun and moon signs are in real conflict.

Your Moon Is in Aries

A fire moon, you are excitable, impulsive, explosive, rarely stand still, loathe tranquillity and are constantly seeking challenges. You are also strongly independent, take criticism badly and tend to dominate others emotionally. Underneath you can be quite insecure. Your moods never last long but others find your constantly changing reactions rather unreliable. Well-known Aries moons are Marlon Brando, the Duchess of York, Lauren Bacall, Luciano Pavarotti, Martina Navratilova and John Cleese.

Your Aries Moon to Their Aries Moon

Earplugs are a must for the neighbours as your eruptions can be spectacular, if short-lived. You will have problems keeping track of each other since both of you leap around like grasshoppers on hot tarmac. Certainly you like the same things, but the constant need for adventure and excitement is likely to pull you apart faster than it keeps you together. You both have a habit of insisting on your own way and will tolerate no interference. Not much room for give and take. This match could have a noisy ending.

Your Aries Moon to Their Taurus Moon

What nourishes you is the thrills, spills, drama of high adventure and a constantly changing life. That is Taurus' absolute horror. Taureans are nourished by the unchangingness of a secure home base, the kind of regular physical contact you would find stifling and, worst of all, they are deeply possessive. Certainly they will keep your feet anchored to the floor, will organize financial stability and give you more constant affection and comfort than you ever dreamed of. But you will dislike their laziness, stubbornness and resistance to change and will find their sensuality a little gross. They can be achingly slow.

Your Aries Moon to Their Gemini Moon

Your comfort demands paradoxically that you keep on the move. So, even more, does theirs. But are you ever going to meet as you both jitterbug about? These are the two moons who most frequently change their minds. What you wanted 10 minutes ago is not what you want now. How are agreements ever to hold together? You are the pushier of the pair, demanding your own way, irritably if necessary. They will adapt but one day they will also fly away. Neither of you is well tuned in to the body, so meals will be erratic. Sex will be fabulous and fiery initially, but boredom will creep in rapidly.

Your Aries Moon to Their Cancer Moon

Bad news this, really. You want space to fly around madly, chopping and changing your mind at whim, not really having obligations or commitments. They want a cosy home and family set-up with everyone tied in together. They feel the pain of separation more than most. Their emotional storms and insecurities will irritate you. Certainly they will provide you with a wonderful domestic life, a well decorated home, good cooking, all the comforts. But it does come at a price. They brood, they smother and have an extreme sensitivity to criticism that your rather abrasive approach would not improve.

Your Aries Moon to Their Leo Moon

Instant passion, but will it last? Two fiery moons together always make for higher noise levels, and with one proviso this could work well. You want to generate a constant feeling of being alive at home, which means never sitting still. They are more fixed and stubborn but they adore the flamboyant lifestyle and together you will set up a wonderful pad, throw great parties and rave it up all over town in the best places. The main problem is that you go your own way, speaking your mind very bluntly. They have a fragile if overblown vanity which dents very easily. You hate their sulks.

Your Aries Moon to Their Virgo Moon

Both of you are quite insecure but show it in entirely different ways. You zip around like a thing possessed. They sit and worry endlessly about trivia. You would never understand or sympathize with their phobias, fears and anxieties. They will certainly adapt to your need for no interference, would organize you a well-run home with good food and keep the medicine cabinet stocked. But is it enough? Sex would become a problem as they can be prudish and you have short-lived enthusiasms. Their nagging about tidiness will drive you daft.

Your Aries Moon to Their Libra Moon

They are thoughtful, sweet, generally considerate and will organize you a beautiful home with a collection of really classy friends. But it may all prove a touch pretentious or precious after a while. You have tastes for high excitement and will speak your mind no matter what, which will ruffle their feathers enormously. You could not care less about social niceties. They blush at the tiniest gaffe. You are fiery, they are cool. Sex would be a problem since you would lose interest and they basically dislike anything too sweaty or passionate.

Your Aries Moon to Their Scorpio Moon

You fly free, they cling on with the tenacity of an octopus. You want change, excitement and new thrills all the time. You will not tolerate interference, they are possessive and manipulative. They are fixed, stubborn, more security-conscious than you and certainly a great deal more jealous. They may hide their hurts and feelings very well – until, that is, their need for revenge gets out to play. Initially the earth will move since your fiery passions can be hot and they are certainly sensual, but will it last? The Duchess of York has an Aries moon. Prince Andrew has a Scorpio moon. Need I say more?

Your Aries Moon to Their Sagittarius Moon

A spectacular firework display with all the bells and whistles going at the same time. That is your initial coming together. The down side is that neither of you stands still. Certainly neither of you is jealous, which helps enormously. But you tend to hop around like a grasshopper and they take off across the open planes at the slightest provocation, so you could drift apart rapidly. You need a joint scheme or joint hopes for the future strong enough to bond you together at the points where your notoriously short-lived enthusiasm sags.

Your Aries Moon to Their Capricorn Moon

You have hot blood rushing through your veins and need a sense of aliveness. They are rather gloomy, self-doubting types with low self-esteem who need to work like maniacs to prove they are worthy of the love they rarely find time for in their busy schedules. Their reserve would bother you. Your brashness would offend their social sensibilities. It could end up a very chilly, detached relationship indeed, where business was the priority. Your moods would never coincide. You want sex. They want to read the accounts. They want a cuddle. You want to dash out.

Your Aries Moon to Their Aquarius Moon

An exciting, communicative, never dull match – but it is difficult to make a real exclusive match with an Aquarius moon because they fear one-to-one commitment. To some extent so do you fear loss of personal freedom so it could work, though you would eventually have less and less time together. They love to startle and shock, which bothers some but would enchant you. Sex could be a problem since they are rather removed from their bodies and you are not well attached to yours. Eating would be erratic.

Your Aries Moon to Their Pisces Moon

They are supersensitive to emotional atmosphere and nuances. Even at your most vain you would never describe yourself as that. You would endlessly be treading on corns you could not see and then have to watch them withdraw into their oyster shells for protection. Their timidity would exasperate you. They always feel like martyrs and their self-pity would pall. At a pinch they could make you gentler and you could make them more courageous. But it is hardly a match made in heaven.

Your Moon Is in Taurus

An earth moon and the most sensual, you are nourished by your senses. Whatever feels, smells, looks and tastes good makes you purr like a pussycat. You are affectionate, demonstrative, very tactile and highly sensual. Love has to be expressed in tangible ways or you do not think it exists. Stability and security are more important to you than almost anything. Sudden change, especially at home, is difficult. Jealousy, possessiveness and obstinacy can create emotional problems. Diana Ross, Elton John, Imelda Marcos, Mick Jagger, Bill Clinton and Prince Charles belong to this cuddliest of moons.

Your Taurus Moon to Their Aries Moon

You first reaction in an emotional crisis is to feed yourself and sit still. Theirs is to leap off into activity. You are placid, affectionate and possessive. They are highly insecure, outspoken and very independent. They certainly will offer you a comfortable, not to say luxurious base in life but you are highly different animals. You would find their passive resistance to anything that does not fit in with their needs impossibly irritating. Arguments over your wandering feet would run and run.

Your Taurus Moon to Their Taurus Moon

You would provide each other with every comfort under the sun. You share the same tastes in good food, luxuriously easy homes, wonderfully sensuous clothes and endless cuddles. You could certainly grow fat together! Both of you are practical but together you could do with a spark more vision or imagination, otherwise your world may become very narrow, even slightly gross. Obstinacy certainly would create a problem as neither of you would give way. Both of you are jealous but usually faithful.

Your Taurus Moon to Their Gemini Moon

A bull and a grasshopper may well have something to offer each other, but as a settled relationship it leaves a lot to be desired. Your rootedness would drive their flyaway nature to distraction. You would feel unsettled because they never sit still for long. Although placid you are possessive and they hate being fenced in. You are into the body, are affectionate, cuddly, constant and sensual. They are into their heads and rather switch on/switch off in their sexual needs.

Your Taurus Moon to Their Cancer Moon

This could run and run. Both of you are into comfort, security, luxurious homes, good food and not too many upheavals. You might fight eventually over the children since moon Cancer likes to smother and dominate while you are possessive in your own way. But you are an excellent match. You can provide an anchor for their moodiness and hyper-sensitivity in a warm, affectionate way. Your solidly physical approach to sex might in the long term prove problematic since they want an all-family relationship, not necessarily just an exclusively one-to-one commitment.

Your Taurus Moon to Their Leo Moon

The bull and the lion together make a mighty awesome pair. Obstinacy will be the greatest problem here since neither of you gives way easily at home. On the other hand both of you are loyal, faithful and good at staying put, which is a major plus factor. You are practical, good at food, furnishings, gardening and clothes. They are wonderful with children, parties, sport and fun. You will keep the domestic machine running smoothly. They will add sparkle. Their vanity and extravagance may irk you but both of you have a steady sex drive.

Your Taurus Moon to Their Virgo Moon

You will enjoy many happy hours together in the kitchen, the garden, having a quiet cuddle or planning new decorations. Both of you are earthy and tuned in to physical comforts. Moon Virgo's endless worries and anxieties will drive you slightly daft but you are patient and their tidiness, if not carried to extremes, counterbalances your laziness. Sex could be a minor problem since they have to be coaxed out of a prudishness that is sometimes (but not always) superficial.

Your Taurus Moon to Their Libra Moon

Aesthetic, cultural, elegant and luxurious, your home life will appear to be a dream of comfort and good taste. You need a solid, happy family base and Libra has a magic touch. They are slightly over-sensitive to the approval of others and may find some of your basic ways a minor social embarrassment. Sex could be a barrier since you are in need of constant physical reassurance. They are an airy Moon, not well in tune with the body and slightly fastidious. What nourishes you sexually will not fit their needs. But they are loyal.

Your Taurus Moon to Their Scorpio Moon

A seethingly passionate and jealous combination this which will either provide endless arguments and real agony or could, with subtle handling, provide real ecstasy as well. Neither of you likes a home life in constant upheaval and both can be faithful. Both of you are fairly preoccupied with sex – you, admittedly, from a more physical viewpoint; they because they want to journey to Nirvana through sex. You will not understand all their motivations but the trip will bring you pleasure. But this is a match which has the seeds of its own destruction buried deep inside. Neither of you is the forgiving type.

Your Taurus Moon to Their Sagittarius Moon

A difficult combination to make work unless your suns are in each other's moon sign. You are nourished by clinging on firmly to a comfortable, luxurious home with a highly cuddly relationship inside. They fly free at the first whiff of jealousy and hate being anchored. They are nourished by books, conversation and travel. Certainly they would adapt to you in some respects. You could also offer them much in the way of practical help in their domestic life. But sex would become eventually an unbridgeable gulf because you need such different things.

Your Taurus Moon to Their Capricorn Moon

Two earth moons together normally suggests great physical comfort, a solid, well-run home, good food and a luxuriant garden. An idyllic domestic base. But you might find your Capricorn moon is rarely there. They sadly lack self-esteem and feel that only by achieving in the big outside world will they be accepted. So the love they chase gets further away. They can seem cool, distant and over-serious to you, who basically want demonstrative affection, lots of cuddles and a regular sex life. They can be indulgent sexually but they can also be celibate for periods. They would also want you to help them in their social climbing, which you would hate.

Your Taurus Moon to Their Aquarius Moon

You live on earth. They live in outer space. You are tuned in to the body, domestic comforts, physical sex and a great many cuddles. They are nourished by erudite conversation, constant travel, not too much close contact and certainly no heavy one-to-one commitments. Their insistence on going their own way and filling your house with group meetings and friends would drive you spare eventually. Your jealousy would nag constantly. Both of you are also highly obstinate and would insist your way was the one to be followed.

Your Taurus Moon to Their Pisces Moon

A sweet, protective combination this, with you providing a shell inside which they could become more confident. You are good at the practical, physical life – making a solid, comfortable home, giving cuddles and demonstrating your affection openly. They appear wispy, frightened creatures but they do have an amazing emotional sensitivity if they feel safe enough to open up. Both of you need peace and bliss – for different reasons but it gets you to the same place. They are highly adaptable, which helps, because you like to dig your heels in.

Your Moon Is in Gemini

An air moon, you think first and try not to feel too deeply. A real butterfly, you hate sitting still. Your emotional reactions change constantly and this upsets others who sometimes find you cool, too detached or unreliable. Boredom is your great bugbear in life and being stuck in a rut is almost unbearable. Your enthusiasms are strong but are rarely long-lived. You hate being pinned down and stability is never an attractive idea. Nourishment comes from reading, talking and knowing a lot. You are not well tuned in to your body or your physical needs, or at least do not stand still enough to comfort yourself on a constant basis. John McEnroe, Goldie Hawn, Tom Jones and Brigitte Bardot are your type, as was Sigmund Freud.

Your Gemini Moon to Their Aries Moon

You talk endlessly, are quick-witted, resourceful and have been known to chop and change your mind and your feelings with great frequency. Thus you will have no problem keeping up with their antics, firework displays and excitements. You are adaptable where they leap in to take the initiative. You will not take offence at their brashness. But the match could lack depth of feeling or body connection. Both of you have dangerously low boredom thresholds.

Your Gemini Moon to Their Taurus Moon

On the up side they will give your endless fidgetiness some stability. They are placid, affectionate and good at organizing the practical comforts of existence. You are adaptable and will bend happily round their obstinacy. But their jealousy and possessiveness will frighten you. Their constant need for sex and physical affection will feel at times crude or gross to you, certainly wearing. Their need for an unchanging lifestyle will give you nightmares. Ruts and routines make you feel ill. You are not basically in tune.

Your Gemini Moon to Their Gemini Moon

You certainly have the same emotional reactions, will have no shortage of topics of conversation and will live in a library of a house, full of telephones! But will you ever get together? You are both so changeable and so fast moving you may just drift apart. You need a mate who will bring you into your feelings and body, not join you up in your head. The relationship could be superficial. Both of you analyse feelings rather than experience them. You need more warmth, more anchoring.

Your Gemini Moon to Their Cancer Moon

You with an adaptable air moon want chat, ideas and a great deal of variety. They, having a watery emotional moon, want a settled home and family base, close ties and life much as it has always been. You might feel stifled, even bored by the sameness that feeds them. Their jealousy would be sparked by your wandering eye and feet. Certainly they would provide you with a wonderful home, beautiful meals and all the comforts. But you would not understand their moodiness and hyper-sensitivity. They would find your cool, analytic approach rather chilling.

Your Gemini Moon to Their Leo Moon

You like variety. They like flamboyance. You want stimulating chat at home; as long as they get to be centre of attention they will converse with great style. They will provide an anchor for your wandering moods since they are more fixed. Your adaptability will come in handy with their stubbornness. They adore the five-star lifestyle, which is not necessarily your wish but you like the excitement that goes with it. Their extravagances may well begin to pall and you will not suffer their arrogance or fragile vanity easily.

Your Gemini Moon to Their Virgo Moon

A lovely combination with just a few drawbacks. On the up side you are both adaptable, so long, drawn-out arguments are less likely. They are practical and tidy so will organize the domestic set-up to perfection, leaving you free to read and chat on the phone. They are reasonably self-sufficient so will not fuss as you wander off after your own interests. What could be a problem is their constant worrying about everything under the sun, for which you would have little sympathy. Their obsessive need to keep order might wear thin as well. But mainly the tendency you both have to analyse feelings before letting them develop could kill the relationship before it takes root.

Your Gemini Moon to Their Libra Moon

Airy moons together certainly means there will be no shortage of stimulating chat or books lying around the house. Both of you are nourished by ideas, thoughts, theories and looking at the meaning of life. But you do lack connection to your deeper feelings. You constantly analyse them before they can develop. Libra likes everything to be so harmonious that no difficult feelings are ever aired. You might find it a little dull eventually and you would never understand their excessive sensitivity to other people's opinion.

Your Gemini Moon to Their Scorpio Moon

This should not work at all because you think and they feel. You fly around and they hold on tight. But despite your rather flibberty-gibbet moods you do have a leaning for the wild side of life, at least for short periods. You hate being fenced in and loathe jealousy, which are both moon Scorpio traits, but you have an attraction/revulsion for all those turbulent depths, that steamy passion, that preoccupation with sex. For a time you will stay and love passionately. Then you will take fright and run. They will never forgive you.

Your Gemini Moon to Their Sagittarius Moon

Life will never be dull, never be the same, and may eventually never be lived together. Both of you are driven by a need not to be chained down emotionally and you will both fly off at the first whiff of possessiveness. Conversation will never be lacking since both of you have wide-ranging interests and are nourished by books, travel and wild theories. But as a match this lacks an anchor, depth of feeling and true commitment. Sex could be fiery then cool off. Neither of you has a high boredom threshold. Long reins can lead to increasing distance and eventually to no connection at all.

Your Gemini Moon to Their Capricorn Moon

This could be a little intellectual or too businesslike to make a real love match. You hardly sit still long enough to feel deeply while they work like maniacs to prove their worth. Both of you in different ways can be too cool. You need warmer mates all round who will give you affection without tying you down. They could certainly organize your home for you but they might hardly be there. They can also be judgemental, which would not suit your rather rebellious side. You do not care about social respectability. They do.

Your Gemini Moon to Their Aquarius Moon

You will pass like two spaceships out in the galaxy. Only remote contact is likely. You are restless beyond belief and they are positively scared of one-to-one commitment. You will have friends galore but passionate moments may get fewer and farther between after the first flush has worn off. Intellectual interests will dominate your relationship – but is talking shop a good basis for a lifelong partnership? Feelings will find it difficult to get a look in and neither of you is good with too much physical intimacy. You would need grounding from earth or water suns to help you to nourish the relationship when it threatened to dry up, as it surely would.

Your Gemini Moon to Their Pisces Moon

Both of you are adaptable, restless creatures, so sulky, brooding silences are hardly likely if you argue. You never keep a feeling for long and in 10 minutes will have forgotten your gripe anyway.

This could work better than an air/water mix might suggest. Pisces moon is deeply sensitive but often hides away in its day-dreams as a protection, so they would not swamp you with feelings. At times they might be hurt by your rather cool, analytical approach. They are sweet, sympathetic creatures and would look after you well, sacrificing themselves in the process.

Your Moon Is in Cancer

A water moon, you feel deeply and intensely and fear separation. You are home- and family-orientated and deeply attached to the past. Your sentimentality often does not let you change old habit patterns or let childhood memories go. Domestic and emotional security are hugely important to you. You only let mother's apron strings go when you can set up an adult family for yourself. You are desperately sensitive to the pain of separation, which can make you emotionally manipulative or smothering. You hate criticism and hear it even when not intended. If wounded by the slightest thing you withdraw into moody, broody silences, snapping your shell shut. You gain great comfort from creating a beautiful home, decorating in style, cooking well and entertaining rather elegant friends. Famous Cancer moons include Harrison Ford, Prince William, Princess Margaret, Tatum O'Neal, Liza Minnelli and Norman Mailer.

Your Cancer Moon to Their Aries Moon

Not an ideal match since their abrasive, rather self-centred style will wound and irritate you. You need harmony at home within the bounds of your own emotional ups and downs. But they crash around, never sitting still, being fiery, noisy, explosive and none too considerate of your needs. You may sense they will embarrass you socially, which you loathe since you need approval from significant people. You want a family. They want to be themselves. You are reasonably controlling and they hate interference.

Your Cancer Moon to Their Taurus Moon

You both aim straight for a solid, settled, luxuriously comfortable home life. Taurus is earthy and fixed so needs to be rooted. You hate letting childhood and the past go. Both of you are driven to organize a domestic machine that positively purrs along. They are more sexually-orientated than you, always tactile and very affectionate. They will help anchor your emotional highs and lows. Both of you are jealous but equally both of you are faithful once settled.

Your Cancer Moon to Their Gemini Moon

Not a wonderful package since you feel and they think. You clutch and they hop out of your reach. You would never understand the way their feelings appear and disappear. You can be moody but they are a complete enigma. At times they feel cool, having been wonderfully enthusiastic 10 minutes ago. Just as you are having an intimate smooch they start to analyse what the emotions are, which freeze-dries them before they have had a chance to develop. They are quick-witted and talk a very great deal. You really want a sensitive, intuitive mate who can protect you – not one who can write a thesis on you.

Your Cancer Moon to Their Cancer Moon

Moody, magnificent, very deeply felt and positively oceanic with all its storms, tempests, undercurrents and calm patches this match might make you feel overwhelmed at times since you would have no one to hang on to through the roller-coasters of your feelings, which do need either an anchor or some detachment to give you a perspective on them. You certainly both want a settled, beautiful family home and would cook wonderful meals together. But you would both be trying to play top dog at home, and two hyper-sensitive souls together could be a little precious. The sulks would be very long. Each full moon time of the month would be a nightmare.

Your Cancer Moon to Their Leo Moon

Not a bad match since both of you basically want a happy, luxurious home life with rather upwardly mobile friends. You are nourished by security and the patterns of the past. They are fixed, hate upheavals and in their own way have their roots firmly attached to traditional values. They are marginally more extravagant than you, always wanting to live the five-star way, which could provoke arguments. But they can be good with domestic finances. Deciding who rules the household could eventually become a problem since both of you like to be in control of the family tribe.

Your Cancer Moon to Their Virgo Moon

This can be a sensitive, refined mating, with you providing emotional comfort, a happy home environment, energy and determination and they providing practical expertise on the domestic front and know-how about food, health and bodies. They love to be of service and you adore being looked after. They can nag, nark and worry overmuch, which is a bore. Their obsessive tidiness is good – up to a point – since it allows you to be lazy. But beyond that point it becomes tiresome. Both of you are affectionate but not exactly sensual, so you will settle happily into your own sexual routine.

Your Cancer Moon to Their Libra Moon

What this has going for it is a shared liking for an elegant social life, a beautiful, luxury home base and not too much emotional hassle. They want harmony above all else and, though at times you may find that a little shallow, they will keep the peace. Both of you need social approval so will not attract embarrassment by speaking or acting out of place. They may seem a little cool at times because they are an air moon. You feel, they think. But they are thoughtful and do need a mate in life, so they will move your way.

Your Cancer Moon to Their Scorpio Moon

On the outside no one will see the depths of intensity and feeling contained in this relationship. The sulks and agonies may be out of sight but the hidden ecstasies are there as well. With two water moons you have to expect overwhelming feelings at times, but Scorpio moons are tightly controlled and fixed so they will stabilize you a touch. Neither of you forgives lightly (if at all), but both of you are fairly faithful once settled. They are more preoccupied with sex than you, which could be the major drawback. In time you like more generalized family cuddles than endless, exclusive passion.

Your Cancer Moon to Their Sagittarius Moon

You want a happy homestead with roses at the door and children in the garden. They want the open plains and as few obligations and commitments as they can manage. You would feel deeply wounded by their need to shoot like an arrow from a bow at a moment's notice. They are excitable, fiery, restless and slightly inconsiderate when it comes to other people's needs. You are thin-skinned and need protection and to be made to feel secure. Your jealousy would become a problem. Your aims are different and they might prove a social embarrassment. You want to look good. They could not care less.

Your Cancer Moon to Their Capricorn Moon

Opposite sign moons often want totally different comforts in life, as in this case. You want home. They want work. You hate being far from happy domesticity and the family while they stay overlong at the office. Their self-esteem is low so they think they have to earn affection. You could do them a great deal of good by teaching them about their essential value and getting them connected to their feelings, but it would be a long, slow job. They can be cool and judgemental while you are deeply sensitive to slights, criticisms and disapproval. Your moods would never be in sync.

Your Cancer Moon to Their Aquarius Moon

A horrible combination unless you have overwhelmingly positive sun connections. You are emotional, needy, protective, possessive and a traditionalist at heart who is keen on social approval. They are wild, wacky eccentrics who think more than they feel and are positively scared of one-to-one commitment. They love being one of the crowd, which is fine because you like friends as well but would make you miss having a real relationship at the centre of it. You need a settled family base while they would feel stifled by it. What nourishes you repels them. They like thinking, talking and travelling.

Your Cancer Moon to Their Pisces Moon

A dream of a match with both of you billing and cooing, protecting each other's hyper-sensitivities and happy as two oysters sharing the same shell. You want a happy home. They just want somewhere to let their defences down. Basically very timid creatures, they often hide away their beautiful, sympathetic natures to avoid rejection or being hurt, which you understand totally. They are adaptable so would not rock the boat. Their slight air of self-pity or constant martyrdom may irk you, but this is a small price to pay.

Your Moon Is in Leo

A fire moon, you act first and think later. Entertaining, charmingly persuasive and rather grand, with a great deal of personal magnetism, you certainly like to make an impression. A prima donna at heart you want your place in the spotlight but you also love children, games and fun. You adore the luxuries and extravagances of life, always wanting to travel first class and to stay only in five-star hotels. Criticism is not something you take at all kindly to, being easily wounded. Indeed vanity and pride can be your downfall. Your stubbornness is also a stumbling block to happiness at home unless your mate is flexible. Famous Leo moons are Queen Elizabeth II, Prince Philip, Barbra Streisand, Clint Eastwood, Margaret Thatcher, Jane Fonda, Dolly Parton and Patrick Swayze.

Your Leo Moon to Their Aries Moon

Fiery, fun-loving and (at least initially) passionate this is a real snap, crackle and pop relationship. You may not always appreciate their blunt, rather tactless approach because your ego is fragile. But you will share similar interests in a thrill-filled, adventurous lifestyle. Boredom is not likely. They are less stubborn than you but do like to win, which could cause the odd ruction. Neither of you is any good at getting down into the depths of your feelings or facing the darker side of life, however, so the stormy passages may be difficult to negotiate.

Your Leo Moon to Their Taurus Moon

This could be a glorious indulgence in all that is decadently and expensively wicked in life. Comfort definitely comes first. It could also be a tough struggle since neither of you gives way easily, if at all, at home. They would want power, you would want all the attention. In good moments you would flirt, cuddle and adore every passion-filled minute. In bad times you would sulk like crazy while they got slightly bitter. It could just work because both of you need constancy and security.

Your Leo Moon to Their Gemini Moon

This has real possibilities because they can adjust to your whims while you sail on rather grandly. You want limelight, admiration and a flamboyant lifestyle. They want fun, excitement, constant movement and stimulating chat. There is not much depth of feeling here. The highs would be wonderful but you would get lost in the low patches. They might even flit off because they are wanderers at heart. You could be exasperated by their lack of staying power. They would make fun of your puffed-up, grand ideas and take wicked delight in teasing you.

Your Leo Moon to Their Cancer Moon

Home would be magnificent as both of you adore a luxurious pad. You could get all the attention while they mothered you, cooked for you and kept the domestic organization running. But both of you in different ways are slightly hyper-sensitive, certainly to criticism, which could create very long sulks indeed. Your fire and their water could be a boiling combination or one that damps the flames fairly quickly. But you are both family-orientated, domestic creatures who can be faithful once settled.

Your Leo Moon to Their Leo Moon

Who is going to be the star and who the audience? You would both be scrabbling for the limelight all the time. Both of you are stubborn, demanding and fairly determined to suit yourselves. Really you need a flexible moon, not another fixed one. Certainly both of you can be warm, persuasive and charming, so the initial contacts could be delicious, but in the long term you would find it an expensive relationship, not very practical, and given to explosive fights.

Your Leo Moon to Their Virgo Moon

Your need to be the centre of attention and live flamboyantly will be happily complemented by their flexibility, common sense and practical efficiency. Their tidiness and nagging may drive you to distraction but it is a small price to pay for being allowed to live like a lord while they do the skivvying. They worry more than you so you help to give them confidence, courage and sparkle. At those times when their anxieties are right they will counter-balance your lack of realism. They will not upset your vanity too much, though they will not understand your need for grand living.

Your Leo Moon to Their Libra Moon

A wonderfully sociable match, this. Together you will throw the best parties in the most elegant house in the neighbourhood. They like to keep the peace so will not upset your vanity. You adore being admired and they are hugely tactful. Money could be a problem since both of you have expensive tastes, to put it mildly. What the relationship lacks is much depth of feeling or connection to the body. You might drift apart just because of this superficiality. But if you do manage to stay the course, neither of you is a wanderer.

Your Leo Moon to Their Scorpio Moon

A steamy connection, this, which no doubt sometimes works but the struggles are long and awesome to behold. Both of you are fiercely stubborn. You want attention and admiration. They want control and are not above undermining you with a real stinging remark which will wound your vanity greatly. They have greater depth, indeed really turbulent feelings that you slightly distrust. If you have compatible suns you could make a go of it, as long as you sort out the power struggles before they get too destructive.

Your Leo Moon to Their Sagittarius Moon

Two fire moons together are delighted with the thrills, adventures and fun of a high-speed, non-stop social and sporting life. But what happens in the quiet moments in the months when you have to economize and life gets dull? You will sulk because you need luxuries to keep you happy. They will fly away because they hate being fenced in, especially by tedious commitments. You need to have a more earthy connection through the suns for this to work well long term.

Your Leo Moon to Their Capricorn Moon

You have both similar aims in terms of a good lifestyle – something traditional, secure and rather grand. You adore being admired and they feel unworthy so they will not be grabbing your limelight. Their earthiness could be a help at home since you tend to be wildly impractical. The one drawback is that they tend to work non-stop so you may never see them. It is also a fairly cool combination at the end of the day, more concerned with outer appearance than inner warmth. You need to tap into their sensuality.

Your Leo Moon to Their Aquarius Moon

You want attention while they want freedom to roam, which is going to cause friction. Basically they fear one-to-one commitment and insist on a life full of friends. You are not deeply jealous but do like a settled home and family life, which makes them claustrophobic. You might also be embarrassed by their rather shocking behaviour at times. They put it on just to wind everyone else up, you included. They can also be horribly honest, which will not suit your fragile vanity.

Your Leo Moon to Their Pisces Moon

Quite a sweet combination because they are sympathetic and adaptable while you are flamboyant and attention-seeking. They do need protecting since they deeply fear rejection, but once they feel safe to trust you they will make your life a haven of bliss. They are not so emotional they will make you feel swamped. They can disappear happily into their day-dreams so do not demand too much from you, though they will always be happy to sacrifice themselves to your every whim. They can go on martyr trips, however, which you will find a minor bore.

Your Moon Is in Virgo

An earth moon, you need to be practical and close to the material world. You can worry more than anyone else under the sun and indeed invent anxieties to keep you going. At times your obsessive tidiness and endless fussing about details drives mates to distraction but you can keep a home running efficiently and are conscientious. Deep down inside you are rather frightened of your emotions. On the outside you can look prudish and rather critical, but once you soften your rigid need to keep order everywhere you can be quite sensual. Learning to let your hair down is crucial. Famous versions are Shirley MacLaine, Jack Nicholson, Madonna, Princess Anne, Dustin Hoffman, Sean Connery, Edward Kennedy and Robert Redford.

Your Virgo Moon to Their Aries Moon

A schoolteacher marrying a circus acrobat! Not really a compatible pairing. You want a tidy, ordered existence while they want constant noise, excitement and challenge. They would worry you to death with the chaos they leave trailing behind them. Certainly you would help them to be more practical, but is it worth it? They could show you what it is like to have more trust in life, but at the end of the day you would write them off as hopeless gamblers. Their brashness would upset your tender sensitivities.

Your Virgo Moon to Their Taurus Moon

A happy coupling of two earthy, home-loving souls. You share common interests in comfort, good food, gardening and small animals. They are more demonstratively affectionate than you, which will help to iron out your wrinkles. Also their solidity will wind your anxiety levels down. Their stubbornness will not bother you excessively since you are adaptable by nature and happy to be of service. You work too hard, which will suit their lazy nature, but then you are not happy being idle. Between you, you do need a little more vision in your lives.

Your Virgo Moon to Their Gemini Moon

Restless, talkative (in the extreme) and rather highly strung together, this can work well because you both basically want to fit round each other. You worry too much while they flit around in a slightly unsettling fashion. But boredom will never be a problem. Your practical side will help to ground them while their airy intuition will teach you to see problems in a different light. Your home will be packed full of books. Sometimes moon Geminis can be wild, wayward and none too faithful. You are not desperately jealous but you do hurt if rejected.

Your Virgo Moon to Their Cancer Moon

Both of you have highly nourishing moons. You connect to practical matters, the body, the garden and small animals. They connect to feelings, food and beautiful environments. They are moody, but in a different way to your highly strung anxiety, so you can cope with their full moon blues while they soothe your endless worries. Both of you are sensitive to emotional hurts so will not intentionally cause damage by wandering or abandoning each other without thought.

Your Virgo Moon to Their Leo Moon

You can certainly cope with them, but do you need to? They love entertaining, being grand, looking flamboyant and travelling first class. You do not need all that show and, although you can adapt to their stubbornness, at the end of the day you need to ask yourself why you are doing it all. Certainly they will bring you the sparkle, *chutzpah* and courage that is lacking in your life. You will organize the practical facts of life that they regard as beneath them. They are warm as long as they are being admired. You might grow to hate all the parties since you have to do all the work.

Your Virgo Moon to Their Virgo Moon

The nervous tension levels would be off the Richter Scale since both of you have an endless supply of anxious concerns. You would just give each other more to worry about. The nagging and obsessive tidiness would get to ridiculous levels. Both of you need a more amiable, laid back moon to mate with. Then your better qualities of practicality and warmth can appear. You would both be too narrow-minded together, only concerned with your shared hypochondria and with what is material in life. You need more vision.

Your Virgo Moon to Their Libra Moon

You like order and they like harmony. Both of you are refined, sensitive, easily embarrassed in public by social gaffes and want a beautiful home. You match well since your practical flair combines with their elegant taste. It could be a touch cool at times if you are standing on the sidelines and they are being snobbish, which happens. But neither of you would rock the boat too much. You might get tired of all the socializing and living on the outside that moon Librans tends to do. You care less about appearances and social reputation.

Your Virgo Moon to Their Scorpio Moon

This could be hot, could be horrible. It depends on whether or not you are an over-controlled, rigid Virgo moon. If you are it will not work, what with their torrid preoccupation with sex and living life in the depths. If on the other hand you are open to passion this could be earth-shaking. You would never quite get to the bottom of their feelings, which are highly private, but you would provide them with a solid practical base. Being a fixed moon and very strong emotionally they would keep you from worrying as much as you sometimes can.

Your Virgo Moon to Their Sagittarius Moon

A restless, energetic, talkative combination, this, which would never stay bored for long. Neither of you is good at sitting still, though they tend to fly further afield than you when the mood strikes. Your infinite capacity for worrying about everything under the sun would not meet with sympathy from their optimistic, unrealistic, rather reckless temperament, however. They would liven you up but you are fairly incompatible types. They hate being fenced in while you like a semblance of order around. It could be fun while it lasts.

Your Virgo Moon to Their Capricorn Moon

Earthy common sense abounds between you, but will it kill passion? Both of you are rather too practical and workaholic and tend to sit on your feelings. If you can open up then both of you have depths of sensuality, but it will take time. You worry endlessly while they feel unworthy of being loved if they do not achieve a great deal. They tend to work long hours at the office and you might find you never have the time or inclination to relax together, which would eventually undermine your warmth towards each other.

Your Virgo Moon to Their Aquarius Moon

Not wonderful since you basically need someone to calm you down and ease your highly strung nerves while they take the greatest delight in stirring up the atmosphere. They love being bizarre and shocking just to see the effect. They are frightened of one-to-one commitment and you can over-control your feelings so the match might end up very distant and cool. You could adapt to their rather stubborn ways, but why would you want to? You are sensitive and want a tidy life. They are disorganized hippies whose lifestyle would make you shriek.

Your Virgo Moon to Their Pisces Moon

Happy as bunnies down a burrow you have a great deal to offer one another if they are not too wimpish and you can keep your obsessive tidying and narking under control. They retreat into day-dreams because they fear rejection and facing life's harsher realities. You can provide a perfectly protective cocoon for them with your practical skills. They will teach you to soften down your workaholic tendencies and make you less rigid. Both of you are sympathetic, caring, adaptable types who would not intentionally hurt one another. You might find yourselves very indecisive at home.

Your Moon Is in Libra

An air moon, you always think before you feel. Life to you should be a graceful business with everyone being tactful, charming and kind all the time. You can come across as insincere because you agree too much just to keep the peace. You like your house to be elegant, your friends to be upwardly mobile and your mate to be hard-working yet supportive. Your love of beautiful surroundings, good food and luxuries gives you expensive habits. Class matters more to you than it should and you are certainly over-sensitive about the approval of those around you. The idle, the unemployed and the great unwashed hold no fascination whatsoever for you. Richard Chamberlain, George Bush, Henry Kissinger, Fidel Castro and Patty Hearst are this type.

Your Libra Moon to Their Aries Moon

You want peace while they want excitement. You are the soul of tact and are desperate for approval while they crash around, dropping clangers, tramping on sensitive corns and being generally over-impulsive. They would make you wince from one end of the weekend to the other. You lack between you much connection to the harsher realities or deeper feelings in life, and would eventually drift apart because there was too little to nourish and recharge the relationship.

Your Libra Moon to Their Taurus Moon

A shared taste in elegant, comfortable, not to say luxurious living will draw you together. They are demonstratively affectionate, which will warm your rather laid back soul. Sex might prove a problem because they want constant, tangible expressions of love while you can take it or leave it. You are more concerned with outer appearances and social approval than they are, but they can help to ground you and keep life rolling along at a practical level. They can be stubborn but you rarely dig your heels in for long.

Your Libra Moon to Their Gemini Moon

Two airy moons together are intellectually stimulating but leave much to be desired emotionally and physically. You have a tendency to like life to be too nice. They do not but are uncomfortable around intense feelings. You could end up gliding across the surface and drawing further apart. They might be a little wild for you socially since they have a quirky sense of humour and can embarrass you. But if you do last your home will be full of books, visitors and a high level of interest.

Your Libra Moon to Their Cancer Moon

Two essentially different energies, you can get along happily because both of you want an elegant, well-organized home life.

They can be emotionally more roller-coaster than you understand but they are not sharp-edged nor vindictive. You like calm, harmony and peace above all else and might find their ups and downs wearing. They tend to retreat and sulk if misunderstood but on the whole you are supremely tactful. They will be exceptionally caring, will cook well and will love to mother you. What may cause problems is your rather cool, laid back approach to the emotional subtleties of life.

Your Libra Moon to Their Leo Moon

You suit each other like a dream, will strive hard to make yourselves accepted by all the best people, will only eat in the best restaurants together and will create a sumptuous palace of a home. Both of you are traditionalists, keen to keep up appearances and horribly extravagant. You do lack, however, a depth in the relationship and need to work at ways of nourishing yourselves that is not just all on the surface. You have to *feel* good together, emotionally and physically, as well as looking good.

Your Libra Moon to Their Virgo Moon

A quietly compatible pairing since they are adaptable and you resourceful. They are sensitive, refined and not prone to crashing into social gaffes. They may criticize more than you might like and certainly they worry obsessively, which becomes a bore. But your airy way of spreading harmony about the place will put them at their ease. They can help to keep the everyday running of the home ticking over nicely since they are practical and earthy. You add a touch of taste. This match could at times by too cool and detached. You need to work to keep up the warmth.

Your Libra Moon to Their Libra Moon

You would spend all your time racing around to ask what the other one wanted! It sounds divine but really you need an anchor, not an echo. Both of you would chat charmingly and intelligently, would entertain superbly and generally be an asset to the social scene. But you ultimately lack feeling together. The relationship needs deeper connections to body and heart before it will have the inner strength and stability to last long term. More nourishment needs to come from your sun signs.

Your Libra Moon to Their Scorpio Moon

You skate like a dragonfly across the surface of life, glittering colourfully, while they plunge into the murky depths. Their intensity and turbulence of feeling would frighten you. Your rather superficial need to keep up appearances and be socially acceptable would appal them. They control their feelings tightly so you would never quite know what was going on but would suspect (rightly) that they were always trying to control you and gain the upper hand. You have difficulty facing up to the harsher realities of life while they adore wallowing in the mire. Not too in tune.

Your Libra Moon to Their Sagittarius Moon

This has promise as long as they are not too rough a diamond. You can put a veneer of good manners on them while they give you more courage, sparkle and spontaneity. You are a traditionalist and, dare it be said, a snob at heart. They are more devil-may-care, reckless, even gamblers in their souls. But they are warm and communicative while they stand still. You like intellectual stimulation and do not mind too much if they fly free, which they will, frequently. Neither of you is especially jealous though you do hate the humiliation of being seen to be rejected. You do need more depth in the relationship.

Your Libra Moon to Their Capricorn Moon

This can be cool, too businesslike and hold together for the sake of status and reputation, but it can also work well. You are both traditionalists and slightly snobbish, wanting to be accepted. Home will be elegant, your entertaining impeccable and friends rather classy. They work too hard since they never feel worthy of love unless it is earned. You might find they are never there, though you can settle for the shell of a relationship if it looks good enough from the outside. If you can banish their workaholic tendencies they are warm, earthy and practical. You can soothe them, make them feel accepted. They can cuddle you.

Your Libra Moon to Their Aquarius Moon

Two airy moons should have an initial attraction, though you are ultimately too cool and 'up in your heads' for a relationship to last for ever. Even an early attraction may falter because you are super-sensitive to social embarrassments and they are bizarre, eccentric and given to slightly shocking displays. They love to see the effect they have on others. Your sensibilities might not stand it. Also you do really want a relationship. They really do not. They are scared of one-to-one commitment and much prefer to move in groups or with friends.

Your Libra Moon to Their Pisces Moon

Blissful, sensitive, refined, caring, creative – what more can you ask for? Air/water mixes do not generally work, but here it can. You want harmony. They want peace. You are tactful, charming and thoughtful. They are self-sacrificing, sympathetic and caring. You would give a great deal to each other. You would never feel swamped by their emotions because they drift gently off into day-dreams much of the time. They can be a touch self-pitying, feeling themselves martyred, but given a protective environment this will disappear.

Your Moon Is in Scorpio

A water moon, you are deep, dark, intensely private, secretive and passionate, an enigma even to intimate lovers. As a matter of pride you never let anyone see the turbulent intensity of emotions churning inside you though you are extremely jealous and possessive. If you are hurt or betrayed you absolutely never let on but will never forgive. You plot and plan revenge for years afterwards. Your romantic life is never taken lightly or with a laugh – it is life or death, love or hate. There is no wishy-washy in-between stage. If lovers leave or are abandoned you absolutely never stay friends afterwards. Your feelings are always tightly controlled.

In true Scorpionic fashion you are fairly preoccupied with sex. Through the sexual act you hope to achieve a higher union. Famous moon Scorpios are Warren Beatty, Nelson Mandela, the Queen Mother, Raquel Welch, Bette Midler, Steven Spielberg, Kevin Costner, Gerard Depardieu, Princess Caroline, Liz Taylor and Prince Andrew.

Your Scorpio Moon to Their Aries Moon

You exist in the subterranean depths of your emotions. They leap up agitatedly if as much as a sniff of a feeling gets remotely heavy. They are fireflies and speed merchants where you want to be locked in an intense clinch most of the time. You would constantly be trying to grasp an untamable energy. Your jealousy and possessiveness would drive you and them crackers. Their insecure, over-independent stance which pushes them into dominating others would soon fall foul of your need to be in control.

Your Scorpio Moon to Their Taurus Moon

Two mighty strong personalities coming together can either be an explosion of passion or end in catastrophic bitterness. Both of you are jealous, stubborn, fairly power-hungry and very immovable. You more obviously fight for control but they are past masters at the art of passive resistance. They just smile lazily and dig their heels in deeper. Certainly they are cuddly, will surround you with every imaginable comfort and are demonstratively affectionate. But you may find them too materialistic and lacking in your depth of vision. Not bad if you can stand the struggle.

Your Scorpio Moon to Their Gemini Moon

Better than it might appear, but certainly not perfect. They are basically butterflies who never sit on one flower for long. They flit restlessly around, which would raise your hackles instantly. You like to possess, to control, to sink into the depths with your mate. The positive note, at least for the short term, is that they do have a leaning towards the dark side of life which suits you admirably. In the long term, though, your turbulent feelings would threaten to envelope and therefore frighten them. They like staying up in their heads, in their thoughts and ideas, which you would find far too cool and unemotional.

Your Scorpio Moon to Their Cancer Moon

A wonderfully intuitive, empathetic connection would exist between you since you are both water moons. You would swirl, toss, roll and sink on the rise and fall of your feelings. Admittedly at times you would feel you were cast adrift together on a rudderless raft because both of you are highly impressionable. But you are more fixed and in control, which is a help. The problems could come long term as you like to dominate and Cancer will gradually try to take over. You also want an exclusive, intense sexual/emotional relationship. They really prefer a more familial, all-cuddles-together type of contact.

Your Scorpio Moon to Their Leo Moon

Not favourable since they fly high and you like to sink low. They are fiery, scared of emotions and adore admiration while you do not care about appearances. You want to be in an intensely private, exclusive affair. Their extravagance and arrogance would irk you; your need to control would bother them. Certainly both of you have a fairly steady sexuality though it comes from different motives. They can be selfish but at best are heart-centred. You are more loin-centred.

Your Scorpio Moon to Their Virgo Moon

This is supposed to be a gas, but . . . you need to watch what kind of Virgo moon you pick. Some can be ravers, highly sensual and earthily warm. Others can be dried up old prunes, fastidiously and obsessively tidy, supreme naggers. Guess which you would like? They will always be less emotionally intense than you but they can help to keep your home life running smoothly at a practical level. They will tend to your medical needs, understand your diet and look after your pets. They will adapt where you are stubborn and you could help to loosen their rigid approach.

Your Scorpio Moon to Their Libra Moon

Not basically in tune since they are fastidiously 'nice', rather class-conscious, fairly cool, laid back and unemotional where you revel in the murky depths of your more intense passions. You want committed union, a real soul mate, and ongoing good sex. They want a colourful social life, upwardly mobile friends and nothing that smells bad. You would frighten them with your stormy undercurrents and they would exasperate you with what looked like superficiality. You think the agonies are worth it for the ecstasies that come along as well. They want total harmony all the time.

Your Scorpio Moon to Their Scorpio Moon

Bliss. Both of you understand each other like a dream and nothing will ever be too emotionally stretching or too much of a challenge for either of you. Here is someone who can understand your most hidden desires, your darkest yearnings and deepest passions. No other sign in the zodiac understands you like one of your own. The fights and sulks will certainly be long and could be bitter. You will both have to curb your instincts for revenge. Try to be more flexible and tolerant. Your sex lives could be the envy of the neighbourhood, except that you'd never kiss and tell.

Your Scorpio Moon to Their Sagittarius Moon

Not a happy mating since you are basically opposite energies. They are fiery, freedom-loving, over-talkative, over-optimistic gamblers at heart, not well connected to their bodies. You are deep, dark, sexy and need an exclusive one-to-one commitment. They would start to feel suffocated and promptly escape. Your jealousy would be terribly out of control. They refuse to admit there is a dark side to life and hate facing the harsher realities. You have utter contempt for those who cannot live at your level. Sex would be an abyss between you.

Your Scorpio Moon to Their Capricorn Moon

Find the right Capricorn moon: some can be earthy, sensual and rather decadent. But most feel so unworthy of love and admiration that they work 90-hour weeks to earn acceptance, thereby never being available for the relationships they so desperately want. You are not one for a workaholic, absent partner and you are too robust to enjoy supporting a fragile heart. If they are truly connected to their bodies and more indulgent side then certainly you could operate well together, though possibly over the long term you might find them too materialistic and lacking in your sense of vision. You can be quite spiritual as well as highly sexual.

Your Scorpio Moon to Their Aquarius Moon

No, in a word. Nothing worse. They are more scared of one-to-one commitment than almost any other moon sign. Every time you wanted a twosome they would invite six friends along to brighten the atmosphere. You do not appreciate your romantic life being made into a permanent party or group meeting. You want sex, they want conversation. They love the theory of sex, you appreciate the practice. Both of you are hugely stubborn and would not give way to each other's quite contradictory needs. They fly away at the first whiff of jealousy while you really cannot help your tendency to possess.

Your Scorpio Moon to Their Pisces Moon

This could be bliss as long as you curb your octopus tendencies and do not pick an over-timid, wispy Pisces moon. They can be such scared creatures they hardly emerge from their shells in case they get hurt. They can spend their lives day-dreaming or indulging various addictions as an escape from a relationship. You would feel chilled out and exasperated by them. They can be slippery, evasive souls when they do not want to be pinned down. Certainly you are both water moons so there should be a depth of emotional understanding. They are kind, caring and very self-sacrificing and would adapt to your rather fixed ways.

Your Moon Is in Sagittarius

Fire is in your veins and the wanderlust is in your feet. You need freedom and wide open spaces more than anything in your emotional life. Being fenced in or committed to long-term relationships can make you panic. Lovers have to be friends as well and you can sustain 'spacier' relationships than most people. Your honesty is at times a touch harsh since you rarely stop to think of the consequences on someone else's fragile ego. You need a robust mate. Honesty and naïvety are your more beguiling character traits. What is most important is that you have strong beliefs by which to live your life. Famous Sagittarius moons of the past and present include Ivana Trump, Donald Trump, Pablo

Picasso, Dame Joan Sutherland, Kitty Kelley and Stephen King.

Your Sagittarius Moon to Their Aries Moon

Noisy, volatile and impulsive, you would always be getting yourselves into impossible scrapes but boredom would never get a look in. The only problems come when life slows down or hits problems. Neither of you is well equipped to face the harsher realities of life or to connect with your feelings, which always happens when you come to rest. Your similarities will provide an initial magnetic attraction but over the long term both of you need more of an anchor, a mate with common sense and an emotional/physical warmth to contain you without making you feel trapped.

Your Sagittarius Moon to Their Taurus Moon

A firefly and a bull, you do not make a compatible couple. You are flyaway, freedom-loving and scared of being possessed or pulled down too much into your body. They are solid, earthy, jealous, immovable and need constant emotional and sexual reassurance about your love. Certainly they would provide you with every comfort but they would also expect you to share their needs and indulgences. They can be blinkered and they do loathe change. You adore constant movement, even moving house often, which they would hate.

Your Sagittarius Moon to Their Gemini Moon

Not much stability, solidity or common sense between you but the conversations will sparkle. You are both grasshoppers who adore philosophizing about life. You can both be romantic in short bursts in your own way. Fidelity can be a problem as neither of you has much staying power. Both of you avoid facing feelings so you lack ways of nourishing the relationship when it becomes dry. Difficult patches would be harder to overcome since both of you lack the resources to do anything other than either think or run. It will be fun but you need an anchor, not a playmate.

Your Sagittarius Moon to Their Cancer Moon

You walk down different roads in life. They want home, family, a secure commitment and emotional empathy. You want freedom, excitement, bright conversation and not too much feeling. You distrust those hidden undercurrents that in moon Cancer grow stronger with age. Certainly they would provide you with a wonderful home base, but they would become more possessive as the years went by. They cannot stand separation. They quite like you as one of the family rather than as a lover, but you would still feel fenced in.

Your Sagittarius Moon to Their Leo Moon

Two fire moons together are noisy, volatile, warm and passionate, at least in the early stages. The main problem is how to keep the flames burning, since neither of you is well connected to your feelings or your bodies. Moon Leos are more settled, home-orientated and stubborn than you, which would provide you with an anchor. Their ego really requires a constant mate, however, while you quite like to be flying free whenever it suits. Your strong, not always tactful opinions would also ruffle their fragile, if over-blown, egos. They desperately need to be admired. This would irk you. Together your extravagances could get well out of hand.

Your Sagittarius Moon to Their Virgo Moon

Restless, energetic and very chatty together, you could do a great deal worse. Their obsessive tidiness and nagging might drive you spare but they would keep the boring practicalities of life ticking over for you. Your sunny, outgoing confidence would give them courage and maybe(!) stop them nagging. Both of you are adaptable so sulks would not be long lived, though indecisiveness could be a drawback. They are not jealous and are fairly self-sufficient so would not try to fence you in. But you need to soften down their rigid outlook.

Your Sagittarius Moon to Their Libra Moon

Fire to air moon creates a lively atmosphere, excellent, stimulating conversation and usually a great social life. They are a touch class-conscious and too 'nice' for you. You are prone to sailing into over-honest, rather tactless opinions that would have them wincing, especially if you are out on the social circuit. They desperately want harmony and respectability. They will bring you a touch of grace, elegance and charm while you will bring them courage, fire and more directness. However, neither of you is good at facing the horrible realities of life. When the stormy times came you would fly off and they would politely look the other way. You need more depth.

Your Sagittarius Moon to Their Scorpio Moon

You would feel as if you were trapped in a spider's web. What nourishes you is freedom, flying high in your ideas and staying friendly rather than feeling suffocated. They on the other hand need intense, passionate, ongoing exclusive relationships. Your sexual needs are so different neither of you would ever be wholly pleased. Their jealousy would be aroused by your escapist tactics and would bother both of you. You would never, never, ever understand what is going on within them. They are private, secretive and manipulative where you are open, gullible, naïve and staggeringly honest.

Your Sagittarius Moon to Their Sagittarius Moon

You light each other up with your ideas, your beliefs about life, your travel plans and your wide social circle of friends. But will it ever hang together? The flames of two fire moons can burn out fairly fast, so the early passion just suddenly disappears one day. You both need so much freedom that you could drift apart without noticing it. Neither of you is good at commitment nor at setting up a practical home. Finances would always be in chaos. It seems a shame since both of you are ultimately so likable, but a more solid moon mate would be better for you.

Your Sagittarius Moon to Their Capricorn Moon

Their judgemental side probably bothers you but this could be better than it looks. You dislike being fenced in and need elbow room. They feel unworthy of being loved so have to work like maniacs to prove their value. You certainly do not object to fairly absent partners and their practical streak would be an asset around the house when they are there. Realistic you are not, so they might keep a curb on spending and run the budget sensibly. You would always feel slightly weighed down by them because you are basically optimistic. They are born pessimists. But some of each might rub off on the other, which would be no bad thing.

Your Sagittarius Moon to Their Aquarius Moon

Wild, wacky, way out and always on the go, this could be an uproarious combination. Both of you are reckless in different ways, so boredom is never going to be a problem. Both of you like being pals, adore friends and will have a house full of people. But what happens when life slows down, the parties stop and you have only each other to face across an echoing room? They are more scared if anything than you of one-to-one commitment. Neither of you is well connected to your feelings, so when the rough times come you will be lost. You may find it difficult to sustain the relationship over the long term because you have no ways of nourishing it.

Your Sagittarius Moon to Their Pisces Moon

Fire and water do not mix, they say, but you could almost make a go of this match. Both of you are adaptable, not very intense personalities. You like freedom and they are the least jealous of the emotional signs, partly because they escape into their daydreams and therefore might not even notice your absence. They are highly sensitive so might object to your rather blunt way of speaking. They can withdraw very fast into their shell. But they are basically kind, caring, sympathetic souls who will sacrifice their own needs to suit yours. Your outgoing optimism will be good for them as long as you keep them safe.

Your Moon Is in Capricorn

An earth moon, you are tuned in to the material world. Emotionally life was tough for you in the beginning so you have ended up feeling unworthy. You think love for you has to be earned by achievement, which is quite the wrong way round. You have to learn that you can be wanted for just being you. Certainly you can be successful but your ambitions often drive away the very relationships you need. In a crisis you can be superb and you are always practical.

When you can relax you are indulgent, earthy, almost decadent at times, though this does not occur often. Luckily you mellow through the years, warming up as you age. You will sacrifice almost anything to achieve your ends in life and have been known to be ruthless. Others see you as cold. Famous Capricorn moons are Barbara Bush, Albert Gore, John Major, Michael Douglas, Norman Schwarzkopf, Christina Onassis, Mia Farrow and Arnold Schwarzenegger.

Your Capricorn Moon to Their Aries Moon

A rather gritty combination, this, you might find your moods never matched. You are cautious, rather pessimistic and approach emotions tentatively, whereas they take the bull by the horns and charge. Neither of you is at home in your feelings. Your self-esteem is low while they appear to be over-confident though their insecurity is all too evident. They never stand still and you rarely stop working, so you might find making meaningful connections difficult. You are earthy and practical. They seem unrealistic and rather abrasive.

Your Capricorn Moon to Their Taurus Moon

You purr in each other's company, cuddling up close. You just adore their way of constantly demonstrating their affection. Both of you are earthy and indulgent, though you try to hide what you see as your more 'lazy' side away. They will provide you with every comfort and make you enjoy it. Their stubbornness will not bother you, especially, because you just flit off to work when the going gets stormy. They are possessive but that can feel like security and support to you as long as they do not start issuing orders. Both of you are manipulative in different ways, which you need to watch.

Your Capricorn Moon to Their Gemini Moon

A rather cool combination because you work too hard and they think too much. Neither of you is into feeling in depth, which could be the stumbling block to long-term intimacy. They are basically butterflies who never settle for long in one mood, in one place or with one face. They are not necessarily unfaithful, just rather casual. You would find your earthy side needed more physical contact. Your judgemental streak would also come out rather destructively to point out their shortcomings. At the end of the day you need someone who can make you feel more valued. They would hardly know how.

Your Capricorn Moon to Their Cancer Moon

Opposite moon signs can be a blessing or a curse depending on which are involved. At best your moods will always be slightly out of sync. They want to make love when you want to sleep. You want to cut the grass when they want to go on the town. They will certainly provide you with a wonderful home base, great cooking, elegantly upmarket friends and lots of sympathetic support. In time they might even make you learn to value yourself more as a human being. But they are jealous and might not take kindly to your long working hours or constant need to keep doing. Your criticisms will wound them.

Your Capricorn Moon to Their Leo Moon

Definitely an upwardly mobile pair socially, you would put great stress in being seen in all the right places with the right friends. They are gloriously extravagant, needing to live life the five-star way. You are a traditionalist, a tiny bit of a snob and constantly striving to prove you are acceptable. It could work but ultimately you both put more value on outer appearances than on how you feel. You always feel unwanted and unworthy, which their rather egocentric approach might emphasize. As far as they are concerned you need to give them all the attention, whereas you really need to give more to yourself.

Your Capricorn Moon to Their Virgo Moon

Cosy, cuddly and comfortable or cool, overworked and rather rigid: this combination could work either way. Both of you have the capacity to indulge and to be sensual but they need to loosen up and forget about keeping life tidy. You need to stop trying to achieve to earn love. If you can get into your bodies and down into the depths of your feelings (which might be painful at first) you would find this match offers both of you a great deal. They are adaptable and rather highly strung, so will fit in with your ways and rely on your advice. They are helpful, keen to serve and generally kind when their perfectionist streak is kept under control.

Your Capricorn Moon to Their Libra Moon

Gritty though a not impossible combination, this. Your moods will never quite be in sync but you both have relatively similar aims in life. Both of you are sensitive to social approval, are snobbish, class-conscious and want to know the right people and live in an elegant home. If this sounds a touch chilly, it might end up that way. Ulterior motives of a material nature never suit the heart's intentions. Moon Librans can come across as superficial because they are so determined to keep the peace and to please. But you are at times happy enough being left to work hard and not be embroiled in heavy emotional scenes. They are not jealous.

Your Capricorn Moon to Their Scorpio Moon

A heavyweight relationship which will only work long term if you are willing to get into your feelings – not easy when you have always felt unwanted and unloved. They have turbulent, intense emotions that they need to live out in close, exclusive twosomes. Each of you in different ways is highly sexual, though you often repress your physical needs for the sake of ambition. You might find their possessiveness a bore when you wanted to escape back to the office. Both of you have a way of cutting corners and manipulating for your own ends that could cause problems.

Your Capricorn Moon to Their Sagittarius Moon

Do pessimists and optimists cancel each other out? You are basically very different energies. They are reckless, impulsive, outspoken, outgoing, true adventurers at heart. You are cautious, defensive, hard-working and rather judgemental. They fly high on a Pollyanna trip with their heads in the clouds, you walk resolutely on the ground facing reality in all its bleakness. You need to be nurtured more, taught to love yourself. They are shockingly and undiplomatically blunt in their opinions. You might end up feeling worse. Certainly you would regard them as fools at times. Highly compatible sun signs would be needed.

Your Capricorn Moon to Their Capricorn Moon

A very gloomy, over-worked, pessimistic pair you would make, with both of you feeling you had to out-vie the other in achievements to earn acceptance. You would both spend so long in the office you might never meet. It could become very cold indeed. There is, however, a flip side to you which is earthy, sensual and quite decadent; whether you would bring that out with another over-defensive Capricorn moon is questionable. Your vision of life together would be too practical, too materialistic. You need more *chutzpah* (daring), sparkle and optimism.

Your Capricorn Moon to Their Aquarius Moon

If you want a distant non-relationship this has much to recommend it. Your workaholic tendencies keep you away from home a great deal and they positively fly scared of heavy one-to-one commitments. Neither of you is good with feelings and you distrust being swamped by emotions you cannot control. They might not always suit you socially because they adore startling or shocking others by doing or saying bizarre things just to see the effect they have. You would cringe with embarrassment. They would find your judgements stuffy and tedious. They are stubborn and would not give way easily. Doubtful.

Your Capricorn Moon to Their Pisces Moon

You could do your strong, protective act, providing them with a solid, secure home base while they would float around caring for your every need, making you feel loved and valued. They are the most adaptable, least jealous of the water signs. If your absences were prolonged at work they would just drift off into their daydreams. What you might have to watch is that both of you are slightly addictive by nature. That could get out of hand. You would need to soften to make a good match of it. They could teach you in quiet ways to appreciate your feelings.

Your Moon Is in Aquarius

An air sign, you think first, analyse your feelings next and then most often forget them. Emotional involvements make you nervous and you would much prefer to be one of a crowd of friends. You can be rebellious, idiosyncratic and downright eccentric at times, often just to make a point. Your sense of humour is always to hand, and startling companions is one of your hobbies. Underneath your bravado, however, lurks a sense of insecurity about one-to-one relationships. Your connection to your feelings and your body is lacking, so you become too impersonal and detached. Sensuality is difficult for you. You need warm mates who do not cling too hard. Famous moon Aquarius types past and present include Princess Diana, Woody Allen, Princess Stephanie, Prince Edward, Joanne Woodward and Andy Warhol.

Your Aquarius Moon to Their Aries Moon

The wit will sparkle, the jokes be raw and fast, no punches pulled, no offence taken. Both of you are verbally robust and not overly sensitive about your feelings. But this could be a problem long term since you do not know what to do when life's stormy passages push you into your depths. You do live too high, too recklessly both of you, and could burn out fast or in time just drift apart since neither of you will stand being fenced in. They also like to dominate, which you will just ignore.

Your Aquarius Moon to Their Taurus Moon

Two hugely stubborn, entirely opposite personalities, you neither want the same things emotionally nor will you give way even marginally to suit one another. You want freedom, change, excitement and space. They want security, no change, a solid rooted existence with them firmly in control. Their possessiveness, though often hidden behind a lazy smile, would unnerve you. They certainly would provide you with all the comforts, but you are less concerned with cuddles, indulgences and the like than most. You would feel suffocated by their very physical approach and fenced in by their need to be together, especially sexually.

Your Aquarius Moon to Their Gemini Moon

Bright, breezy, fast-moving and highly talkative together, you would think life and love was made for you at the beginning. But together you'd have more of an intellectual contact than any other kind. You fear close involvement and they rarely stand still. Their moods change like the wind and what you agreed yesterday would be out of the window today. The amusement factor is high but the durability factor doubtful. When the going got tough both of you would be off like a shot. Neither of you is connected well enough to your bodies or your feelings. There is little to nourish the relationship long term or recharge its batteries. Words are not enough.

Your Aquarius Moon to Their Cancer Moon

The pits, frankly! You are scared of being trapped. They are crab like in their attempts to hang on to mates for security and comfort. Certainly in time they will not want a totally exclusive relationship. You will be added in as just one more of the family, but their jealousy will always be a problem. You basically distrust emotions and they, being a water moon, have undercurrents that make your hair stand on end. You do not understand what makes them tick because they are not sensible, thinking creatures like yourself. They feel! They will find you too detached, cool and evasive.

Your Aquarius Moon to Their Leo Moon

Opposites do not necessarily attract. You are a slightly eccentric soul who loves to waken up parties with a shock or a bizarre happening. Apart from the fact that they loathe embarrassing exhibitions they also want all the admiration and attention going. They can be rather uppity and arrogant while you are gloriously un-snobbish, highly tolerant and fond of the world's oddballs. Your friends would be very different. Being an air/fire mix, together you would lack a certain practical, grounding quality, and there is not enough feeling. You are not inherently suited but if you do get together watch for burnout.

Your Aquarius Moon to Their Virgo Moon

This could just work, though it would be cool. They can be highly self-sufficient, rather intact people so would not mind your tendency to wander off. They are more reclusive than you and might not appreciate all the friends you drag into their quiet space, but they will provide you with a well-run home life. They can be naggers and great critics and, being rather traditional, will not always appreciate your hippy attitudes. This is a 5 out of 10 but it could work.

Your Aquarius Moon to Their Libra Moon

Two air moons together can be too cool, too detached and rather up-in-the-head. On top of that you are quite different personalities. They are rather well-bred, slightly snobbish and highly sensitive to other people's opinion. You are wild, way out, quite eccentric and do not give a toss about approval. Indeed you will positively seek to embarrass or startle others as a way of making them sit up and take notice. Certainly they are not jealous or possessive and would not seek to corral you. But they would try to turn you into a 'proper' person, which you would resist strenuously.

Your Aquarius Moon to Their Scorpio Moon

The absolute worst. You will never make this work since you run a mile from the experiences they regard as essential. They want to plunge into the depths of intense, turbulent feelings, to intertwine passionately with a soul mate. Your hackles rise at the very thought. You are scared of close one-to-one commitment and would insist on bringing a few friends along to ease the atmosphere. They are secretive where you are open. They are jealous where you are tolerant. They want exclusive rights where you like open relationships. Sex would become an abyss as you fight to stay out of your body and they want to drag you firmly into it.

Your Aquarius Moon to Their Sagittarius Moon

No shortage of excitement here or instant fireworks. You both love thrills, spills and adventure. Neither of you appreciates tight, exclusive relationships, but there is the possibility that fairly soon you could drift apart as you pursue your separate interests. There is not enough emotional or physical contact to keep the relationship fed, watered and nourished. Both of you live up in your heads, your ideas and your theories, but it really is not enough. Certainly both of you can stand each other's savagely direct jokes. When it ends you will stay pals for ever.

Your Aquarius Moon to Their Capricorn Moon

Cool, maybe even workmanlike – but is it what you want? They work like maniacs, longer hours than anyone you have ever seen, which certainly would not make you feel trapped or fenced in.

But what is there to hold you together? You are wacky while they are traditional. They like to fit in while you insist on being eccentric just to stand out. Their rather saturnine judgemental streak would exasperate you. Your friends would never mix. Yours are oddballs and hippies. Theirs are leaders in the community.

Your Aquarius Moon to Their Aquarius Moon

You can talk for several years non-stop together, with sparks flying and a high level of interest. But passion? Forget it. You are both so laid back you are practically computers; together you will devise theories that make sex obsolete. You will probably co-author a book about sex rather than do it! Certainly neither of you likes being fenced in and neither of you is jealous, so that seems to work. But you need a mate who can warm you a little without making you feel overwhelmed, who can bring you just a touch more into your body.

Your Aquarius Moon to Their Pisces Moon

Not ideal on the face of it but this pairing can work, just. They are deeply sensitive, caring souls who will make sure you have every comfort. Nor are they so emotional that they will make you feel trapped. If ignored, which they may feel as you zip off, they will just disappear into their day-dreams. Both of you have a way of making partners feel they are not being exclusively related to, which suits both of you. You will feel too cool and laid back to them at times, so you need to warm up. They will teach you gently to be more caring. Watch your shock tactics – they will unsettle Pisces moons and make them withdraw in a hurry.

Your Moon Is in Pisces

A water moon, you are deeply sensitive and often hesitate to indicate your feelings in case you are rejected. Romantic opportunities often slide by as your timidity prevents you making a play. If you do find a protected space you are one of the world's beautiful people, calm, giving, caring and sympathetic. Taking on board the world's suffering sometimes brings you down, but giving to others feels like your role in life. Sometimes you feel martyred and self-pitying because your efforts are taken for granted. Then you escape into your day-dreams, fantasies and often addictions as a way of escaping from a reality that feels too harsh for you. Famous Pisces moon people are Michael Jackson, Hillary Clinton and Paul Newman; the late Grace Kelly and Elvis Presley were also this moon sign.

Your Pisces Moon to Their Aries Moon

Will you ever venture out of your oyster shell, what with them crashing around, causing waves and voicing opinions so direct they go straight through your thin skin? No doubt they could give you more courage, sparkle and dynamism, but you are great opposites. Your timid sensitivity in matters of home and heart really is not well suited to their rather inconsiderate way of behaving. You like peace apart from anything else, while they live in a constant battlefield. You would never feel protected since they change so frequently you reckon they can never be relied on.

Your Pisces Moon to Their Taurus Moon

A good match, this, since both of you like security, if for different reasons. You waft around in the breeze and never feel strong enough for the harsher realities of life. They will provide you with a comfortable emotional base and a sense of protection. Your adaptable nature will fit in with what they want. They are stubborn and not good about tolerating anyone else's needs; you are self-sacrificing, so that will hardly matter. Sex could be a problem since you can be fairly platonic while they like constant physical reassurance.

Your Pisces Moon to Their Gemini Moon

A restless, flyaway pair who are not essentially on the same wavelength, but it could work. They are chatty, changeable and never stand still, often coming across as cool and rather unemotional. You are equally changeable but can get your emotional sustenance from day-dreams, so will not always notice if they are absent in body or in spirit. You will be fairly indecisive together and rather impractical at home, which could be a problem. But the very fact that neither of you is stubborn and neither of you is really happy with a madly committed intimate relationship gives it hope.

Your Pisces Moon to Their Cancer Moon

Blissful. Your emotional sensitivities match wonderfully well. You will feel safe enough to really open up and express your most tender feelings. They will give you a protective shell, a happy home base and a settled family life. They are jealous but you probably will see that as positive because it means you will not be rejected. You can care for them, quite intuitively knowing what they need, which will make them happy. They are more decisive and energetic than you, while you have a flexibility they lack.

Your Pisces Moon to Their Leo Moon

Self-sacrificing, sensitive and adaptable as you are, you could be reasonably good at coping with their slightly over-blown ego, self-centred needs, stubbornness and touchy pride. In return you would get an extravagant lifestyle, flamboyant parties and friends and a lesson in how to be more outgoing and confident. You can cope with being ignored because you feed yourself on your day-dreams, though at the end of the day you need to ask yourself why you are settling for less than you want. Neither of you is practical.

Your Pisces Moon to Their Virgo Moon

This could click. Both of you are sensitive and unlikely to tramp on the other's vulnerable spots. They are more practical and can help to organize a smoothly run home, healthy eating habits and order to your chaos. They will worry endlessly, as you do, which is not helpful. They will also nag constantly, which you will ignore as you disappear into your day-dreams. Both of you are flexible, not especially jealous and rather restless, so anger will not stay in the air for long.

Your Pisces Moon to Their Libra Moon

This could be cool but it could also be workable. You both share rather aesthetic, elegant tastes in clothes and home décor. Both want a life full of peace, harmony and no arguments. Neither of you is hugely physical so you will not feel too weighed down by their demands. They want a relationship but nothing too overwhelming, since they are an air sign. You might at times find them unemotional, too cool and detached. But the pluses undoubtedly outweigh the minuses. They are quite snobbish and adore throwing parties full of upmarket people, so you will be drawn out of your shell.

Your Pisces Moon to Their Scorpio Moon

You have to be robust to cope with this, but the rewards could be great. Two water moons together make for a highly intense emotional scenario. They adore being plunged into the turbulence of their deepest feelings, which you understand though you are a more timid creature. They are fairly preoccupied with sex, which on the whole you are not. But you have an intuitive understanding of each other, which helps. Being the stronger, they will offer you the protection you need and a solid base in life. They may object as you disappear into your day-dreams since they want an ongoing, exclusive, one-to-one commitment. You may appear evasive to them.

Your Pisces Moon to Their Sagittarius Moon

Restless, flexible and always on the go, you are basically different types – but it does sometimes hold together. They are fiery, sometimes brash, want freedom, hate being fenced in and are stimulating conversationalists. You are sensitive, timid, emotional, sympathetic and self-sacrificing. Their directness may wound your sensitivities at times, but curiously for a water moon you do not mind if you do not have a totally exclusive relationship. You are never totally satisfied with real human beings and often disappear into day-dreams for emotional nourishment, so you might not mind their absences. Neither of you is hugely jealous and you are very good at putting yourself out for others.

Your Pisces Moon to Their Capricorn Moon

This can be a cool, workmanlike compromise that offers much of what you need. They are practical, energetic and decisive, which helps prop up the chaos in your life. They, sadly, always think they are unworthy of love unless they earn it by achievements, so they spend long hours at the office. You will help gently to give them more self-esteem but not mind being left to your day-dreams most of the time. As an earth sign they have a sensual, indulgent side that is sometimes kept repressed since ambitions always come first. You are never very happy about too physical a relationship, but you should not be overtaxed here.

Your Pisces Moon to Their Aquarius Moon

This does not sound custom-built for an ideal match but oddly it can be since neither of you minds space. They are positively scared of intense one-to-one commitments and will always invite six friends along to ease the atmosphere. You can be quite happy to disappear into your dream world and have your own problems about coming down to earth to form a real live relationship. Dreams and the movies always provide much nicer mates! You can gently bring more feeling into their lives, since they are very abrasive and airy, up in their heads. They think, they do not feel. They will give you more detachment on emotions and teach you to stand back a bit. They will at times be too sharp or too honest, which will hurt.

Your Pisces Moon to Their Pisces Moon

Two deeply sensitive, indecisive orphans together could offer each other much in the way of empathy, but this is not really a great idea when it comes to coping with the world. If you ever got together in the first place, that is, since both of you are so terrified of rejection that you hardly dare voice your feelings. Neither of you is practical, indeed you tend to live in a certain amount of chaos, which would be doubled in a relationship. Highly impressionable, you would both be swept around by the slightest stimulus both from outside the relationship and within it. Both of you need an anchor and a stronger protector.

MOON TO SUN:
YIN AND YANG

Your Moon to Their Sun

The sun sign (your birthday sign) is the essence of your personality, who you really are, your identity. It dictates career, talents – what you do and how you do it in the outside world. It is, if you will, the 'masculine' side of your personality, the inheritance from your father. Your 'feminine' side comes from your moon sign – it tells you what nourishes you, comforts you and makes you purr contentedly in your emotional life. It is the inheritance from your mother.

In short, your sun sign tells you what you ought to do, what your responsibilities are and what your aims in life are about. Your moon, on the other hand, is about what you want emotionally. In a perfect match your moon sign should be in your partner's sun sign. Thus Paul Newman, an Aquarius with a Pisces moon is married, long term, to Joanne Woodward, a Pisces with an Aquarius moon.

If your moon is nourished by what kind of personality your mate is, how he or she lives life, not emotionally but in reality, at work, with friends and in his or her interests, then you have a really strong connection that gives you a foundation for a good relationship. If your moon is not made comfortable by the essential being of your lover then you may adore him in bed or appreciate her goulash but you will not respect his or her talents, career ambitions or way of handling responsibility.

A compatible moon will support a mate in everything he or she wants to do in the outside world. An out of sync moon will be continually undermining a lover by suggesting changes just to suit its own needs. The desires of one half need to match the sense of duty or ambition in the other for life to run smoothly and successfully.

Your Moon Is in Aries

Your Aries Moon to Their Aries Sun

Brilliant. You feel good about them being active, courageous, slightly foolhardy but glamorously reckless as you see it. It bothers you not at all that they are brash, abrasive firecrackers. The truth is you cannot be happy without a life of adventure. You love their competitive streak and hard drive to win all the time. Others may wince at their lack of social niceties when it comes to getting their own way. You praise it.

Your Aries Moon to Their Taurus Sun

Teeth-achingly irritating. You cannot envisage how anyone can be that slow, that rooted, that security-conscious and so unchanging! You want a fireball of a lover who will make you glow with pride at all the high-flying exploits. Respecting someone who will happily work for results in 10 years' time is not the same. You are nourished by crazy schemes and wild gambles. They take pride in being practical. You would constantly be narking at them (quite unfairly) for being clodhoppers and dunderheads.

Your Aries Moon to Their Gemini Sun

You feel happiest around partners who move non-stop and there is, apart from an Aries, none more fidgety than a Gemini. Your mate probably does three jobs on the trot, talks endlessly and wittily, thinks up magic schemes at the drop of a hat and is never to be found where he or she was yesterday. Boredom is not a problem. You do not even mind the shortcuts Geminis are known to take at work, as you adore opportunists.

Your Aries Moon to Their Cancer Sun

Surprisingly, you appreciate their initiative, their creative talents, their career drive and their flair. Cancerians are not just stay-at-home-and-read-the-recipe-book types. They are go-getters in the world. You will not always understand their motivations or ways of handling inter-personal relationships at work because they are emotionally moody. And your moods will not be in sync a lot of the time – when they want to work, you want to make love. When they are smoochy, you will be ready to rave. Not ideal, but it could be worse.

Your Aries Moon to Their Leo Sun

You adore their flamboyant way of attacking the world, their talent for entertaining others and for getting positions of authority where they attract attention and admiration. Supporting their fragile egos when dented by unappreciative bosses or adverse criticism from workmates will not come easily to you. You like competitive people, whereas Leo likes being on the winner's podium but does not necessarily see why it should go through the hassle of getting there. You will not respect their cowardice and insecurity. They will hate your hard-hitting opinions.

Your Aries Moon to Their Virgo Sun

Not really. What you feel comfortable around is constant movement, excitement, challenge and people who are hard-driving go-getters. Virgo is too neat, precise and self-effacing to keep you happy. You would not see the point in their constant worrying and nit-picking because you do not .see the point of a meticulous job well done. You need an adventurer, a competitor, a winner.

Your Aries Moon to Their Libra Sun

Not a hopeful match since you appreciate a lively, combative mate while Libra is always trying to calm ruffled feathers. Librans are resourceful and energetic at work but their indecisiveness would drive you spare since they rarely make up their minds in less than a week. You do it in half a second. Male Librans are soft, sweet creatures whom you would secretly despise because they do not have your courage. Female Librans are clear-cut, more 'masculine', certainly more argumentative – but they fuss too much about doing the socially acceptable thing.

Your Aries Moon to Their Scorpio Sun

If ambition makes you purr (which it does), then Scorpio should suit your book, though they have a very different approach than your hash, crash-and-bash version. You have immense respect for their way of making miracles happen, of doing the impossible. You do not understand one smidgen about them and rather distrust what you fear are manipulative qualities hidden inside them (you are right). At the end of the day they care less about winning the race than getting the upper hand and wielding the power.

Your Aries Moon to Their Sagittarius Sun

Their devil-may-care, reckless, optimistic approach to life suits you down to the ground. They are full of hope, vision and dreams of grand schemes to come. They never stand still so you will hardly be bored. They will not even notice when you call a spade a spade, because if anything their tongue is rougher than yours. They will certainly not feel fenced in because you will give them a long rein. All this presupposes a feckless Sagittarius. There are deeply intellectual, rather narrow-minded ones, who will deeply disapprove of you.

Your Aries Moon to Their Capricorn Sun

You appreciate their ambition, their will to win, their initiative. At times you do not entirely support their need to be always moving up in the world for class-conscious reasons – though, since you like winners, this is hardly a huge problem. You may find them a touch serious, self-doubting and downright gloomy for your tastes and inclined to settle into fairly slow-moving professions. They scale the peaks, but with long-term goals in mind. You only ever see three days ahead. Your moods will be constantly out of sync.

Your Aries Moon to Their Aquarius Sun

You do not mind their eccentricity, strongly independent streak, nor even their need to take constant risks at work. But you may needle them occasionally because you are more competitive than they. You like winners. They want to be one of the crowd. They will provide you with excitement, good conversation and not too much in the way of restriction. You certainly will not possess them.

Your Aries Moon to Their Pisces Sun

No, in a word, unless you want a browbeaten mate. You appreciate brave warriors who confront the world, who make things happen by force if necessary, adventurers and heroes. Pisceans are vague, sometimes timid creatures who can certainly be highly successful though you just cannot see how. They would slither away from you, disappearing in a puff of smoke if you tried to argue with them, which is one of your life's pleasures.

Your Moon Is in Taurus

Your Taurus Moon to Their Aries Sun

Not a happy match, since everything you not only appreciate but absolutely need they make great strides to avoid. They are fast-moving, constantly changing adventurers. You want a mate who will offer you security, comfort and constant cuddles. You would frequently point out the practical flaws in their schemes, missing their grand vision. You would threaten to put their flame out.

Your Taurus Moon to Their Taurus Sun

What a dream. You would cuddle and smooch endlessly, live a life of unchanging comforts and probably grow a wonderful garden together for 45 years. You respect their practical skills and way of completing long-term projects. They are no short-distance sprinters, but you do not mind. You can wait for results. Both of you appreciate the same luxuries, which means you never have to argue or give way to one another.

Your Taurus Moon to Their Gemini Sun

Everything you appreciate, respect, admire and need is singularly lacking here. They are butterflies where you want an oxen. They are restless, short-distance enthusiasts where you need a marathon runner who can pace him- or herself steadily with the long term in view. Geminis react with horror to the unchangingness of your lifestyle, to your possessiveness and your sheer earthy solidity. They need speed, you need security.

Your Taurus Moon to Their Cancer Sun

A happy pairing since you like security, a rooted existence and all the home comforts while they adore a harmonious family life. You admire (even if you do not quite understand) their initiative, drive and resourcefulness out in the world and their creative flair. You can sometimes undermine them by pointing out the practical flaws in their schemes, thereby killing the flame of inspiration. But on the whole you are good together.

Your Taurus Moon to Their Leo Sun

Their extravagant lifestyle to some extent feeds your need for comfort. You certainly like eating, drinking and dressing well. But you do not understand their over-obvious grasping for attention and their willingness to settle for a position in the world that offers a shiny outward appearance but may be fairly hollow inside. You certainly do not respect their unrealistic, impractical wish to be grand without putting in the necessary legwork to earn it. They need someone who will better prop up their fragile egos.

Your Taurus Moon to Their Virgo Sun

Adorable. You love their way of working conscientiously, especially when the rewards come home to you. They slave self-sacrificingly to be of service, are meticulous, practical and usually to the point. You are lazier than they so may not always support their need to go 16 times over every tiny detail. They appreciate your efforts to provide comfort at the end of a long, hard day.

Your Taurus Moon to Their Libra Sun

You are different energies but you do appreciate their initiative, flair, drive and ambition. You do not even mind their indecisiveness since you can be quite slow to make up your own mind. Their way of working to provide an elegantly tasteful home and indulgent lifestyle suits you down to the ground. Where things could come unstuck is in their need to be distant and not physically intimate, as well as their rather superior view of your more earthy habits.

Your Taurus Moon to Their Scorpio Sun

Your moods would not exactly be in sync – you want to cuddle, they want to plot a conspiracy. They want a deeply passionate encounter just when you want to trim the hedge. But you do have an appreciation for their incredible determination, drive and staying power. Their secrecy would worry you, but on the other hand you are not invasive and are usually happy to leave them to do their thing. Both of you like a settled lifestyle.

Your Taurus Moon to Their Sagittarius Sun

Unless you have a fiery sun this will never work. You only purr with a contented, rooted life full of home comforts, cuddles and reliable mates with pension schemes. Sagittarians are great talkers and wonderfully inspirational but really fairly impractical at heart. You would constantly be pointing out the flaws in their schemes, calling them unrealistic and crushing their inspiration. They would fly away from your possessiveness.

Your Taurus Moon to Their Capricorn Sun

Happy as bunnies down a burrow, this works well – with one proviso. You admire their earthy initiative, practical ambitions and way of setting long-term goals. You are equally a long-distance runner, though lazier at heart. What could be a problem is their over-serious, rather judgemental approach to life, which will keep them away from your cuddles too much and cause them to frown on your indulgences.

Your Taurus Moon to Their Aquarius Sun

No. This would be a constant see-saw or tug of war. Certainly you appreciate their ability to stand solid in the face of change, but they are eccentric, oddball creatures while you are basically traditional at heart. They like to roam, to think, to talk endlessly and mull over madcap schemes. You would not understand their interests, which are ultra-modern and usually high tech. Your earthiness would eventually threaten to suffocate them.

Your Taurus Moon to Their Pisces Sun

You might suit them better than they suit you, but you could complement each other not badly. You would never understand their vague, impractical way of floundering through work – though they do seem to come up trumps more often than not. You would offer them a solid home base and all the physical comforts, though perhaps with a touch too much contact. You need to understand that they have the vision you lack slightly. So appreciate their creative flair and you could help them to turn dreams into reality.

Your Moon Is in Gemini

Your Gemini Moon to Their Aries Sun

You are more weighed down by boredom, lack of excitement and routine than anything else in the world, so they should suit you admirably. Their lives are a constant run of thrills, spills, adventures and noisy arguments. They have drive, ambition and real killer competitive instincts that you secretly admire though you lack these traits yourself. They will adore your witty chat.

Your Gemini Moon to Their Taurus Sun

You cannot by any stretch of your ingenuity see how to admire such a slow, placid (in your view dull), earthy creature. They think long term; you cannot think beyond the moment. You adore a constantly changing kaleidoscope of a life while they like it always the same. You would always be pouring scorn on their very solid virtues and talents, while they would make you feel fenced in, weighed down and possessed.

Your Gemini Moon to Their Gemini Sun

Wonderfully compatible. You admire their ability to hold down three jobs at once, keep up a witty flow of chat, maintain a wide circle of intriguing friends and have so many different interests. You need a versatile mate and this is it. You even have a sneaking admiration for their way of cutting corners and being opportunistic. You will never stop talking together.

Your Gemini Moon to Their Cancer Sun

You certainly appreciate their way of making it in the world with initiative, drive, creative flair and energy, even if you do not totally understand their methods. They have an emotional approach to work as well as home life and can be moody, which does not sit well with you. They will also make you feel fenced in. Their sense of security demands that they keep you close.

Your Gemini Moon to Their Leo Sun

You adore their flamboyance and all the excitement that goes with it, though you do not entirely understand their demanding need for constant attention. They may find your restless way of flitting around rather irksome. Your boredom threshold is much lower than theirs, which could cause friction. You are much less snobbish and could be guilty at times of cutting them down to size, which would not appeal.

Your Gemini Moon to Their Virgo Sun

Your moods would often be out of tune but you both share a basic fidgetiness that could draw you together. Neither of you likes boredom or standing still too long. You do not quite understand their conscientious need to doublecheck all work 16 times or to be quite so helpful. But they are not jealous and would not make you feel trapped. You would never be short of conversation.

Your Gemini Moon to Their Libra Sun

You might envy their upwardly mobile ambitions in society but you do not share them. Certainly you would worry about their delicately balanced sensibilities. You like slightly more robust types. Nevertheless you appreciate their initiative, drive, determination and ambition. They would not always take to your way of shocking others with your wonderfully direct opinions that sometimes rock the boat.

Your Gemini Moon to Their Scorpio Sun

You loathe their way of trying to possess you, but you have a sneaking admiration for their way of driving hard for success, cutting corners if need be and pulling the right strings to make their miracles work. You quite like a walk on the wild side and will happily supply them with ideas, knowing full well that your enthusiasm span is too short for you to make them work. At the end of the day, however, you are different energies.

Your Gemini Moon to Their Sagittarius Sun

You share similar outlooks in life and wide-ranging interests. You adore their constant up-beat enthusiasm for almost everything they are involved in. Your moods would not always be in tune since you are opposite signs in the zodiac. When you wanted to be together, they would want to work. When you wanted to have a stimulating chat they could be full of fiery passion. Neither of you is possessive.

Your Gemini Moon to Their Capricorn Sun

You appreciate their drive, ambition, determination and resourcefulness, though you think them a mite too serious and too conscientious. You would not object when they exhibited a ruthless desire to get to where they want, since you have been known to cut corners yourself. They suit half of your needs but do not quite fulfil the bright, reckless, fun-loving half of you. They would think you shallow and unreliable.

Your Gemini Moon to Their Aquarius Sun

Just what you want – someone as flighty, chatty and devil-may-care as yourself. You would back them up to the hilt in their madcap schemes and ultra-modern ideas and would never feel hemmed in because they are as distant as you. You would wonder slightly at their staying power, since they are more fixed than you, but their range of interests is so wide that you would never become bored. They would appreciate your bright, inventive ideas.

Your Gemini Moon to Their Pisces Sun

You will be permanently perplexed at the way their minds work, even though they are as adaptable as you. They never seem to think matters through. They intuit and float their way through life. Both of you are off the ground, though in different ways. They would probably not satisfy your need for constant intellectual stimulation; you might feel to them a little cool and cutting.

Your Moon Is in Cancer

Your Cancer Moon to Their Aries Sun

You have a distant admiration for their flair, drive and ambition in the outside world, but you are not remotely nourished by their ruthless way of trampling over the competition and your more tender feelings. They create a noise and unrest that make your head ache and your insecurities soar. You would make them feel trapped by your jealousy and swamped by the depths of your feelings.

Your Cancer Moon to Their Taurus Sun

You feel secure, contented and relaxed by their solid earthiness, their way of providing themselves and you with the worldly comforts, especially a settled home base. You do not always appreciate their obstinacy and slow, rather lazy pace of attacking work problems. You really want a mate with more drive and initiative. Neither of you minds the other's jealousy.

Your Cancer Moon to Their Gemini Sun

Not a good pairing, since you like the 'wrap-round' factor and they want total freedom. You admire mates who have ambition, resourcefulness and determination. They can certainly be opportunists, but that is hardly the same thing. They are too restless, too much jack-of-all-trades to make you feel really secure. Your possessiveness and emotional intensity would make them nervy. You need a mate with creative flair, not just intellectual ingenuity.

Your Cancer Moon to Their Cancer Sun

Happy as two crabs together by the seashore you fit each other like hand and glove. You appreciate their creative flair, drive, ambition and initiative out in the world, which is all directed towards setting up a settled home base. They will appreciate your tender love, care and support at the end of a hard day. You understand each other's moodiness and hyper-sensitivity to criticism. You will soothe each other.

Your Cancer Moon to Their Leo Sun

You adore their flamboyant, extravagant lifestyle, upmarket
friends, position in society and their desire to settle with a family.
You do not understand why they have to be quite so grand or so
pretentious. Their rather self-centred way of grabbing all the
attention will not make you feel loved and wanted. They will not
really understand your needs. A 5 out of 10.

Your Cancer Moon to Their Virgo Sun

You admire their quiet, refined, conscientious, practical way of
going about their career. They never let anyone down or cut
corners. You may not quite understand why they have to be so
pernickety about details, but at least you will never feel insecure.
Their self-sufficiency may at times make you feel cut out but they
are warm, self-sacrificing and keen to be of service. Eating with
them will be a shared pleasure.

Your Cancer Moon to Their Libra Sun

Your moods may be out of sync and they will at times seem cool,
detached and too unemotional, but you are nourished by many
of the things they also crave. Both of you like a good home life.
You bring comfort and love. They bring taste, elegance and
harmony. You do admire their initiative, ambition and energy out
in the world. They make things happen without creating too
many waves. They certainly need a mate in life, though not a
possessive one.

Your Cancer Moon to Their Scorpio Sun

You are nourished to some extent by all their emotional intensity,
courage, determination and deep, dark ambition. But you are
wary of their stinging remarks, which can wound you to the
quick. Although this is a highly emotional connection you will

never totally understand what goes on in their hidden depths – and the sulks in your relationship could be long and brooding.

Your Cancer Moon to Their Sagittarius Sun

No. Not a happy mating. You want a lover with initiative, ambition and a self-starting mechanism. They are certainly fire-flies, but they tend to race around agitatedly with their heads in the clouds rather than focus on the central goal. They will also resent being forced to be practical or hand money over to set up home. You will make them feel fenced in and rather swamped by your feelings, which they will not understand. Their blunt opinions will have you in the vapours.

Your Cancer Moon to Their Capricorn Sun

You certainly appreciate their ambition, determination and initiative and very much respect their conscientiousness. Both of you like upwardly mobile friends, are traditionalists at heart and like the grand lifestyle. But you need a mate who comes home occasionally, not one who works a 90-hour week. You always want sensitive handling because you are so emotional, while Capricorns they can be cold, even ruthless at times, when it comes to getting their own way.

Your Cancer Moon to Their Aquarius Sun

In no way! You give each other the horrors. You admire traditional values while they are unreconstructed hippies, boffins or at least state-of-the-art merchants. They adore being eccentric, standing out as individuals at all costs, which will make you wince with embarrassment. You clutch and cling, which will make them flee. Life to you is about relationship. An enjoyable life to them means avoiding too much intimacy.

Your Cancer Moon to Their Pisces Sun

An adorable mix, though you may slightly object to Pisceans' rather vague way of proceeding in the world. But you admire their creativity and their intuition, which is often inspired, and their sensitive way of handling work relationships as well as you. You can help them find more ambition and drive without frightening them. With the happy home base you provide they will have more courage.

Your Moon Is in Leo

Your Leo Moon to Their Aries Sun

A maybe yes, maybe no combination, this. You certainly admire their fiery drive in the world, their competitive, adventurous spirit and, if their need to win makes them successful, their ability to provide you with a sumptuous lifestyle. But what nourishes you most is being centre of attention and being allowed to take the credit for all the successes going. They are not going to tread delicately round your fragile ego and your vanity. They are certainly not going to hand over the winner's rosette meekly to you.

Your Leo Moon to Their Taurus Sun

On the up side you appreciate their tenacity, their staying power and their practical skills, which you almost totally lack. But you are both hugely stubborn and you loathe giving way. Taurus can also be rather basic and earthy, which does not suit your need for grandness. You would much prefer a mate who was a high-flying person of some social standing. Taurus could not care less about appearances. Your mate would taunt you about your unrealistic streak and your arrogance.

Your Leo Moon to Their Gemini Sun

You certainly appreciate Geminis' versatile talents and way of making a success in life, though you do not always adore their way of cutting corners. At times you fear they could cause you minor humiliation because they do not care about social respectability, which you do, deeply. They can dent your pride by being too blunt at times and maybe even by wandering off. Rejection makes you crumple.

Your Leo Moon to Their Cancer Sun

Leos have the drive, initiative, creative flair and resourcefulness in their career which you adore. They also mix in rather upmarket circles, which suits you down to the ground. You will not understand their moodiness or rather emotional way of approaching work problems. They will not understand your need for constant exclusive attention. They quite like to be noticed as well.

Your Leo Moon to Their Virgo Sun

Virgos are not nearly grand enough nor flamboyant enough at work for you really to appreciate their meticulous talents. On the other hand they will not be grabbing the spotlight from you and will sort out the tedious, practical details of your life. Their adaptability and willingness to be of service will turn them into a willing slave, but at the end of the day you are highly different energies.

Your Leo Moon to Their Libra Sun

A wonderfully compatible mix. You love Libra's resourceful, energetic, ambitious way in the world that still manages to be graceful and well bred. Librans are good at adapting to the needs of others and will put themselves out considerably for you. Both of you love a grand lifestyle, good taste and snobbish friends. They will happily allow you to be centre of attention and their diplomatic, peace-loving side will mean they never dent your vanity.

Your Leo Moon to Their Scorpio Sun

Not a superbly compatible combination, this. You will certainly appreciate Scorpio's staying power, stamina and hard-driving ambition. But you cannot understand Scorpio's overwhelming need for power and secrecy or its desire to manipulate. Scorpios could not care less whether they get attention or not (which you do), as long as they hold the whip. Their stinging tongue will reduce your fragile ego to a deflated balloon at times. Both of you are hugely stubborn.

Your Leo Moon to Their Sagittarius Sun

You applaud your Sagittarian's courage, way of following fantasies and idealistic aspirations. You even forgive the unrealistic ideas that are not grounded in common sense. But you wince at the sharp opinions that do not always take into account your tender ego. You hate criticism. Sagittarians never stop to think of the effect of what they say. They will adapt to your obstinacy. But they may also fly away.

Your Leo Moon to Their Capricorn Sun

You find Capricorn's ambitions to rise to the top of the pile admirable in the extreme. Both of you are traditional, rather snobbish and always mix in the best circles. Your need for attention may cause you to complain when your Capricorn spends long hours at the office, so it can be a cooler combination than you might like. But you cannot have it all ways. Capricorns have been known to be stingy, so they may complain about your extravagances.

Your Leo Moon to Their Aquarius Sun

Not in a million years. You cannot envisage how anyone could have such oddball ideas about work. You respect power, prestige, status and a glowing reputation. Aquarians thrive on humanitarian ideals and madcap schemes that would make you feel the laughing stock of the neighbourhood. Both of you are stubborn and would not give way. They would scorn your extravagances and deride your need to be so grand.

Your Leo Moon to Their Pisces Sun

You will support Pisceans to the hilt if they are successful. They are superbly intuitive and can sometimes turn their dreams into reality. But if they are a vague, wispy, timid non-triers you are not the one to support their tentative efforts. They certainly will not be able to provide you with the lifestyle you need. Certainly they are elegant, sympathetic, kind creatures who will adapt to your needs – but you need a regal mate of position in the world who can reflect well on you.

Your Moon Is in Virgo

Your Virgo Moon to Their Aries Sun

You respect hard workers with practical common sense who are conscientious and helpful. So this is hardly going to fit. You have picked a reckless adventurer who certainly can be successful but who never seems to take time to think, let alone plan. Ariens have been known to push the competition ruthlessly aside and they take great pleasure in winning. Their egocentricity makes you wince, though you could do with more of it yourself. You would nag them endlessly. They would run eventually.

Your Virgo Moon to Their Taurus Sun

All that earthy strength, solidity and common sense makes you purr. You envy Taureans' staying power, which you lack, though at times you may find them a touch ponderous and lazy. You adapt where they are obstinate. They have an honesty and straightforwardness that you find highly appealing and they never do anything that does not have a practical outcome. They smile benignly at your narking and are slow to rouse to irritation. Together you may find it difficult to get new projects rolling.

Your Virgo Moon to Their Gemini Sun

You light up at Gemini's quick wits, bright flow of ideas, snappy way with words and non-stop ability to keep three jobs on the go at once. What you are less chirpy about is its way of cutting corners sometimes at work, its impracticality and short-lived enthusiasms. You are fidgety. Geminis can seem like jacks-of-all-trades, which is not your style. They do not understand your obsessive need for order.

Your Virgo Moon to Their Cancer Sun

You appreciate Cancer's resourcefulness, initiative, creative flair and drive out in the world. Cancerians are not just home-loving recluses. Their moodiness and emotional way of approaching problems are, however, not yours, and can cause you to carp a little – especially when they fall foul of workmates. You think they brew up storms that are unnecessary. Your narking does not go down well, since they are deeply sensitive creatures.

Your Virgo Moon to Their Leo Sun

You look with awe and wonder at Leos' ability to grab all the spotlight for themselves (which you would never do) and their tendency to grab the credit even when they have not earned it.

You basically do not respect what drives them on, their need for status and importance. What is important to you is a job well done that helps others. They will hate your nit-picking and carping. Certainly you can be adaptable where they are stubborn and self-sacrificing, but neither of you is really suited to the other.

Your Virgo Moon to Their Virgo Sun

Ideal. You settle down and forget about nagging and worrying endlessly because you know your partner will do a job you can respect. Virgos probably work too hard, which means you see them less than you like, but that is better than having a lazy, unemployed lump who hangs round your neck all day. Together you will pin every last tiny detail down and never have the paperwork out of place. The tension levels could sometimes rise a little and you might be indecisive together.

Your Virgo Moon to Their Libra Sun

You do like Libra's elegant yet resourceful way of pushing its ambitions in the world. Librans may not always be as practical as you would like but they are hard-working, fair-minded and generally try to keep the peace. They will appreciate your helpful comments about detail, though will not like being nagged because it ruffles their calm. They love your ability to keep order at home, which makes them feel that life is in balance.

Your Virgo Moon to Their Scorpio Sun

Not an ideal match since you not understand Scorpio's driving need for power, habit of manipulating (which never seems to you quite straight) or in-built secrecy. You respect hard-working, conscientious types who do a job well for its own sake and try to serve others fairly. Scorpios scorn what they regard as obsessive principles, which yours would seem to them to be. You certainly would adapt to their rather obstinate ways, but maybe more out of fear than respect.

Your Virgo Moon to Their Sagittarius Sun

You certainly appreciate Sagittarians' wide-ranging ideas and intellectually stimulating approach. You even slightly envy their eternal optimism – but you have scant respect for their unrealistic, devil-may-care approach that often leaves jobs half done. Your constant need for order and endless worrying about detail would eventually weigh them down and dry up their inspiration.

Your Virgo Moon to Their Capricorn Sun

An earth moon to an earth sun has distinct possibilities. You both share a respect for hard work, the practicalities of life and, when there is time, the indulgences of the body. You will not always have as much of Capricorns as you want because they are workaholics, even more than you. They can also be a touch sombre in their younger years, which makes you anxious. You dislike their ruthlessness and attitude that the ends justify the means. They will never sympathize with your endless worrying.

Your Virgo Moon to Their Aquarius Sun

There are few common factors here at all. You appreciate the solid, traditional virtues in life while Aquarians are wild, eccentric, ultra-modern and not very grounded. Certainly you appreciate those who serve the world and they often are humanitarian. But you wince at their need to stand out as individuals and their uncompromising way of not bending to circumstance. They will fly away if you nag at them or try to tidy them up.

Your Virgo Moon to Their Pisces Sun

Successful Pisceans may be, but you will worry endlessly about how in their impractical muddle they manage to get results at all, never mind repeat them. You will be constantly trying to bring order to their chaos, which will help them but may not be entirely nourishing and relaxing for you. They are sympathetic and caring at heart, which will soothe you. You may do more for them than they for you.

Your Moon Is in Libra

Your Libra Moon to Their Aries Sun

You basically respect people who are nice, fair in their dealings, diplomatic and do not make too much of a rumpus. So this is hardly going to work. Ariens crash through life being abrasively competitive and sweeping social niceties aside in their fight to be the winner. You would be on tenterhooks in your social life about what clanger they were going to drop next. They would dismiss your comments with scorn.

Your Libra Moon to Their Taurus Sun

Taurus' pace of operation will make your teeth ache but, unless they are thoroughly rough, you do appreciate Taureans' pleasant, steadfast approach and their taste in the comforts of life. They can be lazier than you appreciate but they will bring practical common sense to your rather up-in-the-head life. Sex may be a problem since they need constant physical reassurance while you do not.

Your Libra Moon to Their Gemini Sun

You like Gemini's bright, sparkling wit, flow of ideas and wonderful ways with words. But you are not sure whether you really respect its jack-of-all-trades versatility. You certainly do not appreciate the way certain Geminis cut corners or are less than straightforward in their dealings. They will pour scorn on your social ambitions and need for everything to be so nice all the time. They quite like walking on the wild side.

Your Libra Moon to Their Cancer Sun

Your moods will be out of sync and Cancerians may clutch more than you like, but you do admire their ambition, drive, energy and creative flair out in the world. They are not just stay-at-home creatures. Basically you do not understand their emotional moodiness or way of blowing up storms of misunderstandings with workmates. They are hyper-sensitive where you would suppress your vulnerabilities just to keep the peace. They find you cool but adore you.

Your Libra Moon to Their Leo Sun

Terribly grand together. You adore Leo's extravagant lifestyle, classy friends and high social status. Leos may be stubborn, prickly and rather arrogant but your diplomacy can cope and they do have warm-hearted moments. You could wish that they showed more initiative. They can be very fixed. They will like your way of adapting to their needs, your well-bred manners and elegant tastes.

Your Libra Moon to Their Virgo Sun

You appreciate people who are hard-working, refined and do not make waves. Virgos may be a little dull for your rather more colourful, social tastes, but it is not a bad match. When you throw parties they will do the work. They will not embarrass you by being too ruthless, dishonest or manipulative at work. They will appreciate your way of soothing them peacefully at the end of a long day. Neither of you is over-emotional.

Your Libra Moon to Their Libra Sun

Ideal. You adore similar things, have the same aims in life and fit together like hand in glove. You like people who have social aspirations and energy, drive, initiative and creative flair. You need a mate you can converse with, who thinks deeply. Librans are wise and just though a touch indecisive, which you understand. This will be a slightly cool contact, so you must watch when the stormy times come. Neither of you likes handling difficult feelings.

Your Libra Moon to Their Scorpio Sun

Not really. You like 'nice', well-bred, straightforward people who have justice as their aim. Scorpios certainly work hard, which you appreciate, but they can be dark, devious and manipulative about gaining their end – which is power. You will hate being dragged into their emotional depths. You like a colourful, glittering life on the surface where all is calm and harmony. They will pour scorn on what they see as your superficiality.

Your Libra Moon to Their Sagittarius Sun

Conversations will sparkle until your Sagittarian starts voicing over-blunt opinions, but there certainly is an intellectual rapport and a shared interest in the fate of society. You appreciate the Sagittarian mind. But you are not relaxed by its sometimes crazy lifestyle, short-lived enthusiasms and rather reckless approach to career matters. You prefer a steadier, more respectable type. Sagittarians will not understand your hyper-sensitivity to other people's opinion and will tell you so in no uncertain manner. Your friends will be very different.

Your Libra Moon to Their Capricorn Sun

Cool but workable. You appreciate Capricorn's hard work, initiative, determination and ambition. You loathe lazy loafers who sponge through life. Both of you are traditionalists at heart and slightly snobbish, so you will share an elegant home, classy friends and a professionally useful social life. Capricorns work too hard and too long; you can be too laid back and unemotional. The relationship could eventually wither away from lack of attention and warmth.

Your Libra Moon to Their Aquarius Sun

An air moon to an air sign should work, but you are very unlike Aquarius. You want niceness, social approval, an elegant home, classy friends and status in the community. Aquarians genuinely love being the oddball, have no social ambitions whatsoever and will happily mix with anyone from tramps to kings. They would embarrass you with their eccentricities. You like to fit in harmoniously. They make a strenuous effort not to. You will converse well at the beginning but it will not last.

Your Libra Moon to Their Pisces Sun

This can be just OK. Pisceans are not as resourceful or dynamic as you might like but they can have a way of floating intuitively towards success. You are nourished by their creative flair, their sympathy, caring and adaptability. You will like them if they do rise to the top but will not be so happy if they stay wispy, timid and reclusive. You need standing in the eyes of the world. They will appreciate your way of creating peace at home.

Your Moon Is in Scorpio

Your Scorpio Moon to Their Aries Sun

No. These are really opposite personalities with contradictory needs and desires. You are deep, dark, secretive and rather respect people who aim for power and are strategic, even devious. Ariens are open and straightforward, crashing ahead with little forethought and less planning – never mind tactics. They can be successful since they like winning but they are not ultimately concerned with power. They also wander and hate being possessed, so your jealous side would never be at peace.

Your Scorpio Moon to Their Taurus Sun

You understand and admire Taurus' persistence though question its application at times. Taureans can be lazy. Both of you are hugely stubborn and neither gives way easily. They do not quite have the edge of wit or cunning that you like and, irritatingly, will not be manipulated by you. Both of you can be deeply passionate, though you are sexual in a feeling way where they are sexual in a highly physical way. They will certainly supply you with comforts aplenty.

Your Scorpio Moon to Their Gemini Sun

You may initially be attracted to Gemini's dark side, agile wit, cunning and way of handling problems by bending every which way. But at the end of the day you will find Geminis too superficial, too changeable, lacking in staying power and absent of any real intuitive understanding of life. You need a more intense mate who can share your turbulent depths. Your jealousy would be set off by their wandering eye. Their need not to be fenced in would eventually cause a break.

Your Scorpio Moon to Their Cancer Sun

You really appreciate Cancerians' creative flair, ambition and resourcefulness out in the world, as well as their interest in setting up a happy family base. Their interests are shorter lived than you might like. They are great starters, not such great finishers – but they do have more initiative than you, which helps. Your emotional sensitivities are highly compatible so you can be of help to them and they will protect your vulnerabilities and not betray you.

Your Scorpio Moon to Their Leo Sun

No. What you admire Leos do not represent. What they like revolts you. You need a powerful mate of cunning, wit, strength and persuasiveness. Leo is open, attention-seeking, an entertainer at heart and will seem naïvely puffed up or empty to you. You will never understand why they put appearances above everything else when you know it is what goes on behind the scenes that really counts. They will distrust the depths of your feelings, will assume you are always manipulating (rightly) and shy clear of your ruthlessness.

Your Scorpio Moon to Their Virgo Sun

You need a partner to grapple with and self-sufficient Virgo may not be quite it. Certainly you respect Virgos' earthy persistence, their hard work and their way with details. But you find them tediously straitlaced at work and elsewhere. They want to be of service and refuse to manipulate or get involved in a power struggle to win. You need a mate who is willing to walk in the mud to find the gold nuggets. They seem too fastidious. They are fearful of your emotional depths and your stinging tongue.

Your Scorpio Moon to Their Libra Sun

Absolutely not. Librans are colourful, bright, straightforward, fair-minded and live life on the surface. You live life in the depths and respect those who are willing to work in secret and are good tacticians, willing to cut corners if necessary to gain power. Librans are too scared of losing social approval to do anything as risky and will loathe your stinging tongue. They need relationships but nothing too emotional or sexual.

Your Scorpio Moon to Their Scorpio Sun

A match made, if not in heaven, then certainly in your favourite place. You adore Scorpio's strength, determination to work miracles against all the odds, its cunning and ruthlessness. You also share a wildly sentimental outlook on family matters. Jealousy and obstinacy are the greatest drawbacks, since neither of you budges or lets go. But then neither of you minds a good tussle. Scorpios will give you all the passion you ever wanted.

Your Scorpio Moon to Their Sagittarius Sun

Not a chance. Sagittarians are either heady intellectuals or flyaway adventurers. You respect neither greatly. People who think too much you dismiss as lightweight. Those who do not have staying power come even lower down your love list. They regard you with horror as a walking octopus with stinging tentacles. They want freedom, not to be possessed. They live on the cloud tops, not on the ocean floor.

Your Scorpio Moon to Their Capricorn Sun

Certainly you admire Capricorn's ambition, persistence, resourcefulness and way of getting to high positions of authority and power. But you do not appreciate a mate who works so hard you are always left home alone. Capricorns also incline to being chilly. They do have a sensual, indulgent side, but it is often repressed in favour of ambition. That is beyond your under-standing. They would not quite trust the depths of your feelings and would always be suspicious of your manipulative tendencies.

Your Scorpio Moon to Their Aquarius Sun

Not a hope. Aquarians represent most things you either do not understand or cannot respect. Power is not on their agenda, neither are they cunning or ruthless. Certainly they have endurance, which you like, but basically they want to be one of a democratic group at work, not the one pulling the reins of control. They dislike your need to possess and will run from jealousy at the drop of a hat.

Your Scorpio Moon to Their Pisces Sun

You can help them but they probably do little to relax you. Pisceans can either be intuitive, creative successes in the world, though impractical, or they can be vague, wispy, frightened non-triers. The latter you would dismiss with contempt, and even the former you would forever be chivvying to make them stand up straighter and fight harder. They would care for you though shrink from your acid tongue. Both of you can do better.

Your Moon Is in Sagittarius

Your Sagittarius Moon to Their Aries Sun

Your heart lifts at their fiery, adventurous escapades, their wild schemes that can end in high-flying successes and their crashing failures from which they dust themselves down and start again. Ariens are not thoughtful but they never, never fence you in. A fire moon and fire sun guarantee the interest levels and noise levels will be high and boredom will be kept at bay. Neither of you is tactful or practical.

Your Sagittarius Moon to Their Taurus Sun

No. You want an adventurer or a thinker. Someone who can soar in life. Taurus is rooted, placid, steady and very earthy. Taureans have long-term staying power which you cannot understand and write off as slowness. They would pour scorn on your brighter ideas as revenge for your blunt judgements of them. Their jealousy would make you feel fenced in and your wandering feet would give them a fit.

Your Sagittarius Moon to Their Gemini Sun

A wonderfully chatty pair, you would always be swapping titbits of information and discussing every subject under the sun.

Gemini's interests are slightly more superficial and shorter lived than yours but you genuinely respect this sign's constant energy and ability to hold down three jobs at once. You will be indecisive, impractical and rather harum-scarum together but you certainly will not be bored.

Your Sagittarius Moon to Their Cancer Sun

A fire moon and a water sun are not good news together. You do appreciate Cancer's energy, drive and creative flair in the outside world but never understand its emotional moodiness. Cancerians fall out with workmates and create storms in a teacup that you cannot fathom. They also dislike your rather blunt opinions. Their jealousy and need to set up a settled family base will make you run. You do not want to be fenced in.

Your Sagittarius Moon to Their Leo Sun

A fire moon with a fire sun make for a spectacular firework display. You appreciate their flamboyance, their way of living an extravagant life. But you do not entirely understand their need to keep up appearances and their rather self-centred approach to work and life. You are more adaptable, fairly democratic and cut straight through the crap very sharply at times. Their fragile egos would deflate in a hurry.

Your Sagittarius Moon to Their Virgo Sun

Both of you are adaptable, which helps, and there are pros and cons. You genuinely admire Virgo's conscientious, practical way of working, which is absolutely not yours. Virgos can keep your life rolling along at an organization level, which is highly nourishing. But you do find them a little straitlaced, even dull. They do not feed your desire for excitement and adventure with their obsessive need for order and control. But they are self-sufficient and will never fence you in – though they will nag at your lack of realism.

Your Sagittarius Moon to Their Libra Sun

Can you keep your opinions toned down? Then this might just work, though Librans can be a touch too calm, harmonious and well-bred for your wilder tastes. You certainly appreciate their initiative, resourcefulness and ambition in the outside world. They have sharp minds and a shared interest with you in the fate of society, so conversations should be deep and meaningful. But they can be a touch snobbish, which you are not. On the up side they are unemotional and will not fence you in.

Your Sagittarius Moon to Their Scorpio Sun

No. You want a high flier, a straightforward, maybe reckless, certainly intellectual mate. You will envy but not understand Scorpio's staying power, which you lack, and certainly dislike its secrecy, cunning and manipulative way of getting power. You hate being crowded or possessed anywhere in your life. Scorpio will make you feel overwhelmed. You both in different ways have sharp opinions. The arguments would flare.

Your Sagittarius Moon to Their Sagittarius Sun

Ideal. You adore Sagittarius' bright mind and wide spread of ideas and share the love of travel. You approve of the idealistic Sagittarian way of tackling career matters, which may not always be realistic but is usually straightforward. Neither of you is practical, which may cause problems, but you are happy to muddle through. Conversation will never be lacking and neither of you will trap the other.

Your Sagittarius Moon to Their Capricorn Sun

A basic optimist with a basic pessimist is not usually a happy match. You certainly appreciate Capricorn's energy, initiative, drive and resourcefulness at work, though you seriously question whether anyone needs to put in those hours just for the sake of turning a buck. You are not as materialistic as they and Capricorns can be hugely judgemental about your lack of practical skills or realistic ambitions.

Your Sagittarius Moon to Their Aquarius Sun

An appreciative mix since you like their eccentricity and complete disinterest in social approval. Aquarians are real one-offs who do their thing for their own sake. They are more determined than you, with more staying power, but you are adaptable so that should not matter. Conversations will always sparkle since both of you have wide interests and a genuine feeling for humanity and the future of society.

Your Sagittarius Moon to Their Pisces Sun

An adaptable pair you can bend to each other – but you will not understand Pisces' lack of courage or pushing power. You basically admire heroes who can go out into the world to make it happen. Pisceans can be successful but they do it obliquely by avoiding confrontations. You will not understand their emotional intuition either, though it often matches your fiery intuition. You would not find them straightforward enough, while your bluntness would make them wince.

Your Moon Is in Capricorn

Your Capricorn Moon to Their Aries Sun

You certainly need an ambitious, resourceful mate who will not fuss if you are never home. Ariens fit this bill. But you really do not admire their rather slapdash, none too realistic way of proceeding. They leap into action without forethought or planning, which offends your cautious nature. They can be lucky but you feel in the depths of your soul they have not earned it by solid toil. They would get cross with your eternally pessimistic outlook and certainly could not teach you to love yourself better.

Your Capricorn Moon to Their Taurus Sun

You adore their earthy practicality and steadiness and rather envy Taureans their way of providing themselves with every comfort under the sun, which you feel is too decadent for you. But they are lazier than you which brings on your stern, disapproving face and they are hugely stubborn. They could teach you to value yourself more by relaxing with your favourite indulgences, but only if you would let them. They certainly do not feel unworthy like you. They reckon they deserve it. Not a bad match.

Your Capricorn Moon to Their Gemini Sun

Not wonderful, although you do appreciate Gemini's energy in tackling so many tasks at once. Geminis certainly will not complain if you work non-stop, which you sometimes do since you never feel worthy of love unless you achieve. You really do not admire their flip approach to career matters and to your way of sometimes cutting corners. You also want social respectability, which is not high on their list of priorities.

Your Capricorn Moon to Their Cancer Sun

You certainly admire their drive, get-up-and-go in the outside world. Cancerians are by no manner of means the stay-at-home cooks and knitters they sometimes have a reputation for being. Their emotional moodiness leaves you cold, but then your slightly hard-edged approach unsettles them. It is not ideal since they would resent being left when you skipped off to work.

Your moods would always be a little out of sync. But it could be worse.

Your Capricorn Moon to Their Leo Sun

You warm to their grand ways and confident approach. Both of you are traditionalists and rather upmarket in ambition, so you would appreciate Leo's way of introducing you to the right people. Your rather stingy streak would not remotely appreciate their extravagances, which can be monumental. But never criticize. Their vanity will not take it. They would not teach you to love yourself – except by example: they love themselves so much some of their approach might rub off on you.

Your Capricorn Moon to Their Virgo Sun

You purr with approval about their quiet, conscientious, practical, workaholic approach to career matters. It is almost on a par with your own. Except that you crave position and possessions. Virgos just like serving others. They are adaptable and would not stand in your way. Your vision (or slight lack of it) is a shared trait and both of you will always work with a purpose to a tangible end. They are refined and will not embarrass you. But the relationship could be cool, too businesslike.

Your Capricorn Moon to Their Libra Sun

You are basically after the same aims in life, which helps. You never feel quite loved or wanted and their tactful but rather detached way of handling relationships will help you gain self-esteem. You certainly appreciate their resourcefulness, initiative and hard-working streak. Especially after the age of 29, Librans buckle to with a will. It could end up a cool pairing, however, since neither of you is good at feelings.

Your Capricorn Moon to Their Scorpio Sun

You certainly appreciate their determination to go at all costs for what they want careerwise. Little is allowed to stand in their way, and even if you would not use the same cunning you certainly think the end justifies the means. But you need to be more in your feelings and your body for this to work well. Scorpios are not just determined careerists, they are also highly intense sexual beings who live in the turbulent depths you normally avoid.

Your Capricorn Moon to Their Sagittarius Sun

You tend to gloom, Sagittarians enthuse. You like hard, dedicated workers. They fly through life at speed, not always with much common sense. They are certainly not practical. They can be highly intellectual or woolly idealists, but you wonder if all these ideas have any real purpose. Your conscientious need to work long hours will suit them because they hate being hemmed in. But you are judgemental of their faults. You are not really in tune.

Your Capricorn Moon to Their Capricorn Sun

Same sign suns and moons should be an ideal pairing but in your case there are dangers – two workaholics never meeting, two pessimists stoking up each other's self-doubt and gloom. Certainly you will have endless respect for your Capricorn's achievements and steady rise in the world, which will perhaps even give you the social position you crave. But you need to watch you are not too narrow in your vision of the world together, maybe too materialistic.

Your Capricorn Moon to Their Aquarius Sun

This has one thing going for it – you may never be home because you are a workaholic and an Aquarian will never notice because the house will be full of friends. You are not basically compatible since you are a traditionalist – a snob, even – and highly practical while Aquarians are democratic egalitarians who have no sense of their social position. They are more tolerant than you of the world's lame ducks and humanitarian/eco/green causes. They would also embarrass you with their oddball ways and friends.

Your Capricorn Moon to Their Pisces Sun

Their impracticality and vague approach to work will drive you spare, but Pisceans are refined, kind, adaptable souls who can sometimes be miraculously successful, which would suit you. Their lack of confidence exasperates you because you are fairly hard-driving, but they would in gentle ways teach you to value yourself more. You could help them greatly at work with your earthy sense of organization.

Your Moon Is in Aquarius

Your Aquarius Moon to Their Aries Sun

You appreciate their courage, sparkle and sense of adventure but are rather contemptuous of their lack of staying power. Ariens are great starters and terrible finishers while you really like partners who get on track and stay there. They are more ruthless than you appreciate. You are a humanitarian, democratic soul while they are out-and-out winners – me first. They love your independent stance and lack of jealousy, but perhaps they might want for more passion.

Your Aquarius Moon to Their Taurus Sun

Not a happy match. You certainly do appreciate their staying power and stamina but their aims seem so rooted, so materialistic. Taureans would not give you any sense of inspiration, idealistic vision or humanitarian purpose behind their aims, and these considerations are all-important to you. Plus you like expansive, uncommitted relationships. They are possessive, jealous and hate insecurity. Your flightiness would give them nightmares.

Your Aquarius Moon to Their Gemini Sun

A zippy, chatty combination. You adore their bright, witty, agile minds and slick way with words. You may envy their way of doing three jobs at once. What you do not totally respect is their Neptunian way of approaching career matters, which can be evasive, rather slippery and fairly opportunistic at times. You would prefer a steadier, more straightforward way. Geminis will certainly not make you feel hemmed in, nor will the conversation ever flag, but it could all be too cool.

Your Aquarius Moon to Their Cancer Sun

You admire anyone who can get results, which with Cancer's energy, initiative and resourcefulness is very possible. But you do not understand the emotional moodiness that can brew up storms in a teacup with workmates. Cancerians' need for a happy home base can make you feel restricted and tied, though they are not always keen on highly exclusive relationships as long as they have the family around. Your blunt, abrasive, not always sensitive way of expressing yourself can cause trouble since they hurt easily.

Your Aquarius Moon to Their Leo Sun

You respect their steadiness, staying power and persistence but not much else. Their need to be flamboyant, grand, extravagant and always centre of attention passes you by completely. Leos are egocentric where you are egalitarian. You like being part of a democratic group; they want to be monarch. They want you to be at their feet all the time; you like space. Your outspoken opinions would offend them deeply. Your moods would always be out of sync.

Your Aquarius Moon to Their Virgo Sun

You really admire those who have the courage to be pioneers, to stand out as oddballs if necessary to fight for a just cause. Virgos will be self-sacrificing and serve others but they can be rather timid, self-effacing and slightly straitlaced for your tastes. You do not understand their obsessive need to double-check every detail; they certainly wince at some of your tactics. The conversations will be good because both of you are thinkers and communicators.

Your Aquarius Moon to Their Libra Sun

An air moon to an air sun should work well, except that your rather unconventional needs and approach does not suit their terribly traditional, slightly class-conscious way of living. You admire their thoughtful minds and their interest in justice. You appreciate their coolness and lack of jealousy. But you do not really take to their seemingly superficial social outlook. Librans want everyone to be harmonious, well-bred and well-washed. You adore oddballs, hippies – all of life's rich mix.

Your Aquarius Moon to Their Scorpio Sun

Not in a million years. You give each other nightmares. Scorpios have a deep, dark, secretive, power-hungry, manipulative way of going about their career aims and love lives. You want space, the truth out in the open, no ties and ambitions that do not include getting others under your thumb. Their jealousy would haunt you and you would raise their hackles instantly because you shy clear of exclusive relationships. You are both stubborn and neither would ever give way.

Your Aquarius Moon to Their Sagittarius Sun

An air moon to a fire sun promises plenty of sparkle, excitement, noise and good conversation, especially here since Sagittarians have wide-ranging intellectual interests and a quite philosophical approach to life that suits you down to the ground. You do not entirely appreciate their rather restless approach to work. They never seem to stay long on track. But they will never make you feel hemmed in and even your abrasive opinions will wash over them.

Your Aquarius Moon to Their Capricorn Sun

Not a total success since you do not appreciate their traditionalist lifestyle and upmarket aims. You also find them too materialistic and not caring enough about the philosophical issues that appeal to you. Certainly Capricorns are never going to crowd you since they work such long hours. You will be free to wander. But you will never agree on friends. They like the leaders in the community. You adore oddballs, eccentrics and pioneers.

Your Aquarius Moon to Their Aquarius Sun

Ideal except that you may not meet very often. Both of you adore being one of a crowd or being out there doing your own thing. When your paths do cross the conversation will be lively, inventive and inspired. You like their steadiness, their way of disregarding convention to push ahead with the ideas they consider important. Neither of you is jealous but both of you are hugely stubborn.

Your Aquarius Moon to Their Pisces Sun

You cannot understand their vague, meandering way of proceeding in the world. Certainly Pisceans can be successful, but you can never quite work out how. You do share a similar interest in helping to make the world a better place, but you are very different types. They will not make you feel hemmed in because they disappear so frequently into their day-dreams they may not notice your absence. Your sharp, sometimes tactless opinions may upset them.

Your Moon Is in Pisces

Your Pisces Moon to Their Aries Sun

You would be a quivering wreck within a week! You adore deeply sensitive, creative, kind, sympathetic souls. Ariens hash, crash and bash their way through life in a fiery way, rather inconsiderate of the needs of others. You might envy their courage, dash and resilience in the face of setbacks because they just bounce back. But they certainly do not nourish you where you need it most. You would withdraw into your shell and never come out. They would get exasperated – if they noticed at all.

Your Pisces Moon to Their Taurus Sun

You adore their earthy solidity and their protectiveness. Even their jealousy makes you feel wanted. But you are not sure you want quite so much physical attention. You are highly different personalities so this is a complementary match. Taureans could help you by being practical. You are adaptable so will not stand in their way, though you can feel a martyr. They are fairly self-indulgent and this could ultimately prove a problem since your needs, where they differed, would not even be considered.

Your Pisces Moon to Their Gemini Sun

You love agile minds, versatile talents and restless souls, so Geminis suit you admirably though they can be a touch cool, detached and unemotional. You both have a fairly intuitive approach to career matters, so neither of you is practical. Neither of you is great at making decisions, either. But the drawback is that they will not stay around to give you the protection you need. Their wandering feet will drive you back into your day-dreams.

Your Pisces Moon to Their Cancer Sun

Lovely. You envy their initiative, drive and creative flair out in the world. Cancerians make it all happen where you can be rather wandered and vague. Their nest-building tendencies and emotional sensitivities will give you all the sympathetic protection you ask for. You are adaptable so will equally care for their needs. Neither of you is desperate to have a totally exclusive relationship, so that is fine as well.

Your Pisces Moon to Their Leo Sun

You adore the tinge of glamour, romance and adventure about their lives. Leos tend to try to live out their fantasies where you just dream yours. You positively envy (though you do not understand) their way of pushing themselves forward to grab all the attention. You can adapt to their egocentric ways but you will end up getting precious little in return at times, since they assume you are there solely for their needs.

Your Pisces Moon to Their Virgo Sun

Opposite signs do not always complement each other, but you two probably do. Both of you are sensitive and refined. Virgos have a practical streak, which you lack, and can help to give you a place in the world. They do nark on and worry almost as much as you, which is not helpful. But they are ultimately kind-hearted and want to serve. You can help them be more creative. They ground you. At times your moods will be out of sync.

Your Pisces Moon to Their Libra Sun

Lovely even though you are water to air. You want peace, bliss, harmony and taste in your life. So do Librans. You admire their drive, initiative, energy and ambition to get things done as gracefully as possible. They are not practical but they are good at starting new projects, which you are not. They will work hard to provide the good life for both of you. Their diplomacy means you will never feel attacked. Your kindness will help bring them in touch with their feelings.

Your Pisces Moon to Their Scorpio Sun

A water moon and water sun should be fine together, but you are terribly sensitive and Scorpios are fiercely robust. You look with awe on their iron determination, miracle-making talents and ruthlessness about getting power, all of which makes you wilt. As long as you can persuade yourself that their strong, manipulative talents are all being used for you and not against you, then you could manage nicely. But you would always be slightly suspicious. They are sentimental at home so would surprise you with kindness.

Your Pisces Moon to Their Sagittarius Sun

You love variety in life but whether all this noise, excitement and strong opinion is really what nourishes you is questionable. Deeply sensitive water and rather inconsiderate fire do not generally make a good mix. Sagittarians mean well but they have a way of putting their feet in their mouths or rubbing you up the wrong way. Their reckless way of approaching some work problems also does not make you feel protected. Neither of you is practical, which is a drawback.

Your Pisces Moon to Their Capricorn Sun

There are possibilities here but it is a cool match, with you perhaps being locked away at home while Capricorns work manically long hours. They will not always appreciate your vagueness and you will not always take kindly to their rather judgemental, materialistic approach to life. What it has going for it is their practical, earthy, ambitious side, which could provide the solid home and lifestyle within which you could feel protected.

Your Pisces Moon to Their Aquarius Sun

You feel for the suffering of the world while Aquarians actively work to help humanitarian causes. Neither of you wants (for different reasons) a really committed, exclusive relationship, so you will not mind if they wander off and they will not notice if you retreat into your dream world. But at the end of the day you are very different personalities. They may not give you quite enough emotional sustenance. They live in their heads, their ideas, their ideals and their inventive schemes.

Your Pisces Moon to Their Pisces Sun

Ideal. Two deeply emotionally sensitive souls clinging to each other. You understand their fears, phobias and anxieties and will help them to put their dreams into action. Pisceans need someone to give them practical help. You can't do this but you will give them inner confidence and admiration. They in turn will never laugh at your worries and pain. You are just tuned in to the same wavelength.

HOW THE GREAT MATE

*Sample Relationships
of the Rich and Famous*

Prince Charles

Scorpio Sun Taurus Moon

Intensely passionate, deeply private, very stubborn, rather sensual but also fairly split, Prince Charles can never quite get his head and his heart together. With his sun and moon in opposite zodiac signs he grew up seeing his parents as quite incompatible personalities. What they could not get together in their marriage he cannot get together in his head. What he wants romantically is never what he ought to be doing. Desire and duty fight an unending battle.

The tragedy for someone with as detached and downright cold a childhood as he had is that his Taurus moon craves physical contact. As a child he needed more cuddles than most yet he had a mother who put duty before her children. He was handled by paid nannies, then dispatched early to a brutally insensitive public school regime.

Both his highly sexual Scorpio sun and his earthy Taurus moon want intensely close relationships. He is looking for a soul mate though he will not find one until he learns to separate from his childhood and its destructive influences. All the intimate publicity surrounding his marriage and love affair must have been exceptionally difficult for his highly secretive Scorpio sun.

Princess Diana

Cancer Sun Aquarius Moon

Highly emotional yet very detached, home-loving yet terrified of intimate relationships, very jealous and quick to take offence, in her own way Princess Diana is as confused about herself as her now-estranged husband. Her Cancer sun makes her keen to set up family early, compulsively caring, rather moody and quick to take offence. Her separation from her mother in childhood must have been especially difficult for her and the arrival of the 'wicked stepmother' in the guise of Raine Spencer, the last straw.

Cancerians need mothering and find it difficult to cut the apron strings, but once they do they instantly set up a household of their own that they can organize. The women especially turn into matriarchs who like to rule the roost and want to turn out perfect children. Cancerians although they look motherly do not always produce happy, well-adjusted youngsters – Nancy Reagan and Rose Kennedy are two others.

Diana's Aquarius moon is frightened of anything too committed or close. Friends are preferable to intimate clinches. Certainly it wants to steer clear of physical passion. Aquarius does not like the flesh and despite her public cuddling she is not really tactile in private. Her inner conflict between mind and body has been fought out in her bulimia.

Their Relationship

Together his Scorpio sun and her Cancer sun are a good match, though her increasing power as she grew older was always going to be a problem. Scorpios are controlling and dislike being pushed around. Both of them are highly sensitive, rather sulky and over-impressionable to the slightest stimulus. When the going got tough he would dig his heels in while she would set her fertile mind to work at finding a new scenario in which to play queen bee.

Their moons are a plain disaster, both to each other and hers to his sun. His Taurus moon is stubborn, indulgent and wants constant physical reassurance. Her Aquarius moon is stubborn, distant and prefers kissing fingertips across a room than anything closer. His Scorpio sun views with complete horror her emotional needs because they are so far removed from his. His friendship with Camilla Parker Bowles must have been devastating for her Cancerian jealousy, but her Aquarius moon oddly would not really mind at all if it was let off the hook of too much intimacy. At the end of the day Charles' physical, sexual and spiritual needs are so compelling that no Aquarius moon was ever going to fulfil them.

Prince Andrew

Pisces Sun Scorpio Moon

An overwhelmingly emotional personality, he plays life by his gut instincts. With a water sun and water moon he is highly impressionable to the slightest stimulus and is much more at the mercy of his feelings than he ever lets on. Curiously he is the only one of the Royal children who has a balanced view of his parents. He grew up perceiving them as well matched and happy together – and indeed he was known as the 'loved' child, being the Queen's favourite. His Pisces sun makes him adaptable, at times rather timid or evasive but basically kind. He has creative potential, as his photography shows.

His tightly controlled Scorpio moon is, however, stubborn, deeply jealous and very turbulent – but takes great pride in never displaying the depths of its hurt. The breakdown of his marriage was not only a blow to his pride but also to his possessive nature. Sometimes very watery personalities find it easier to protect their feelings by serving in charitable or helping organizations rather than relating too closely. That way they can get nourished and still remain within their own self-protective cocoon.

Duchess of York

Libra Sun Aries Moon

An air/fire mix, Sarah is volatile, impulsive, over-excitable, extremely noisy and given to wild outbursts. She lacks contact with her feelings or with common sense. Libra women tend to be fairly 'masculine' and argumentative in their approach. They make good career women (à la Maggie Thatcher) but they do find it tricky to play the softer, more 'feminine', motherly roles in life. They are always their father's daughters. The Duchess does find it difficult to cope with the harsher side of life or to negotiate stormy emotional times. Her solution is to fly away.

With her insecure Aries moon in the opposite sign to her Libra sun she grew up in a split home with separated parents. So, like Prince Charles, she has great difficulty get her head and heart together. When she has settled with one partner she promptly fancies someone tastier across the fence. Never does she feel totally satisfied. She will probably always feel pulled in two opposite directions.

Their Relationship

Basically there was nothing in common that was ever going to hold these two together. At a pinch Libra sun and Pisces sun can make a go of it – they can share creative tastes together and are both reasonably kind souls. But the moons together are a disaster and neither moon fits the other's sun in any way. His Scorpio moon wants deep passion, sensuality and ongoing intimacy – in private. Her Aries moon has nightmares about being settled or possessed. Tranquillity makes her feel ill and she is not well connected to her body or her physical passions. Certainly lust will flare for a brief spell but her enthusiasm wanes quickly. Air/fire people burn out because they have nothing with which to nourish themselves or their relationships. Her Libra sun is also terrified of his Scorpio moon – it wants to stay glittering on the surface, socializing madly, not to be tucked away out of sight. His Pisces sun is basically peace-loving and will not appreciate the noise levels of an Aries moon crashing around at home, raising the rafters. They should have consulted an astrologer before they embarked!

Kenneth Branagh

Sagittarius Sun Virgo Moon

A fire/earth type, he is a real steamroller, able to keep going long after weaker souls have dropped by the wayside. His grand fantasies and fiery enthusiasms can be turned into reality by that earthy moon, which is meticulous about getting every last detail right. His sun and moon are at rather gritty angles so he is driven on by a sense that he is never totally satisfied by anything he does in life. If it is what he wants then his conscience nags him to be somewhere else. If he is doing what his duty tells him then he feels deprived. Restlessness is probably his biggest fault with a mutable sun and moon. He cannot sit still. He also worries himself silly. A settled suburban marriage would never have suited him since he needs not to be fenced in, but he is not stubborn and will adapt happily to any difficulties.

Emma Thompson

Aries Sun Cancer Moon

A fiery, dynamic Aries, Emma is straightforward to a fault and almost severe in her approach to work and the world. She tends to open her mouth without thinking of the consequences. Like her husband her sun and moon are at gritty angles so she is always going to be on the move, never being entirely happy with her life emotionally or professionally. Chock-a-block with initiative and resourcefulness she will never be short of work or new projects. She will never be one to let the grass grow under her feet. Her split between her Cancer moon – which wants home, family and calm – and her Aries sun – which takes fright at just the thought of these pursuits – will keep her on edge. Being a fire/water type she is given to extremes of mood and wild outbursts but she is highly creative.

Their Relationship

Two fire suns together generate a great deal of heat, enthusiasm, hope and passion. The initial attraction would be instant because fire never wastes time. The danger is of an equally fast burnout, but here earth and water moons provide ballast and emotional nourishment. Theirs will be a noisy relationship, full of amiable arguments. She is the more decisive, he the more adaptable. Her Cancer moon suits his Virgo moon nicely, since both like a reasonably well-ordered home life with all the home comforts. Her Cancer moon does not sit well with his Sagittarius sun, however. She wants a close family – he wants freedom. But then she is used to not getting quite what she wants because her moon does not sit easily with her own fiery sun. His Virgo moon is reasonably quiet, tidy and concerned with detail; it will not appreciate her Aries sun's harum-scarum approach but then his own Sagittarius sun is much the same.

Bill Clinton

Leo Sun Taurus Moon

A match for Mick Jagger, who shares the same sun and moon placings, President Clinton is an entertainer at heart: colourful, attention-seeking and with a deeply sensual streak. He was certainly never designed for the quiet life. A fire/earth mix he is a real steamroller, with more energy than 10. His sun and moon are at odds with one another, suggesting that his heart is never where his head says it ought to be. He settles one place emotionally and promptly thinks the grass is greener on the other side of the fence. This desire/duty conflict comes from a childhood in which he never had the experience of a happy adult relationship.

For all his loud display of confidence, like most Leos he is deeply insecure inside, fearing that his life is a con and that inside there is only emptiness. He cannot bear criticism, which is why he deflects it so quickly. His fragile ego just wants the credit, not the kicks. His Taurus moon craves physical contact, is highly tactile and needs ongoing sexual reassurance. Physical comforts are his weak spot. His tastes are extravagant.

Hillary Clinton

Scorpio Sun Pisces Moon

Deeply emotional, very private, highly impressionable and not the strong ice queen she appears, Hillary rarely displays the depths of her feelings or her hurts. Her Pisces moon is so scared of rejection it withdraws instantly into its shell at the first scent of danger. She may look as if she took betrayal on the chin, but beware – Scorpio does not forgive nor forget. It gets revenge. Maybe years later, but it will come.

With a water sun and moon she may find more solace in caring for others in a wider sense in public than in trusting her feelings too openly in a close relationship. The Pisces moon in particular is good at being self-sacrificing, almost making a martyr of itself. But she desperately needs a sensitive, caring partner who understands the turbulence of her feelings and her vulnerabilities. Her mood swings will be extreme, sometimes violently so, and she may appear unreliable just because she so over-reacts – not in a thinking way but with the full force of her gut feelings. Another Scorpio might be best.

Their Relationship

Looking at it cynically, he wants the attention, the glitter, the glamour, the outer shell while she wants the power. It is no love match made in heaven, that is for sure. His Leo sun is self-centred and rather emotionally insensitive. He wants to be surrounded by courtiers who attend to his needs. He is not made for the give and take of a relationship. Hillary's Scorpio sun, on the other hand, wants control, intensity, passion, exclusivity. She has no respect for what he is or how he goes about his affairs. Certainly there is his Taurus moon, which can offer some physical reassurance to her Scorpio sun. It is a stubbornly difficult match but this pairing does help. Both are hugely jealous in their own ways and not given to making concessions. Their togetherness is a minor miracle.

Sophia Loren

Virgo Sun Aquarius Moon

Hard-working, conscientious, earthy and practical but rather distant, Sophia has a fairly self-sufficient approach to life. Her Virgo sun suits her for a job that requires physical attention to detail and gives her a warm heart and a need to be of service. Her

Aquarius moon is bright, intelligent but rather scared of close one-to-one commitment. She will have appreciated a career that necessitated breaks in her marriage as she travelled on location to act in films. An earth/air mix she can come across as cool and she certainly is not given to impulse decisions, though she worries about details a great deal.

Carlo Ponti

Sagittarius Sun Capricorn Moon

A fire/earth mix, Carlo has boundless energy especially when it comes to turning his fantasies into reality. Sagittarius sun people always have bigger and better ideas than everyone else, but often they fizzle out. His Capricorn moon gives him the practical skills to ground the visions and make money out of them. He always felt he had to earn money with this moon before he could be loved, so he has been driven always to succeed. He has always been too serious, maybe even coming across as cold despite his fiery sun, because his childhood was a struggle emotionally or financially.

Their Relationship

They are well matched since two mutable (adaptable) signs together are never stubborn but fit round difficulties and new circumstances. His Capricorn moon, which is really a workaholic at heart, strikes a chord with her over-conscientious Virgo sun. His optimistic, freedom-loving Sagittarius sun fits extremely well with her Aquarius moon, which cannot bear to be possessed.

Woody Allen

Sagittarius Sun Aquarius Moon

A fire/air personality, Woody is excitable, impulsive, unpredictable and freedom-loving but not good at coping with reality. Sagittarians can either be wild adventurers or overly intellectual and slightly dogmatic. They certainly are always armchair philosophers who think about society and its future. His Aquarius moon is scared of one-to-one involvement and not well connected to the body or the physical passions. He can be fixed about his needs at home and will not bend easily to accommodate the needs of others, though out in the world he is flexible enough. Burnout is a danger because he cannot get nourished either by his feelings or the earthier side of physical comforts. Fire/air people come unstuck when they are forced to face the harsher realities of life. Usually through suffering they learn to plumb their depths to find the inner strength and stability they lack.

Mia Farrow

Aquarius Sun Capricorn Moon

An air/earth mix, Mia is cool and at times comes across, with her Capricorn moon, as downright cold. She thinks a great deal but is practical as well. Her Aquarius sun makes her slightly eccentric, an oddball who goes her own way. She dislikes highly possessive, too intimate relationships and will run at the first whiff of jealousy. Her Capricorn moon sadly gave her the idea in childhood that she was unwanted and unworthy of love and that she had to earn acceptance. So she rarely sits still but is constantly on the go, frequently pushing away the very love she is seeking to earn. She can be ruthless at getting her own way. The ends justify the means as far as she is concerned, especially in her home life.

Their Relationship

His distant Aquarius moon certainly fits her Aquarius sun perfectly. They share similar outlooks, similar interests and though both are stubborn they can rub along not badly. Her essential being nourishes him deeply, or at least it did when they met. His Sagittarius sun also appreciates her Aquarius sun, since both are freedom-loving, fairly deep thinking and share broad humanitarian interests. What probably withered the relationship is that neither actually wants to relate intimately over any length of time. Long-term commitment is difficult for both. Certainly an earth moon should have helped, though it has no cross connections and hers is in Capricorn – the least warm of the earth moons and one that puts work as a higher priority than love. It was not a catastrophic relationship by any manner of means, but there was little to hold it together.

Tatum O'Neal

Scorpio Sun Cancer Moon

Intensely emotional, given to wild extremes of mood, highly jealous and fairly controlling, 'little Miss Tantrum' (as she was known in childhood) does not find it easy to settle in a calm relationship. She desperately wants home, family and a sexual, sensual relationship but is too over-reactive to manage it easily. Her Scorpio sun is hugely private, determined, power-hungry and vindictive, though sentimental when it comes to her family. Her Cancer sun is particularly broody and sensitive to criticism or rejection. She is socially charming, appearing at ease, so few know the turmoil of emotions that churn inside her. She will get stronger as she ages. What she needs is an emotionally sensitive partner who understands her vulnerabilities. Sometimes watery personalities find refuge in public work: they find it easier getting the attention or thanks of a great many people than trying to cope with the highs and lows of one close relationship.

John McEnroe

Aquarius Sun Gemini Moon

Airy, chatty, freedom-loving, not emotional, cool, detached and rather outspoken, John is very up-in-his head. An oddball and an eccentric from his Aquarius sun it is important to him to stand out as an individual. He loathes compromise in any form either at work or at home because it feels as if part of himself is being given up. Too much air puts him out of touch with his feelings so he cannot understand other people's needs.

His Gemini moon makes him extremely restless. He needs to be constantly on the move, always doing, which is not conducive to a settled emotional life. His disconnection from his body and his heart in particular will continue until he comes down to face the darker side of life, through suffering. Once he learns compassion he will cope better. His highly strung nervous tension comes from a head full of too many thoughts, worries and ideas.

Their Relationship

Neither of the two suns or the two moons like each other, nor do the cross aspects match. Scorpio is passionate, possessive and power-hungry. Aquarius is egalitarian, distant and fears intimacy. He would be frightened of being drawn into her watery net. He distrusts all feelings and would fear her manipulative tendencies. She would be dismayed by his lack of closeness on all counts. His Gemini moon does certainly want to walk for a short while on the wild side, but never for long. Her Cancer moon is less concerned with career than with having a settled family. There seems little there to have brought them together in the first place, never mind to keep them spliced.

Paul Newman

Aquarius Sun Pisces Moon

An air/water mix, Paul is pulled between his thoughts and his feelings. Highly sensitive, especially with a Pisces moon, he wants to escape into dream time. Highly creative, he can put across his visions but he needs careful handling. Rather at odds with himself he both fears close involvements and yet desperately needs emotional protection. His Aquarius sun makes him a true eccentric, one who stands out on his own and walks his own road. From this side he would rather be with a group of friends than in a one-to-one relationship. But his moon is deeply scared of rejection and needs a soft pillow for its head.

Joanne Woodward

Pisces Sun Aquarius Moon

Another water/air mix, Joanne is also pulled between two opposing sides of her nature. Her Pisces sun is creative, caring, kind, rather vague and highly emotional; her Aquarius moon fears close involvement and really wants space. She will be evasive emotionally at times because Pisces can disappear into its day-dreams at the drop of a hat to get away from harsh reality. She will come across to those close to her as rather diffuse and quite difficult to pin down.

Their Relationship

A miracle of good sense with two slightly-out-of-sorts-with-themselves people finding a similar soul. This is ideal with the opposing sun and moon signs matching. His need for kindness and sympathy is well met by her Pisces sun. Her need for freedom and no heavy intensity is well served by his Aquarius sun. The marriage will not always have been easy but there is enough emotional nourishment from the water sun and water moon to give it sustenance through the dry patches.

Mick Jagger

Leo Sun Taurus Moon

A fire/earth personality, Mick is a real powerhouse of energy, determination and – with both Leo and Taurus – indulgence. He is Leo so he craves attention, colour, flamboyance and noise in his life. Leos are entertainers *par excellence* and quite grandly regal with it. They are always desperately sensitive about their reputations and loathe the slightest whiff of criticism. With a Taurus moon, Mick wants every imaginable comfort that his senses could dream of. Highly tactile, he needs constant physical reassurance of his lovability and is highly sensual. Stubborn was never the word for him. He can dig his heels in further than anyone else and does not understand about the give and take of normal relationships. 'I do what I want and you do what I want' – only then are Leos happy. Add indulgent Taurus in and a mate can forget her needs totally. You take the whole package or you leave it. With his sun and moon at gritty angles his head and heart never agree. What he wants is never what he has got. His desire/duty conflict means his wandering eye is always a danger.

Jerry Hall

Cancer Sun Aries Moon

Emotional, possessive, family-orientated and highly resourceful, Jerry is a strong personality though at times over-impressionable. Her head and heart do not agree so she is always pulled between career and home and never totally satisfied with any relationship.

Her sun will make her increasingly matriarchal on the home front though her fiery moon keeps her constantly on the move looking for new challenges. Tranquillity is not in her nature. She is jealous, though that may ease as she ages and her children come to replace her lover as the object of her exclusive affection. But she will not find letting them go easy. As a water/fire personality she is given to explosive outbursts and fiery displays of emotion. She is surprisingly sensitive to what others think.

Their Relationship

Her fire moon to his fire sun certainly can make for a good firework display, with plenty of heat, inspired ideas and mutual ideals. Her rather upfront, often tactless opinions could offend his vanity. His Taurus moon is in theory not a bad match for her Cancer sun, since both are security-conscious and fairly home-based. But with 90-degree angles between their individual suns and moons neither is a settled personality, so they must always have been a restless couple. Her Cancer sun does not fit with his Leo sun really at all – certainly both like the grand lifestyle but Cancer needs more emotional warmth while Leo just wants all the attention. Her Cancer sun must also have hurt acutely at his betrayals, though she is capable of getting her own back with her Aries moon that dashes into reckless action without a moment's hesitation.

APPENDIX

FIND YOUR MOON SIGN

Times, Dates and Places

If mathematics is not your forte, do not panic. The basic rules for finding your exact moon sign are extremely simple. It is always helpful to know your exact time of birth.

Rule 1: Your birth time needs to be converted into Greenwich Mean Time (= London time). If you are in New York you are five hours behind London time; in Delhi you are five hours ahead. The Time Zone Map on page 342 will give you a guide to time conversion.

Rule 2: The position of the moon given in the tables in this chapter is at midnight on every other day (from January 1st 1920 to December 31st 1999). The moon moves approximately one degree every two hours. So if you were born at 10 in the morning (Greenwich Mean time) add five degrees to the midnight position.

For example, 1st February 1920 on Table 2 reads 25Ge. This means the moon was 25 degrees into the sign of Gemini at midnight on 1st February. If you were born at 6 a.m., add 3 degrees; at noon, add 6 degrees; at 6 p.m., add 9 degrees; midnight, 12

degrees, 6 a.m. next day, 15 degress; 12 noon next
day, 18 degrees; 6 p.m. next day, 21 degrees.
Remember, however, that the signs only go up to 30
degrees. So once you reach 29 degrees Gemini you
move into Cancer. To give another example, after 29
degrees Scorpio you move into Sagittarius. The moon
moves through the signs in the usual order.

Rule 3: If you are still in doubt, hovering in the grey area
between signs and given that there are the added
complications of summertime changes of one hour in
certain countries, of more than one hour during war
time and shifting time zones during this century, then
you have several options. First and easiest is to phone
a friendly consulting astrologer who can calculate it
off the top of his or her head. Second is to get a
printed computerized horoscope (for details write to
Marjorie Orr, PO Box 3125, London NW3 5QB). Third
is to phone the embassy of the country in which you
were born. They will know the status of time changes
in the year you were born.

Rule 4: If you are in a hurry, look at the two moon signs
which you are trying to decide between. Then read
the entries for both in this book – i.e., Cancer sun
Aries moon and Cancer sun Taurus moon. Decide for
yourself or ask your nearest and dearest which
sounds most like you. Good luck!

TIME ZONES AROUND THE WORLD

Key to Astrological Symbols and Qualities

Aries ♈ (the Ram): Ar – fire, cardinal

Taurus ♉ (the Bull): Ta – earth, fixed

Gemini ♊ (the Twins): Ge – air, mutable

Cancer ♋ (the Crab): Cn – water, cardinal

Leo ♌ (the Lion): Le – fire, fixed

Virgo ♍ (the Virgin): Vi – earth, mutable

Libra ♎ (the Scales): Li – air, cardinal

Scorpio ♏ (the Scorpion): Sc – water, fixed

Sagittarius ♐ (the Archer): Sg – fire, mutable

Capricorn ♑ (the Goat): Cp – earth, cardinal

Aquarius ♒ (the Water-bearer): Aq – air, fixed

Pisces ♓ (the Fish): Pi – water, mutable

Table: Moon Signs 1920–2000

1920

	Jan	Feb	Mar	Apr	May	Jun	Jul	Aug	Sep	Oct	Nov	Dec
1	2Ta	25Ge	19Cn	11Vi	16Li	2Sg	4Cp	20Aq	7Ar	14Ta	7Cn	16Le
3	1Ge	24Cn	17Le	7Li	11Sc	26Sg	28Cp	15Pi	4Ta	12Ge	6Le	14Vi
5	1Cn	23Le	15Vi	2Sc	5Sg	19Cp	23Aq	10Ar	1Ge	10Cn	3Vi	10Li
7	0Le	20Vi	12Li	27Sc	29Sg	13Aq	17Pi	7Ta	29Ge	9Le	0Li	6Sc
9	29Le	16Li	7Sc	20Sg	22Cp	8Pi	13Ar	5Ge	28Cn	7Vi	26Li	0Sg
11	26Vi	11Sc	1Sg	14Cp	17Aq	4Ar	11Ta	4Cn	27Le	4Li	22Sc	25Sg
13	21Li	5Sg	24Sg	8Aq	12Pi	2Ta	9Ge	3Le	25Vi	0Sc	16Sg	18Cp
15	15Sc	28Sg	18Cp	4Pi	9Ar	1Ge	10Cn	3Vi	22Li	26Sc	10Cp	12Aq
17	8Sg	23Cp	13Aq	1Ar	8Ta	1Cn	10Le	1Li	18Sc	20Sg	4Aq	6Pi
19	2Cp	18Aq	9Pi	29Ar	8Ge	1Le	9Vi	27Li	12Sg	14Cp	28Aq	1Ar
21	27Cp	14Pi	7Ar	29Ta	8Cn	0Vi	6Li	22Sc	6Cp	8Aq	23Pi	27Ar
23	22Aq	11Ar	5Ta	28Ge	7Le	27Vi	2Sc	16Sg	0Aq	2Pi	19Ar	25Ta
25	18Pi	9Ta	3Ge	27Cn	4Vi	23Li	26Sc	10Cp	24Aq	28Pi	17Ta	25Ge
27	14Ar	7Ge	2Cn	24Le	1Li	17Sc	19Sg	4Aq	20Pi	25Ar	17Ge	26Cn
29	12Ta	5Cn	0Le	21Vi	26Li	11Sg	13Cp	28Aq	17Ar	23Ta	17Cn	25Le
31	10Ge		27Le		20Sc		7Aq	24Pi		22Ge		24Vi

1921

	Jan	Feb	Mar	Apr	May	Jun	Jul	Aug	Sep	Oct	Nov	Dec
1	7Li	24Sc	3Sg	17Cp	19Aq	3Ar	7Ta	27Ge	21Le	0Li	20Sc	25Sg
3	3Sc	18Sg	27Sg	11Aq	13Pi	29Ar	5Ge	27Cn	21Vi	29Li	17Sg	20Cp
5	28Sc	12Cp	21Cp	5Pi	8Ar	26Ta	4Cn	28Le	21Li	26Sc	12Cp	14Aq
7	21Sg	6Aq	15Aq	0Ar	4Ta	25Ge	4Le	28Vi	18Sc	22Sg	6Aq	8Pi
9	15Cp	0Pi	9Pi	26Ar	2Ge	25Cn	4Vi	26Li	14Sg	16Cp	0Pi	2Ar
11	9Aq	24Pi	4Ar	22Ta	1Cn	24Le	3Li	22Sc	8Cp	10Aq	24Pi	26Ar
13	3Pi	19Ar	29Ar	20Ge	29Cn	23Vi	0Sc	17Sg	2Aq	4Pi	19Ar	23Ta
15	27Pi	15Ta	26Ta	18Cn	28Le	20Li	25Sc	11Cp	26Aq	28Pi	15Ta	20Ge
17	23Ar	13Ge	23Ge	17Le	26Vi	16Sc	20Sg	5Aq	20Pi	23Ar	12Ge	19Cn
19	19Ta	12Cn	22Cn	15Vi	23Li	11Sg	14Cp	29Aq	14Ar	19Ta	10Cn	19Le
21	18Ge	12Le	21Le	23Li	19Sc	5Cp	8Aq	23Pi	9Ta	16Ge	8Le	17Vi
23	18Cn	12Vi	20Vi	10Sc	14Sg	29Cp	2Pi	17Ar	5Ge	13Cn	6Vi	15Li
25	19Le	10Li	18Li	6Sg	9Cp	23Aq	26Pi	12Ta	2Cn	11Le	4Li	12Sc
27	18Vi	7Sc	15Sc	1Cp	3Aq	17Pi	20Ar	8Ge	1Le	10Vi	2Sc	8Sg
29	16Li		11Sg	25Cp	27Aq	11Ar	16Ta	6Cn	0Vi	9Li	29Sc	4Cp
31	12Sc		5Cp		21Pi		13Ge	6Le		7Sc		28Cp

1922

	Jan	Feb	Mar	Apr	May	Jun	Jul	Aug	Sep	Oct	Nov	Dec
1	10Aq	24Pi	3Ar	19Ta	24Ge	16Le	25Vi	18Sc	8Cp	12Aq	26Pi	28Ar
3	4Pi	18Ar	27Ar	14Ge	21Cn	14Vi	23Li	15Sg	2Aq	6Pi	20Ar	22Ta
5	28Pi	13Ta	22Ta	11Cn	19Le	13Li	21Sc	11Cp	27Aq	29Pi	14Ta	18Ge
7	22Ar	9Ge	18Ge	9Le	18Vi	11Sc	18Sg	6Aq	20Pi	23Ar	9Ge	14Cn
9	17Ta	6Cn	15Cn	8Vi	17Li	8Sg	14Cp	0Pi	14Ar	17Ta	4Cn	11Le
11	14Ge	6Le	14Le	8Li	16Sc	5Cp	9Aq	24Pi	8Ta	12Ge	1Le	9Vi
13	13Cn	7Vi	14Vi	7Sc	14Sg	1Aq	3Pi	17Ar	2Ge	7Cn	28Le	7Li
15	13Le	7Li	15Li	6Sg	10Cp	25Aq	27Pi	11Ta	28Ge	4Le	26Vi	5Sc
17	13Vi	5Sc	14Sc	2Cp	5Aq	19Pi	21Ar	6Ge	25Cn	2Vi	26Li	4Sg
19	12Li	2Sg	11Sg	27Cp	29Aq	13Ar	15Ta	3Cn	24Le	2Li	25Sc	2Cp
21	9Sc	27Sg	6Cp	21Aq	23Pi	7Ta	11Ge	1Le	24Vi	2Sc	24Sg	29Cp
23	5Sg	22Cp	1Aq	15Pi	17Ar	3Ge	8Cn	1Vi	24Li	2Sg	21Cp	24Aq
25	0Cp	16Aq	25Aq	9Ar	12Ta	0Cn	7Le	1Li	23Sc	0Cp	16Aq	18Pi
27	25Cp	9Pi	18Pi	3Ta	7Ge	28Cn	7Vi	0Sc	21Sg	26Cp	11Pi	12Ar
29	19Aq		12Ar	28Ta	4Cn	27Le	6Li	28Sc	17Cp	20Aq	4Ar	6Ta
31	13Pi	6Ta			2Le		4Sc	25Sg		14Pi		1Ge

1923

	Jan	Feb	Mar	Apr	May	Jun	Jul	Aug	Sep	Oct	Nov	Dec
1	13Ge	2Le	10Le	2Li	11Sc	3Cp	9Aq	25Pi	9Ta	11Ge	27Cn	2Vi
3	10Cn	1Vi	9Vi	2Sc	11Sg	1Aq	5Pi	19Ar	3Ge	6Cn	23Le	29Vi
5	7Le	0Li	9Li	2Sg	9Cp	27Aq	0Ar	13Ta	27Ge	1Le	20Vi	28Li
7	5Vi	29Li	9Sc	0Cp	6Aq	22Pi	23Ar	7Ge	23Cn	28Le	20Li	28Sc
9	4Li	27Sc	7Sg	27Cp	1Pi	15Ar	17Ta	2Cn	20Le	27Vi	20Sc	29Sg
11	2Sc	24Sg	4Cp	22Aq	25Pi	9Ta	11Ge	28Cn	18Vi	27Li	21Sg	28Cp
13	0Sg	20Cp	0Aq	16Pi	19Ar	3Ge	7Cn	26Le	18Li	27Sc	19Cp	25Aq
15	27Sg	16Aq	25Aq	10Ar	12Ta	28Ge	3Le	24Vi	17Sc	26Sg	16Aq	20Pi
17	24Cp	10Pi	19Pi	3Ta	6Ge	23Cn	0Vi	23Li	16Sg	24Cp	12Pi	14Ar
19	20Aq	4Ar	13Ar	27Ta	1Cn	20Le	28Vi	21Sc	14Cp	20Aq	6Ar	8Ta
21	14Pi	28Ar	6Ta	22Ge	26Cn	17Vi	26Li	19Sg	10Aq	15Pi	0Ta	2Ge
23	8Ar	22Ta	0Ge	17Cn	23Le	15Li	24Sc	17Cp	5Pi	9Ar	23Ta	26Ge
25	2Ta	4Ge	25Ge	13Le	20Vi	14Sc	23Sg	13Aq	0Ar	3Ta	17Ge	21Cn
27	26Ta	29Ge	20Cn	11Vi	19Li	13Sg	21Cp	9Pi	24Ar	26Ta	11Cn	16Le
29	21Ge	26Cn	18Le	10Li	19Sc	12Cp	17Aq	3Ar	18Ta	20Ge	6Le	12Vi
31	18Cn		17Vi		19Sg		13Pi	27Ar		14Cn		9Li

1924

	Jan	Feb	Mar	Apr	May	Jun	Jul	Aug	Sep	Oct	Nov	Dec
1	23Li	17Sg	12Cp	2Pi	7Ar	22Ta	25Ge	10Le	28Vi	5Sc	29Sg	8Aq
3	22Sc	16Cp	9Aq	28Pi	1Ta	16Ge	19Cn	5Vi	25Li	4Sg	28Cp	5Pi
5	22Sg	14Aq	6Pi	22Ar	25Ta	10Cn	13Le	2Li	24Sc	3Cp	25Aq	2Ar
7	21Cp	10Pi	1Ar	16Ta	19Ge	4Le	8Vi	29Li	22Sg	1Aq	22Pi	27Ar
9	19Aq	6Ar	26Ar	10Ge	13Cn	29Le	5Li	27Sc	20Cp	28Aq	17Ar	21Ta
11	16Pi	0Ta	20Ta	4Cn	7Le	25Vi	2Sc	26Sg	18Aq	25Pi	12Ta	15Ge
13	11Ar	24Ta	14Ge	28Cn	2Vi	22Li	1Sg	25Cp	16Pi	21Ar	6Ge	9Cn
15	5Ta	18Ge	8Cn	24Le	29Vi	22Sc	1Cp	23Aq	12Ar	16Ta	0Cn	2Le
17	28Ta	13Cn	3Le	21Vi	28Li	22Sg	1Aq	21Pi	7Ta	10Ge	24Cn	26Le
19	22Ge	8Le	29Le	20Li	29Sc	22Cp	29Aq	17Ar	2Ge	4Cn	18Le	21Vi
21	17Cn	5Vi	27Vi	20Sc	29Sg	21Aq	26Pi	12Ta	26Ge	27Cn	13Vi	18Li
23	13Le	2Li	26Li	20Sg	28Cp	18Pi	22Ar	6Ge	19Cn	22Le	9Li	16Sc
25	9Vi	1Sc	26Sc	19Cp	26Aq	13Ar	16Ta	0Cn	14Le	18Vi	8Sc	16Sg
27	6Li	29Sc	24Sg	16Aq	22Pi	7Ta	10Ge	24Cn	10Vi	15Li	8Sg	16Cp
29	4Sc	29Sg	22Cp	12Pi	16Ar	1Ge	3Cn	19Le	7Li	15Sc	8Cp	16Aq
31	3Sg		19Aq		10Ta		28Cn	15Vi		14Sg		14Pi

1925

	Jan	Feb	Mar	Apr	May	Jun	Jul	Aug	Sep	Oct	Nov	Dec
1	28Pi	15Ta	23Ta	7Cn	8Le	23Vi	28Li	19Sg	12Aq	20Pi	11Ta	15Ge
3	24Ar	9Ge	17Ge	0Le	2Vi	19Li	25Sc	18Cp	12Pi	19Ar	7Ge	10Cn
5	18Ta	2Cn	11Cn	24Le	28Vi	17Sc	25Sg	19Aq	11Ar	16Ta	2Cn	4Le
7	12Ge	26Cn	4Le	20Vi	25Li	17Sg	25Cp	18Pi	8Ta	12Ge	26Cn	27Le
9	6Cn	20Le	29Le	16Li	23Sc	17Cp	25Aq	16Ar	4Ge	6Cn	20Le	21Vi
11	29Cn	15Vi	24Vi	14Sc	22Sg	16Aq	24Pi	13Ta	28Ge	0Le	14Vi	16Li
13	23Le	11Li	21Li	13Sg	22Cp	14Pi	21Ar	8Ge	22Cn	24Le	9Li	13Sc
15	18Vi	7Sc	18Sc	11Cp	20Aq	11Ar	16Ta	2Cn	16Le	18Vi	5Sc	11Sg
17	14Li	5Sg	16Sg	9Aq	17Pi	7Ta	11Ge	25Cn	10Vi	13Li	3Sg	11Cp
19	11Sc	4Cp	14Cp	7Pi	14Ar	2Ge	5Cn	19Le	5Li	10Sc	2Cp	10Aq
21	9Sg	3Aq	13Aq	4Ar	10Ta	26Ge	28Cn	13Vi	0Sc	7Sg	0Aq	9Pi
23	9Cp	2Pi	11Pi	1Ta	5Ge	19Cn	22Le	8Li	27Sc	5Cp	29Aq	7Ar
25	9Aq	0Ar	9Ar	26Ta	29Ge	13Le	16Vi	3Sc	24Sg	3Aq	26Pi	4Ta
27	9Pi	27Ar	5Ta	21Ge	23Cn	7Vi	11Li	0Sg	23Cp	2Pi	24Ar	29Ta
29	6Ar		0Ge	14Cn	16Le	1Li	7Sc	28Sg	21Aq	0Ar	20Ta	24Ge
31	2Ta		25Ge		10Vi		4Sg	27Cp		28Ar		18Cn

1926

	Jan	Feb	Mar	Apr	May	Jun	Jul	Aug	Sep	Oct	Nov	Dec
1	0Le	14Vi	23Vi	10Sc	16Sg	8Aq	17Pi	10Ta	29Ge	2Le	16Vi	18Li
3	24Le	9Li	18Li	6Sg	14Cp	7Pi	16Ar	6Ge	23Cn	26Le	10Li	13Sc
5	18Vi	3Sc	13Sc	3Cp	11Aq	5Ar	13Ta	1Cn	17Le	19Vi	4Sc	8Sg
7	12Li	29Sc	9Sg	1Aq	10Pi	3Ta	9Ge	26Cn	11Vi	13Li	0Sg	5Cp
9	7Sc	27Sg	6Cp	29Aq	8Ar	0Ge	5Cn	20Le	4Li	8Sc	26Sg	3Aq
11	5Sg	27Cp	5Aq	29Pi	7Ta	26Ge	29Cn	13Vi	28Li	3Sg	22Cp	1Pi
13	4Cp	27Aq	5Pi	28Ar	4Ge	21Cn	23Le	7Li	23Sc	29Sg	20Aq	29Pi
15	4Aq	27Pi	5Ar	26Ta	0Cn	15Le	17Vi	1Sc	19Sg	25Cp	18Pi	28Ar
17	4Pi	26Ar	4Ta	22Ge	25Cn	8Vi	11Li	26Sc	16Cp	24Aq	17Ar	25Ta
19	3Ar	23Ta	1Ge	17Cn	19Le	2Li	5Sc	23Sg	14Aq	23Pi	16Ta	23Ge
21	0Ta	18Ge	27Ge	11Le	12Vi	27Li	1Sg	21Cp	15Pi	23Ar	14Ge	19Cn
23	26Ta	12Cn	21Cn	4Vi	7Li	23Sc	29Sg	21Aq	15Ar	23Ta	11Cn	14Le
25	21Ge	6Le	14Le	29Vi	2Sc	20Sg	28Cp	22Pi	14Ta	20Ge	6Le	8Vi
27	15Cn	0Vi	8Vi	23Li	28Sc	19Cp	28Aq	21Ar	12Ge	16Cn	0Vi	2Li
29	9Le		2Li	19Sc	26Sg	18Aq	28Pi	20Ta	8Cn	10Le	24Vi	26Li
31	3Vi		27Li		24Cp		26Ar	16Ge		4Vi		21Sc

1927

	Jan	Feb	Mar	Apr	May	Jun	Jul	Aug	Sep	Oct	Nov	Dec
1	3Sg	22Cp	0Aq	23Pi	2Ta	24Ge	29Cn	15Vi	29Li	2Sg	17Cp	24Aq
3	0Cp	21Aq	29Aq	23Ar	1Ge	21Cn	25Le	9Li	23Sc	26Sg	14Aq	21Pi
5	28Cp	21Pi	0Ar	23Ta	0Cn	17Le	19Vi	3Sc	17Sg	21Cp	11Pi	20Ar
7	27Aq	21Ar	0Ta	21Ge	26Cn	11Vi	13Li	27Sc	13Cp	18Aq	11Ar	19Ta
9	26Pi	19Ta	29Ta	17Cn	21Le	5Li	7Sc	22Sg	10Aq	17Pi	11Ta	19Ge
11	24Ar	16Ge	25Ge	12Le	15Vi	29Li	1Sg	18Cp	9Pi	18Ar	11Ge	18Cn
13	22Ta	11Cn	21Cn	6Vi	9Li	23Sc	27Sg	16Aq	9Ar	18Ta	10Cn	15Le
15	19Ge	6Le	15Le	0Li	3Sc	18Sg	23Cp	15Pi	9Ta	17Ge	7Le	10Vi
17	15Cn	0Vi	9Vi	24Li	27Sc	14Cp	21Aq	15Ar	8Ge	15Cn	2Vi	5Li
19	10Le	24Vi	3Li	18Sc	22Sg	11Aq	20Pi	14Ta	5Cn	11Le	26Vi	28Li
21	4Vi	18Li	27Li	12Sg	18Cp	9Pi	19Ar	11Ge	1Le	5Vi	20Li	22Sc
23	28Vi	12Sc	21Sc	8Cp	15Aq	8Ar	17Ta	8Cn	26Le	29Vi	14Sc	16Sg
25	22Li	6Sg	15Sg	4Aq	12Pi	6Ta	15Ge	4Le	20Vi	23Li	8Sg	11Cp
27	16Sc	2Cp	11Cp	2Pi	11Ar	5Ge	11Cn	29Le	14Li	17Sc	2Cp	7Aq
29		11Sg	8Aq	2Ar	11Ta	2Cn	8Le	23Vi	8Sc	11Sg	27Cp	4Pi
31	8Cp		8Pi		10Ge		3Vi	17Li		5Cp		2Ar

1928

	Jan	Feb	Mar	Apr	May	Jun	Jul	Aug	Sep	Oct	Nov	Dec
1	16Ar	9Ge	3Cn	23Le	28Vi	12Sc	15Sg	0Aq	19Pi	27Ar	21Ge	29Cn
3	14Ta	7Cn	0Le	18Vi	22Li	6Sg	9Cp	26Aq	18Ar	26Ta	19Cn	27Le
5	13Ge	4Le	26Le	13Li	15Sc	0Cp	4Aq	23Pi	16Ta	25Ge	17Le	23Vi
7	12Cn	0Vi	22Vi	7Sc	9Sg	24Cp	0Pi	21Ar	14Ge	23Cn	13Vi	18Li
9	9Le	26Vi	16Li	0Sg	3Cp	20Aq	27Pi	19Ta	12Cn	20Le	8Li	12Sc
11	5Vi	20Li	10Sc	24Sg	27Cp	16Pi	24Ar	13Ge	10Le	16Vi	3Sc	5Sg
13	0Li	14Sc	4Sg	18Cp	23Aq	14Ar	23Ta	16Cn	7Vi	11Li	26Sc	29Sg
15	24Li	8Sg	28Sg	14Aq	20Pi	13Ta	22Ge	14Le	3Li	6Sc	20Sg	23Cp
17	18Sc	2Cp	23Cp	12Pi	19Ar	13Ge	21Cn	11Vi	27Li	0Sg	14Cp	17Aq
19	12Sg	28Cp	19Aq	11Ar	19Ta	13Cn	19Le	7Li	21Sc	23Sg	8Aq	12Pi
21	7Cp	25Aq	18Pi	11Ta	20Ge	11Le	16Vi	2Sc	15Sg	17Cp	3Pi	9Ar
23	3Aq	24Pi	18Ar	11Ge	19Cn	8Vi	11Li	25Sc	9Cp	12Aq	0Ar	7Ta
25	0Pi	23Ar	17Ta	10Cn	16Le	3Li	6Sc	19Sg	4Aq	8Pi	29Ar	7Ge
27	28Pi	22Ta	16Ge	7Le	12Vi	27Li	29Sc	13Cp	0Pi	6Ar	29Ta	7Cn
29	27Ar	20Ge	14Cn	3Vi	7Li	21Sc	23Sg	9Aq	28Pi	6Ta	29Ge	7Le
31	25Ta		10Le		1Sc		18Cp	5Pi		6Ge		5Vi

1929

	Jan	Feb	Mar	Apr	May	Jun	Jul	Aug	Sep	Oct	Nov	Dec
1	19Vi	5Sc	12Sc	26Sg	28Cp	13Pi	18Ar	10Ge	4Le	12Vi	2Sc	6Sg
3	14Li	29Sc	6Sg	20Cp	22Aq	10Ar	16Ta	9Cn	3Vi	10Li	27Sc	0Cp
5	8Sc	22Sg	0Cp	14Aq	18Pi	7Ta	15Ge	9Le	1Li	6Sc	22Sg	24Cp
7	2Sg	16Cp	24Cp	10Pi	15Ar	7Ge	16Cn	9Vi	28Li	1Sg	15Cp	17Aq
9	26Sg	11Aq	19Aq	7Ar	14Ta	7Cn	16Le	7Li	24Sc	26Sg	9Aq	11Pi
11	20Cp	6Pi	15Pi	5Ta	14Ge	7Le	15Vi	3Sc	18Sg	19Cp	3Pi	6Ar
13	14Aq	2Ar	12Ar	4Ge	13Cn	6Vi	12Li	28Sc	11Cp	13Aq	29Pi	3Ta
15	9Pi	29Ar	10Ta	3Cn	12Le	2Li	7Sc	21Sg	5Aq	8Pi	25Ar	1Ge
17	5Ar	27Ta	8Ge	1Le	9Vi	28Li	1Sg	15Cp	0Pi	4Ar	24Ta	1Cn
19	3Ta	25Ge	6Cn	29Le	5Li	22Sc	25Sg	9Aq	25Pi	1Ta	23Ge	2Le
21	1Ge	24Cn	4Le	26Vi	1Sc	16Sg	18Cp	4Pi	22Ar	29Ta	22Cn	1Vi
23	0Cn	23Le	2Vi	21Li	25Sc	9Cp	12Aq	29Pi	19Ta	27Ge	21Le	29Vi
25	0Le	21Vi	29Vi	16Sc	19Sg	3Aq	7Pi	25Ar	17Ge	26Cn	19Vi	25Li
27	29Le	17Li	25Li	10Sg	13Cp	27Aq	2Ar	22Ta	15Cn	24Le	15Li	20Sc
29	27Vi		20Sc	4Cp	6Aq	22Pi	28Ar	20Ge	14Le	22Vi	11Sc	15Sg
31	22Li		14Sg		1Pi		26Ta	19Cn		19Li		8Cp

1930

	Jan	Feb	Mar	Apr	May	Jun	Jul	Aug	Sep	Oct	Nov	Dec
1	20Cp	5Pi	14Pi	1Ta	7Ge	0Le	10Vi	1Sc	19Sg	22Cp	6Pi	8Ar
3	14Aq	29Pi	9Ar	27Ta	5Cn	29Le	8Li	27Sc	13Cp	16Aq	0Ar	2Ta
5	8Pi	24Ar	4Ta	25Ge	4Le	27Vi	4Sc	22Sg	7Aq	10Pi	24Ar	29Ta
7	2Ar	20Ta	0Ge	23Cn	2Vi	24Li	0Sg	16Cp	1Pi	4Ar	20Ta	26Ge
9	28Ar	18Ge	28Ge	22Le	0Li	20Sc	25Sg	10Aq	25Pi	28Ar	17Ge	25Cn
11	25Ta	18Cn	27Cn	20Vi	28Li	16Sg	19Cp	4Pi	19Ar	24Ta	14Cn	24Le
13	24Ge	18Le	26Le	19Li	24Sc	11Cp	13Aq	28Pi	14Ta	20Ge	13Le	22Vi
15	25Cn	18Vi	26Vi	16Sc	20Sg	5Aq	7Pi	22Ar	10Ge	18Cn	11Vi	20Li
17	25Le	17Li	24Li	12Sg	14Cp	28Aq	1Ar	17Ta	7Cn	16Le	9Li	17Sc
19	24Vi	13Sc	21Sc	7Cp	8Aq	22Pi	25Ar	14Ge	6Le	15Vi	7Sc	13Sg
21	22Li	8Sg	16Sg	1Aq	2Pi	17Ar	21Ta	12Cn	6Vi	14Li	5Sg	9Cp
23	17Sc	2Cp	11Cp	24Aq	26Pi	13Ta	19Ge	12Le	6Li	13Sc	1Cp	4Aq
25	12Sg	26Cp	4Aq	19Pi	22Ar	11Ge	19Cn	13Vi	5Sc	10Sg	26Cp	28Aq
27	6Cp	20Aq	28Aq	14Ar	18Ta	10Cn	19Le	12Li	2Sg	6Cp	20Aq	21Pi
29	29Cp		23Pi	10Ta	17Ge	10Le	19Vi	10Sc	28Sg	0Aq	14Pi	15Ar
31	23Aq		18Ar		16Cn		18Li	6Sg		24Aq		10Ta

1931

	Jan	Feb	Mar	Apr	May	Jun	Jul	Aug	Sep	Oct	Nov	Dec
1	23Ta	13Cn	21Cn	14Vi	23Li	14Sg	19Cp	5Pi	19Ar	22Ta	9Cn	16Le
3	20Ge	12Le	20Le	14Li	22Sc	11Cp	15Aq	29Pi	13Ta	16Ge	5Le	13Vi
5	19Cn	13Vi	21Vi	14Sc	20Sg	7Aq	9Pi	23Ar	7Ge	12Cn	3Vi	12Li
7	19Le	12Li	21Li	12Sg	16Cp	1Pi	3Ar	17Ta	3Cn	9Le	2Li	11Sc
9	18Vi	10Sc	20Sc	8Cp	11Aq	25Pi	26Ar	12Ge	1Le	8Vi	2Sc	10Sg
11	17Li	7Sg	16Sg	3Aq	5Pi	18Ar	21Ta	9Cn	0Vi	8Li	2Sg	8Cp
13	14Sc	2Cp	12Cp	27Aq	29Pi	13Ta	17Ge	7Le	0Li	9Sc	0Cp	5Aq
15	10Sg	27Cp	6Aq	20Pi	22Ar	9Ge	14Cn	7Vi	0Sc	8Sg	27Cp	0Pi
17	5Cp	21Aq	0Pi	14Ar	17Ta	5Cn	13Le	6Li	29Sc	5Cp	22Aq	24Pi
19	0Aq	15Pi	23Pi	8Ta	13Ge	3Le	12Vi	5Sc	26Sg	1Aq	16Pi	18Ar
21	24Aq	8Ar	17Ar	3Ge	9Cn	2Vi	11Li	3Sg	22Cp	26Aq	10Ar	12Ta
23	18Pi	2Ta	11Ta	29Ge	7Le	0Li	9Sc	0Cp	17Aq	20Pi	4Ta	6Ge
25	11Ar	27Ta	6Ge	26Cn	5Vi	28Li	6Sg	25Cp	11Pi	13Ar	28Ta	2Cn
27	6Ta	23Ge	2Cn	24Le	3Li	26Sc	3Cp	20Aq	4Ar	7Ta	23Ge	29Cn
29	1Ge		0Le	23Vi	2Sc	23Sg	28Cp	14Pi	28Ar	1Ge	19Cn	26Le
31	28Ge		29Le		0Sg		23Aq	7Ar		26Ge		24Vi

1932

	Jan	Feb	Mar	Apr	May	Jun	Jul	Aug	Sep	Oct	Nov	Dec
1	8Li	1Sg	26Sg	15Aq	18Pi	2Ta	5Ge	21Cn	10Vi	18Li	12Sg	20Cp
3	6Sc	29Sg	22Cp	9Pi	12Ar	26Ta	29Ge	17Le	9Li	18Sc	11Cp	17Aq
5	5Sg	25Cp	17Aq	3Ar	6Ta	21Ge	25Cn	15Vi	8Sc	17Sg	8Aq	13Pi
7	3Cp	21Aq	12Pi	27Ar	29Ta	16Cn	21Le	13Li	7Sg	15Cp	4Pi	8Ar
9	0Aq	16Pi	6Ar	20Ta	24Ge	11Le	18Vi	11Sc	5Cp	12Aq	29Pi	2Ta
11	25Aq	10Ar	0Ta	14Ge	18Cn	8Vi	16Li	10Sg	2Aq	7Pi	23Ar	25Ta
13	20Pi	3Ta	24Ta	9Cn	14Le	6Li	15Sc	8Cp	28Aq	2Ar	17Ta	19Ge
15	14Ar	27Ta	18Ge	5Le	11Vi	4Sc	14Sg	5Aq	23Pi	26Ar	10Ge	13Cn
17	7Ta	22Ge	13Cn	2Vi	10Li	4Sg	12Cp	2Pi	17Ar	20Ta	4Cn	8Le
19	2Ge	18Cn	10Le	1Li	10Sc	3Cp	10Aq	27Pi	11Ta	13Ge	29Cn	4Vi
21	27Ge	16Le	8Vi	2Sc	10Sg	2Aq	6Pi	21Ar	5Ge	7Cn	23Le	0Li
23	24Cn	15Vi	8Li	2Sg	10Cp	28Aq	1Ar	15Ta	29Ge	2Le	21Vi	28Li
25	22Le	15Li	9Sc	1Cp	7Aq	23Pi	25Ar	9Ge	24Cn	28Le	19Li	28Sc
27	20Vi	14Sc	8Sg	28Cp	3Pi	17Ar	19Ta	3Cn	20Le	26Vi	19Sc	28Sg
29	19Li	12Sg	6Cp	24Aq	27Pi	11Ta	13Ge	29Cn	18Vi	26Li	20Sg	27Cp
31	17Sc		2Aq		21Ar		8Cn	26Le		27Sc		25Aq

1933

	Jan	Feb	Mar	Apr	May	Jun	Jul	Aug	Sep	Oct	Nov	Dec
1	9Pi	24Ar	2Ta	16Ge	18Cn	4Vi	9Li	2Sg	25Cp	3Pi	22Ar	26Ta
3	4Ar	18Ta	26Ta	10Cn	12Le	0Li	7Sc	1Cp	24Aq	0Ar	17Ta	20Ge
5	28Ar	12Ge	20Ge	4Le	8Vi	28Li	7Sg	1Aq	22Pi	26Ar	12Ge	14Cn
7	22Ta	6Cn	14Cn	0Vi	5Li	28Sc	7Cp	29Aq	18Ar	21Ta	5Cn	7Le
9	16Ge	1Le	9Le	27Vi	4Sc	29Sg	7Aq	27Pi	13Ta	15Ge	29Cn	2Vi
11	10Cn	27Le	5Vi	26Li	5Sg	28Cp	5Pi	23Ar	8Ge	9Cn	23Le	27Vi
13	5Le	24Vi	3Li	26Sc	5Cp	27Aq	2Ar	18Ta	1Cn	3Le	18Vi	23Li
15	1Vi	21Li	2Sc	25Sg	4Aq	23Pi	27Ar	11Ge	25Cn	28Le	15Li	22Sc
17	27Vi	20Sc	1Sg	24Cp	1Pi	18Ar	21Ta	5Cn	20Le	24Vi	14Sc	22Sg
19	25Li	18Sg	29Sg	21Aq	27Pi	12Ta	15Ge	29Cn	16Vi	21Li	14Sg	23Cp
21	23Sc	16Cp	27Cp	17Pi	21Ar	6Ge	9Cn	24Le	13Li	20Sc	14Cp	22Aq
23	22Sg	14Aq	24Aq	12Ar	15Ta	0Cn	3Le	20Vi	11Sc	20Sg	13Aq	20Pi
25	21Cp	11Pi	20Pi	6Ta	9Ge	24Cn	28Le	17Li	9Sg	18Cp	10Pi	16Ar
27	19Aq	7Ar	15Ar	0Ge	3Cn	18Le	23Vi	14Sc	8Cp	16Aq	6Ar	11Ta
29	16Pi		10Ta	24Ge	27Cn	13Vi	20Li	12Sg	6Aq	13Pi	2Ta	5Ge
31	12Ar		4Ge		21Le		17Sc	11Cp		9Ar		29Ge

1934

	Jan	Feb	Mar	Apr	May	Jun	Jul	Aug	Sep	Oct	Nov	Dec
1	11Cn	25Le	4Vi	22Li	29Sc	22Cp	1Pi	22Ar	9Ge	12Cn	25Le	27Vi
3	4Le	20Vi	29Vi	19Sc	28Sg	21Aq	29Pi	18Ta	4Cn	6Le	19Vi	22Li
5	28Le	16Li	26Li	17Sg	26Cp	19Pi	26Ar	13Ge	27Cn	29Le	14Li	19Sc
7	23Vi	12Sc	23Sc	16Cp	25Aq	16Ar	21Ta	7Cn	21Le	24Vi	11Sc	17Sg
9	19Li	10Sg	20Sg	14Aq	22Pi	12Ta	16Ge	0Le	15Vi	19Li	8Sg	16Cp
11	16Sc	9Cp	19Cp	12Pi	19Ar	7Ge	10Cn	24Le	10Li	15Sc	7Cp	15Aq
13	15Sg	9Aq	18Aq	9Ar	15Ta	1Cn	3Le	18Vi	5Sc	12Sg	5Aq	14Pi
15	16Cp	8Pi	17Pi	6Ta	10Ge	25Cn	27Le	13Li	2Sg	10Cp	3Pi	12Ar
17	16Aq	7Ar	14Ar	2Ge	4Cn	18Le	21Vi	8Sc	29Sg	8Aq	1Ar	8Ta
19	15Pi	3Ta	11Ta	26Ge	28Cn	12Vi	16Li	5Sg	28Cp	7Pi	29Ar	4Ge
21	12Ar	28Ta	6Ge	20Cn	22Le	7Li	12Sc	3Cp	27Aq	5Ar	25Ta	29Ge
23	8Ta	22Ge	0Cn	14Le	16Vi	3Sc	10Sg	3Aq	26Pi	3Ta	21Ge	24Cn
25	2Ge	16Cn	24Cn	8Vi	12Li	1Sg	9Cp	3Pi	25Ar	0Ge	16Cn	17Le
27	26Ge	10Le	18Le	4Li	9Sc	1Cp	10Aq	3Ar	22Ta	26Ge	9Le	11Vi
29	20Cn		13Vi	1Sc	8Sg	1Aq	10Pi	1Ta	18Ge	20Cn	3Vi	5Li
31	13Le		8Li		7Cp		8Ar	27Ta		13Le		0Sc

1935

	Jan	Feb	Mar	Apr	May	Jun	Jul	Aug	Sep	Oct	Nov	Dec
1	13Sc	3Cp	12Cp	5Pi	14Ar	5Ge	10Cn	25Le	9Li	13Sc	0Cp	7Aq
3	11Sg	3Aq	11Aq	5Ar	12Ta	1Cn	4Le	19Vi	3Sc	8Sg	27Cp	5Pi
5	10Cp	3Pi	11Pi	4Ta	10Ge	26Cn	28Le	12Li	28Sc	3Cp	25Aq	4Ar
7	10Aq	3Ar	12Ar	2Ge	6Cn	20Le	22Vi	7Sc	24Sg	0Aq	23Pi	2Ta
9	10Pi	2Ta	10Ta	28Ge	1Le	14Vi	16Li	2Sg	21Cp	29Aq	23Ar	1Ge
11	8Ar	28Ta	7Ge	23Cn	24Le	8Li	11Sc	29Sg	21Aq	29Pi	22Ta	28Ge
13	5Ta	23Ge	2Cn	16Le	18Vi	3Sc	7Sg	27Cp	21Pi	0Ta	21Ge	25Cn
15	1Ge	17Cn	26Cn	10Vi	12Li	29Sc	5Cp	27Aq	21Ar	29Ta	17Cn	20Le
17	26Ge	11Le	20Le	4Li	8Sc	26Sg	4Aq	28Pi	20Ta	26Ge	12Le	14Vi
19	20Cn	5Vi	13Vi	29Li	4Sg	25Cp	4Pi	27Ar	17Ge	22Cn	6Vi	7Li
21	14Le	28Vi	8Li	25Sc	1Cp	24Aq	3Ar	25Ta	13Cn	16Le	0Li	2Sc
23	8Vi	23Li	2Sc	21Sg	29Cp	22Pi	1Ta	21Ge	7Le	9Vi	24Li	26Sc
25	2Li	18Sc	28Sc	18Cp	27Aq	20Ar	28Ta	16Cn	1Vi	3Li	18Sc	23Sg
27	26Li	14Sg	24Sg	16Aq	25Pi	18Ta	24Ge	10Le	25Vi	27Li	14Sg	20Cp
29	22Sc		21Cp	15Pi	24Ar	14Ge	19Cn	4Vi	18Li	22Sc	10Cp	18Aq
31	19Sg		20Aq		21Ta		13Le	27Vi		17Sg		16Pi

1936

	Jan	Feb	Mar	Apr	May	Jun	Jul	Aug	Sep	Oct	Nov	Dec
1	1Ar	23Ta	17Ge	5Le	8Vi	22Li	25Sc	11Cp	1Pi	9Ar	3Ge	10Cn
3	29Ar	20Ge	13Cn	29Le	2Li	16Sc	20Sg	8Aq	0Ar	9Ta	2Cn	8Le
5	27Ta	16Cn	8Le	23Vi	26Li	11Sg	16Cp	6Pi	0Ta	9Ge	29Cn	3Vi
7	24Ge	11Le	2Vi	17Li	20Sc	6Cp	13Aq	5Ar	29Ta	7Cn	24Le	28Vi
9	20Cn	6Vi	26Vi	11Sc	14Sg	3Aq	11Pi	4Ta	27Ge	3Le	19Vi	22Li
11	15Le	0Li	20Li	5Sg	10Cp	0Pi	9Ar	2Ge	23Cn	28Le	13Li	16Sc
13	10Vi	23Li	14Sc	0Cp	6Aq	28Pi	7Ta	0Cn	18Le	22Vi	7Sc	9Sg
15	3Li	17Sc	8Sg	26Cp	3Pi	27Ar	6Ge	26Cn	13Vi	16Li	1Sg	4Cp
17	27Li	12Sg	3Cp	23Aq	2Ar	26Ta	3Cn	22Le	7Li	10Sc	25Sg	29Cp
19	22Sc	8Cp	0Aq	22Pi	2Ta	24Ge	0Le	17Vi	1Sc	4Sg	19Cp	25Aq
21	17Sg	6Aq	29Aq	23Ar	1Ge	22Cn	26Le	11Li	25Sc	28Sg	15Aq	22Pi
23	14Cp	6Pi	29Pi	23Ta	0Cn	18Le	21Vi	5Sc	19Sg	23Cp	12Pi	20Ar
25	13Aq	6Ar	0Ta	22Ge	27Cn	13Vi	15Li	28Sc	14Cp	19Aq	11Ar	19Ta
27	12Pi	6Ta	29Ta	19Cn	22Le	7Li	8Sc	23Sg	10Aq	17Pi	10Ta	19Ge
29	11Ar	4Ge	27Ge	14Le	17Vi	1Sc	3Sg	19Cp	9Pi	17Ar	11Ge	18Cn
31	10Ta		23Cn		11Li		28Sg	16Aq		18Ta		15Le

1937

	Jan	Feb	Mar	Apr	May	Jun	Jul	Aug	Sep	Oct	Nov	Dec
1	29Le	14Li	22Li	6Sg	8Cp	25Aq	1Ar	24Ta	17Cn	25Le	13Li	17Sc
3	24Vi	8Sc	16Sc	29Sg	3Aq	21Pi	29Ar	23Ge	15Le	21Vi	8Sc	10Sg
5	18Li	1Sg	9Sg	24Cp	28Aq	19Ar	28Ta	21Cn	12Vi	17Li	2Sg	4Cp
7	12Sc	26Sg	3Cp	20Aq	26Pi	19Ta	28Ge	20Le	8Li	11Sc	25Sg	28Cp
9	6Sg	21Cp	29Cp	18Pi	25Ar	19Ge	27Cn	17Vi	3Sc	5Sg	19Cp	22Aq
11	0Cp	17Aq	26Aq	17Ar	26Ta	19Cn	25Le	13Li	27Sc	29Sg	13Aq	17Pi
13	25Cp	15Pi	24Pi	17Ta	26Ge	17Le	22Vi	7Sc	21Sg	23Cp	9Pi	14Ar
15	22Aq	14Ar	23Ar	17Ge	25Cn	14Vi	17Li	1Sg	15Cp	18Aq	6Ar	13Ta
17	19Pi	12Ta	23Ta	15Cn	22Le	9Li	11Sc	25Sg	10Aq	14Pi	5Ta	13Ge
19	17Ar	10Ge	21Ge	12Le	17Vi	3Sc	5Sg	19Cp	6Pi	12Ar	5Ge	13Cn
21	15Ta	8Cn	19Cn	8Vi	12Li	26Sc	29Sg	14Aq	4Ar	12Ta	5Cn	13Le
23	14Ge	5Le	15Le	3Li	6Sc	20Sg	23Cp	11Pi	3Ta	11Ge	4Le	11Vi
25	12Cn	2Vi	11Vi	27Li	29Sc	14Cp	18Aq	9Ar	1Ge	10Cn	2Vi	7Li
27	10Le	27Vi	6Li	21Sc	23Sg	9Aq	15Pi	7Ta	0Cn	8Le	28Vi	2Sc
29	6Vi		0Sc	14Sg	17Cp	5Pi	12Ar	5Ge	28Cn	5Vi	23Li	25Sc
31	2Li		24Sc		12Aq		10Ta	3Cn		1Li		19Sg

1938

	Jan	Feb	Mar	Apr	May	Jun	Jul	Aug	Sep	Oct	Nov	Dec
1	1Cp	16Aq	25Aq	13Ar	20Ta	13Cn	22Le	13Li	29Sc	1Cp	15Aq	17Pi
3	25Cp	11Pi	21Pi	11Ta	19Ge	13Le	20Vi	9Sc	23Sg	25Cp	9Pi	12Ar
5	19Aq	7Ar	17Ar	9Ge	18Cn	11Vi	17Li	3Sg	17Cp	19Aq	5Ar	9Ta
7	14Pi	4Ta	15Ta	8Cn	17Le	7Li	12Sc	27Sg	11Aq	14Pi	1Ta	8Ge
9	10Ar	2Ge	13Ge	6Le	14Vi	3Sc	6Sg	20Cp	5Pi	10Ar	29Ta	8Cn
11	8Ta	0Cn	11Cn	4Vi	10Li	27Sc	0Cp	14Aq	1Ar	6Ta	28Ge	7Le
13	6Ge	0Le	9Le	1Li	6Sc	21Sg	24Cp	9Pi	27Ar	4Ge	27Cn	6Vi
15	6Cn	29Le	8Vi	27Li	0Sg	15Cp	17Aq	4Ar	24Ta	2Cn	26Le	4Li
17	6Le	27Vi	5Li	22Sc	24Sg	8Aq	12Pi	0Ta	21Ge	0Le	23Vi	0Sc
19	5Vi	23Li	1Sc	16Sg	18Cp	3Pi	7Ar	27Ta	20Cn	29Le	20Li	25Sc
21	3Li	18Sc	26Sc	10Cp	12Aq	28Pi	3Ta	25Ge	19Le	27Vi	16Sc	20Sg
23	28Li	12Sg	20Sg	3Aq	6Pi	24Ar	1Ge	24Cn	18Vi	24Li	11Sg	14Cp
25	22Sc	6Cp	14Cp	28Aq	2Ar	22Ta	0Cn	24Le	16Li	20Sc	5Cp	7Aq
27	16Sg	0Aq	8Aq	24Pi	29Ar	22Ge	1Le	23Vi	12Sc	15Sg	29Cp	1Pi
29	9Cp		3Pi	21Ar	28Ta	22Cn	1Vi	21Li	7Sg	9Cp	23Aq	25Pi
31	4Aq		29Pi		28Ge		29Vi	17Sc		3Aq		20Ar

1939

	Jan	Feb	Mar	Apr	May	Jun	Jul	Aug	Sep	Oct	Nov	Dec
1	3Ta	24Ge	3Cn	27Le	5Li	26Sc	0Cp	15Aq	0Ar	3Ta	22Ge	0Le
3	1Ge	24Cn	2Le	26Vi	3Sc	21Sg	25Cp	9Pi	24Ar	29Ta	19Cn	28Le
5	1Cn	24Le	2Vi	25Li	0Sg	16Cp	18Aq	3Ar	19Ta	25Ge	17Le	26Vi
7	1Le	24Vi	2Li	22Sc	26Sg	10Aq	12Pi	27Ar	15Ge	22Cn	16Vi	24Li
9	1Vi	23Li	1Sc	18Sg	20Cp	4Pi	6Ar	22Ta	12Cn	21Le	14Li	22Sc
11	0Li	19Sc	27Sc	12Cp	14Aq	28Pi	1Ta	19Ge	12Le	21Vi	13Sc	19Sg
13	27Li	14Sg	22Sg	6Aq	8Pi	23Ar	27Ta	18Cn	12Vi	20Li	10Sg	15Cp
15	22Sc	8Cp	16Cp	0Pi	2Ar	19Ta	25Ge	18Le	12Li	19Sc	7Cp	9Aq
17	17Sg	1Aq	10Aq	24Pi	28Ar	17Ge	25Cn	19Vi	11Sc	16Sg	2Aq	3Pi
19	11Cp	25Aq	4Pi	19Ar	24Ta	16Cn	25Le	18Li	8Sg	11Cp	26Aq	27Pi
21	4Aq	19Pi	28Pi	15Ta	22Ge	17Le	25Vi	16Sc	3Cp	6Aq	19Pi	21Ar
23	28Aq	14Ar	23Ar	12Ge	21Cn	15Vi	23Li	12Sg	27Cp	29Aq	13Ar	16Ta
25	22Pi	9Ta	19Ta	10Cn	20Le	12Li	19Sc	6Cp	21Aq	23Pi	8Ta	13Ge
27	17Ar	5Ge	16Ge	8Le	18Vi	9Sc	15Sg	0Aq	15Pi	18Ar	4Ge	11Cn
29	12Ta		13Cn	7Vi	16Li	5Sg	9Cp	24Aq	9Ar	13Ta	2Cn	10Le
31	9Ge		12Le		12Sc		3Aq	18Pi		9Ge		9Vi

1940

	Jan	Feb	Mar	Apr	May	Jun	Jul	Aug	Sep	Oct	Nov	Dec
1	23Vi	15Sc	8Sg	26Cp	29Aq	12Ar	14Ta	1Cn	22Le	0Li	23Sc	0Cp
3	21Li	12Sg	4Cp	20Aq	22Pi	6Ta	10Ge	29Cn	21Vi	0Sc	22Sg	28Cp
5	18Sc	7Cp	29Cp	14Pi	16Ar	1Ge	6Cn	28Le	21Li	0Sg	20Cp	24Aq
7	15Sg	2Aq	23Aq	7Ar	10Ta	27Ge	4Le	27Vi	20Sc	28Sg	15Aq	18Pi
9	10Cp	26Aq	17Pi	1Ta	5Ge	24Cn	3Vi	26Li	18Sg	24Cp	10Pi	12Ar
11	5Aq	20Pi	10Ar	26Ta	1Cn	22Le	1Li	24Sc	14Cp	19Aq	3Ar	5Ta
13	29Aq	13Ar	4Ta	21Ge	28Cn	20Vi	29Li	21Sg	9Aq	13Pi	27Ar	29Ta
15	23Pi	7Ta	29Ta	17Cn	25Le	19Li	27Sc	17Cp	4Pi	6Ar	21Ta	25Ge
17	17Ar	2Ge	24Ge	15Le	24Vi	17Sc	24Sg	13Aq	28Pi	0Ta	15Ge	21Cn
19	11Ta	28Ge	21Cn	14Vi	23Li	15Sg	21Cp	7Pi	21Ar	24Ta	11Cn	17Le
21	7Ge	27Cn	20Le	14Li	22Sc	12Cp	16Aq	1Ar	15Ta	18Ge	7Le	15Vi
23	4Cn	27Le	20Vi	13Sc	20Sg	8Aq	11Pi	24Ar	9Ge	14Cn	4Vi	13Li
25	4Le	27Vi	20Li	12Sg	17Cp	3Pi	4Ar	18Ta	4Cn	10Le	2Li	11Sc
27	4Vi	27Li	20Sc	9Cp	12Aq	26Pi	28Ar	13Ge	1Le	8Vi	2Sc	10Sg
29	3Li	25Sc	17Sg	4Aq	7Pi	20Ar	22Ta	9Cn	0Vi	8Li	1Sg	8Cp
31	2Sc		13Cp		0Ar		18Ge	7Le		8Sc		6Aq

1941

	Jan	Feb	Mar	Apr	May	Jun	Jul	Aug	Sep	Oct	Nov	Dec
1	19Aq	3Ar	12Ar	25Ta	29Ge	16Le	23Vi	16Sc	9Cp	16Aq	4Ar	7Ta
3	14Pi	27Ar	5Ta	19Ge	23Cn	13Vi	21Li	14Sg	6Aq	12Pi	28Ar	0Ge
5	8Ar	21Ta	29Ta	14Cn	19Le	11Li	20Sc	13Cp	3Pi	7Ar	22Ta	24Ge
7	1Ta	15Ge	23Ge	10Le	17Vi	10Sc	19Sg	11Aq	28Pi	1Ta	15Ge	18Cn
9	25Ta	11Cn	19Cn	8Vi	16Li	10Sg	18Cp	7Pi	23Ar	25Ta	9Cn	13Le
11	20Ge	8Le	16Le	8Li	16Sc	10Cp	16Aq	2Ar	17Ta	19Ge	4Le	9Vi
13	16Cn	6Vi	15Vi	8Sc	17Sg	8Aq	12Pi	27Ar	10Ge	13Cn	29Le	5Li
15	13Le	5Li	15Li	8Sg	16Cp	4Pi	7Ar	21Ta	5Cn	8Le	26Vi	4Sc
17	11Vi	4Sc	14Sc	7Cp	13Aq	29Pi	1Ta	14Ge	0Le	4Vi	25Li	4Sg
19	9Li	3Sg	13Sg	4Aq	8Pi	23Ar	24Ta	9Cn	26Le	3Li	26Sc	4Cp
21	8Sc	0Cp	11Cp	29Aq	2Ar	16Ta	19Ge	5Le	25Vi	2Sc	26Sg	4Aq
23	6Sg	27Cp	7Aq	23Pi	26Ar	10Ge	14Cn	2Vi	24Li	3Sg	26Cp	1Pi
25	4Cp	23Aq	2Pi	17Ar	19Ta	5Cn	9Le	0Li	23Sc	2Cp	23Aq	27Pi
27	1Aq	17Pi	26Pi	11Ta	13Ge	0Le	6Vi	28Li	22Sg	0Aq	18Pi	22Ar
29	27Aq		20Ar	4Ge	8Cn	26Le	4Li	27Sc	20Cp	26Aq	13Ar	15Ta
31	21Pi		14Ta		3Le		2Sc	25Sg		22Pi		9Ge

1942

	Jan	Feb	Mar	Apr	May	Jun	Jul	Aug	Sep	Oct	Nov	Dec
1	21Ge	7Le	15Le	3Li	11Sc	5Cp	13Aq	3Ar	19Ta	21Ge	5Le	7Vi
3	15Cn	2Vi	11Vi	2Sc	11Sg	4Aq	11Pi	29Ar	13Ge	15Cn	29Le	2Li
5	10Le	29Vi	9Li	1Sg	10Cp	2Pi	7Ar	23Ta	7Cn	9Le	24Vi	29Li
7	6Vi	26Li	7Sc	0Cp	9Aq	28Pi	2Ta	17Ge	1Le	4Vi	22Li	29Sc
9	2Li	24Sc	5Sg	28Cp	6Pi	23Ar	26Ta	11Cn	26Le	0Li	20Sc	29Sg
11	29Li	23Sg	4Cp	25Aq	1Ar	17Ta	20Ge	5Le	21Vi	27Li	20Sg	29Cp
13	28Sc	21Cp	2Aq	22Pi	26Ar	11Ge	14Cn	29Le	18Li	26Sc	19Cp	28Aq
15	28Sg	20Aq	29Aq	17Ar	20Ta	5Cn	8Le	25Vi	16Sc	25Sg	18Aq	25Pi
17	27Cp	17Pi	25Pi	12Ta	14Ge	29Cn	3Vi	21Li	14Sg	23Cp	15Pi	21Ar
19	26Aq	13Ar	21Ar	6Ge	8Cn	23Le	28Vi	19Sc	12Cp	21Aq	11Ar	16Ta
21	22Pi	8Ta	15Ta	29Ge	2Le	18Vi	24Li	17Sg	10Aq	18Pi	7Ta	10Ge
23	18Ar	2Ge	9Ge	23Cn	26Le	15Li	22Sc	16Cp	8Pi	15Ar	1Ge	4Cn
25	12Ta	25Ge	3Cn	18Le	22Vi	13Sc	22Sg	15Aq	6Ar	10Ta	25Ge	28Cn
27	6Ge	20Cn	27Cn	14Vi	20Li	13Sg	22Cp	14Pi	2Ta	5Ge	19Cn	21Le
29	29Ge		23Le	11Li	19Sc	13Cp	21Aq	11Ar	27Ta	29Ge	13Le	16Vi
31	24Cn		19Vi		20Sg		19Pi	7Ta		23Cn		11Li

1943

	Jan	Feb	Mar	Apr	May	Jun	Jul	Aug	Sep	Oct	Nov	Dec
1	24Li	15Sg	25Sg	19Aq	27Pi	17Ta	21Ge	6Le	20Vi	24Li	14Sg	22Cp
3	22Sc	15Cp	24Cp	17Pi	24Ar	12Ge	15Cn	29Le	15Li	20Sc	11Cp	20Aq
5	22Sg	15Aq	23Aq	15Ar	20Ta	6Cn	9Le	23Vi	10Sc	17Sg	9Aq	18Pi
7	22Cp	15Pi	23Pi	12Ta	16Ge	0Le	2Vi	18Li	6Sg	14Cp	8Pi	16Ar
9	22Aq	13Ar	21Ar	8Ge	10Cn	24Le	26Vi	13Sc	4Cp	13Aq	6Ar	13Ta
11	21Pi	9Ta	17Ta	2Cn	4Le	18Vi	21Li	10Sg	3Aq	12Pi	4Ta	10Ge
13	18Ar	4Ge	12Ge	26Cn	27Le	13Li	18Sc	9Cp	3Pi	11Ar	1Ge	5Cn
15	13Ta	28Ge	6Cn	19Le	22Vi	9Sc	16Sg	9Aq	2Ar	9Ta	27Ge	29Cn
17	7Ge	21Cn	0Le	14Vi	18Li	8Sg	16Cp	9Pi	1Ta	6Ge	21Cn	23Le
19	1Cn	15Le	24Le	9Li	15Sc	7Cp	16Aq	9Ar	28Ta	1Cn	15Le	17Vi
21	25Cn	10Vi	18Vi	6Sc	14Sg	7Aq	16Pi	6Ta	23Ge	25Cn	9Vi	11Li
23	18Le	5Li	14Li	4Sg	13Cp	6Pi	14Ar	2Ge	17Cn	19Le	3Li	6Sc
25	13Vi	0Sc	11Sc	3Cp	12Aq	4Ar	10Ta	27Ge	11Le	13Vi	28Li	3Sg
27	7Li	27Sc	8Sg	1Aq	10Pi	1Ta	6Ge	21Cn	5Vi	8Li	25Sc	2Cp
29	3Sc		6Cp	29Aq	7Ar	26Ta	0Cn	14Le	29Vi	3Sc	23Sg	1Aq
31	1Sg		4Aq		4Ta		24Cn	8Vi		0Sg		1Pi

1944

	Jan	Feb	Mar	Apr	May	Jun	Jul	Aug	Sep	Oct	Nov	Dec
1	15Pi	7Ta	29Ta	16Cn	18Le	2Li	4Sc	21Sg	12Aq	20Pi	14Ta	21Ge
3	13Ar	3Ge	25Ge	10Le	12Vi	26Li	0Sg	19Cp	12Pi	21Ar	13Ge	18Cn
5	10Ta	28Ge	19Cn	4Vi	6Li	22Sc	27Sg	19Aq	12Ar	21Ta	10Cn	13Le
7	6Ge	22Cn	13Le	27Vi	0Sc	18Sg	25Cp	19Pi	12Ta	18Ge	5Le	7Vi
9	1Cn	16Le	7Vi	22Li	26Sc	16Cp	24Aq	18Ar	10Ge	15Cn	0Vi	1Li
11	26Cn	10Vi	1Li	17Sc	22Sg	14Aq	23Pi	16Ta	5Cn	9Le	23Vi	25Li
13	19Le	4Li	25Li	12Sg	20Cp	13Pi	22Ar	13Ge	0Le	3Vi	17Li	20Sc
15	13Vi	28Li	20Sc	9Cp	17Aq	11Ar	19Ta	8Cn	24Le	27Vi	11Sc	15Sg
17	7Li	23Sc	15Sg	7Aq	16Pi	9Ta	16Ge	3Le	18Vi	20Li	6Sg	12Cp
19	1Sc	19Sg	13Cp	5Pi	14Ar	6Ge	11Cn	27Le	11Li	15Sc	2Cp	9Aq
21	27Sc	18Cp	11Aq	5Ar	13Ta	2Cn	6Le	21Vi	5Sc	9Sg	29Cp	7Pi
23	25Sg	17Aq	11Pi	4Ta	11Ge	28Cn	0Vi	14Li	0Sg	5Cp	26Aq	5Ar
25	24Cp	18Pi	11Ar	2Ge	7Cn	22Le	24Vi	8Sc	25Sg	2Aq	24Pi	3Ta
27	25Aq	18Ar	10Ta	29Ge	2Le	16Vi	18Li	3Sg	22Cp	0Pi	23Ar	2Ge
29	24Pi	16Ta	8Ge	24Cn	26Le	10Li	12Sc	29Sg	20Aq	29Pi	22Ta	29Ge
31	23Ar		4Cn		20Vi		8Sg	27Cp		29Ar		26Cn

1945

	Jan	Feb	Mar	Apr	May	Jun	Jul	Aug	Sep	Oct	Nov	Dec
1	8Le	23Vi	2Li	16Sc	19Sg	7Aq	15Pi	9Ta	1Cn	8Le	24Vi	27Li
3	3Vi	17Li	25Li	10Sg	14Cp	4Pi	13Ar	7Ge	28Cn	3Vi	18Li	21Sc
5	27Vi	11Sc	19Sc	5Cp	10Aq	3Ar	12Ta	4Cn	23Le	27Vi	12Sc	15Sg
7	21Li	5Sg	13Sg	1Aq	8Pi	2Ta	11Ge	1Le	18Vi	21Li	6Sg	9Cp
9	15Sc	1Cp	9Cp	29Aq	7Ar	1Ge	9Cn	27Le	13Li	15Sc	0Cp	4Aq
11	10Sg	28Cp	6Aq	28Pi	7Ta	0Cn	6Le	22Vi	7Sc	9Sg	24Cp	0Pi
13	7Cp	27Aq	5Pi	29Ar	7Ge	28Cn	2Vi	16Li	0Sg	3Cp	20Aq	27Pi
15	4Aq	27Pi	6Ar	29Ta	6Cn	24Le	26Vi	10Sc	24Sg	28Cp	17Pi	26Ar
17	3Pi	26Ar	6Ta	28Ge	3Le	18Vi	20Li	4Sg	19Cp	25Aq	16Ar	25Ta
19	2Ar	25Ta	5Ge	24Cn	28Le	12Li	14Sc	29Sg	16Aq	23Pi	17Ta	25Ge
21	0Ta	22Ge	2Cn	19Le	22Vi	6Sc	8Sg	25Cp	15Pi	23Ar	17Ge	24Cn
23	28Ta	18Cn	28Cn	14Vi	16Li	0Sg	4Cp	22Aq	15Ar	24Ta	16Cn	21Le
25	25Ge	13Le	22Le	7Li	10Sc	25Sg	0Aq	21Pi	15Ta	23Ge	13Le	17Vi
27	21Cn	7Vi	16Vi	1Sc	4Sg	21Cp	27Aq	21Ar	14Ge	21Cn	9Vi	12Li
29	17Le		10Li	25Sc	29Sg	18Aq	26Pi	20Ta	12Cn	17Le	3Li	6Sc
31	11Vi		4Sc		24Cp		24Ar	18Ge		12Vi		29Sc

1946

	Jan	Feb	Mar	Apr	May	Jun	Jul	Aug	Sep	Oct	Nov	Dec
1	11Sg	27Cp	5Aq	24Pi	2Ta	25Ge	3Le	23Vi	9Sc	11Sg	24Cp	27Aq
3	6Cp	23Aq	2Pi	23Ar	2Ge	25Cn	1Vi	19Li	3Sg	4Cp	19Aq	23Pi
5	1Aq	20Pi	0Ar	23Ta	2Cn	23Le	28Vi	13Sc	26Sg	28Cp	15Pi	20Ar
7	27Aq	18Ar	29Ar	22Ge	0Le	19Vi	23Li	7Sg	20Cp	23Aq	12Ar	19Ta
9	24Pi	17Ta	28Ta	20Cn	27Le	14Li	17Sc	0Cp	15Aq	20Pi	11Ta	19Ge
11	22Ar	15Ge	26Ge	17Le	22Vi	8Sc	10Sg	25Cp	12Pi	18Ar	11Ge	20Cn
13	20Ta	13Cn	23Cn	13Vi	17Li	2Sg	4Cp	20Aq	9Ar	18Ta	11Cn	19Le
15	19Ge	10Le	20Le	8Li	11Sc	25Sg	28Cp	16Pi	8Ta	17Ge	10Le	16Vi
17	18Cn	7Vi	16Vi	2Sc	5Sg	19Cp	23Aq	13Ar	6Ge	15Cn	7Vi	12Li
19	16Le	3Li	11Li	26Sc	28Sg	14Aq	20Pi	11Ta	4Cn	13Le	3Li	7Sc
21	12Vi	27Li	5Sc	19Sg	22Cp	9Pi	16Ar	9Ge	2Le	10Vi	27Li	1Sg
23	8Li	21Sc	29Sc	13Cp	17Aq	6Ar	14Ta	8Cn	0Vi	6Li	22Sc	24Sg
25	2Sc	15Sg	23Sg	8Sq	13Pi	4Ta	13Ge	6Le	26Vi	1Sc	15Sg	18Cp
27	25Sc	9Cp	17Cp	4Pi	11Ar	4Ge	13Cn	4Vi	22Li	25Sc	9Cp	12Aq
29	19Sq		12Aq	2Ar	10Ta	4Cn	12Le	1Li	17Sc	19Sg	3Aq	6Pi
31	14Cp		10Pi		10Ge		10Vi	27Li		12Cp		2Ar

1947

	Jan	Feb	Mar	Apr	May	Jun	Jul	Aug	Sep	Oct	Nov	Dec
1	15Ar	7Ge	17Ge	10Le	19Vi	8Sc	11Sg	26Cp	11Pi	15Ar	5Ge	13Cn
3	13Ta	6Cn	16Cn	9Vi	15Li	2Sg	5Cp	20Aq	6Ar	12Ta	3Cn	13Le
5	12Ge	6Le	15Le	6Li	11Sc	26Sg	29Cp	14Pi	2Ta	9Ge	2Le	11Vi
7	13Cn	5Vi	13Vi	2Sc	6Sg	20Cp	22Aq	9Ar	28Ta	7Cn	0Vi	8Li
9	13Le	3Li	11Li	27Sc	0Cp	14Aq	17Pi	5Ta	26Ge	5Le	28Vi	5Sc
11	11Vi	29Li	7Sc	22Sg	23Cp	8Pi	12Ar	2Ge	25Cn	4Vi	25Li	0Sg
13	8Li	24Sc	2Sg	15Cp	17Aq	3Ar	8Ta	0Cn	24Le	2Li	21Sc	25Sg
15	3Sc	18Sg	26Sg	9Aq	12Pi	0Ta	7Ge	0Le	23Vi	0Sc	16Sg	19Cp
17	28Sc	11Cp	19Cp	4Pi	8Ar	28Ta	6Cn	0Vi	22Li	26Sc	11Cp	13Aq
19	21Sg	5Aq	13Aq	0Ar	5Ta	28Ge	7Le	29Vi	18Sc	21Sg	5Aq	6Pi
21	15Cp	0Pi	9Pi	27Ar	5Ge	28Cn	7Vi	27Li	13Sg	15Cp	28Aq	1Ar
23	9Aq	26Pi	5Ar	26Ta	4Cn	28Le	5Li	23Sc	7Cp	9Aq	23Pi	26Ar
25	3Pi	22Ar	2Ta	24Ge	4Le	26Vi	1Sc	17Sg	1Aq	3Pi	18Ar	23Ta
27	29Pi	19Ta	0Ge	23Cn	2Vi	22Li	26Sc	11Cp	25Aq	28Pi	15Ta	22Ge
29	25Ar		28Ge	21Le	29Vi	17Sc	20Sg	4Aq	19Pi	24Ar	14Ge	22Cn
31	23Ta		26Cn		25Li		14Cp	28Aq		21Ta		22Le

358   A Lover's Guide

1948

	Jan	Feb	Mar	Apr	May	Jun	Jul	Aug	Sep	Oct	Nov	Dec
1	7Vi	28Li	20Sc	6Cp	8Aq	21Pi	24Ar	11Ge	3Le	12Vi	5Sc	11Sg
3	5Li	24Sc	15Sg	0Aq	2Pi	16Ar	20Ta	10Cn	3Vi	12Li	3Sg	8Cp
5	2Sc	19Sg	10Cp	24Aq	26Pi	12Ta	17Ge	9Le	4Li	11Sc	0Cp	3Aq
7	27Sc	13Cp	3Aq	18Pi	21Ar	9Ge	16Cn	10Vi	3Sc	9Sg	25Cp	27Aq
9	22Sg	6Aq	27Aq	12Ar	16Ta	7Cn	16Le	10Li	0Sg	5Cp	19Aq	21Pi
11	16Cp	0Pi	21Pi	8Ta	14Ge	6Le	15Vi	8Sc	26Sg	29Cp	13Pi	15Ar
13	9Aq	24Pi	16Ar	4Ge	11Cn	5Vi	14Li	4Sg	20Cp	23Aq	7Ar	9Ta
15	3Pi	19Ar	11Ta	1Cn	10Le	3Li	11Sc	29Sg	14Aq	17Pi	1Ta	5Ge
17	27Pi	14Ta	7Ge	29Cn	8Vi	1Sc	7Sg	23Cp	8Pi	11Ar	27Ta	2Cn
19	22Ar	10Ge	4Cn	27Le	6Li	27Sc	2Cp	17Aq	2Ar	5Ta	23Ge	1Le
21	18Ta	8Cn	3Le	26Vi	4Sc	23Sg	26Cp	11Pi	26Ar	0Ge	21Cn	29Le
23	15Ge	8Le	2Vi	25Li	1Sg	18Cp	20Aq	5Ar	21Ta	27Ge	18Le	28Vi
25	15Cn	9Vi	2Li	23Sc	27Sg	12Aq	14Pi	29Ar	16Ge	24Cn	17Vi	26Li
27	16Le	9Li	1Sc	19Sg	22Cp	6Pi	8Ar	24Ta	13Cn	22Le	15Li	23Sc
29	16Vi	7Sc	28Sc	14Cp	16Aq	0Ar	2Ta	20Ge	12Le	21Vi	13Sc	20Sg
31	15Li		24Sg		10Pi		28Ta	18Cn		20Li		16Cp

1949

	Jan	Feb	Mar	Apr	May	Jun	Jul	Aug	Sep	Oct	Nov	Dec
1	28Cp	13Pi	22Pi	6Ta	10Ge	29Cn	7Vi	1Sc	23Sg	29Cp	15Pi	17Ar
3	23Aq	7Ar	15Ar	1Ge	6Cn	27Le	6Li	29Sc	19Cp	24Aq	9Ar	11Ta
5	17Pi	1Ta	9Ta	26Ge	2Le	25Vi	4Sc	26Sg	14Aq	18Pi	2Ta	5Ge
7	11Ar	25Ta	4Ge	22Cn	0Vi	23Li	2Sg	22Cp	9Pi	12Ar	26Ta	0Cn
9	5Ta	21Ge	29Ge	20Le	29Vi	22Sc	29Sg	18Aq	3Ar	5Ta	20Ge	25Cn
11	0Ge	19Cn	27Cn	20Vi	28Li	20Sg	26Cp	12Pi	26Ar	29Ta	16Cn	22Le
13	27Ge	18Le	26Le	20Li	28Sc	18Cp	22Aq	6Ar	20Ta	23Ge	12Le	19Vi
15	25Cn	18Vi	27Vi	20Sc	26Sg	14Aq	16Pi	0Ta	14Ge	19Cn	9Vi	17Li
17	25Le	18Li	27Li	18Sg	23Cp	8Pi	10Ar	24Ta	10Cn	16Le	8Li	16Sc
19	24Vi	17Sc	26Sc	15Cp	18Aq	2Ar	4Ta	19Ge	7Le	14Vi	7Sc	16Sg
21	23Li	13Sg	23Sg	10Aq	12Pi	26Ar	28Ta	15Cn	6Vi	14Li	7Sg	14Cp
23	20Sc	9Cp	19Cp	4Pi	6Ar	20Ta	24Ge	13Le	6Li	14Sc	6Cp	12Aq
25	16Sg	4Aq	13Aq	28Pi	0Ta	15Ge	21Cn	13Vi	6Sc	14Sg	4Aq	7Pi
27	12Cp	28Aq	7Pi	21Ar	24Ta	12Cn	19Le	12Li	5Sg	12Cp	29Aq	1Ar
29	7Aq		1Ar	15Ta	19Ge	9Le	18Vi	11Sc	3Cp	8Aq	23Pi	25Ar
31	1Pi		24Ar		16Cn		17Li	9Sg		3Pi		19Ta

1950

	Jan	Feb	Mar	Apr	May	Jun	Jul	Aug	Sep	Oct	Nov	Dec
1	1Ge	17Cn	25Cn	14Vi	22Li	16Sg	24Cp	13Pi	28Ar	0Ge	14Cn	18Le
3	26Ge	14Le	22Le	14Li	23Sc	16Cp	22Aq	8Ar	22Ta	24Ge	9Le	14Vi
5	22Cn	12Vi	21Vi	14Sc	23Sg	14Aq	18Pi	2Ta	16Ge	18Cn	5Vi	11Li
7	19Le	11Li	20Li	14Sg	21Cp	10Pi	12Ar	26Ta	10Cn	14Le	2Li	10Sc
9	16Vi	9Sc	20Sc	12Cp	18Aq	4Ar	6Ta	20Ge	6Le	10Vi	2Sc	10Sg
11	14Li	7Sg	18Sg	9Aq	13Pi	28Ar	0Ge	15Cn	2Vi	9Li	2Sg	11Cp
13	12Sc	5Cp	15Cp	4Pi	7Ar	22Ta	24Ge	11Le	0Li	9Sc	2Cp	10Aq
15	11Sg	2Aq	11Aq	28Pi	1Ta	15Ge	19Cn	7Vi	29Li	8Sg	1Aq	7Pi
17	9Cp	28Aq	7Pi	22Ar	25Ta	10Cn	15Le	5Li	28Sc	7Cp	28Aq	3Ar
19	6Aq	23Pi	1Ar	16Ta	19Ge	5Le	11Vi	3Sc	27Sg	5Aq	24Pi	27Ar
21	2Pi	17Ar	25Ar	9Ge	13Cn	1Vi	8Li	2Sg	24Cp	1Pi	18Ar	21Ta
23	27Pi	11Ta	19Ta	4Cn	8Le	28Vi	6Sc	0Cp	21Aq	26Pi	12Ta	14Ge
25	21Ar	4Ge	13Ge	28Cn	4Vi	26Li	5Sg	28Cp	17Pi	21Ar	6Ge	8Cn
27	15Ta	29Ge	7Cn	25Le	2Li	25Sc	4Cp	25Aq	12Ar	15Ta	29Ge	3Le
29	9Ge		3Le	23Vi	1Sc	25Sg	2Aq	21Pi	6Ta	9Ge	23Cn	28Le
31	4Cn		0Vi		1Sg		0Pi	16Ar		2Cn		23Vi

1951

	Jan	Feb	Mar	Apr	May	Jun	Jul	Aug	Sep	Oct	Nov	Dec
1	7Li	29Sc	10Sg	3Aq	10Pi	28Ar	2Ge	16Cn	1Vi	6Li	26Sc	5Cp
3	4Sc	28Sg	8Cp	0Pi	6Ar	22Ta	25Ge	10Le	27Vi	3Sc	25Sg	5Aq
5	3Sg	27Cp	6Aq	27Pi	1Ta	16Ge	19Cn	5Vi	23Li	1Sg	24Cp	3Pi
7	4Cp	26Aq	4Pi	22Ar	26Ta	10Cn	13Le	0Li	20Sc	29Sg	22Aq	0Ar
9	3Aq	23Pi	1Ar	17Ta	20Ge	4Le	7Vi	26Li	18Sg	28Cp	20Pi	26Ar
11	2Pi	19Ar	27Ar	11Ge	13Cn	28Le	3Li	23Sc	17Cp	26Aq	16Ar	21Ta
13	28Pi	13Ta	21Ta	5Cn	7Le	23Vi	29Li	22Sg	16Aq	23Pi	12Ta	15Ge
15	23Ar	7Ge	15Ge	29Cn	2Vi	20Li	28Sc	22Cp	14Pi	20Ar	7Ge	9Cn
17	17Ta	1Cn	9Cn	24Le	28Vi	19Sc	27Sg	21Aq	12Ar	16Ta	1Cn	3Le
19	11Ge	25Cn	3Le	20Vi	26Li	19Sg	28Cp	20Pi	8Ta	11Ge	24Cn	27Le
21	5Cn	21Le	29Le	18Li	25Sc	19Cp	27Aq	17Ar	3Ge	5Cn	18Le	21Vi
23	29Cn	17Vi	25Vi	17Sc	26Sg	19Aq	25Pi	12Ta	27Ge	28Cn	13Vi	16Li
25	24Le	14Li	23Li	16Sg	25Cp	17Pi	22Ar	7Ge	20Cn	22Le	8Li	14Sc
27	20Vi	11Sc	22Sc	16Cp	24Aq	13Ar	16Ta	1Cn	15Le	17Vi	6Sc	13Sg
29	17Li		21Sg	14Aq	20Pi	8Ta	10Ge	24Cn	9Vi	14Li	5Sg	13Cp
31	15Sc		19Cp		16Ar		4Cn	19Le		12Sc		14Aq

1952

	Jan	Feb	Mar	Apr	May	Jun	Jul	Aug	Sep	Oct	Nov	Dec
1	28Aq	19Ar	10Ta	26Ge	27Cn	11Vi	14Li	2Sg	24Cp	3Pi	25Ar	2Ge
3	26Pi	15Ta	5Ge	20Cn	21Le	6Li	10Sc	0Cp	24Aq	2Ar	23Ta	28Ge
5	23Ar	9Ge	0Cn	13Le	15Vi	2Sc	8Sg	0Aq	24Pi	1Ta	20Ge	23Cn
7	18Ta	3Cn	23Cn	7Vi	10Li	29Sc	7Cp	1Pi	23Ar	29Ta	15Cn	17Le
9	12Ge	27Cn	17Le	2Li	7Sc	28Sg	7Aq	0Ar	21Ta	25Ge	9Le	10Vi
11	6Cn	21Le	11Vi	28Li	5Sg	28Cp	7Pi	29Ar	16Ge	19Cn	3Vi	4Li
13	0Le	15Vi	6Li	25Sc	4Cp	27Aq	5Ar	25Ta	11Cn	13Le	26Vi	29Li
15	24Le	9Li	2Sc	23Sg	2Aq	25Pi	2Ta	20Ge	5Le	7Vi	21Li	26Sc
17	18Vi	5Sc	29Sc	21Cp	1Pi	22Ar	28Ta	14Cn	28Le	1Li	17Sc	23Sg
19	12Li	2Sg	26Sg	20Aq	28Pi	18Ta	23Ge	8Le	22Vi	26Li	15Sg	22Cp
21	9Sc	0Cp	25Cp	18Pi	25Ar	14Ge	17Cn	1Vi	17Li	22Sc	13Cp	21Aq
23	6Sg	0Aq	24Aq	16Ar	22Ta	8Cn	11Le	25Vi	12Sc	18Sg	11Aq	20Pi
25	6Cp	29Aq	23Pi	13Ta	17Ge	2Le	4Vi	20Li	8Sg	16Cp	9Pi	18Ar
27	6Aq	29Pi	21Ar	9Ge	12Cn	26Le	28Vi	15Sc	5Cp	14Aq	7Ar	15Ta
29	6Pi	27Ar	18Ta	4Cn	5Le	19Vi	23Li	11Sg	3Aq	12Pi	5Ta	11Ge
31	5Ar		13Ge		29Le		18Sc	9Cp		11Ar		6Cn

1953

	Jan	Feb	Mar	Apr	May	Jun	Jul	Aug	Sep	Oct	Nov	Dec
1	19Cn	3Vi	12Vi	27Li	1Sg	21Cp	29Aq	23Ar	15Ge	20Cn	5Vi	7Li
3	13Le	27Vi	6Li	22Sc	27Sg	19Aq	28Pi	21Ta	10Cn	14Le	29Vi	1Sc
5	7Vi	21Li	0Sc	17Sg	24Cp	17Pi	26Ar	18Ge	5Le	8Vi	22Li	25Sc
7	0Li	15Sc	25Sc	14Cp	22Aq	15Ar	24Ta	13Cn	29Le	2Li	17Sc	21Sg
9	24Li	11Sg	20Sg	12Aq	21Pi	14Ta	21Ge	8Le	23Vi	26Li	11Sg	17Cp
11	20Sc	9Cp	18Cp	11Pi	20Ar	11Ge	17Cn	2Vi	17Li	20Sc	7Cp	14Aq
13	17Sg	9Aq	17Aq	11Ar	19Ta	8Cn	12Le	26Vi	10Sc	14Sg	3Aq	11Pi
15	16Cp	9Pi	17Pi	10Ta	17Ge	3Le	6Vi	20Li	5Sg	10Cp	1Pi	10Ar
17	16Aq	9Ar	17Ar	8Ge	13Cn	28Le	29Vi	14Sc	0Cp	7Aq	29Pi	8Ta
19	15Pi	8Ta	16Ta	5Cn	8Le	21Vi	23Li	9Sg	27Cp	5Pi	29Ar	7Ge
21	14Ar	5Ge	14Ge	0Le	2Vi	15Li	18Sc	5Cp	26Aq	5Ar	28Ta	5Cn
23	12Ta	0Cn	9Cn	24Le	25Vi	10Sc	14Sg	3Aq	27Pi	5Ta	27Ge	1Le
25	8Ge	24Cn	3Le	17Vi	19Li	6Sg	11Cp	3Pi	27Ar	5Ge	24Cn	27Le
27	3Cn	18Le	27Le	11Li	14Sc	3Cp	10Aq	3Ar	27Ta	3Cn	19Le	21Vi
29	27Cn		21Vi	6Sc	10Sg	1Aq	9Pi	3Ta	24Ge	29Cn	13Vi	15Li
31	21Le		15Li		7Cp		9Ar	1Ge		23Le		9Sc

1954

	Jan	Feb	Mar	Apr	May	Jun	Jul	Aug	Sep	Oct	Nov	Dec
1	21Sc	7Cp	15Cp	5Pi	13Ar	7Ge	14Cn	3Vi	18Li	20Sc	5Cp	9Aq
3	16Sg	4Aq	12Aq	5Ar	14Ta	6Cn	12Le	28Vi	12Sc	14Sg	29Cp	5Pi
5	12Cp	3Pi	12Pi	5Ta	14Ge	4Le	7Vi	22Li	6Sg	8Cp	25Aq	2Ar
7	10Aq	2Ar	12Ar	5Ge	12Cn	29Le	2Li	16Sc	0Cp	3Aq	23Pi	1Ta
9	8Pi	1Ta	11Ta	3Cn	8Le	24Vi	26Li	10Sg	25Cp	1Pi	23Ar	1Ge
11	6Ar	0Ge	10Ge	29Cn	3Vi	18Li	20Sc	5Cp	22Aq	0Ar	23Ta	1Cn
13	5Ta	27Ge	7Cn	24Le	27Vi	12Sc	14Sg	1Aq	21Pi	0Ta	23Ge	0Le
15	3Ge	23Cn	3Le	19Vi	21Li	6Sg	9Cp	28Aq	21Ar	0Ge	22Cn	27Le
17	0Cn	18Le	27Le	12Li	15Sc	1Cp	5Aq	27Pi	21Ta	29Ge	19Le	23Vi
19	27Cn	13Vi	22Vi	6Sc	9Sg	26Cp	3Pi	26Ar	19Ge	26Cn	14Vi	17Li
21	22Le	7Li	15Li	0Sg	4Cp	22Aq	1Ar	24Ta	16Cn	22Le	9Li	11Sc
23	17Vi	1Sc	9Sc	24Sg	29Cp	20Pi	29Ar	22Ge	12Le	17Vi	2Sc	5Sg
25	11Li	24Sc	3Sg	19Cp	25Aq	18Ar	27Ta	19Cn	8Vi	11Li	26Sc	29Sg
27	4Sc	19Sg	27Sg	16Aq	23Pi	17Ta	26Ge	16Le	2Li	5Sc	20Sg	23Cp
29	29Sc		23Cp	14Pi	22Ar	16Ge	23Cn	11Vi	27Li	29Sc	14Cp	19Aq
31	24Sg		20Aq		22Ta		20Le	6Li		23Sg		15Pi

1955

	Jan	Feb	Mar	Apr	May	Jun	Jul	Aug	Sep	Oct	Nov	Dec
1	28Pi	21Ta	2Ge	25Cn	2Vi	19Li	22Sc	6Cp	21Aq	26Pi	18Ta	26Ge
3	26Ar	20Ge	0Cn	22Le	27Vi	13Sc	15Sg	0Aq	17Pi	24Ar	17Ge	26Cn
5	25Ta	18Cn	28Cn	18Vi	22Li	7Sg	9Cp	25Aq	15Ar	23Ta	16Cn	24Le
7	25Ge	16Le	25Le	13Li	16Sc	0Cp	3Aq	21Pi	13Ta	22Ge	14Le	21Vi
9	24Cn	13Vi	21Vi	7Sc	10Sg	24Cp	28Aq	18Ar	11Ge	20Cn	11Vi	17Li
11	22Le	9Li	17Li	1Sg	3Cp	19Aq	24Pi	16Ta	9Cn	17Le	7Li	12Sc
13	18Vi	3Sc	11Sc	25Sg	27Cp	14Pi	21Ar	14Ge	7Le	15Vi	2Sc	6Sg
15	13Li	27Sc	5Sg	19Cp	22Aq	11Ar	19Ta	13Cn	5Vi	11Li	27Sc	29Sg
17	7Sc	21Sg	28Sg	13Aq	18Pi	10Ta	19Ge	12Le	2Li	6Sc	21Sg	23Cp
19	1Sg	15Cp	23Cp	10Pi	17Ar	10Ge	18Cn	10Vi	28Li	0Sg	14Cp	17Aq
21	25Sg	11Aq	18Aq	8Ar	16Ta	10Cn	18Le	7Li	22Sc	24Sg	8Aq	11Pi
23	20Cp	7Pi	16Pi	8Ta	17Ge	9Le	16Vi	2Sc	16Sg	18Cp	3Pi	7Ar
25	25Aq	5Ar	15Ar	8Ge	16Cn	7Vi	12Li	27Sc	10Cp	12Aq	29Pi	4Ta
27	12Pi	4Ta	14Ta	7Cn	15Le	3Li	6Sc	20Sg	4Aq	7Pi	26Ar	3Ge
29	9Ar		13Ge	5Le	11Vi	28Li	0Sg	14Cp	29Aq	4Ar	26Ta	4Cn
31	7Ta		11Cn		7Li		24Sg	9Aq		3Ta		4Le

1956

	Jan	Feb	Mar	Apr	May	Jun	Jul	Aug	Sep	Oct	Nov	Dec
1	19Le	9Li	0Sc	15Sg	17Cp	1Pi	4Ar	23Ta	15Cn	24Le	17Li	23Sc
3	17Vi	5Sc	25Sc	9Cp	11Aq	26Pi	0Ta	21Ge	15Le	23Vi	14Sc	18Sg
5	14Li	29Sc	19Sg	3Aq	5Pi	22Ar	28Ta	21Cn	15Vi	22Li	10Sg	12Cp
7	9Sc	23Sg	13Cp	27Aq	1Ar	20Ta	27Ge	21Le	14Li	19Sc	4Cp	6Aq
9	3Sg	17Cp	7Aq	23Pi	28Ar	19Ge	28Cn	21Vi	11Sc	14Sg	28Cp	0Pi
11	26Sg	11Aq	1Pi	19Ar	26Ta	19Cn	28Le	19Li	6Sg	9Cp	22Aq	24Pi
13	20Cp	5Pi	27Pi	17Ta	25Ge	19Le	27Vi	15Sc	1Cp	2Aq	16Pi	19Ar
15	14Aq	1Ar	24Ar	15Ge	24Cn	17Vi	24Li	10Sg	24Cp	26Aq	11Ar	16Ta
17	8Pi	27Ar	21Ta	14Cn	23Le	14Li	19Sc	4Cp	18Aq	21Pi	8Ta	14Ge
19	4Ar	24Ta	19Ge	12Le	20Vi	9Sc	13Sg	28Cp	12Pi	16Ar	6Ge	13Cn
21	0Ta	22Ge	17Cn	10Vi	17Li	4Sg	7Cp	22Aq	8Ar	13Ta	4Cn	13Le
23	28Ta	21Cn	15Le	7Li	13Sc	28Sg	1Aq	16Pi	3Ta	10Ge	3Le	12Vi
25	27Ge	20Le	14Vi	3Sc	7Sg	22Cp	25Aq	11Ar	0Ge	8Cn	2Vi	10Li
27	27Cn	19Vi	12Li	29Sc	1Cp	16Aq	19Pi	6Ta	27Ge	6Le	29Vi	6Sc
29	27Le	17Li	8Sc	23Sg	25Cp	10Pi	14Ar	3Ge	25Cn	5Vi	26Li	2Sg
31	26Vi		3Sg		19Aq		10Ta	1Cn		3Li		27Sg

1957

	Jan	Feb	Mar	Apr	May	Jun	Jul	Aug	Sep	Oct	Nov	Dec
1	9Cp	23Aq	2Pi	17Ar	22Ta	12Cn	21Le	15Li	5Sg	10Cp	25Aq	27Pi
3	3Aq	17Pi	26Pi	13Ta	19Ge	11Le	20Vi	13Sc	1Cp	5Aq	19Pi	20Ar
5	27Aq	11Ar	21Ar	9Ge	16Cn	10Vi	19Li	9Sg	26Cp	28Aq	12Ar	15Ta
7	20Pi	6Ta	16Ta	5Cn	14Le	8Li	16Sc	4Cp	20Aq	22Pi	7Ta	11Ge
9	15Ar	2Ge	12Ge	3Le	13Vi	5Sc	12Sg	28Cp	13Pi	16Ar	2Ge	8Cn
11	10Ta	0Cn	9Cn	2Vi	11Li	2Sg	7Cp	23Aq	7Ar	10Ta	28Ge	6Le
13	7Ge	29Cn	8Le	2Li	9Sc	28Sg	2Aq	16Pi	1Ta	5Ge	25Cn	4Vi
15	6Cn	0Vi	8Vi	1Sc	7Sg	23Cp	26Aq	10Ar	26Ta	1Cn	23Le	2Li
17	7Le	0Li	8Li	29Sc	3Cp	17Aq	20Pi	4Ta	21Ge	28Cn	21Vi	0Sc
19	7Vi	29Li	7Sc	25Sg	27Cp	11Pi	13Ar	29Ta	19Cn	27Le	20Li	28Sc
21	6Li	26Sc	4Sg	20Cp	21Aq	5Ar	8Ta	26Ge	18Le	26Vi	19Sc	25Sg
23	3Sc	21Sg	29Sg	13Aq	15Pi	0Ta	4Ge	24Cn	18Vi	26Li	17Sg	21Cp
25	29Sc	15Cp	23Cp	7Pi	9Ar	26Ta	1Cn	24Le	18Li	25Sc	13Cp	16Aq
27	24Sg	9Aq	17Aq	1Ar	4Ta	23Ge	1Le	25Vi	17Sc	23Sg	9Aq	11Pi
29	18Cp		11Pi	26Ar	1Ge	22Cn	1Vi	24Li	14Sg	18Cp	3Pi	4Ar
31	12Aq		5Ar		28Ge		1Li	22Sc		13Aq		28Ar

1958

	Jan	Feb	Mar	Apr	May	Jun	Jul	Aug	Sep	Oct	Nov	Dec
1	10Ta	27Ge	5Cn	26Le	4Li	28Sc	5Cp	23Aq	8Ar	10Ta	25Ge	0Le
3	6Ge	25Cn	3Le	26Vi	4Sc	26Sg	2Aq	18Pi	2Ta	4Ge	20Cn	27Le
5	3Cn	24Le	2Vi	26Li	4Sg	24Cp	27Aq	12Ar	25Ta	28Ge	17Le	24Vi
7	1Le	24Vi	3Li	26Sc	2Cp	19Aq	22Pi	5Ta	20Ge	24Cn	14Vi	23Li
9	0Vi	24Li	3Sc	24Sg	29Cp	14Pi	16Ar	29Ta	16Cn	21Le	14Li	22Sc
11	29Vi	21Sc	1Sg	20Cp	24Aq	8Ar	9Ta	24Ge	13Le	20Vi	14Sc	22Sg
13	27Li	18Sg	28Sg	15Aq	18Pi	1Ta	4Ge	21Cn	12Vi	21Li	14Sg	20Cp
15	25Sc	14Cp	24Cp	9Pi	11Ar	26Ta	29Ge	19Le	12Li	21Sc	13Cp	18Aq
17	21Sg	9Aq	18Aq	3Ar	5Ta	21Ge	26Cn	18Vi	12Sc	20Sg	9Aq	13Pi
19	17Cp	3Pi	12Pi	26Ar	29Ta	17Cn	24Le	18Li	11Sg	17Cp	5Pi	7Ar
21	12Aq	27Pi	6Ar	20Ta	24Ge	14Le	23Vi	16Sc	8Cp	13Aq	29Pi	1Ta
23	7Pi	21Ar	29Ar	15Ge	20Cn	12Vi	21Li	14Sg	4Aq	8Pi	22Ar	24Ta
25	0Ar	14Ta	23Ta	10Cn	17Le	10Li	19Sc	11Cp	29Aq	2Ar	16Ta	19Ge
27	24Ar	9Ge	18Ge	7Le	15Vi	9Sc	17Sg	7Aq	23Pi	26Ar	10Ge	14Cn
29	18Ta		14Cn	5Vi	14Li	7Sg	14Cp	2Pi	17Ar	19Ta	5Cn	10Le
31	14Ge		11Le		13Sc		10Aq	26Pi		13Ge		7Vi

1959

	Jan	Feb	Mar	Apr	May	Jun	Jul	Aug	Sep	Oct	Nov	Dec
1	21Vi	14Sc	24Sc	17Cp	23Aq	9Ar	12Ta	26Ge	12Le	17Vi	8Sc	17Sg
3	18Li	12Sg	23Sg	13Aq	18Pi	3Ta	5Ge	20Cn	8Vi	15Li	8Sg	17Cp
5	17Sc	10Cp	20Cp	9Pi	12Ar	27Ta	29Ge	16Le	6Li	14Sc	8Cp	16Aq
7	16Sg	7Aq	16Aq	3Ar	6Ta	21Ge	24Cn	13Vi	4Sc	14Sg	6Aq	13Pi
9	14Cp	3Pi	12Pi	27Ar	0Ge	15Cn	20Le	10Li	3Sg	12Cp	3Pi	8Ar
11	12Aq	29Pi	7Ar	21Ta	24Ge	10Le	16Vi	8Sc	1Cp	10Aq	28Pi	2Ta
13	8Pi	23Ar	1Ta	15Ge	18Cn	6Vi	13Li	6Sg	29Cp	6Pi	23Ar	26Ta
15	3Ar	16Ta	24Ta	9Cn	13Le	3Li	11Sc	5Cp	26Aq	1Ar	17Ta	20Ge
17	27Ar	10Ge	18Ge	4Le	9Vi	1Sc	10Sg	3Aq	22Pi	26Ar	11Ge	13Cn
19	20Ta	5Cn	13Cn	0Vi	7Li	1Sg	9Cp	1Pi	18Ar	20Ta	4Cn	8Le
21	15Ge	1Le	9Le	29Vi	7Sc	1Cp	8Aq	27Pi	12Ta	14Ge	28Cn	2Vi
23	10Cn	28Le	6Vi	29Li	7Sg	0Aq	6Pi	22Ar	6Ge	8Cn	23Le	28Vi
25	6Le	27Vi	5Li	29Sc	7Cp	28Aq	2Ar	16Ta	0Cn	2Le	19Vi	25Li
27	3Vi	26Li	5Sc	29Sg	6Aq	24Pi	26Ar	10Ge	24Cn	27Le	17Li	24Sc
29	1Li		5Sg	27Cp	2Pi	18Ar	20Ta	4Cn	20Le	24Vi	16Sc	25Sg
31	29Li		3Cp		27Pi		14Ge	29Cn		23Li		25Cp

1960

	Jan	Feb	Mar	Apr	May	Jun	Jul	Aug	Sep	Oct	Nov	Dec
1	10Aq	29Pi	20Ar	5Ge	7Cn	21Le	25Vi	14Sc	7Cp	16Aq	8Ar	13Ta
3	8Pi	25Ar	15Ta	29Ge	1Le	16Vi	21Li	13Sg	6Aq	15Pi	4Ta	8Ge
5	4Ar	19Ta	9Ge	22Cn	25Le	12Li	19Sc	12Cp	6Pi	12Ar	0Ge	3Cn
7	29Ar	13Ge	3Cn	17Le	20Vi	10Sc	18Sg	12Aq	4Ar	9Ta	24Ge	26Cn
9	23Ta	7Cn	27Cn	12Vi	18Li	10Sg	19Cp	12Pi	1Ta	4Ge	18Cn	20Le
11	16Ge	1Le	22Le	9Li	17Sc	10Cp	19Aq	10Ar	26Ta	28Ge	12Le	14Vi
13	10Cn	26Le	18Vi	8Sc	16Sg	10Aq	18Pi	6Ta	20Ge	22Cn	6Vi	9Li
15	5Le	22Vi	15Li	7Sg	16Cp	9Pi	14Ar	0Ge	14Cn	16Le	1Li	6Sc
17	29Le	19Li	13Sc	6Cp	15Aq	5Ar	9Ta	24Ge	8Le	11Vi	28Li	4Sg
19	25Vi	16Sc	11Sg	4Aq	12Pi	0Ta	4Ge	18Cn	3Vi	6Li	26Sc	4Cp
21	22Li	14Sg	9Cp	2Pi	8Ar	25Ta	27Ge	12Le	28Vi	3Sc	26Sg	5Aq
23	19Sc	13Cp	8Aq	28Pi	3Ta	19Ge	21Cn	6Vi	24Li	2Sg	25Cp	4Pi
25	18Sg	12Aq	5Pi	24Ar	28Ta	12Cn	15Le	2Li	22Sc	0Cp	24Aq	1Ar
27	18Cp	10Pi	2Ar	19Ta	22Ge	6Le	9Vi	28Li	20Sg	29Cp	21Pi	28Ar
29	18Aq	7Ar	28Ar	13Ge	15Cn	0Vi	5Li	25Sc	18Cp	27Aq	18Ar	23Ta
31	16Pi		23Ta		9Le		1Sc	23Sg		24Pi		17Ge

1961

	Jan	Feb	Mar	Apr	May	Jun	Jul	Aug	Sep	Oct	Nov	Dec
1	29Ge	14Le	22Le	8Li	13Sc	4Cp	13Aq	6Ar	26Ta	0Cn	15Le	16Vi
3	23Cn	8Vi	17Vi	4Sc	10Sg	3Aq	12Pi	4Ta	22Ge	25Cn	8Vi	10Li
5	17Le	2Li	11Li	0Sg	9Cp	2Pi	10Ar	0Ge	16Cn	18Le	2Li	5Sc
7	11Vi	27Li	7Sc	28Sg	7Aq	0Ar	7Ta	25Ge	10Le	12Vi	27Li	2Sg
9	5Li	23Sc	3Sg	26Cp	5Pi	27Ar	3Ge	19Cn	3Vi	6Li	23Sc	29Sg
11	1Sc	21Sg	1Cp	24Aq	3Ar	23Ta	28Ge	13Le	27Vi	1Sc	20Sg	28Cp
13	28Sc	21Cp	0Aq	23Pi	0Ta	19Ge	22Cn	6Vi	22Li	27Sc	17Cp	26Aq
15	27Sg	21Aq	29Aq	21Ar	27Ta	13Cn	16Le	0Li	17Sc	23Sg	15Aq	24Pi
17	28Cp	21Pi	29Pi	19Ta	23Ge	7Le	9Vi	24Li	13Sg	20Cp	13Pi	22Ar
19	28Aq	19Ar	27Ar	15Ge	17Cn	1Vi	3Li	20Sc	10Cp	19Aq	12Ar	20Ta
21	27Pi	16Ta	24Ta	9Cn	11Le	25Vi	28Li	17Sg	9Aq	18Pi	10Ta	16Ge
23	24Ar	11Ge	19Ge	3Le	5Vi	19Li	24Sc	15Cp	8Pi	17Ar	7Ge	12Cn
25	20Ta	5Cn	13Cn	27Le	29Vi	16Sc	22Sg	15Aq	8Ar	15Ta	4Cn	6Le
27	14Ge	29Cn	7Le	21Vi	24Li	14Sg	22Cp	15Pi	7Ta	13Ge	28Cn	0Vi
29	8Cn		1Vi	16Li	21Sc	13Cp	22Aq	15Ar	5Ge	8Cn	22Le	24Vi
31	2Le		25Vi		20Sg		22Pi	13Ta		3Le		18Li

1962

	Jan	Feb	Mar	Apr	May	Jun	Jul	Aug	Sep	Oct	Nov	Dec
1	0Sc	17Sg	26Sg	17Aq	26Pi	19Ta	26Ge	13Le	28Vi	1Sc	16Sg	22Cp
3	26Sc	15Cp	24Cp	16Pi	25Ar	17Ge	22Cn	8Vi	22Li	25Sc	12Cp	18Aq
5	23Sg	15Aq	23Aq	17Ar	25Ta	14Cn	17Le	1Li	16Sc	19Sg	8Aq	16Pi
7	22Cp	15Pi	23Pi	16Ta	23Ge	9Le	11Vi	25Li	10Sg	15Cp	5Pi	14Ar
9	22Aq	15Ar	24Ar	14Ge	19Cn	3Vi	5Li	19Sc	6Cp	12Aq	5Ar	14Ta
11	21Pi	13Ta	22Ta	11Cn	13Le	27Vi	29Li	14Sg	3Aq	11Pi	5Ta	13Ge
13	19Ar	10Ge	19Ge	5Le	7Vi	21Li	24Sc	11Cp	3Pi	11Ar	5Ge	11Cn
15	16Ta	5Cn	14Cn	29Le	1Li	16Sc	20Sg	10Aq	3Ar	12Ta	3Cn	7Le
17	13Ge	29Cn	9Le	23Vi	25Li	11Sg	17Cp	9Pi	3Ta	11Ge	0Le	3Vi
19	8Cn	23Le	2Vi	17Li	20Sc	8Cp	16Aq	9Ar	2Ge	8Cn	25Le	27Vi
21	3Le	17Vi	26Vi	11Sc	16Sg	6Aq	15Pi	8Ta	29Ge	4Le	19Vi	20Li
23	27Le	11Li	20Li	6Sg	12Cp	4Pi	14Ar	6Ge	25Cn	28Le	12Li	14Sc
25	20Vi	5Sc	14Sc	2Cp	10Aq	3Ar	12Ta	2Cn	19Le	22Vi	6Sc	9Sg
27	14Li	0Sc	9Sg	29Cp	7Pi	1Ta	9Ge	28Cn	13Vi	16Li	1Sg	5Cp
29	8Sc		5Cp	27Aq	6Ar	29Ta	5Cn	22Le	7Li	10Sc	26Sg	1Aq
31	4Sg		3Aq		5Ta		1Le	16Vi		4Sg		29Aq

1963

	Jan	Feb	Mar	Apr	May	Jun	Jul	Aug	Sep	Oct	Nov	Dec
1	13Pi	6Ta	17Ta	8Cn	14Le	29Vi	2Sc	16Sg	1Aq	7Pi	29Ar	8Ge
3	11Ar	4Ge	15Ge	4Le	9Vi	23Li	25Sc	10Cp	29Aq	6Ar	0Ge	8Cn
5	9Ta	1Cn	12Cn	29Le	3Li	17Sc	20Sg	6Aq	27Pi	6Ta	29Ge	6Le
7	8Ge	28Cn	7Le	24Vi	26Li	11Sg	15Cp	4Pi	26Ar	6Ge	28Cn	3Vi
9	5Cn	23Le	2Vi	18Li	20Sc	6Cp	11Aq	2Ar	25Ta	4Cn	24Le	28Vi
11	2Le	18Vi	27Vi	11Sc	14Sg	1Aq	7Pi	0Ta	24Ge	1Le	19Vi	23Li
13	28Le	12Li	21Li	5Sg	9Cp	27Aq	5Ar	29Ta	21Cn	27Le	14Li	16Sc
15	22Vi	6Sc	14Sc	29Sg	4Aq	24Pi	4Ta	27Ge	17Le	22Vi	7Sc	10Sg
17	16Li	0Sg	8Sg	24Cp	0Pi	23Ar	2Ge	24Cn	13Vi	17Li	1Sg	4Cp
19	10Sc	25Sg	3Cp	21Aq	28Pi	22Ta	1Cn	21Le	8Li	11Sc	25Sg	28Cp
21	4Sg	21Cp	29Cp	19Pi	28Ar	22Ge	29Cn	17Vi	2Sc	4Sg	19Cp	23Aq
23	0Cp	19Aq	26Aq	19Ar	28Ta	20Cn	26Le	12Li	26Sc	28Sg	14Aq	20Pi
25	27Cp	18Pi	26Pi	20Ta	28Ge	18Le	21Vi	6Sc	19Sg	22Cp	10Pi	17Ar
27	24Aq	17Ar	26Ar	20Ge	26Cn	13Vi	16Li	29Sc	14Cp	18Aq	8Ar	16Ta
29	23Pi		26Ta	18Cn	22Le	8Li	10Sc	23Sg	9Aq	15Pi	7Ta	16Ge
31	22Ar		25Ge		17Vi		3Sg	18Cp		14Ar		15Cn

1964

	Jan	Feb	Mar	Apr	May	Jun	Jul	Aug	Sep	Oct	Nov	Dec
1	0Le	19Vi	10Li	25Sc	27Sg	11Aq	16Pi	6Ta	29Ge	8Le	29Vi	4Sc
3	28Le	15Li	5Sc	18Sg	20Cp	6Pi	12Ar	5Ge	28Cn	6Vi	25Li	29Sc
5	24Vi	9Sc	29Sc	12Cp	15Aq	3Ar	10Ta	4Cn	26Le	3Li	20Sc	23Sg
7	19Li	3Sg	22Sg	7Aq	11Pi	1Ta	10Ge	3Le	24Vi	29Li	14Sg	16Cp
9	13Sc	26Sg	16Cp	2Pi	8Ar	1Ge	10Cn	2Vi	21Li	24Sc	8Cp	10Aq
11	7Sg	21Cp	11Aq	0Ar	7Ta	1Cn	9Le	0Li	16Sc	18Sg	1Aq	4Pi
13	0Cp	16Aq	8Pi	29Ar	8Ge	1Le	8Vi	26Li	10Sg	12Cp	26Aq	29Pi
15	25Cp	13Pi	6Ar	29Ta	8Cn	29Le	5Li	20Sc	4Cp	5Aq	21Pi	26Ar
17	20Aq	10Ar	5Ta	28Ge	6Le	26Vi	0Sc	14Sg	28Cp	0Pi	18Ar	25Ta
19	17Pi	8Ta	3Ge	26Cn	3Vi	21Li	24Sc	8Cp	22Aq	27Pi	17Ta	25Ge
21	14Ar	7Ge	2Cn	23Le	29Vi	15Sc	17Sg	2Aq	18Pi	25Ar	17Ge	25Cn
23	12Ta	5Cn	29Cn	19Vi	24Li	9Sg	11Cp	27Aq	16Ar	23Ta	17Cn	25Le
25	10Ge	3Le	26Le	15Li	18Sc	2Cp	5Aq	23Pi	14Ta	23Ge	16Le	23Vi
27	9Cn	0Vi	23Vi	9Sc	12Sg	26Cp	0Pi	20Ar	12Ge	21Cn	13Vi	19Li
29	8Le	27Vi	18Li	3Sg	5Cp	21Aq	26Pi	17Ta	10Cn	19Le	9Li	14Sc
31	6Vi		13Sc		29Cp		23Ar	15Ge		16Vi		8Sg

1965

	Jan	Feb	Mar	Apr	May	Jun	Jul	Aug	Sep	Oct	Nov	Dec
1	20Sg	4Aq	12Aq	28Pi	3Ta	25Ge	4Le	27Vi	17Sc	20Sg	4Aq	6Pi
3	13Cp	28Aq	7Pi	25Ar	2Ge	25Cn	4Vi	25Li	12Sg	14Cp	28Aq	0Ar
5	7Aq	23Pi	2Ar	22Ta	0Cn	24Le	2Li	21Sc	6Cp	8Aq	22Pi	25Ar
7	1Pi	18Ar	29Ar	20Ge	29Cn	22Vi	29Li	15Sg	0Aq	2Pi	17Ar	22Ta
9	26Pi	15Ta	25Ta	18Cn	27Le	19Li	24Sc	9Cp	24Aq	26Pi	14Ta	20Ge
11	22Ar	13Ge	23Ge	16Le	25Vi	14Sc	18Sg	3Aq	18Pi	22Ar	11Ge	19Cn
13	19Ta	12Cn	21Cn	15Vi	22Li	9Sg	12Cp	27Aq	13Ar	18Ta	9Cn	18Le
15	18Ge	11Le	20Le	12Li	18Sc	3Cp	6Aq	21Pi	8Ta	15Ge	8Le	17Vi
17	18Cn	11Vi	19Vi	9Sc	13Sg	27Cp	0Pi	16Ar	4Ge	13Cn	6Vi	15Li
19	18Le	10Li	17Li	4Sg	7Cp	21Aq	24Pi	11Ta	2Cn	11Le	4Li	11Sc
21	18Vi	6Sc	14Sc	29Sg	1Aq	15Pi	19Ar	8Ge	0Le	10Vi	1Sc	7Sg
23	15Li	1Sg	9Sg	23Cp	24Aq	10Ar	15Ta	6Cn	0Vi	8Li	28Sc	2Cp
25	10Sc	25Sg	3Cp	16Aq	19Pi	6Ta	13Ge	6Le	29Vi	6Sc	23Sg	26Cp
27	5Sg	19Cp	27Cp	11Pi	14Ar	4Ge	12Cn	6Vi	28Li	3Sg	18Cp	20Aq
29	28Sg		21Aq	6Ar	12Ta	4Cn	12Le	6Li	25Sc	28Sg	12Aq	14Pi
31	22Cp		15Pi		10Ge		13Vi	4Sc		22Cp		8Ar

1966

	Jan	Feb	Mar	Apr	May	Jun	Jul	Aug	Sep	Oct	Nov	Dec
1	20Ar	8Ge	17Ge	8Le	18Vi	10Sc	17Sg	4Aq	18Pi	21Ar	7Ge	13Cn
3	16Ta	6Cn	14Cn	8Vi	17Li	8Sg	12Cp	28Aq	12Ar	15Ta	3Cn	10Le
5	13Ge	6Le	14Le	8Li	15Sc	4Cp	7Aq	21Pi	6Ta	10Ge	0Le	8Vi
7	13Cn	6Vi	14Vi	7Sc	13Sg	29Cp	1Pi	15Ar	1Ge	6Cn	28Le	7Li
9	13Le	6Li	15Li	5Sg	8Cp	23Aq	25Pi	9Ta	26Ge	3Le	27Vi	5Sc
11	13Vi	5Sc	13Sc	1Cp	3Aq	17Pi	19Ar	5Ge	24Cn	2Vi	26Li	3Sg
13	11Li	1Sg	10Sg	25Cp	27Aq	11Ar	13Ta	1Cn	24Le	2Li	25Sc	12Cp
15	8Sc	26Sg	5Cp	19Aq	21Pi	6Ta	10Ge	0Le	24Vi	2Sc	23Sg	27Cp
17	4Sg	20Cp	29Cp	13Pi	15Ar	1Ge	7Cn	0Vi	24Li	1Sg	19Cp	22Aq
19	29Sg	14Aq	22Aq	7Ar	10Ta	29Ge	7Le	1Li	23Sc	28Sg	14Aq	16Pi
21	23Cp	7Pi	16Pi	2Ta	6Ge	27Cn	6Vi	0Sc	20Sg	24Cp	9Pi	10Ar
23	17Aq	1Ar	10Ar	27Ta	4Cn	26Le	6Li	27Sc	15Cp	18Aq	2Ar	4Ta
25	10Pi	25Ar	5Ta	23Ge	1Le	25Vi	4Sc	23Sg	10Aq	12Pi	26Ar	29Ta
27	4Ar	20Ta	0Ge	21Cn	0Vi	23Li	1Sg	18Cp	4Pi	6Ar	21Ta	25Ge
29	29Ar		26Ge	19Le	28Vi	20Sc	26Sg	13Aq	27Pi	0Ta	16Ge	23Cn
31	24Ta		24Cn		26Li		21Cp	7Pi		25Ta		21Le

1967

	Jan	Feb	Mar	Apr	May	Jun	Jul	Aug	Sep	Oct	Nov	Dec
1	5Vi	28Li	8Sc	29Sg	4Aq	20Pi	21Ar	5Ge	22Cn	27Le	20Li	28Sc
3	4Li	26Sc	6Sg	25Cp	29Aq	13Ar	15Ta	0Cn	19Le	27Vi	20Sc	28Sg
5	2Sc	23Sg	3Cp	20Aq	23Pi	7Ta	9Ge	27Cn	18Vi	27Li	20Sg	27Cp
7	29Sc	19Cp	28Cp	14Pi	17Ar	1Ge	5Cn	25Le	18Li	27Sc	18Cp	23Aq
9	26Sg	14Aq	23Aq	8Ar	10Ta	26Ge	2Le	24Vi	17Sc	25Sg	15Aq	19Pi
11	23Cp	8Pi	17Pi	2Ta	5Ge	22Cn	29Le	23Li	15Sg	23Cp	10Pi	13Ar
13	18Aq	2Ar	11Ar	25Ta	29Ge	19Le	28Vi	21Sc	13Cp	18Aq	4Ar	6Ta
15	12Pi	26Ar	4Ta	20Ge	25Cn	17Vi	26Li	19Sg	9Aq	13Pi	28Ar	0Ge
17	6Ar	20Ta	28Ta	15Cn	22Le	15Li	24Sc	16Cp	4Pi	7Ar	21Ta	24Ge
19	0Ta	14Ge	23Ge	12Le	20Vi	14Sc	22Sg	12Aq	28Pi	1Ta	15Ge	19Cn
21	24Ta	11Cn	19Cn	11Vi	19Li	12Sg	19Cp	7Pi	22Ar	24Ta	10Cn	15Le
23	20Ge	9Le	17Le	10Li	19Sc	11Cp	16Aq	2Ar	16Ta	18Ge	5Le	12Vi
25	17Cn	9Vi	17Vi	11Sc	18Sg	8Aq	11Pi	25Ar	9Ge	13Cn	1Vi	9Li
27	16Le	9Li	17Li	10Sg	16Cp	3Pi	5Ar	19Ta	4Cn	8Le	29Vi	8Sc
29	15Vi		17Sc	8Cp	13Aq	28Pi	29Ar	13Ge	0Le	6Vi	28Li	7Sg
31	14Li		16Sg		8Pi		23Ta	8Cn		5Li		6Cp

1968

	Jan	Feb	Mar	Apr	May	Jun	Jul	Aug	Sep	Oct	Nov	Dec
1	20Cp	9Pi	0Ar	14Ta	17Ge	2Le	7Vi	28Li	22Sg	1Aq	21Pi	25Ar
3	18Aq	4Ar	24Ar	8Ge	11Cn	27Le	4Li	26Sc	20Cp	28Aq	16Ar	19Ta
5	14Pi	28Ar	18Ta	2Cn	5Le	24Vi	2Sc	25Sg	18Aq	24Pi	10Ta	13Ge
7	9Ar	22Ta	12Ge	27Cn	1Vi	22Li	1Sg	24Cp	15Pi	19Ar	4Ge	7Cn
9	2Ta	16Ge	6Cn	23Le	29Vi	21Sc	1Cp	23Aq	11Ar	14Ta	28Ge	0Le
11	26Ta	11Cn	1Le	20Vi	28Li	22Sg	0Aq	20Pi	6Ta	8Ge	22Cn	25Le
13	20Ge	7Le	28Le	20Li	28Sc	22Cp	28Aq	15Ar	0Ge	1Cn	16Le	20Vi
15	15Cn	4Vi	27Vi	20Sc	29Sg	20Aq	25Pi	10Ta	23Ge	25Cn	11Vi	17Li
17	12Le	2Li	26Li	20Sg	28Cp	17Pi	20Ar	4Ge	17Cn	20Le	9Li	16Sc
19	8Vi	1Sc	25Sc	18Cp	25Aq	11Ar	14Ta	27Ge	12Le	17Vi	7Sc	16Sg
21	6Li	29Sc	24Sg	15Aq	20Pi	5Ta	7Ge	22Cn	9Vi	15Li	8Sg	16Cp
23	4Sc	27Sg	22Cp	11Pi	14Ar	29Ta	1Cn	17Le	7Li	14Sc	8Cp	16Aq
25	2Sg	25Cp	18Aq	5Ar	8Ta	23Ge	26Cn	14Vi	5Sc	14Sg	7Aq	14Pi
27	1Cp	21Aq	14Pi	29Ar	2Ge	17Cn	21Le	11Li	4Sg	13Cp	5Pi	10Ar
29	29Cp	17Pi	8Ar	23Ta	26Ge	12Le	18Vi	9Sc	3Cp	11Aq	0Ar	4Ta
31	26Aq		3Ta		20Cn		14Li	7Sg		8Pi		28Ta

1969

	Jan	Feb	Mar	Apr	May	Jun	Jul	Aug	Sep	Oct	Nov	Dec
1	10Ge	24Cn	2Le	18Vi	24Li	16Sg	25Cp	18Pi	7Ta	10Ge	24Cn	25Le
3	4Cn	19Le	27Le	15Li	23Sc	16Cp	25Aq	15Ar	2Ge	4Cn	18Le	20Vi
5	28Cn	14Vi	23Vi	13Sc	22Sg	16Aq	23Pi	11Ta	26Ge	28Cn	12Vi	15Li
7	22Le	10Li	20Li	12Sg	21Cp	14Pi	20Ar	6Ge	20Cn	22Le	7Li	12Sc
9	17Vi	7Sc	17Sc	11Cp	20Aq	10Ar	15Ta	0Cn	14Le	16Vi	4Sc	11Sg
11	13Li	5Sg	15Sg	9Aq	17Pi	5Ta	9Ge	23Cn	8Vi	12Li	2Sg	11Cp
13	10Sc	3Cp	14Cp	6Pi	13Ar	0Ge	3Cn	17Le	3Li	9Sc	1Cp	10Aq
15	9Sg	3Aq	12Aq	3Ar	8Ta	24Ge	26Cn	11Vi	29Li	7Sg	0Aq	9Pi
17	9Cp	2Pi	10Pi	29Ar	3Ge	17Cn	20Le	6Li	26Sc	5Cp	28Aq	6Ar
19	9Aq	0Ar	8Ar	24Ta	27Ge	11Le	14Vi	2Sc	24Sg	3Aq	26Pi	2Ta
21	8Pi	26Ar	4Ta	18Ge	21Cn	5Vi	9Li	29Sc	23Cp	2Pi	22Ar	28Ta
23	5Ar	21Ta	28Ta	12Cn	14Le	0Li	6Sc	28Sg	21Aq	29Pi	18Ta	22Ge
25	0Ta	15Ge	22Ge	6Le	9Vi	26Li	4Sg	27Cp	20Pi	26Ar	14Ge	16Cn
27	25Ta	8Cn	16Cn	1Vi	4Li	25Sc	3Cp	27Aq	18Ar	23Ta	8Cn	10Le
29	18Ge		10Le	26Vi	2Sc	25Sg	4Aq	26Pi	15Ta	18Ge	2Le	4Vi
31	12Cn		5Vi		1Sg		3Pi	24Ar	27Ta		12Cn	28Vi

1970

	Jan	Feb	Mar	Apr	May	Jun	Jul	Aug	Sep	Oct	Nov	Dec
1	10Li	28Sc	8Sg	1Aq	10Pi	2Ta	8Ge	24Cn	9Vi	11Li	28Sc	5Cp
3	6Sc	27Sg	6Cp	29Aq	8Ar	28Ta	3Cn	18Le	2Li	6Sc	25Sg	3Aq
5	4Sg	27Cp	5Aq	29Pi	6Ta	24Ge	27Cn	11Vi	26Li	1Sg	22Cp	1Pi
7	4Cp	27Aq	5Pi	27Ar	3Ge	19Cn	21Le	5Li	21Sc	28Sg	20Aq	29Pi
9	4Aq	27Pi	5Ar	25Ta	28Ge	13Le	15Vi	0Sc	18Sg	25Cp	18Pi	27Ar
11	4Pi	25Ar	3Ta	20Ge	23Cn	6Vi	9Li	25Sc	15Cp	24Aq	17Ar	25Ta
13	3Ar	21Ta	0Ge	15Cn	17Le	0Li	3Sc	22Sg	15Aq	23Pi	16Ta	22Ge
15	29Ar	16Ge	25Ge	9Le	10Vi	25Li	0Sg	21Cp	15Pi	23Ar	13Ge	17Cn
17	25Ta	10Cn	19Cn	2Vi	5Li	22Sc	28Sg	21Aq	15Ar	22Ta	9Cn	12Le
19	19Ge	4Le	12Le	27Vi	0Sc	20Sg	28Cp	22Pi	13Ta	19Ge	4Le	6Vi
21	13Cn	28Le	6Vi	22Li	27Sc	19Cp	28Aq	21Ar	11Ge	14Cn	28Le	29Vi
23	7Le	22Vi	1Li	18Sc	25Sg	18Aq	27Pi	18Ta	6Cn	8Le	22Vi	24Li
25	1Vi	16Li	26Li	15Sg	24Cp	17Pi	25Ar	14Ge	0Le	2Vi	16Li	19Sc
27	25Vi	12Sc	22Sc	13Cp	22Aq	15Ar	22Ta	9Cn	24Le	26Vi	11Sc	16Sg
29	19Li		19Sg	11Aq	21Pi	12Ta	18Ge	3Le	17Vi	20Li	7Sg	14Cp
31	15Sc		16Cp		18Ar		12Cn	27Le		15Sc		13Aq

1971

	Jan	Feb	Mar	Apr	May	Jun	Jul	Aug	Sep	Oct	Nov	Dec
1	27Aq	20Ar	0Ta	20Ge	25Cn	9Vi	11Li	25Sc	12Cp	18Aq	11Ar	19Ta
3	26Pi	18Ta	28Ta	16Cn	19Le	3Li	5Sc	20Sg	10Aq	17Pi	11Ta	19Ge
5	24Ar	15Ge	24Ge	11Le	13Vi	27Li	0Sg	17Cp	9Pi	18Ar	11Ge	17Cn
7	21Ta	10Cn	10Cn	4Vi	6Li	21Sc	26Sg	16Aq	9Ar	18Ta	9Cn	13Le
9	18Ge	5Le	14Le	28Vi	0Sc	17Sg	23Cp	15Pi	9Ta	17Ge	5Le	8Vi
11	13Cn	29Le	7Vi	22Li	25Sc	14Cp	21Aq	14Ar	7Ge	14Cn	0Vi	2Li
13	8Le	22Vi	1Li	16Sc	21Sg	11Aq	20Pi	13Ta	4Cn	9Le	24Vi	26Li
15	2Vi	16Li	25Li	11Sg	17Cp	9Pi	18Ar	11Ge	0Le	3Vi	18Li	20Sc
17	26Vi	10Sc	19Sc	7Cp	14Aq	7Ar	16Ta	7Cn	24Le	27Vi	12Sc	15Sg
19	19Li	5Sg	14Sg	4Aq	12Pi	6Ta	14Ge	3Le	18Vi	21Li	6Sg	10Cp
21	14Sc	1Cp	10Cp	2Pi	11Ar	4Ge	11Cn	27Le	12Li	15Sc	1Cp	6Aq
23	10Sg	0Aq	8Aq	1Ar	10Ta	1Cn	6Le	21Vi	6Sc	9Sg	26Cp	3Pi
25	7Cp	29Aq	8Pi	1Ta	9Ge	28Cn	1Vi	15Li	0Sg	4Cp	23Aq	1Ar
27	7Aq	0Ar	8Ar	1Ge	7Cn	23Le	25Vi	9Sc	24Sg	29Cp	21Pi	0Ta
29	6Pi		8Ta	29Ge	3Le	17Vi	19Li	3Sg	20Cp	27Aq	20Ar	29Ta
31	6Ar		7Ge		27Le		13Sc	28Sg		26Pi		27Ge

1972

	Jan	Feb	Mar	Apr	May	Jun	Jul	Aug	Sep	Oct	Nov	Dec
1	11Cn	29Le	20Vi	5Sc	7Sg	23Cp	29Aq	21Ar	14Ge	23Cn	12Vi	16Li
3	8Le	24Vi	14Li	28Sc	1Cp	19Aq	26Pi	19Ta	12Cn	19Le	6Li	10Sc
5	4Vi	18Li	8Sc	22Sg	26Cp	15Pi	24Ar	18Ge	9Le	15Vi	1Sc	3Sg
7	28Vi	12Sc	2Sg	17Cp	22Aq	14Ar	23Ta	16Cn	5Vi	10Li	24Sc	27Sg
9	22Li	6Sg	26Sg	13Aq	20Pi	13Ta	22Ge	13Le	1Li	4Sc	18Sg	21Cp
11	16Sc	1Cp	21Cp	11Pi	19Ar	13Ge	21Cn	10Vi	25Li	28Sc	12Cp	16Aq
13	10Sg	27Cp	18Aq	10Ar	19Ta	12Cn	18Le	5Li	19Sc	21Sg	6Aq	11Pi
15	6Cp	25Aq	17Pi	11Ta	20Ge	10Le	14Vi	29Li	13Sg	15Cp	2Pi	8Ar
17	2Aq	24Pi	17Ar	11Ge	18Cn	6Vi	9Li	23Sc	7Cp	10Aq	29Pi	7Ta
19	0Pi	23Ar	17Ta	9Cn	15Le	1Li	3Sc	17Sg	2Aq	7Pi	28Ar	7Ge
21	28Pi	22Ta	16Ge	6Le	10Vi	25Li	27Sc	12Cp	29Aq	5Ar	29Ta	7Cn
23	26Ar	19Ge	13Cn	1Vi	5Li	29Sc	21Sg	7Aq	27Pi	5Ta	29Ge	6Le
25	25Ta	16Cn	9Le	26Vi	29Li	13Sg	16Cp	4Pi	27Ar	6Ge	28Cn	4Vi
27	23Ge	12Le	4Vi	20Li	22Sc	7Cp	12Aq	3Ar	26Ta	5Cn	25Le	0Li
29	20Cn	7Vi	29Vi	13Sc	16Sg	3Aq	9Pi	1Ta	25Ge	3Le	21Vi	24Li
31	16Le		23Li		11Cp		7Ar	0Ge		29Le		18Sc

1973

	Jan	Feb	Mar	Apr	May	Jun	Jul	Aug	Sep	Oct	Nov	Dec
1	0Sg	14Cp	22Cp	8Pi	14Ar	7Ge	16Cn	8Vi	27Li	0Sg	13Cp	15Aq
3	24Sg	9Aq	17Aq	6Ar	14Ta	7Cn	15Le	6Li	22Sc	24Sg	7Aq	9Pi
5	18Cp	5Pi	14Pi	5Ta	14Ge	7Le	14Vi	1Sc	16Sg	17Cp	1Pi	5Ar
7	13Aq	1Ar	11Ar	4Ge	13Cn	5Vi	10Li	26Sc	9Cp	11Aq	27Pi	2Ta
9	8Pi	29Ar	10Ta	3Cn	11Le	1Li	5Sc	19Sg	3Aq	6Pi	25Ar	1Ge
11	5Ar	27Ta	8Ge	1Le	8Vi	26Li	29Sc	13Cp	28Aq	3Ar	23Ta	1Cn
13	2Ta	25Ge	6Cn	28Le	4Li	20Sc	23Sg	7Aq	24Pi	0Ta	23Ge	2Le
15	1Ge	24Cn	4Le	24Vi	29Li	14Sg	16Cp	2Pi	21Ar	29Ta	22Cn	0Vi
17	0Cn	22Le	1Vi	20Li	23Sc	8Cp	10Aq	28Pi	19Ta	27Ge	20Le	28Vi
19	0Le	20Vi	28Vi	14Sc	17Sg	1Aq	5Pi	24Ar	17Ge	26Cn	18Vi	24Li
21	28Le	16Li	24Li	8Sg	11Cp	26Aq	1Ar	22Ta	15Cn	24Le	14Li	19Sc
23	25Vi	10Sc	18Sc	2Cp	4Aq	21Pi	27Ar	20Ge	13Le	21Vi	9Sc	13Sg
25	20Li	4Sg	12Sg	26Cp	29Aq	18Ar	25Ta	19Cn	11Vi	17Li	4Sg	7Cp
27	15Sc	28Sg	6Cp	20Aq	25Pi	16Ta	24Ge	18Le	9Li	13Sc	28Sg	0Aq
29	8Sg		0Aq	16Pi	23Ar	16Ge	24Cn	16Vi	5Sc	8Sg	22Cp	24Aq
31	2Cp		25Aq		22Ta		24Le	24Li		2Cp		18Pi

1974

	Jan	Feb	Mar	Apr	May	Jun	Jul	Aug	Sep	Oct	Nov	Dec
1	1Ar	20Ta	0Ge	23Cn	2Vi	23Li	29Sc	14Cp	29Aq	2Ar	19Ta	26Ge
3	27Ar	18Ge	28Ge	21Le	0Li	19Sc	23Sg	8Aq	23Pi	27Ar	16Ge	24Cn
5	25Ta	17Cn	27Cn	20Vi	27Li	14Sg	17Cp	2Pi	18Ar	23Ta	14Cn	23Le
7	24Ge	18Le	26Le	18Li	23Sc	9Cp	11Aq	26Pi	13Ta	20Ge	12Le	22Vi
9	25Cn	17Vi	25Vi	15Sc	18Sg	2Aq	5Pi	20Ar	9Ge	17Cn	11Vi	19Li
11	25Le	16Li	23Li	10Sg	12Cp	26Aq	29Pi	16Ta	7Cn	16Le	9Li	16Sc
13	24Vi	12Sc	20Sc	5Cp	6Aq	20Pi	24Ar	13Ge	6Le	15Vi	7Sc	12Sg
15	20Li	7Sg	15Sg	28Cp	0Pi	15Ar	20Ta	12Cn	6Vi	14Li	4Sg	7Cp
17	16Sc	0Cp	9Cp	22Aq	25Pi	12Ta	19Ge	12Le	5Li	12Sc	29Sg	2Aq
19	10Sg	24Cp	2Aq	17Pi	20Ar	10Ge	18Cn	12Vi	4Sc	9Sg	24Cp	25Aq
21	4Cp	18Aq	26Aq	12Ar	18Ta	10Cn	19Le	12Li	1Sg	4Cp	18Aq	19Pi
23	27Cp	12Pi	21Pi	9Ta	16Ge	10Le	19Vi	9Sc	26Sg	28Cp	11Pi	13Ar
25	21Aq	7Ar	17Ar	7Ge	15Cn	9Vi	17Li	5Sg	20Cp	22Aq	6Ar	9Ta
27	15Pi	3Ta	13Ta	5Cn	14Le	7Li	13Sc	29Sg	13Aq	16Pi	1Ta	6Ge
29	10Ar		11Ge	4Le	13Vi	3Sc	8Sg	23Cp	7Pi	10Ar	28Ta	4Cn
31	6Ta		8Cn		10Li		2Cp	17Aq		6Ta		4Le

1975

	Jan	Feb	Mar	Apr	May	Jun	Jul	Aug	Sep	Oct	Nov	Dec
1	19Le	12Li	21Li	11Sg	14Cp	29Aq	0Ar	15Ta	2Cn	9Le	2Li	11Sc
3	18Vi	10Sc	19Sc	6Cp	9Aq	23Pi	24Ar	10Ge	0Le	8Vi	2Sc	9Sg
5	16Li	6Sg	15Sg	1Aq	3Pi	17Ar	19Ta	7Cn	0Vi	9Li	1Sg	7Cp
7	13Sc	1Cp	10Cp	24Aq	26Pi	11Ta	16Ge	6Le	0Li	9Sc	29Sg	3Aq
9	9Sg	25Cp	4Aq	18Pi	21Ar	7Ge	13Cn	6Vi	0Sc	7Sg	25Cp	28Aq
11	4Cp	19Aq	28Aq	12Ar	16Ta	4Cn	12Le	6Li	29Sc	4Cp	20Aq	22Pi
13	28Cp	12Pi	21Pi	7Ta	12Ge	3Le	12Vi	5Sc	24Sg	29Cp	14Pi	16Ar
15	22Aq	6Ar	15Ar	2Ge	8Cn	1Vi	11Li	2Sg	20Cp	24Aq	8Ar	10Ta
17	16Pi	0Ta	10Ta	28Ge	6Le	0Li	8Sc	28Sg	15Aq	17Pi	2Ta	5Ge
19	9Ar	25Ta	5Ge	25Cn	4Vi	28Li	5Sg	23Cp	9Pi	11Ar	26Ta	1Cn
21	4Ta	22Ge	1Cn	24Le	3Li	25Sc	1Cp	18Aq	2Ar	5Ta	22Ge	28Cn
23	0Ge	20Cn	29Cn	23Vi	2Sc	22Sg	26Cp	12Pi	26Ar	0Ge	18Cn	26Le
25	28Ge	20Le	29Le	22Li	0Sg	18Cp	21Aq	5Ar	20Ta	25Ge	15Le	24Vi
27	27Cn	21Vi	29Vi	21Sc	26Sg	13Aq	15Pi	29Ar	15Ge	21Cn	13Vi	22Li
29	27Le		29Li	19Sg	22Cp	7Pi	9Ar	23Ta	11Cn	18Le	12Li	20Sc
31	28Vi		27Sc		17Aq		3Ta	19Ge		17Vi		18Sg

1976

	Jan	Feb	Mar	Apr	May	Jun	Jul	Aug	Sep	Oct	Nov	Dec
1	2Cp	19Aq	19Pi	25Ar	27Ta	14Cn	21Le	13Li	6Sg	14Cp	3Pi	6Ar
3	28Cp	14Pi	4Ar	18Ta	22Ge	10Le	18Vi	11Sc	4Cp	10Aq	27Pi	0Ta
5	24Aq	8Ar	28Ar	12Ge	17Cn	7Vi	16Li	9Sg	0Aq	6Pi	21Ar	23Ta
7	18Pi	1Ta	22Ta	7Cn	13Le	5Li	15Sc	7Cp	26Aq	0Ar	15Ta	17Ge
9	12Ar	25Ta	16Ge	4Le	11Vi	4Sc	13Sg	4Aq	21Pi	24Ar	8Ge	12Cn
11	5Ta	20Ge	11Cn	2Vi	10Li	4Sg	11Cp	0Pi	15Ar	18Ta	2Cn	7Le
13	0Ge	17Cn	9Le	1Li	10Sc	3Cp	9Aq	25Pi	9Ta	11Ge	27Cn	3Vi
15	26Ge	15Le	8Vi	2Sc	10Sg	0Aq	4Pi	19Ar	3Ge	5Cn	23Le	0Li
17	23Cn	15Vi	9Li	2Sg	9Cp	26Aq	29Pi	13Ta	27Ge	1Le	20Vi	28Li
19	21Le	15Li	9Sc	0Cp	6Aq	21Pi	23Ar	7Ge	22Cn	28Le	19Li	28Sc
21	20Vi	14Sc	7Sg	27Cp	1Pi	15Ar	17Ta	1Cn	19Le	26Vi	19Sc	28Sg
23	19Li	11Sg	5Cp	22Aq	25Pi	9Ta	11Ge	28Cn	18Vi	26Li	20Sg	27Cp
25	17Sc	8Cp	0Aq	16Pi	19Ar	3Ge	6Cn	25Le	18Li	26Sc	19Cp	24Aq
27	14Sg	3Aq	25Aq	10Ar	12Ta	28Ge	3Le	24Vi	18Sc	26Sg	16Aq	20Pi
29	11Cp	28Aq	19Pi	4Ta	6Ge	24Cn	0Vi	23Li	17Sg	24Cp	12Pi	14Ar
31	7Aq		13Ar		1Cn		29Vi	22Sc		20Aq		8Ta

1977

	Jan	Feb	Mar	Apr	May	Jun	Jul	Aug	Sep	Oct	Nov	Dec
1	20Ta	4Cn	12Cn	29Le	5Li	28Sc	7Cp	29Aq	17Ar	19Ta	3Cn	6Le
3	14Ge	29Cn	7Le	27Vi	4Sc	28Sg	6Aq	26Pi	11Ta	13Ge	27Cn	0Vi
5	8Cn	26Le	5Vi	26Li	5Sg	28Cp	4Pi	21Ar	5Ge	7Cn	21Le	25Vi
7	4Le	23Vi	3Li	26Sc	4Cp	26Aq	1Ar	15Ta	29Ge	1Le	17Vi	23Li
9	0Vi	21Li	2Sc	25Sg	3Aq	22Pi	25Ar	9Ge	23Cn	26Le	15Li	22Sc
11	27Vi	19Sc	0Sg	23Cp	0Pi	17Ar	19Ta	3Cn	18Le	23Vi	14Sc	22Sg
13	24Li	18Sg	29Sg	20Aq	25Pi	10Ta	13Ge	27Cn	15Vi	21Li	14Sg	23Cp
15	23Sc	16Cp	26Cp	16Pi	20Ar	4Ge	7Cn	23Le	12Li	20Sc	14Cp	22Aq
17	22Sg	13Aq	23Aq	10Ar	13Ta	28Ge	1Le	19Vi	10Sc	19Sg	12Aq	19Pi
19	21Cp	10Pi	19Pi	4Ta	7Ge	22Cn	26Le	16Li	9Sg	18Cp	9Pi	15Ar
21	19Aq	6Ar	14Ar	28Ta	1Cn	17Le	22Vi	14Sc	7Cp	16Aq	5Ar	9Ta
23	15Pi	0Ta	8Ta	22Ge	25Cn	12Vi	19Li	12Sg	5Aq	12Pi	0Ta	3Ge
25	10Ar	24Ta	2Ge	16Cn	20Le	9Li	17Sc	11Cp	3Pi	8Ar	24Ta	27Ge
27	4Ta	17Ge	25Ge	11Le	16Vi	7Sc	16Sg	9Aq	29Pi	3Ta	18Ge	21Cn
29	28Ta		20Cn	7Vi	13Li	6Sg	15Cp	7Pi	25Ar	27Ta	12Cn	15Le
31	22Ge		15Le		13Sc		15Aq	4Ar		21Ge		9Vi

1978

	Jan	Feb	Mar	Apr	May	Jun	Jul	Aug	Sep	Oct	Nov	Dec
1	22Vi	11Sc	22Sc	15Cp	24Aq	15Ar	20Ta	5Cn	19Le	22Vi	10Sc	17Sg
3	18Li	10Sg	20Sg	14Aq	22Pi	10Ta	14Ge	28Cn	13Vi	18Li	8Sg	16Cp
5	16Sc	9Cp	19Cp	11Pi	18Ar	5Ge	8Cn	22Le	8Li	14Sc	6Cp	15Aq
7	15Sg	9Aq	18Aq	9Ar	13Ta	29Ge	1Le	16Vi	4Sc	12Sg	5Aq	14Pi
9	15Cp	8Pi	16Pi	5Ta	8Ge	23Cn	25Le	11Li	1Sg	10Cp	3Pi	11Ar
11	16Aq	6Ar	14Ar	0Ge	2Cn	16Le	19Vi	7Sc	29Sg	8Aq	1Ar	7Ta
13	14Pi	2Ta	9Ta	24Ge	26Cn	10Vi	14Li	4Sg	28Cp	6Pi	28Ar	3Ge
15	11Ar	26Ta	4Ge	18Cn	20Le	5Li	11Sc	3Cp	27Aq	5Ar	24Ta	28Ge
17	6Ta	20Ge	28Ge	12Le	14Vi	2Sc	9Sg	3Aq	26Pi	2Ta	19Ge	22Cn
19	0Ge	14Cn	22Cn	6Vi	10Li	1Sg	9Cp	3Pi	24Ar	28Ta	14Cn	15Le
21	24Ge	8Le	16Le	2Li	8Sc	1Cp	10Aq	2Ar	21Ta	23Ge	7Le	9Vi
23	17Cn	3Vi	11Vi	0Sc	7Sg	1Aq	10Pi	29Ar	16Ge	18Cn	1Vi	3Li
25	12Le	28Vi	7Li	28Sc	7Cp	1Pi	8Ar	25Ta	10Cn	11Le	25Vi	29Li
27	6Vi	25Li	5Sc	27Sg	7Aq	28Pi	4Ta	20Ge	3Le	5Vi	21Li	26Sc
29	2Li		3Sg	26Cp	5Pi	25Ar	29Ta	13Cn	27Le	0Li	18Sc	25Sg
31	28Li		1Cp		2Ar		23Ge	7Le		26Li		25Cp

1979

	Jan	Feb	Mar	Apr	May	Jun	Jul	Aug	Sep	Oct	Nov	Dec
1	10Aq	3Ar	11Ar	1Ge	4Cn	18Le	20Vi	5Sc	23Sg	0Aq	23Pi	2Ta
3	10Pi	1Ta	9Ta	26Ge	29Cn	12Vi	14Li	1Sg	21Cp	29Aq	23Ar	0Ge
5	8Ar	27Ta	5Ge	21Cn	22Le	6Li	9Sc	28Sg	21Aq	29Pi	22Ta	27Ge
7	4Ta	21Ge	0Cn	14Le	16Vi	1Sc	6Sg	27Cp	21Pi	29Ar	19Ge	23Cn
9	0Ge	15Cn	24Cn	8Vi	10Li	28Sc	4Cp	28Aq	21Ar	28Ta	15Cn	18Le
11	24Ge	9Le	18Le	2Li	6Sc	26Sg	4Aq	28Pi	19Ta	25Ge	10Le	12Vi
13	18Cn	3Vi	12Vi	27Li	3Sg	25Cp	4Pi	26Ar	16Ge	20Cn	4Vi	5Li
15	12Le	27Vi	6Li	23Sc	0Cp	24Aq	2Ar	24Ta	11Cn	14Le	27Vi	29Li
17	6Vi	21Li	1Sc	20Sg	29Cp	22Pi	0Ta	19Ge	5Le	7Vi	22Li	25Sc
19	0Li	16Sc	26Sc	18Cp	27Aq	20Ar	27Ta	14Cn	29Le	1Li	17Sc	22Sg
21	24Li	13Sg	23Sg	16Aq	25Pi	17Ta	22Ge	8Le	22Vi	25Li	13Sg	19Cp
23	20Sc	12Cp	21Cp	15Pi	23Ar	13Ge	17Cn	2Vi	16Li	20Sc	10Cp	18Aq
25	18Sg	11Aq	20Aq	13Ar	20Ta	8Cn	11Le	25Vi	11Sc	16Sg	7Sg	16Pi
27	18Cp	12Pi	20Pi	11Ta	17Ge	3Le	5Vi	19Li	6Sg	13Cp	5Pi	14Ar
29	18Aq		19Ar	8Ge	12Cn	26Le	28Vi	14Sc	2Cp	10Aq	3Ar	12Ta
31	18Pi		17Ta		6Le		22Li	9Sg		9Pi		9Ge

1980

	Jan	Feb	Mar	Apr	May	Jun	Jul	Aug	Sep	Oct	Nov	Dec
1	23Ge	10Le	1Vi	15Li	18Sc	5Cp	12Aq	5Ar	28Ta	6Cn	23Le	26Vi
3	19Cn	4Vi	24Vi	9Sc	13Sg	2Aq	10Pi	4Ta	26Ge	2Le	17Vi	20Li
5	14Le	28Vi	18Li	3Sg	9Cp	29Aq	9Ar	2Ge	22Cn	26Le	11Li	13Sc
7	8Vi	21Li	12Sc	29Sg	5Aq	27Pi	7Ta	29Ge	17Le	20Vi	5Sc	8Sg
9	1Li	15Sc	6Sg	25Cp	3Pi	26Ar	5Ge	25Cn	11Vi	14Li	29Sc	3Cp
11	25Li	11Sg	2Cp	23Aq	1Ar	25Ta	2Cn	20Le	5Li	8Sc	23Sg	28Cp
13	20Sc	7Cp	0Aq	22Pi	1Ta	23Ge	29Cn	15Vi	29Li	2Sg	18Cp	24Aq
15	16Sg	6Aq	29Aq	22Ar	1Ge	21Cn	24Le	9Li	23Sc	26Sg	14Aq	22Pi
17	14Cp	6Pi	29Pi	22Ta	29Ge	16Le	19Vi	2Sc	17Sg	21Cp	11Pi	20Ar
19	13Aq	6Ar	29Ar	21Ge	26Cn	11Vi	12Li	26Sc	13Cp	18Aq	10Ar	19Ta
21	12Pi	5Ta	28Ta	17Cn	21Le	4Li	6Sc	21Sg	10Aq	17Pi	10Ta	19Ge
23	11Ar	3Ge	26Ge	12Le	15Vi	28Li	1Sg	18Cp	8Pi	17Ar	10Ge	17Cn
25	9Ta	29Ge	21Cn	6Vi	8Li	23Sc	26Sg	16Aq	9Ar	17Ta	9Cn	14Le
27	6Ge	24Cn	16Le	0Li	2Sc	18Sg	23Cp	15Pi	9Ta	17Ge	6Le	10Vi
29	2Cn	19Le	9Vi	24Li	27Sc	15Cp	22Aq	15Ar	8Ge	15Cn	2Vi	4Li
31	27Cn		3Li		22Sg		21Pi	14Ta		11Le		28Li

1981

	Jan	Feb	Mar	Apr	May	Jun	Jul	Aug	Sep	Oct	Nov	Dec
1	10Sc	24Sg	2Cp	19Aq	25Pi	19Ta	28Ge	19Le	6Li	9Sc	23Sg	26Cp
3	4Sg	20Cp	27Cp	17Pi	25Ar	19Ge	27Cn	15Vi	1Sc	3Sg	17Cp	20Aq
5	29Sg	17Sq	25Aq	17Ar	26Ta	19Cn	24Le	11Li	25Sc	27Sg	11Aq	16Pi
7	24Cp	15Pi	23Pi	17Ta	26Ge	16Le	20Vi	5Sc	19Sg	21Cp	7Pi	14Ar
9	21Aq	13Ar	23Ar	17Ge	24Cn	12Vi	15Li	29Sc	13Cp	16Aq	5Ar	13Ta
11	19Pi	12Ta	22Ta	15Cn	21Le	7Li	9Sc	23Sg	8Aq	13Pi	5Ta	13Ge
13	17Ar	10Ge	21Ge	11Le	16Vi	1Sc	3Sg	17Cp	5Pi	12Ar	5Ge	13Cn
15	15Ta	8Cn	18Cn	6Vi	10Li	24Sc	27Sg	13Aq	3Ar	12Ta	5Cn	13Le
17	14Ge	4Le	14Le	1Li	4Sc	18Sg	22Cp	10Pi	2Ta	11Ge	4Le	10Vi
19	12Cn	0Vi	9Vi	25Li	27Sc	13Cp	17Aq	8Ar	1Ge	10Cn	1Vi	5Li
21	9Le	25Vi	4Li	19Sc	21Sg	8Aq	14Pi	6Ta	0Cn	8Le	26Vi	0Sc
23	5Vi	20Li	28Li	12Sg	16Cp	3Pi	11Ar	5Ge	27Cn	4Vi	21Li	24Sc
25	0Li	13Sc	22Sc	6Cp	11Aq	0Ar	9Ta	3Cn	24Le	29Vi	15Sc	17Sg
27	24Li	7Sg	15Sg	1Aq	7Pi	29Ar	8Ge	1Le	20Vi	24Li	8Sg	11Cp
29	17Sc		10Cp	27Aq	4Ar	28Ta	7Cn	28Le	15Li	18Sc	2Cp	5Aq
31	12Sg		5Aq		4Ta		5Le	24Vi		11Sg		0Pi

1982

	Jan	Feb	Mar	Apr	May	Jun	Jul	Aug	Sep	Oct	Nov	Dec
1	13Pi	4Ta	14Ta	8Cn	16Le	6Li	10Sc	25Sg	9Aq	12Pi	1Ta	8Ge
3	9Ar	2Ge	13Ge	5Le	13Vi	1Sc	4Sg	18Cp	4Pi	8Ar	29Ta	8Cn
5	7Ta	1Cn	11Cn	3Vi	9Li	25Sc	28Sg	12Aq	29Pi	6Ta	28Ge	7Le
7	6Ge	0Le	9Le	29Vi	4Sc	19Sg	22Cp	7Pi	26Ar	4Ge	27Cn	6Vi
9	6Cn	28Le	7Vi	25Li	28Sc	13Cp	15Aq	3Ar	23Ta	2Cn	25Le	3Li
11	6Le	26Vi	4Li	20Sc	22Sg	6Sq	10Pi	29Ar	21Ge	0Le	22Vi	29Li
13	4Vi	22Li	29Li	14Sg	16Cp	1Pi	6Ar	26Ta	19Cn	28Le	19Li	24Sc
15	1Li	16Sc	24Sc	8Cp	10Aq	26Pi	2Ta	25Ge	18Le	26Vi	15Sc	18Sg
17	26Li	10Sg	18Sg	1Aq	4Pi	23Ar	1Ge	24Cn	17Vi	23Li	9Sg	12Cp
19	20Sc	4Cp	11Cp	26Aq	1Ar	22Ta	0Cn	24Le	14Li	19Sc	3Cp	5Aq
21	14Sg	28Cp	6Aq	22Pi	29Ar	22Ge	0Le	22Vi	11Sc	13Sg	27Cp	29Aq
23	8Cp	23Aq	1Pi	20Ar	28Ta	22Cn	0Vi	20Li	5Sg	7Cp	21Aq	23Pi
25	2Aq	19Pi	28Pi	20Ta	28Ge	21Le	28Vi	15Sc	29Sg	1Aq	15Pi	19Ar
27	27Aq	16Ar	26Ar	19Ge	28Cn	19Vi	24Li	9Sg	23Cp	25Aq	11Ar	16Ta
29	23Pi		25Ta	18Cn	26Le	15Li	19Sc	3Cp	17Aq	20Pi	9Ta	16Ge
31	20Ar		24Ge		23Vi		13Sg	27Cp		17Ar		16Cn

1983

	Jan	Feb	Mar	Apr	May	Jun	Jul	Aug	Sep	Oct	Nov	Dec
1	1Le	24Vi	2Li	21Sc	24Sg	8Aq	10Pi	26Ar	14Ge	22Cn	15Vi	24Li
3	1Vi	21Li	0Sc	16Sg	18Cp	2Pi	4Ar	21Ta	12Cn	21Le	14Li	21Sc
5	29Vi	17Sc	26Sc	10Cp	12Aq	26Pi	29Ar	19Ge	11Le	20Vi	12Sc	18Sg
7	26Li	12Sg	20Sg	4Aq	6Pi	21Ar	26Ta	18Cn	12Vi	20Li	9Sg	13Cp
9	21Sc	6Cp	14Cp	28Aq	0Ar	18Ta	25Ge	18Le	12Li	18Sc	5Cp	7Aq
11	15Sg	29Cp	8Aq	22Pi	26Ar	16Ge	25Cn	19Vi	10Sc	15Sg	29Cp	1Pi
13	9Cp	23Aq	2Pi	18Ar	24Ta	16Cn	25Le	18Li	6Sg	9Cp	23Aq	25Pi
15	2Aq	17Pi	26Pi	15Ta	22Ge	15Le	24Vi	15Sc	1Cp	3Aq	17Pi	19Ar
17	26Aq	12Ar	22Ar	12Ge	21Cn	14Vi	22Li	10Sg	25Cp	27Aq	12Ar	15Ta
19	20Pi	8Ta	18Ta	10Cn	19Le	12Li	18Sc	5Cp	19Aq	21Pi	7Ta	12Ge
21	15Ar	5Ge	15Ge	8Le	17Vi	8Sc	13Sg	28Cp	13Pi	16Ar	4Ge	10Cn
23	11Ta	3Cn	13Cn	6Vi	15Li	4Sg	7Cp	22Aq	7Ar	11Ta	1Cn	9Le
25	9Ge	2Le	12Le	5Li	11Sc	28Sg	1Aq	16Pi	2Ta	8Ge	29Cn	9Vl
27	9Cn	2Vi	11Vi	2Sc	7Sg	23Cp	25Aq	10Ar	28Ta	5Cn	28Le	7Li
29	9Le		10Li	29Sc	2Cp	16Aq	19Pi	5Ta	24Ge	3Le	26Vi	4Sc
31	9Vi		7Sc		26Cp		13Ar	1Ge		1Vi		1Sg

1984

	Jan	Feb	Mar	Apr	May	Jun	Jul	Aug	Sep	Oct	Nov	Dec
1	14Sg	0Aq	21Aq	5Ar	9Ta	26Ge	3Le	27Vi	20Sc	27Sg	13Aq	16Pi
3	9Cp	24Aq	15Pi	0Ta	4Ge	24Cn	2Vi	26Li	17Sg	22Cp	8Pi	10Ar
5	3Aq	18Pi	8Ar	24Ta	0Cn	22Le	1Li	24Sc	13Cp	17Aq	1Ar	3Ta
7	27Aq	11Ar	2Ta	20Ge	27Cn	20Vi	29Li	20Sg	8Aq	11Pi	25Ar	28Ta
9	21Pi	6Ta	27Ta	16Cn	25Le	18Li	27Sc	16Cp	2Pi	5Ar	19Ta	23Ge
11	15Ar	1Ge	23Ge	14Le	24Vi	17Sc	23Sg	11Aq	26Pi	28Ar	14Ge	19Cn
13	10Ta	28Ge	20Cn	14Vi	23Li	14Sg	19Cp	5Pi	19Ar	22Ta	9Cn	16Le
15	6Ge	26Cn	20Le	14Li	21Sc	11Cp	14Aq	29Pi	13Ta	17Ge	6Le	14Vi
17	4Cn	27Le	20Vi	13Sc	19Sg	6Aq	8Pi	22Ar	8Ge	12Cn	4Vi	13Li
19	3Le	27Vi	20Li	11Sg	15Cp	0Pi	2Ar	16Ta	3Cn	9Le	2Li	11Sc
21	4Vi	27Li	19Sc	7Cp	10Aq	24Pi	26Ar	11Ge	0Le	8Vi	2Sc	10Sg
23	3Li	24Sc	16Sg	2Aq	4Pi	18Ar	20Ta	8Cn	29Le	8Li	1Sg	7Cp
25	1Sc	20Sg	12Cp	26Aq	28Pi	13Ta	16Ge	6Le	0Li	8Sc	29Sg	4Aq
27	28Sc	15Cp	6Aq	20Pi	22Ar	8Ge	14Cn	6Vi	0Sc	7Sg	26Cp	29Aq
29	23Sg	9Aq	0Pi	14Ar	17Ta	5Cn	13Le	6Li	29Sc	5Cp	22Aq	24Pi
31	18Cp		23Pi		13Ge		12Vi	6Sc		1Aq		17Ar

1985

	Jan	Feb	Mar	Apr	May	Jun	Jul	Aug	Sep	Oct	Nov	Dec
1	29Ar	13Ge	21Ge	9Le	16Vi	10Sc	19Sg	9Aq	27Pi	29Ar	13Ge	17Cn
3	23Ta	9Cn	17Cn	8Vi	16Li	10Sg	17Cp	6Pi	21Ar	23Ta	7Cn	12Le
5	18Ge	7Le	15Le	8Li	16Sc	9Cp	14Aq	1Ar	15Ta	16Ge	2Le	8Vi
7	15Cn	6Vi	15Vi	8Sc	16Sg	6Aq	10Pi	25Ar	8Ge	11Cn	28Le	5Li
9	13Le	6Li	15Li	8Sg	15Cp	2Pi	5Ar	18Ta	3Cn	6Le	26Vi	4Sc
11	11Vi	4Sc	14Sc	6Cp	11Aq	27Pi	29Ar	12Ge	28Cn	3Vi	25Li	4Sg
13	9Li	2Sg	13Sg	2Aq	6Pi	21Ar	22Ta	7Cn	25Le	2Li	26Sc	4Cp
15	8Sc	29Sg	9Cp	27Aq	0Ar	14Ta	17Ge	3Le	24Vi	3Sc	26Sg	3Aq
17	5Sg	25Cp	5Aq	21Pi	24Ar	8Ge	12Cn	1Vi	24Li	3Sg	25Cp	0Pi
19	3Cp	21Aq	0Pi	15Ar	18Ta	3Cn	8Le	0Li	23Sc	2Cp	22Aq	26Pi
21	29Cp	16Pi	24Pi	9Ta	12Ge	29Cn	6Vi	28Li	22Sg	29Cp	17Pi	20Ar
23	25Aq	10Ar	18Ar	2Ge	6Cn	25Le	4Li	27Sc	19Cp	25Aq	11Ar	13Ta
25	19Pi	3Ta	12Ta	27Ge	2Le	23Vi	2Sc	25Sg	15Aq	20Pi	5Ta	7Ge
27	13Ar	27Ta	5Ge	22Cn	28Le	21Li	0Sg	22Cp	11Pi	14Ar	28Ta	1Cn
29	7Ta		0Cn	18Le	26Vi	20Sc	28Sg	18Aq	5Ar	8Ta	22Ge	26Cn
31	1Ge		26Cn		25Li		26Cp	14Pi		1Ge		22Le

1986

	Jan	Feb	Mar	Apr	May	Jun	Jul	Aug	Sep	Oct	Nov	Dec
1	5Vi	26Li	7Sc	0Cp	8Aq	27Pi	1Ta	15Ge	29Cn	2Vi	21Li	28Sc
3	1Li	24Sc	5Sg	28Cp	5Pi	22Ar	24Ta	8Cn	24Le	29Vi	20Sc	29Sg
5	29Li	22Sg	3Cp	25Aq	0Ar	15Ta	18Ge	3Le	20Vi	27Li	20Sg	29Cp
7	28Sc	21Cp	1Aq	20Pi	24Ar	9Ge	12Cn	28Le	17Li	25Sc	19Cp	27Aq
9	27Sg	19Aq	28Aq	15Ar	18Ta	3Cn	6Le	24Vi	15Sc	24Sg	17Aq	24Pi
11	26Cp	16Pi	24Pi	10Ta	12Ge	27Cn	1Vi	21Li	13Sg	23Cp	14Pi	20Ar
13	25Aq	11Ar	19Ar	4Ge	6Cn	21Le	27Vi	18Sc	12Cp	20Aq	10Ar	14Ta
15	21Pi	6Ta	14Ta	27Ge	0Le	17Vi	24Li	17Sg	10Aq	17Pi	5Ta	8Ge
17	16Ar	29Ta	7Ge	21Cn	25Le	14Li	22Sc	16Cp	8Pi	13Ar	29Ta	2Cn
19	10Ta	23Ge	1Cn	16Le	21Vi	12Sc	21Sg	15Aq	5Ar	9Ta	23Ge	26Cn
21	3Ge	18Cn	25Cn	13Vi	19Li	12Sg	21Cp	13Pi	0Ta	3Ge	17Cn	20Le
23	27Ge	13Le	21Le	11Li	19Sc	13Cp	21Aq	10Ar	25Ta	27Ge	11Le	14Vi
25	22Cn	10Vi	19Vi	11Sc	19Sg	12Aq	18Pi	5Ta	19Ge	20Cn	5Vi	10Li
27	18Le	8Li	17Li	11Sg	19Cp	10Pi	14Ar	29Ta	13Cn	15Le	1Li	7Sc
29	15Vi		17Sc	10Cp	18Aq	6Ar	9Ta	23Ge	7Le	10Vi	29Li	6Sg
31	12Li		16Sg		14Pi		3Ge	17Cn		7Li		7Cp

1987

	Jan	Feb	Mar	Apr	May	Jun	Jul	Aug	Sep	Oct	Nov	Dec
1	22Cp	14Pi	22Pi	10Ta	14Ge	28Cn	0Vi	16Li	6Sg	14Cp	8Pi	16Ar
3	22Aq	12Ar	20Ar	6Ge	8Cn	22Le	24Vi	12Sc	4Cp	13Aq	5Ar	12Ta
5	20Pi	7Ta	15Ta	0Cn	1Le	16Vi	20Li	10Sg	3Aq	12Pi	3Ta	8Ge
7	16Ar	2Ge	10Ge	24Cn	25Le	11Li	16Sc	9Cp	3Pi	10Ar	29Ta	3Cn
9	11Ta	26Ge	4Cn	18Le	20Vi	8Sc	15Sg	9Aq	2Ar	8Ta	25Ge	27Cn
11	5Ge	19Cn	28Cn	12Vi	16Li	7Sg	16Cp	9Pi	0Ta	4Ge	19Cn	21Le
13	29Ge	13Le	22Le	8Li	14Sc	7Cp	16Aq	8Ar	26Ta	29Ge	13Le	15Vi
15	23Cn	8Vi	17Vi	5Sc	13Sg	7Aq	15Pi	5Ta	21Ge	23Cn	7Vi	9Li
17	17Le	3Li	13Li	4Sg	13Cp	6Pi	13Ar	1Ge	15Cn	17Le	1Li	5Sc
19	11Vi	29Li	10Sc	2Cp	12Aq	3Ar	9Ta	25Ge	9Le	11Vi	27Li	2Sg
21	6Li	27Sc	7Sg	1Aq	10Pi	20Ar	4Ge	19Cn	3Vi	6Li	24Sc	1Cp
23	3Sc	25Sg	6Cp	29Aq	6Ar	24Ta	28Ge	12Le	27Vi	2Sc	23Sg	1Aq
25	0Sg	24Cp	4Aq	26Pi	2Ta	19Ge	22Cn	6Vi	23Li	29Sc	22Cp	1Pi
27	0Cp	23Aq	3Pi	23Ar	27Ta	13Cn	15Le	1Li	19Sc	27Sg	20Aq	29Pi
29	0Aq		1Ar	19Ta	22Ge	6Le	9Vi	26Li	16Sg	25Cp	18Pi	26Ar
31	0Pi		27Ar		16Cn		4Li	22Sc		23Aq		22Ta

1988

	Jan	Feb	Mar	Apr	May	Jun	Jul	Aug	Sep	Oct	Nov	Dec
1	5Ge	21Cn	11Le	25Vi	29Li	17Sg	25Cp	19Pi	11Ta	17Ge	4Le	5Vi
3	29Ge	14Le	5Vi	20Li	25Sc	15Cp	24Aq	18Ar	8Ge	13Cn	28Le	29Vi
5	24Cn	8Vi	29Vi	15Sc	22Sg	14Aq	23Pi	15Ta	4Cn	7Le	21Vi	23Li
7	17Le	2Li	23Li	11Sg	19Cp	12Pi	21Ar	12Ge	28Cn	1Vi	15Li	18Sc
9	11Vi	26Li	18Sc	8Cp	17Aq	11Ar	18Ta	7Cn	22Le	25Vi	9Sc	14Sg
11	5Li	21Sc	14Sg	6Aq	16Pi	8Ta	15Ge	1Le	16Vi	18Li	5Sg	11Cp
13	0Sc	19Sg	12Cp	5Pi	14Ar	5Ge	10Cn	25Le	9Li	13Sc	1Cp	9Aq
15	26Sc	17Cp	11Aq	5Ar	12Ta	1Cn	4Le	19Vi	3Sc	8Sg	28Cp	7Pi
17	24Sg	18Aq	11Pi	3Ta	9Ge	26Cn	28Le	12Li	28Sc	4Cp	26Aq	5Ar
19	24Cp	18Pi	11Ar	1Ge	5Cn	20Le	22Vi	7Sc	24Sg	1Aq	24Pi	3Ta
21	25Aq	17Ar	9Ta	27Ge	0Le	14Vi	16Li	2Sg	21Cp	0Pi	23Ar	1Ge
23	24Pi	15Ta	6Ge	22Cn	24Le	8Li	10Sc	28Sg	20Aq	29Pi	22Ta	28Ge
25	22Ar	11Ge	2Cn	16Le	18Vi	2Sc	6Sg	27Cp	20Pi	29Ar	20Ge	24Cn
27	19Ta	5Cn	26Cn	10Vi	12Li	28Sc	4Cp	27Aq	21Ar	28Ta	16Cn	19Le
29	14Ge	29Cn	20Le	4Li	7Sc	26Sg	4Aq	27Pi	20Ta	25Ge	11Le	13Vi
31	8Cn		13Vi		3Sg		4Pi	27Ar		21Cn		7Li

1989

	Jan	Feb	Mar	Apr	May	Jun	Jul	Aug	Sep	Oct	Nov	Dec
1	19Li	3Sg	12Sg	0Aq	8Pi	1Ta	10Ge	0Le	17Vi	19Li	4Sg	8Cp
3	13Sc	0Cp	8Cp	29Aq	7Ar	1Ge	8Cn	26Le	11Li	13Sc	28Sg	3Aq
5	9Sg	28Cp	6Aq	28Pi	7Ta	29Ge	5Le	20Vi	4Sc	7Sg	23Cp	29Aq
7	6Cp	27Aq	5Pi	29Ar	7Ge	27Cn	0Vi	14Li	28Sc	1Cp	19Aq	26Pi
9	4Aq	27Pi	5Ar	29Ta	5Cn	22Le	24Vi	8Sc	23Sg	27Cp	17Pi	25Ar
11	3Pi	26Ar	5Ta	27Ge	1Le	16Vi	18Li	2Sg	18Cp	24Aq	16Ar	25Ta
13	2Ar	24Ta	4Ge	23Cn	26Le	10Li	12Sc	27Sg	16Aq	23Pi	17Ta	25Ge
15	0Ta	21Ge	1Cn	18Le	20Vi	4Sc	7Sg	24Cp	15Pi	23Ar	17Ge	23Cn
17	27Ta	17Cn	26Cn	12Vi	14Li	28Sc	2Cp	22Aq	15Ar	24Ta	15Cn	20Le
19	24Ge	12Le	21Le	5Li	8Sc	24Sg	29Cp	21Pi	15Ta	23Ge	12Le	15Vi
21	20Cn	6Vi	15Vi	29Li	2Sg	20Cp	27Aq	20Ar	14Ge	20Cn	7Vi	10Li
23	15Le	29Vi	8Li	23Sc	27Sg	17Aq	26Pi	19Ta	11Cn	16Le	1Li	3Sc
25	9Vi	23Li	2Sc	18Sg	23Cp	15Pi	24Ar	17Ge	7Le	10Vi	25Li	27Sc
27	3Li	17Sc	26Sc	13Cp	20Aq	13Ar	22Ta	14Cn	1Vi	4Li	19Sc	22Sg
29	27Li		21Sg	10Aq	18Pi	12Ta	20Ge	9Le	25Vi	28Li	13Sg	17Cp
31	21Sc		17Cp		17Ar		17Cn	4Vi		22Sc		13Aq

1990

	Jan	Feb	Mar	Apr	May	Jun	Jul	Aug	Sep	Oct	Nov	Dec
1	26Aq	18Ar	28Ar	22Ge	29Cn	17Vi	21Li	4Sg	19Cp	22Aq	11Ar	19Ta
3	23Pi	16Ta	27Ta	20Cn	26Le	12Li	14Sc	28Sg	14Aq	19Pi	11Ta	20Ge
5	21Ar	15Ge	25Ge	16Le	21Vi	6Sc	8Sg	23Cp	11Pi	18Ar	11Ge	20Cn
7	20Ta	13Cn	23Cn	11Vi	15Li	0Sg	2Cp	19Aq	9Ar	17Ta	11Cn	18Le
9	19Ge	10Le	19Le	6Li	9Sc	23Sg	27Cp	15Pi	7Ta	17Ge	9Le	15Vi
11	17Cn	6Vi	14Vi	0Sc	3Sg	18Cp	22Aq	13Ar	6Ge	15Cn	6Vi	10Li
13	15Le	1Li	9Li	24Sc	26Sg	12Aq	18Pi	11Ta	4Cn	12Le	1Li	5Sc
15	11Vi	25Li	3Sc	17Sg	21Cp	8Pi	16Ar	9Ge	2Le	9Vi	26Li	29Sc
17	5Li	19Sc	27Sc	11Cp	15Aq	5Ar	14Ta	8Cn	29Le	4Li	20Sc	22Sg
19	29Li	13Sg	21Sg	6Aq	12Pi	4Ta	13Ge	6Le	25Vi	29Li	14Sg	16Cp
21	23Sc	8Cp	15Cp	3Pi	10Ar	4Ge	12Cn	3Vi	20Li	23Sc	7Cp	10Aq
23	17Sg	3Aq	11Aq	1Ar	10Ta	4Cn	11Le	29Vi	15Sc	17Sg	1Aq	5Pi
25	12Cp	1Pi	9Pi	1Ta	10Ge	3Le	8Vi	24Li	8Sg	10Cp	26Aq	1Ar
27	9Aq	29Pi	8Ar	2Ge	10Cn	0Vi	4Li	19Sc	2Cp	4Aq	22Pi	28Ar
29	6Pi		8Ta	2Cn	8Le	26Vi	29Li	12Sg	26Cp	0Pi	19Ar	27Ta
31	4Ar		8Ge		5Vi		23Sc	6Cp		27Pi		28Ge

1991

	Jan	Feb	Mar	Apr	May	Jun	Jul	Aug	Sep	Oct	Nov	Dec
1	13Cn	4Vi	12Vi	1Sc	4Sg	18Cp	20Aq	7Ar	28Ta	7Cn	0Vi	7Li
3	12Le	2Li	9Li	25Sc	28Sg	12Aq	15Pi	4Ta	26Ge	5Le	27Vi	3Sc
5	10Vi	27Li	5Sc	19Sg	21Cp	6Pi	11Ar	1Ge	25Cn	3Vi	24Li	29Sc
7	7Li	22Sc	0Sg	13Cp	15Aq	1Ar	8Ta	0Cn	24Le	1Li	20Sc	23Sg
9	2Sc	16Sg	23Sg	7Aq	10Pi	29Ar	6Ge	0Le	23Vi	28Li	15Sg	17Cp
11	26Sc	9Cp	17Cp	2Pi	7Ar	28Ta	6Cn	0Vi	20Li	24Sc	9Cp	11Aq
13	19Sg	3Aq	12Aq	28Pi	5Ta	28Ge	7Le	28Vi	16Sc	19Sg	2Aq	4Pi
15	13Cp	28Aq	7Pi	26Ar	4Ge	28Cn	6Vi	25Li	11Sg	13Cp	26Aq	29Pi
17	7Aq	24Pi	4Ar	25Ta	4Cn	27Le	4Li	21Sc	5Cp	6Aq	21Pi	25Ar
19	2Pi	21Ar	1Ta	25Ge	3Le	25Vi	0Sc	15Sg	29Cp	1Pi	17Ar	23Ta
21	28Pi	19Ta	0Ge	23Cn	1Vi	20Li	24Sc	9Cp	23Aq	26Pi	15Ta	22Ge
23	24Ar	17Ge	28Ge	21Le	28Vi	15Sc	18Sg	2Aq	18Pi	23Ar	14Ge	22Cn
25	22Ta	16Cn	26Cn	18Vi	23Li	9Sg	12Cp	26Aq	14Ar	21Ta	13Cn	22Le
27	21Ge	14Le	24Le	14Li	18Sc	3Cp	6Aq	22Pi	11Ta	19Ge	12Le	21Vi
29	21Cn		21Vi	9Sc	12Sg	27Cp	0Pi	17Ar	9Ge	18Cn	10Vi	18Li
31	20Le		18Li		6Cp		25Pi	14Ta		16Le		13Sc

1992

	Jan	Feb	Mar	Apr	May	Jun	Jul	Aug	Sep	Oct	Nov	Dec
1	26Sc	11Cp	1Aq	16Pi	19Ar	8Ge	16Cn	10Vi	2Sc	7Sg	23Cp	25Aq
3	20Sg	4Aq	25Aq	11Ar	16Ta	7Cn	16Le	9Li	29Sc	3Cp	17Aq	19Pi
5	14Cp	28Aq	19Pi	6Ta	13Ge	6Le	15Vi	7Sc	24Sg	27Cp	11Pi	13Ar
7	7Aq	22Pi	14Ar	3Ge	11Cn	5Vi	13Li	3Sg	19Cp	21Aq	5Ar	8Ta
9	1Pi	17Ar	10Ta	0Cn	9Le	3Li	10Sc	27Sg	12Aq	15Pi	0Ta	4Ge
11	25Pi	13Ta	6Ge	28Cn	8Vi	0Sc	6Sg	22Cp	6Pi	9Ar	26Ta	2Cn
13	20Ar	10Ge	4Cn	27Le	6Li	26Sc	0Cp	15Aq	0Ar	4Ta	23Ge	0Le
15	17Ta	8Le	2Le	26Vi	3Sc	21Sg	25Cp	9Pi	24Ar	29Ta	20Cn	29Le
17	15Ge	8Le	2Vi	24Li	0Sg	16Cp	18Aq	3Ar	20Ta	26Ge	18Le	27Vi
19	15Cn	8Vi	1Li	21Sc	25Sg	10Aq	12Pi	27Ar	16Ge	23Cn	16Vi	25Li
21	15Le	8Li	0Sc	17Sg	20Cp	3Pi	6Ar	23Ta	13Cn	21Le	15Li	22Sc
23	15Vi	6Sc	27Sc	12Cp	13Aq	27Pi	1Ta	19Ge	11Le	21Vi	13Sc	19Sg
25	14Li	1Sg	22Sg	6Aq	7Pi	22Ar	27Ta	18Cn	11Vi	20Li	10Sg	14Cp
27	10Sc	26Sg	16Cp	29Aq	2Ar	19Ta	25Ge	18Le	11Li	18Sc	6Cp	9Aq
29	5Sg	19Cp	9Aq	24Pi	27Ar	16Ge	24Cn	18Vi	10Sc	15Sg	1Aq	3Pi
31	29Sg		3Pi		24Ta		24Le	18Li		11Cp		26Pi

1993

	Jan	Feb	Mar	Apr	May	Jun	Jul	Aug	Sep	Oct	Nov	Dec
1	8Ar	23Ta	2Ge	21Cn	29Le	23Li	2Sg	21Cp	7Pi	10Ar	24Ta	28Ge
3	3Ta	20Ge	28Ge	20Le	29Vi	22Sc	29Sg	16Aq	1Ar	3Ta	19Ge	24Cn
5	29Ta	18Cn	26Cn	19Vi	28Li	20Sg	25Cp	10Pi	24Ar	27Ta	14Cn	21Le
7	26Ge	18Le	26Le	20Li	27Sc	16Cp	20Aq	4Ar	18Ta	22Ge	11Le	19Vi
9	25Cn	18Vi	26Vi	19Sc	25Sg	12Aq	14Pi	28Ar	13Ge	17Cn	8Vi	17Li
11	24Le	18Li	27Li	17Sg	21Cp	6Pi	8Ar	22Ta	8Cn	15Le	8Li	16Sc
13	24Vi	16Sc	25Sc	13Cp	16Aq	0Ar	2Ta	17Ge	6Le	14Vi	8Sc	15Sg
15	22Li	12Sg	22Sg	8Aq	10Pi	24Ar	26Ta	14Cn	6Vi	14Li	7Sg	13Cp
17	19Sc	8Cp	17Cp	2Pi	4Ar	18Ta	22Ge	12Le	6Li	15Sc	6Cp	10Aq
19	15Sg	2Aq	11Aq	25Pi	28Ar	14Ge	20Cn	12Vi	6Sc	14Sg	2Aq	5Pi
21	11Cp	26Aq	5Pi	19Ar	23Ta	11Cn	18Le	12Li	5Sg	11Cp	27Aq	29Pi
23	5Aq	20Pi	29Pi	14Ta	18Ge	9Le	18Vi	11Sc	2Cp	6Aq	21Pi	23Ar
25	29Aq	13Ar	22Ar	9Ge	15Cn	7Vi	17Li	9Sg	27Cp	1Pi	15Ar	17Ta
27	23Pi	7Ta	17Ta	5Cn	12Le	6Li	15Sc	5Cp	22Aq	25Pi	9Ta	12Ge
29	17Ar		12Ge	1Le	10Vi	4Sc	12Sg	0Aq	16Pi	18Ar	3Ge	7Cn
31	11Ta		8Cn		9Li		8Cp	25Aq		12Ta		4Le

1994

	Jan	Feb	Mar	Apr	May	Jun	Jul	Aug	Sep	Oct	Nov	Dec
1	18Le	11Li	20Li	13Sg	20Cp	8Pi	11Ar	24Ta	8Cn	12Le	2Li	10Sc
3	16Vi	9Sc	20Sc	11Cp	17Aq	2Ar	4Ta	18Ge	4Le	10Vi	2Sc	10Sg
5	14Li	7Sg	17Sg	7Aq	11Pi	26Ar	28Ta	13Cn	2Vi	9Li	2Sg	10Cp
7	12Sc	4Cp	14Cp	2Pi	5Ar	20Ta	22Ge	9Le	0Li	9Sc	2Cp	9Aq
9	10Sg	0Aq	10Aq	26Pi	29Ar	14Ge	17Cn	7Vi	29Li	8Sg	0Aq	6Pi
11	8Cp	26Aq	5Pi	20Ar	23Ta	8Cn	13Le	5Li	28Sc	7Cp	27Aq	1Ar
13	5Aq	21Pi	0Ar	14Ta	17Ge	4Le	10Vi	3Sc	26Sg	4Aq	22Pi	25Ar
15	1Pi	15Ar	23Ar	8Ge	11Cn	0Vi	8Li	1Sg	24Cp	0Pi	16Ar	19Ta
17	25Pi	9Ta	17Ta	2Cn	7Le	27Vi	6Sc	29Sg	20Aq	25Pi	10Ta	12Ge
19	19Ar	2Ge	11Ge	27Cn	3Vi	26Li	5Sg	27Cp	16Pi	19Ar	4Ge	6Cn
21	13Ta	27Ge	5Cn	24Le	1Li	25Sc	3Cp	24Aq	11Ar	13Ta	27Ge	1Le
23	7Ge	23Cn	1Le	22Vi	1Sc	24Sg	1Aq	20Pi	5Ta	7Ge	22Cn	26Le
25	2Cn	21Le	29Le	22Li	1Sg	23Cp	28Aq	14Ar	28Ta	0Cn	16Le	23Vi
27	29Cn	21Vi	29Vi	23Sc	1Cp	20Aq	24Pi	8Ta	22Ge	25Cn	13Vi	20Li
29	27Le		29Li	22Sg	29Cp	16Pi	18Ar	2Ge	16Cn	20Le	10Li	19Sc
31	26Vi		29Sc		25Aq		12Ta	26Ge		18Vi		18Sg

1995

	Jan	Feb	Mar	Apr	May	Jun	Jul	Aug	Sep	Oct	Nov	Dec
1	3Cp	25Aq	3Pi	21Ar	24Ta	8Cn	11Le	29Vi	20Sc	29Sg	22Aq	29Pi
3	3Aq	22Pi	0Ar	15Ta	17Ge	2Le	6Vi	25Li	18Sg	27Cp	19Pi	24Ar
5	1Pi	17Ar	25Ar	9Ge	11Cn	26Le	2Li	23Sc	16Cp	25Aq	15Ar	19Ta
7	27Pi	11Ta	19Ta	3Cn	5Le	22Vi	29Li	22Sg	15Aq	22Pi	10Ta	13Ge
9	22Ar	5Ge	13Ge	27Cn	0Vi	19Li	27Sc	21Cp	13Pi	19Ar	5Ge	7Cn
11	15Ta	29Ge	7Cn	22Le	27Vi	18Sc	27Sg	21Aq	10Ar	14Ta	29Ge	1Le
13	9Ge	23Cn	1Le	19Vi	25Li	19Sg	27Cp	19Pi	6Ta	8Ge	22Cn	25Le
15	3Cn	19Le	27Le	17Li	25Sc	19Cp	27Aq	16Ar	1Ge	2Cn	16Le	19Vi
17	28Cn	16Vi	25Vi	17Sc	25Sg	18Aq	24Pi	11Ta	24Ge	26Cn	11Vi	15Li
19	23Le	13Li	23Li	16Sg	25Cp	16Pi	20Ar	5Ge	18Cn	21Le	7Li	13Sc
21	20Vi	11Sc	22Sc	15Cp	23Aq	11Ar	14Ta	28Ge	13Le	16Vi	5Sc	12Sg
23	17Li	9Sg	20Sg	13Aq	19Pi	6Ta	8Ge	22Cn	8Vi	13Li	5Sg	13Cp
25	14Sc	8Cp	18Cp	9Pi	14Ar	29Ta	2Cn	17Le	5Li	11Sc	5Cp	13Aq
27	13Sg	6Aq	16Aq	5Ar	9Ta	23Ge	26Cn	12Vi	2Sc	11Sg	4Aq	12Pi
29	12Cp		13Pi	0Ta	2Ge	17Cn	21Le	9Li	0Sg	10Cp	2Pi	9Ar
31	11Aq		8Ar		26Ge		16Vi	6Sc		8Aq		4Ta

1996

	Jan	Feb	Mar	Apr	May	Jun	Jul	Aug	Sep	Oct	Nov	Dec
1	16Ta	1Cn	21Cn	6Vi	9Li	28Sc	7Cp	1Pi	22Ar	27Ta	13Cn	15Le
3	10Ge	25Cn	15Le	1Li	6Sc	28Sg	7Aq	0Ar	19Ta	23Ge	7Le	8Vi
5	4Cn	19Le	10Vi	27Li	4Sg	28Cp	7Pi	28Ar	15Ge	17Cn	1Vi	2Li
7	28Cn	13Vi	5Li	25Sc	3Cp	27Aq	5Ar	23Ta	9Cn	11Le	25Vi	28Li
9	22Le	8Li	1Sc	23Sg	2Aq	25Pi	1Ta	18Ge	3Le	5Vi	20Li	24Sc
11	16Vi	4Sc	28Sc	21Cp	0Pi	21Ar	26Ta	12Cn	26Le	29Vi	16Sc	23Sg
13	11Li	1Sg	26Sg	20Aq	28Pi	17Ta	21Ge	6Le	20Vi	24Li	14Sg	22Cp
15	8Sc	0Cp	25Cp	18Pi	24Ar	12Ge	15Cn	29Le	15Li	20Sc	12Cp	21Aq
17	6Sg	0Aq	24Aq	15Ar	20Ta	6Cn	9Le	23Vi	11Sc	18Sg	11Aq	20Pi
19	6Cp	29Aq	22Pi	11Ta	15Ge	0Le	2Vi	18Li	7Sg	15Cp	9Pi	17Ar
21	6Aq	28Pi	20Ar	7Ge	9Cn	24Le	26Vi	14Sc	5Cp	14Aq	7Ar	14Ta
23	6Pi	26Ar	16Ta	1Cn	3Le	17Vi	21Li	10Sg	3Aq	12Pi	4Ta	9Ge
25	4Ar	21Ta	11Ge	25Cn	27Le	12Li	17Sc	9Cp	3Pi	11Ar	0Ge	5Cn
27	0Ta	16Ge	5Cn	19Le	21Vi	9Sc	15Sg	9Aq	2Ar	9Ta	26Ge	29Cn
29	25Ta	9Cn	29Cn	13Vi	17Li	7Sg	15Cp	9Pi	0Ta	5Ge	21Cn	23Le
31	19Ge		23Le		14Sc		16Aq	8Ar		1Cn		16Vi

1997

	Jan	Feb	Mar	Apr	May	Jun	Jul	Aug	Sep	Oct	Nov	Dec
1	28Vi	14Sc	23Sc	13Cp	22Aq	15Ar	23Ta	12Cn	27Le	0Li	15Sc	19Sg
3	23Li	10Sg	19Sg	11Aq	21Pi	13Ta	20Ge	6Le	21Vi	24Li	10Sg	16Cp
5	18Sc	9Cp	17Cp	11Pi	19Ar	10Ge	15Cn	0Vi	15Li	18Sc	6Cp	13Aq
7	16Sg	9Aq	17Aq	10Ar	18Ta	6Cn	10Le	24Vi	8Sc	13Sg	3Aq	11Pi
9	16Cp	9Pi	17Pi	9Ta	15Ge	2Le	4Vi	18Li	3Sg	9Cp	0Pi	9Ar
11	16Aq	9Ar	17Ar	7Ge	11Cn	26Le	27Vi	12Sc	29Sg	6Aq	29Pi	8Ta
13	16Pi	7Ta	16Ta	3Cn	6Le	19Vi	21Li	7Sg	27Cp	5Pi	28Ar	6Ge
15	14Ar	3Ge	12Ge	28Cn	0Vi	13Li	16Sc	4Cp	26Aq	5Ar	28Ta	4Cn
17	11Ta	28Ge	7Cn	22Le	23Vi	8Sc	12Sg	3Aq	27Pi	5Ta	26Ge	0Le
19	6Ge	23Cn	1Le	15Vi	17Li	4Sg	10Cp	3Pi	27Ar	4Ge	22Cn	25Le
21	1Cn	16Le	25Le	9Li	13Sc	2Cp	10Aq	3Ar	26Ta	1CN	17Le	19Vi
23	26Cn	10Vi	19Vi	4Sc	9Sg	1Aq	9Pi	2Ta	23Ge	27Cn	11Vi	13Li
25	19Le	4Li	13Li	0Sg	7Cp	29Aq	8Ar	0Ge	18Cn	21Le	5Li	7Sc
27	13Vi	28Li	7Sc	26Sg	5Aq	28Pi	6Ta	26Ge	12Le	15Vi	29Li	2Sg
29	7Li		3Sg	24Cp	3Pi	26Ar	3Ge	21Cn	6Vi	8Li	23Sc	28Sg
31	1Sc		29Sg		1Ar		29Ge	15Le		2Sc		25Cp

1998

	Jan	Feb	Mar	Apr	May	Jun	Jul	Aug	Sep	Oct	Nov	Dec
1	9Aq	2Ar	12Ar	5Ge	11Cn	28Le	0Li	14Sc	28Sg	2Aq	23Pi	1Ta
3	8Pi	1Ta	11Ta	2Cn	7Le	22Vi	24Li	8Sg	24Cp	0Pi	22Ar	1Ge
5	6Ar	29Ta	9Ge	28Cn	2Vi	16Li	18Sc	3Cp	22Aq	29Pi	23Ta	1Cn
7	4Ta	26Ge	6Cn	23Le	25Vi	9Sc	12Sg	0Aq	21Pi	0Ta	23Ge	0Le
9	2Ge	22Cn	1Le	17Vi	19Li	4Sg	8Cp	28Aq	21Ar	0Ge	21Cn	26Le
11	29Ge	17Le	26Le	10Li	13Sc	29Sg	5Aq	26Pi	20Ta	28Ge	18Le	21Vi
13	25Cn	11Vi	20Vi	4Sc	7Sg	25Cp	2Pi	25Ar	18Ge	25Cn	12Vi	15Li
15	21Le	5Li	13Li	28Sc	2Cp	22Aq	0Ar	24Ta	15Cn	21Le	6Li	9Sc
17	15Vi	28Li	7Sc	23Sg	28Cp	19Pi	29Ar	22Ge	11Le	15Vi	0Sc	3Sg
19	8Li	22Sc	1Sg	18Cp	25Aq	18Ar	27Ta	19Cn	6Vi	9Li	24Sc	27Sg
21	2Sc	17Sg	26Sg	15Aq	23Pi	17Ta	25Ge	15Le	1Li	3Sc	18Sg	22Cp
23	27Sc	14Cp	22Cp	13Pi	22Ar	15Ge	22Cn	10Vi	24Li	27Sc	12Cp	18Aq
25	22Sg	12Aq	20Aq	13Ar	22Ta	14Cn	19Le	4Li	18Sc	21Sg	8Aq	14Pi
27	20Cp	12Pi	20Pi	13Ta	21Ge	10Le	14Vi	28Li	12Sg	15Cp	4Pi	12Ar
29	18Aq		20Ar	13Ge	19Cn	6Vi	8Li	22Sc	7Cp	-11Aq	2Ar	10Ta
31	18Pi		20Ta		15Le		2Sc	16Sg		8Pi		10Ge

1999

	Jan	Feb	Mar	Apr	May	Jun	Jul	Aug	Sep	Oct	Nov	Dec
1	24Ge	15Le	24Le	11Li	14Sc	28Sg	2Aq	20Pi	12Ta	21Ge	14Le	20Vi
3	23Cn	12Vi	20Vi	5Sc	8Sg	23Cp	27Aq	17Ar	11Ge	20Cn	10Vi	15Li
5	21Le	7Li	15Li	29Sc	1Cp	17Aq	23Pi	15Ta	9Cn	17Le	6Li	10Sc
7	17Vi	1Sc	9Sc	23Sg	26Cp	13Pi	20Ar	14Ge	7Le	13Vi	1Sc	4Sg
9	11Li	25Sc	3Sg	17Cp	21Aq	10Ar	19Ta	13Cn	4Vi	9Li	25Sc	27Sg
11	5Sc	19Sg	27Sg	12Aq	17Pi	10Ta	19Ge	11Le	0Li	4Sc	19Sg	21Cp
13	29Sc	13Cp	21Cp	9Pi	16Ar	10Ge	18Cn	9Vi	26Li	28Sc	12Cp	15Aq
15	23Sg	9Aq	17Aq	8Ar	16Ta	10Cn	17Le	5Li	20Sc	22Sg	6Aq	10Pi
17	18Cp	7Pi	15Pi	8Ta	17Ge	9Le	14Vi	0Sc	14Sg	16Cp	1Pi	6Ar
19	14Aq	5Ar	14Ar	8Ge	16Cn	6Vi	10Li	24Sc	8Cp	10Aq	27Pi	4Ta
21	11Pi	3Ta	14Ta	7Cn	14Le	1Li	4Sc	18Sg	2Aq	6Pi	26Ar	4Ge
23	9Ar	2Ge	13Ge	4Le	10Vi	26Li	28Sc	12Cp	28Aq	3Ar	26Ta	4Cn
25	7Ta	0Cn	11Cn	1Vi	5Li	20Sc	22Sg	7Aq	25Pi	2Ta	26Ge	4Le
27	5Ge	27Cn	8Le	26Vi	29Li	13Sg	16Cp	3Pi	24Ar	2Ge	26Cn	3Vi
29	4Cn		3Vi	20Li	23Sc	7Cp	11Aq	0Ar	23Ta	2Cn	24Le	29Vi
31	2Le		29Vi		17Sg		7Pi	28Ar		0Le		25Li

2000

	Jan	Feb	Mar	Apr	May	Jun	Jul	Aug	Sep	Oct	Nov	Dec
1	7Sc	21Sg	11Cp	25Aq	29Pi	19Ta	28Ge	21Le	13Li	17Sc	2Cp	4Aq
3	1Sg	15Cp	5Aq	21Pi	27Ar	19Ge	28Cn	20Vi	9Sc	13Sg	26Cp	28Aq
5	24Sg	9Aq	0Pi	18Ar	26Ta	19Cn	28Le	18Li	5Sg	7Cp	20Aq	22Pi
7	18Cp	4Pi	26Pi	16Ta	25Ge	18Le	26Vi	14Sc	29Sg	0Aq	14Pi	18Ar
9	12Aq	29Pi	23Ar	15Ge	24Cn	16Vi	22Li	8Sg	22Cp	24Aq	10Ar	15Ta
11	7Pi	26Ar	20Ta	14Cn	22Le	13Li	17Sc	2Cp	16Aq	19Pi	7Ta	14Ge
13	2Ar	23Ta	18Ge	12Le	19Vi	8Sc	11Sg	26Cp	11Pi	15Ar	5Ge	13Cn
15	29Ar	22Ge	17Cn	9Vi	16Li	2Sg	5Cp	20Aq	6Ar	12Ta	4Cn	13Le
17	27Ta	21Cn	15Le	6Li	11Sc	26Sg	29Cp	14Pi	2Ta	10Ge	3Le	12Vi
19	27Ge	20Le	13Vi	2Sc	6Sg	20Cp	23Aq	9Ar	29Ta	8Cn	1Vi	9Li
21	27Cn	18Vi	10Li	27Sc	29Sg	14Aq	17Pi	5Ta	27Ge	6Le	29Vi	5Sc
23	26Le	15Li	6Sc	21Sg	23Cp	8Pi	12Ar	2Ge	25Cn	4Vi	25Li	1Sg
25	24Vi	11Sc	1Sg	15Cp	17Aq	3Ar	9Ta	1Cn	24Le	2Li	21Sc	25Sg
27	21Li	5Sg	25Sg	9Aq	11Pi	29Ar	7Ge	0Le	23Vi	29Li	16Sg	19Cp
29	15Sc	29Sg	19Cp	3Pi	7Ar	28Ta	6Cn	0Vi	21Li	25Sc	11Cp	13Aq
31	9Sg		13Aq		5Ta		6Le	29Vi		20Sg		6Pi